D0884408

ISLAM

From Medina to the Magreb and from the
Indies to Istanbul

ARCHITECTURE IN CONTEXT is dedicated to my wife Juliet.
This volume is dedicated to Tunku Munirah
and to the memory of her father,
Tunku Mustapha bin Tunku Besar Burhanuddin.
CT

adgell, Christopher, 19
slam : from Medina to
he Magreb and from the
008.
3305221236130
          07/16/10

ISLAM
From Medina to the Magreb and from the Indies to Istanbul

Christopher Tadgell

Routledge
Taylor & Francis Group

ARCHITECTURE IN CONTEXT III

First published 2008 by Routledge
2 Park Square, Milton Park, Abingdon, Oxon, OX14 4RN

Simultaneously published in the USA and Canada by Routledge
270 Madison Avenue, New York, NY10016

Routledge is an imprint of the Taylor & Francis Group, an informa business

© 2008 Christopher Tadgell
pictures 1.16, 2.15c, d reproduced by kind permission of James Morris
picture 1.66 reproduced by kind permission of Warwick Ball
pictures 1.104a,c, 1.114a, c, 1.122a, d, 1.123c, d, 1.124a, d, e, g reproduced by kind
permission of Pam Jacobson
picture 2.143f reproduced by kind permision of Jenny Sandys
picture 2.157a reproduced by kind permission of Louise Nicholson
ASI = Archaeological Survey of India

Series design by Claudia Schenk
Image processing and drawings by Mark Wilson
Produced by Categorical Books
Printed and bound in China by Everbest Printing Co. Ltd

All rights reserved. No part of this book may be reprinted or reproduced
or utilised in any form or by any electronic, mechanical, or other means, now known
or hereafter invented, including photocopying and recording, or in any information
storage or retrieval system, without permission in writing from the publishers

British Library Cataloguing in Publication Data
A catalogue record for this book is available from the British Library
Library of Congress Cataloging-in-Publication Data
A catalogue record for this book has been requested

ISBN13 978–0–415–43609–0 (hbk)

CONTENTS

1.1

ISLAM: INTRODUCTION

1.2a

THE FOUNDATION OF ISLAM

The dramatic career of the great religion which first claimed the submission (*islam*) of the Arabs began with the mission of the Prophet Muhammad who was born into the Quraishi tribe at Mecca c. 570 and died in Medina in 632. A practical man who claimed no power of intercession with God and disclaimed the miraculous, he is acknowledged by his followers to have been the hand with which God wrote his definitive Word enshrined in the Koran.**1.1, 1.7**

THE PROPHET MUHAMMAD AND HIS MISSION

Paganism was in retreat from monotheism in 6th-century Arabia: from Christianity in the north, Zoroastrianism in the north-east and Judaism in both Palestine and Ethiopia, to which Jews had fled from the depredations of Nebuchadnezzar in the 6th century BCE. It was with Ethiopia

›1.2 MECCA, THE KA'BA: (a) Abraham and Ismail building the shrine; (b) Abd' al-Mutallib al-Quraishi, Mohammad's grandfather, guarding the door (16th-century Turkish miniatures from the Kiab school).

The goal of Muslim pilgrimage, the Ka'ba was originally the dry-stone enclosure of a spring: it is believed to be the first building dedicated to the one true God and to incorporate material sent from heaven (meteorites, most significantly the black stone of the south-west corner).

Having been repudiated by Abraham, Hagar and her son Ismail were revived by the waters of the miraculous spring after their desert wanderings: Abraham later found his son there and together they built the sanctuary over foundations believed to have been laid by Adam. Defiled by the images of other religions imported into Mecca with trade, in 608 it was rebuilt with a timber roof supported by six columns. Later in the 7th century, after Muhammad had vented his wrath on the images, the precinct was developed as the pre-eminent place of worship in Islam.

The sacred compound, walled to exclude all but the select, descends from the ancient Semitic sanctuaries of Mesopotamia. The sanctuary was enlarged under the Ottomans in the 16th century.

1.2b

>**1.3 MUHAMMAD AND HIS VISION OF THE ARCHANGEL GABRIEL:** revealing his sacred mission to him in the Night of Destiny which is placed towards the end of Ramadan in 609 (Kitab siyar-i Nabi, 1594; Istanbul, Topkapi Library).

that the traders of the Arabian coastal Hijaz were most readily in contact. Their principal city, Mecca, was recognized by them as the site revealed by God to the Patriarch Abraham for the primary monument to monotheism – though, by the 6th century, it had become the prime repository for the numerous idols and emblems of pan-Arabian tribes. The shelter was the enigmatic structure known as the Ka'ba in its exclusive compound (*haram*) whose traditional guardians were the Quraishi.[1.2]

Muhammad, a merchant who had travelled extensively in the area and was used to dealing with foreigners, seems first to have been bent on reviving the faith of the Jewish patriarch in his mission to alert his fellow man of impending apocalypse. In the 'Night of Destiny' the Archangel Gabriel appeared to him while he was in retreat on Mount Hira and revealed his appointment as the Apostle of God.[1.3]

Monotheism is asserted as the fundamental truth. The Judaic prophetical lineage is acclaimed. The fall of Adam, the devil and, hence, God's predestination of good and evil are accepted: so too is the concept of the ministering angel and the intermediate spirit (*jinn*) which may work for the angel or the devil. Christ is acknowledged as of prime significance as a teacher, leading man to redemption from the Fall, but not as the son of God: like all the Judaic prophets before him, he had been inspired by God. But Muhammad was taken further in the light of his vision of Gabriel: God favoured him with direct revelation. At first this was recorded by his guided hand, later it was delivered through him in a trance-like state and transcribed: either way, divine dictation was unquestionably definitive.

Muhammad was constrained to confide only in his closest relations as he foresaw accusations of insufferable arrogance, at least, countering his claim to be the hand and mouth of God. In 612, however, his wife Khadijah and his

The Archangel took Muhammad on a spiritual journey to Jerusalem and from thence – from a rocky outcrop on Mount Moriah believed to derive from the altar of Solomon's Temple – up through seven heavens where he met the Prophets (here Moses, who had previously been the instrument of God's dictation) before contemplating the supreme Unseen.

father-in-law Abu Bakr persuaded him to embark on public preaching. As his success was mainly with the poor, he excited the opposition of the wealthy – including the leaders of his own Quraishi tribe. In 619, his following still small and the ranks of his enemies increasing, he lost his most fervent supporter with the death of Khadijah: anguish was assuaged with another vision, the 'Night Journey to Heaven' on which he was led, via Jerusalem, by Gabriel.**1·4**

Threatened with death in his birthplace, in 622 he took refuge in Yathrib – subsequently named Medina al-Nabi, 'Town of the Prophet' – where he met sympathy for his cause. From his house there, the first building to be dedicated to his new religion, he challenged Mecca with a

›1.5 THE PROPHET PREDICTING HIS DEATH AND TAKING LEAVE OF HIS COMPANIONS IN MEDINA, in the 11th year of Islam = 632 (Kitab siyar-i Nabi, 1594; Istanbul, Topkapi Library).

compilation of his revelations which were later enshrined in the Koran. After many vicissitudes, the faithful won the right of pilgrimage to the Ka'ba and their faith infiltrated Mecca: excluded again, Muhammad and his followers were provoked into invading in force in 630. The opposition surrendered and the Prophet returned triumphant to his native city. There he proclaimed his new law and cleansed the Ka'ba of the intrusive idols: introduced over centuries of trade, the very multiplicity of the religions represented by those idols may well have prompted a syncretism which inspired the quest for the unity of God in the Hijaz. Muhammad returned to his humble house in Medina, led a farewell pilgrimage from there to the Holy City in 632 and died soon after returning home again.[1.5]

EXPANSION OF THE NEW FAITH

Muhammad had seen many Arabian tribes enrolled in his cause before his death and the peninsula was wholly converted within two years. Islam then rapidly spread into the Palestinian heartland of the Judeo-Christian tradition. A largely Arab army of the Byzantine emperor Heraclius (610–41) was subverted and decisively defeated at Yarmuk, and Damascus was taken soon afterwards in 636. Jerusalem followed two years later. The Sasanians were defeated at Qadisiyya and their capital, Ctesiphon, was taken in 637. Iraq submitted before the year was out and most of Iran followed over the next twenty years. Egypt was invaded in 639 and Alexandria surrendered in 642.

The faith spread like wildfire from Egypt along the north coast of Africa through the zeal of the Arab conquerors, followed by equally zealous settlers, and because the Berber tribes roaming the area preferred it to Christianity. By 720 it had taken Spain and was soon pressing up into France: in the latter its triumph was ephemeral, in the former it was sustained for centuries.

East from Iran, Islam ultimately passed along the great trade route known as the Silk Road to China, but it was never to be predominant there. In 681 the Arabs were encamped below the Oxus (Amu Darya) with their sights set on Khorasan, the remotest Sasanian province: in the event that was the easternmost theatre of their enduring conquest but its autonomy was sustained from its capital, Merv. To the south-east, Sind was taken in 711 and Muslim colonies were established in India from the 8th century, but Islam was not a substantial force in the Indian subcontinent until after the Delhi sultanate was established in 1190. From India, the faith crossed with commerce to overwhelm the Buddhist and Hindu kingdoms of the East Indies where its dominance is sustained.

CALIPHATE AND SCHISM

Muhammad had preached a doctrine in which there was no distinction between religious and secular life. He was the head of the body of the faithful. After his death, his principal companions in tribal council appointed in turn as caliph – *khalifa*, 'successor' to supreme authority – four of his Quraishi tribal kinsmen related to him by marriage: Abu Bakr (632–34), Muhammad's companion on the flight to Medina, father of his wife A'isha and his designated successor; Omar (634–44), father of another of Muhammad's wives and Abu Bakr's designated successor; Othman (644–56), a member of the Umayyad clan and a son-in-law of the Prophet, appointed by a Meccan tribal council and killed for venality by Medinian rebels; Ali, husband of the Prophet's daughter Fatima, appointed by the rebels but opposed by Othman's Umayyad kinsman Mu'awiya, scion of a Meccan trading family who had been made governor of Syria.**1.6**

The rival claims of Ali and Mu'awiya, contested indecisively, were submitted to hardly more decisive arbitration.

›1.6 THE PROPHET WITH HIS DAUGHTER FATIMA AND SON-IN-LAW, ALI (Kitab siyar-i Nabi, 1594; Istanbul, Topkapi Library).

Ali's forces were revolutionary in origin but the most fanatical rejected him for agreeing to human arbitration in a matter that was for God alone to decide. The governor of Syria, with conservative tribal backing and a disciplined army, ultimately gained the upper hand and was acclaimed in Jerusalem in 660. Ali was assassinated within a year.

Mu'awiya, based on Damascus in so far as peripatetic tribal tradition allowed, proved able and magnanimous in exercising the principal duties of the caliphate: to promote the Koranic doctrine, enforce justice, sustain an exchequer and defend the faith in holy war (*jihad*) against enemies from within and without. For nearly a century the best of his successors proved no less dedicated and under them the foundations of a specifically Islamic culture were laid in the codification of Koranic dogma and the distinction of the *hadith* traditions built around the Prophet's collected sayings and accounts of his life (*sunna*).

From the interpretation of the Koran, guided in part by scrutiny of the *hadith*, the several schools of the *sharia* legal system began to emerge. Yet pragmatism acknowledged the force of custom which, though often inconsistent with Islam, proved resistant to eradication: examples range from submission to the political authority of the dynasty to belief in the superhuman nature of Muhammad and even the classification of his descendants (*sayyids*) as superior in contradiction to the essential egalitarian tenor of Koranic prescription.

As empire was obviously inconsistent with the caliph's prime duty personally to lead the faithful in prayer, Mu'awiya delegated the responsibility to an *imam* (leader) – and the central office was replicated in all the mosques of Islam. As for prayer, so too for government: recognizing that an empire incorporating many once-great states was beyond personal rule, he clothed himself in imperial majesty but delegated authority to ministers in council (*diwan*) – of whom one was inevitably to emerge as a special aide (*vizier*) – and began the establishment of a bureaucracy. The process was furthered in the next century when those states reasserted themselves as autonomous provinces, acknowledging the authority of the caliph as primarily spiritual. And the natural conclusion of that was political dissolution.

Submitting to Mu'awiya's rule, as success required, the Arab majority (*Sunni*, the followers of the *Sunna* 'path' of tradition) were the orthodox faction which maintained their tribal practice of appointment to leadership. Yet the great Umayyad also recognized that tribal election to supreme authority in a rapidly expanding empire was impractical, that nomination was preferable and that his power, like that of his imperial predecessors, lay with the army. Before he died in 680 he secured a general oath of allegiance to his son Yazid, nominated as his successor on the precedent set by Muhammad's designation of Abu Bakr and the latter's promotion of Omar. Challenged by the minority 'party' of Ali (*Shi'ah*), this provoked schism.

There were to be many Islamic factions of varied longevity but the Shi'ah – with factions of its own – was by far the most significant. Swelled by converts from the ancient realms of Babylonia and Persia with their tradition of quasi-divine kingship, it maintained as an article of faith that the caliphate was God-given and not open to human arbitration or appointment. For them the only line of legitimate succession as leader lay with the descent of the Prophet's blood through his daughter and son-in-law: most were to recognize twelve *imams*, the minority seven, and both (Ithna'ashariyyas and Isma'ilis respectively) await the second coming of their last, lost leader.

The Shi'ites first recognized Ali's sons, Hasan and Husayn, as successive *imams*. Undermined by dissension in the ranks of his opposition to the Umayyads, the former retired to Medina within a year and died in 670. Killed at Karbala in October 680, Husayn became the holiest of martyrs to the Shi'ite cause, after Ali, and though the debacle was due to the desertion of his erstwhile followers, opprobrium was heaped on the Umayyad regime of Yazid.

1.7a

THE KORAN AND ITS REQUIREMENTS

The central dogma on which Islam rests concerns the unity of God (Allah) and the finality of Muhammad's prophethood. The essence of God is inapprehensible and knowledge of him depends upon the ninety-nine names he gives himself in his revelations to Muhammad. These are enshrined in the Koran.[1.1, 1.7]

>1.7 **KORAN:** (a) page from 9th-century edition, Egypt or Iraq; (b) leaf from 14th-century reading stand, Turkestan (both New York, Metropolitan Museum of Art).

1.7b

As the book of law, the Koran imposes the conditions for submission and defines the consequent moral obligations of the Muslim: the 'five pillars' of Islam. These are the affirmation of the creed ('There is no god but Allah and Muhammad is His apostle'); prayer five times a day; fasting for the month of the revelation of the Koran (Ramadan, the ninth month of the lunar calendar); the giving of a prescribed proportion of income (at least) as alms to the faith and the poor; and pilgrimage to Mecca (*hadj*) at least once at the prescribed time of year for all able to afford it. Sunnis and Shi'ites are in accord on the essentials but the latter add 'Ali is God's vicar [*wali*]' to the creed and constitute from Ali's descendants an extensive company of saints whose shrines, emanating grace (*baraka*), may be the object of pilgrimage instead of Mecca.

Of the five pillars of the faith, prayer and its requirements constitute the prime progenitor of Muslim architecture. The Koran specifies dawn, noon, evening and nightfall as the times of prayer but *hadith* distinguishes sunset and dusk. On the Muslim sabbath, Friday, noon prayer is congregational at least for the male members of the community, to receive moral instruction. The service (*salat*) of prayer must be preceded by the washing of face,

›1.8 PRAYER: in the Mishqal Palli Mosque, Calikut.

hands and feet in a strictly defined manner. It includes affirmation of the creed and the recital of passages from the Koran in a cycle of prescribed physical positions, culminating in semi-prostration on a mat protecting the worshipper from the impurities of the ground.[1.8]

Mosque (masjid) is the generic term for the place of Muslim prostration, local, communal or private, detached or part of a larger complex of communal facilities – or associated with events of special significance. Its prototype was the ubiquitous courtyard house.[1.9]

While formal provision is often made for the modest area required for individual or family worship, the principal place of worship is clearly the centre of its community of Muslims called on Friday to the congregational (*jum'a* or *jami*) noon prayers, hence Jum'a- or Jami-masjid (congregational mosque). Then the prayers were punctuated with a sermon (*khutba*) on political as well as moral issues, as well as affirmation of loyalty to those in authority. Thus the complex needed clear acoustics and lines of sight as well as enough space to accommodate the considerable number of mats involved in an enclosure defending sanctity from pollution.

Naturally, in defining the requirements of prayer the Koran moulded Muslim building and governed its embellishment – perhaps to a degree further than intended. Idols are proscribed as the work of the devil (in Chapter v, along with wine and games of chance), but the text does not necessarily extend to all representation of the animate in art – as strict Muslims have taken it to do in accordance with the dogma that only God is Creator and that the creators of images of his creation are impious impostors.

The resurrection of the Biblical ban on idolatry should be seen in the light of the growing significance of icons in Byzantium, just as stressing the Judaic unity of God denied Christian Trinitarianism. Moreover, as Islam rejected the conception of God in human form – central to Christianity – and listened only to the austere Word, anthropomorphic embellishment in the venerable tradition still vital in the lands first conquered by the Muslims naturally ceded to the calligraphic representation of Koranic texts. The highest form of Islamic art, calligraphy was supplemented by other stylized abstractions – geometry in particular – and flora.[1.7] However, Muslim palace builders rarely recognized such restriction.

MOSQUE DEVELOPMENT

On fleeing from Mecca in 622 and settling in Medina, the Prophet presided over the first centre of his faith from an extensive adjunct to his own house for the informal accommodation of the community of his followers. The evolution of this complex is obscure and it is premature to call it a mosque, but it reputedly incorporated the elements that were to constitute the canonical place of Muslim congregational prayer: the main components of a house with any social pretensions, these are a court with a verandah to provide cover for a limited number of worshippers before the main hall and a shelter for the Prophet's followers to either side of the entrance opposite. The latter ensured that the court would retain its social significance as well as

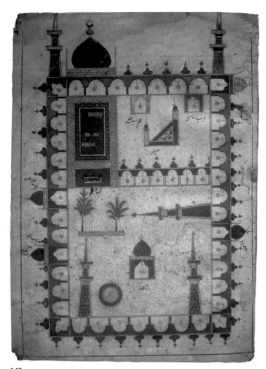

1.10

›1.10 MADINA AL-NABI: THE PROPHET'S MOSQUE (16th-century Turkish miniature).

The courtyard, the enlarged precinct of the Prophet's house partially surrounded by verandahs and with chambers to its south, is archetypical in much of the Middle East – if not in the southern Arabian Yemeni domain, where high-rise blocks are timeless (**1.12a** and see AIC1, pages 179ff.). The identity of the domestic court and the religious sanctuary was not merely fortuitous in a society that made no distinction between religious and secular life. The image shows the later features of the typical mosque: the niche (mihrab) in the centre of the upper range marking the spot where the Prophet habitually stood when leading prayer, the ablution fountain (in the centre of the outer court) and the corner towers (minarets). The Prophet's bedroom was endowed with a cenotaph representing his tomb, reputedly when the complex was rebuilt under the Umayyad caliph at the beginning of the 8th century (see **1.33**). The mosque was again rebuilt by the Ottoman Turks in 1849.

›1.11 MECCA, THE KA'BA IN ITS SANCTUARY (16th-century Turkish miniature).

1.11

catering for the new religious activity. Essentially, that embraced the administration of justice – in accordance with Koranic law, of course – and education ranging from the rudimentary at the humble parish level to abstruse theological enquiry at the highest intellectual level of the great metropolitan foundations – or was to do so as the faith developed.**1.10**

Prayer – by the ritually cleansed in the fountain usually associated with the entrance to the court – was originally directed towards Jerusalem but in 624 the Prophet aligned its axis (qibla) with the Ka'ba in Mecca to distinguish the Muslim from Jew and Christian.[1.2, 1.11] It focused on the cubical Ka'ba which was indicated by a small stone cube until a niche (mihrab) was introduced early in the 8th century: this reputedly marked the place where Muhammad habitually stood as prayer leader, off centre, and it was primarily designed to enhance the presence of the community leader at prayer but it was central to the qibla wall in subsequent mosques with increasing elaboration. From the 9th century the mihrab was joined by a pulpit (minbar) with steps leading up to a canopied throne: derived from the traditional seat of judgement, this is traditionally left vacant as the preserve of absent authority – Muhammad himself – and the *imam* or preacher (*khatib*) takes the top step. At the centre of power, where the main Jami-masjid was the scene of acclamation and proclamation, an enclosure (maqsura) was usually provided for the ruler.

The derivation of the religious from the secular is not unusual and as the religious and secular were to be inseparable in Islam *ab initio*, the pre-eminence of the Prophet's mosque as a model hardly needs explaining but the accidents of survival leave the line of development from it difficult to trace. Regularized, its features appeared immediately in San'a[1.12a] and in the new Muslim towns such as Basra (635), Kufa (638) or Fustat (Old Cairo, 641) to provide garrisons in conquered territory with a place of congregation for Friday prayer. These are all lost or entirely reworked but according to early chroniclers the one at Kufa, at least, had a gallery of pillaged columns against the qibla wall.

As Muslim builders followed their conquering leaders, refining primitive trabeation by adapting Christian and

1.12a

›ARCHITECTURE IN CONTEXT »ISLAM: INTRODUCTION

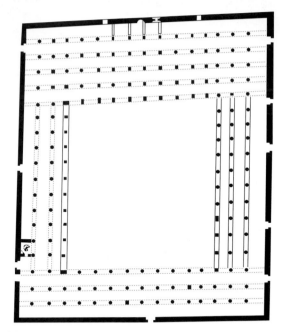

1.12b @ 1:1000

By the time of Muhammad, the palaces of south Arabia attributed to the Queen of Sheba had long disappeared: they lived on in inspirational legend which drew the image of twenty-storey buildings from the less astounding actuality of the typical tower house. If secular building was generally elevated over a square groundplan, so too were the places of worship. The Muslims followed the tradition: their first formal prayer halls were cubes with internal columns, like the Ka'ba.

The main mosques of the Yemeni capital are reputed to have been founded in the Prophet's lifetime. The Jami-masjid dominating the scene here enshrines a replica of the Ka'ba: its courtyard was probably developed with a five-bay prayer-hall to the north (three-bay riwaqs to the other sides) early in the 8th century to cater for the regular prayers of the expanding body of the faithful.

Antique precincts or reusing materials pillaged from them, the shelter provided for worshippers developed into a multi-columned or arcaded hall whose bays were invariably multiplied to a greater extent in length than in depth to provide maximum exposure of the individual to the view of *imam* and mihrab. Ultimately it was usual for the outer range to return around the other sides of the court to form galleries (riwaqs), as in the Prophet's mosque. The central range was distinguished to assert the qibla: this was usually the axis opened by the main entrance, on the opposite side of the court, beside a tower (minar) which asserted the presence of the mosque in the urban fabric.[1.12]

The development of arcading tended to respond to the need to support pitched roofing over generous space. However, in places remote from the Romanized centres of civilization – especially on the road to the East – trabeation survived in forms ranging from the most primitive to

1.13a

**›1.13 THE SILK ROAD IN XINJIANG, TUR-
FAN, GREAT MOSQUE,** 18th century: (a) exterior,
(b) interior.

A landmark in the advance of Islam to one of the few
substantial oases on the section of the Silk Road which
skirts the south of the Gobi Desert, this mosque – many
times restored – preserves the most primitive form of
prayer hall.

1.13b

the high sophistication traditional in China. The pyrami-
dal-roofed vernacular was dominant in the Indies – at least
until modern times. And so too, of course, was the Sub-
Saharan adobe tradition.**1.13–1.16**

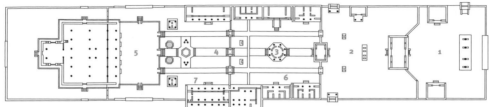

1.14a @ 1:2000

1.14b

1.14c

›1.14 CHINA, XI'AN, QINGZHEN-SI: (a) plan with (1) outer court and timber screen, (2) stele court with stone screen, (3) octagonal minaret, (4) inner court, (5) prayer hall terrace, (6) school for teaching Islam (madrasa), (7) bath house and accommodation for pilgrims, (b) entrance screen (paifeng), (c) octagonal minaret, (d) gate to inner court with fountain, (e) ablution tank, (f) prayer hall and terrace.

Founded in 742, the present form dates from the early 16th century, but the complex was restored in the early 17th and late-18th centuries, and (thoroughly) in the 1980s. As always with mosques east of Mecca, it is orientated with the wall sealing the prayer hall to the west indicating the direction of prayer.

Built almost entirely in accordance with the Chinese trabeated tradition, like the main mosque of Beijing but unlike most of the many mosques which line the Silk Road through Xinjiang, it is now entered from the north. The first (eastern) courtyard is dominated by the timber screen. The main gate, on the principal axis, leads to a stele court. Beyond is a second gate leading to the court of the octagonal minaret, flanked by the lecture hall and residential cells of the madrasa. Triple stone portals lead to the inner court with fountain and ablution tank, flanked by a bath house and accommodation for pilgrims. From this steps lead through a second set of triple portals to a prayer platform immediately before the seven-bay prayer hall.

1.14d

1.14e

1.14f

1.15a

Following the traditional Javanese style, the royal Masjid Agung at Solo was built by Sultan Pakubuono III beside his Kasunanan Palace (transported five years earlier from Kartasura). The multi-tiered pyramidal roof (joglo) covers a palatial hall (pendopo, see AIC2, pages 328–329) beyond the main prayer hall which is itself an elongated pendopo. By that time the formula was well represented in Malaysia.

1.15b

1.15c

1.15d

›1.16 SUB-SAHARAN AFRICA, MALI: Djenné, Friday Mosque (13th-century foundation in the reign of Sultan Koi Kunboro, rebuilt and augmented many times, most recently in 1906–07 under the direction of Ismaila Traoré, head of Djenné's guild of masons).

1.16

›ARCHITECTURE IN CONTEXT »ISLAM: INTRODUCTION

DEATH AND BURIAL

The example of the provision made for the burial of the Prophet in his establishment at Medina was to inspire the development of the second most important Muslim building type: the tomb. Unlike the mosque itself, however, that was ultimately to honour Koranic prescription more in the breach than in the letter.

Islam requires burial for the dead, the body being laid flat with the face turned towards Mecca, if possible in a vaulted chamber allowing the incumbent room to sit up when called to account. *Hadith*, rather than the Koran, proscribes funerary monuments: the Prophet reputedly discouraged the cult of the dead. Strict orthodoxy left the Muslim place of burial open to the sky but allowed the grave to be marked at ground level by a commemorative tablet and a recumbent stone – reflecting the position of the body below – inscribed with the ninety-nine names of God.**1.17**

As shade was a blessing, a canopy was deemed admissible by the less doctrinaire – and great was to be the import of that licence. Moreover, wishing to be buried within the orbit of 'benign influence' (*baraka*), many endowed the graves of holy men exuding mystic grace and provided themselves with associated tomb chambers. Hence, too, tombs were incorporated in the design of mosques after the precedent reputedly set at Medina but the type remains undocumented for more than a century after the Prophet's death.

The conquest of lands with strong traditions of holy places associated with entombment – and, indeed, of the secular mausoleum – prompted the introduction of the shrine commemorating martyrdom (mashhad). A canopy dome enshrined the sacred rock on Jerusalem's Mount Moriah little more than half a century after the Prophet's apotheosis there. The development of the heterodox Shi'ite cult of Ali and his descendants furthered the practice: a canopy was reputedly erected over the grave of Ali soon after it was identified at Najaf and – like the tomb of Ali's son Husayn at Karbala – this had achieved impressive durability by the late-9th century. Thereafter a variety of more-or-less substantial canopies proliferated over the graves of the eminent – orthodox as well as heterodox, princes as well as saints – often as the centrepieces of teaching colleges, hospitals or hospices designed to surpass the normal requirements of charity – and to veil pretension.

1.18a

INHERITANCE

The towns taken by the forces of Islam from highly sophisticated western and eastern civilizations – Christian and
Classical – were among the richest and most magnificent
ever seen.[1.18a, 1.19, 1.24a] Still dynamic and sustained by
scarcely flagging trade, many of them were to acquire new
splendour within half a millennium of the promulgation
of the Faith – an era of commercial sterility and urban
eclipse in most of feudal Europe. Punctuating the world
from Spain and Roman Africa to Mesopotamia and Iran
– a world unified in faith and commerce but only briefly
centred on one great capital, like Rome or Babylon – that

1.18c

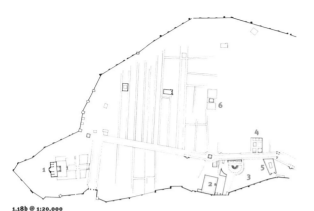

1.18b @ 1:20,000

›1.18 PALMYRA: (a) view of remains from the west with 'Diocletian's camp' in the foreground; (b) plan of main urban area c. 300 CE with (1) Diocletian's camp, (2) agora, (3) theatre, (4) baths, (5) sanctuary of Nebo, (6) sanctuary of Baal; (c) tomb tower.

›1.19 DAMASCUS: (a) plan of the central area (early 20th century) showing the Hellenistic grid partially obscured and in particular (1) the main east–west artery (the *decumanus maximus* in Roman times, the Biblical New Testament's 'Street Called Straight'), (2) the main north–south artery (the Roman *cardo maximus*, partially obscured by Muslim development), (3) the temenos of the Roman Temple of Jupiter Damascenus (c. 15 CE in origin) in which the Great Mosque replaced the church of S John the Baptist which had itself replaced the temple cella, (4) the site of the Hellenistic agora, (5) the Arabic palace, Temple of Jupiter; (b, c) temenos of Jupiter, remains of the temple propylaea and reconstruction with the basilican church of S John the Baptist in place of the original cella.

development was inevitably eclectic too: the Classical formal order, rarely preserved unobscured, was usually overlayed and expanded organically especially with market arcades (souks) providing the arteries of communication and integration like the major and minor blood vessels which bring life to all parts of a body. And so too with the world body served by the network of intercontinental trade arteries where – apart from the fort – the dominant extra-urban building type was the arcaded court catering for travellers and their caravans (caravanserai).

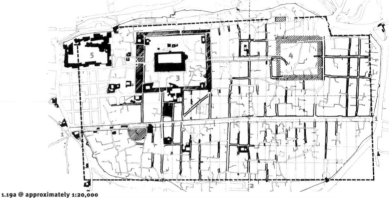

1.19a @ approximately 1:20,000

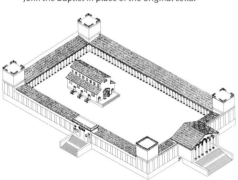

1.19c

1.19b

Between the arteries, the body of the archetypical town in the typically hot and dry Muslim world consists largely of courtyards, domestic, civic and religious. Responding to the order of planning or the waywardness of natural growth, these are the orifices of air and light and the hubs of commerce, social and political – like agora or forum, atrium or peristyle and their ancient eastern ancestors. And, of course, like their grandest predecessors, they were framed by the community's most important buildings – the palace of the ruler in due course, but first the Jami-masjid which provided the community with its focus.

The Arab conquerors in the name of Islam had an acute sense of sacred space, forbidden (*haram*) except for pre-scribed devotion in accordance with venerable formulas – like the Ka'ba precinct. The orientation and protection of such space were always to be the first objectives of Muslim builders. With no native monumental tradition of building to draw upon, as we have already noted they read-ily adapted what they found to augment their liturgical needs. Thus, as bases for further conquest were established in old or new settlements, the Muslims developed their essentially urban tradition to meet the requirements of prayer in widely varied ways – not least the vernacular, as we have seen.**1.14–1.17**

Climate and materials available locally determine form and style generally, of course, but in the Fertile Crescent – the cradle of civilization arching from Syria and Palestine through the course of the great rivers Tigris and Euphrates – the first Muslims drew on the most sophisticated of Antique monumental traditions. To the west they were indebted to Christian Byzantium and its Roman men-tors.**1.18, 1.19** To the east they absorbed the imperial Parthian and Sasanian synthesis of the Hellenistic, the Roman and the ancient Persian for both religious and sec-ular purposes – in so far as these may be distinguished in

1.20a @ approximately 1:1000

›**1.20 THE PARTHIAN AND SASANIAN LEGACY:** (a) Assur (early 1st century CE?), plan; (b, c) Firozabad (c. 250), plan of palace and court view to iwan; (d) Qasr-i Shirin, Imarat I-Kusraw (c. 590), plan; (e) Ctesiphon, Sasanian palace (mid-6th century), view from north-east; (f) Sarvistan, general view with domed cubical chamber (qubba); (g–i) Gira (between Firozabad and Kazarun), fire temple, plan, elevation and section (5th century, after Herzfeld, no scale); (j) Naqsh-i Rustam (site of the imperial Achaemenid tombs and of a rectangular tower which may be a Zoroastrian funerary monument), model fire temples.

The Assur palace has the earliest-known four-iwan plan. If the general approach to planning in terms of a warren of rooms about a nuclear court is traditionally Mesopotamian, like the dominant arch, the eclecticism of the Parthians is marked not only by the dressing in terms borrowed from the Roman theatrical scenae frons, but also by the inclusion of a columned hall descended through the Achaemenids from the Urar-tians – and, ultimately from the tent.

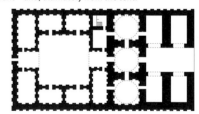

1.20b @ 1:2000

The main court façade of Firozabad, facing north, was dominated by the great central iwan (now largely fallen) in which the king could have sat in public audi-ence. It led to three great domed rooms well suited to more exclusive reception and private audience. Beyond these was a court flanked by the royal apartments with iwans to the north and south. The traditional tripartite division of the oriental palace has rarely been clearer.

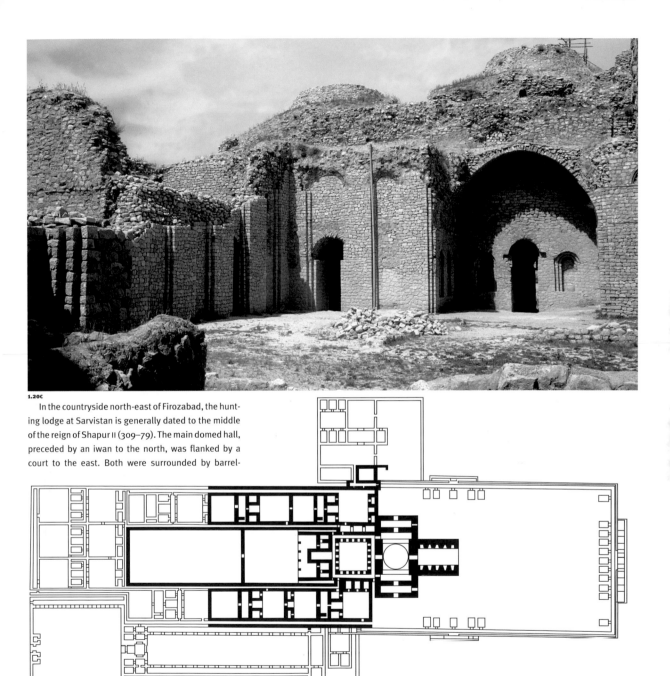

1.20C

In the countryside north-east of Firozabad, the hunting lodge at Sarvistan is generally dated to the middle of the reign of Shapur II (309–79). The main domed hall, preceded by an iwan to the north, was flanked by a court to the east. Both were surrounded by barrel-

1.20d @ approximately 1:2500

1.200

›ARCHITECTURE IN CONTEXT »ISLAM: INTRODUCTION

1.20f

1.20j

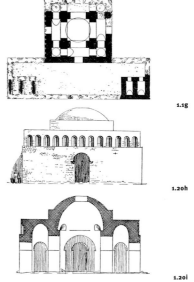

1.1g

1.20h

1.20i

strict orthodoxy.**1.20** In between, the example was set by their Semitic relatives in outpost like Hatra or Petra**1.21, 1.22** and by the elusive Ghassanid Arabic clients of the great 6th-century Byzantine imperialist, Justinian. The combination of appropriated motifs was generally uncanonical – in the Hellenistic sense of the authoritative – and exotic traditions asserted themselves as the conquest moved east and west, promoting provincial diversity but also enriching the style of the caliph's own works as conscription drew labour from all over the empire.

vaulted halls, the larger ones to the north and south with shallow aisles defined by truncated columns – as in a basilica. The subsidiary domed space in the northwest corner (to the left here) may have been a fire temple: the typical Iranian fire temple is a freestanding domed cube open to all four sides – chahar-taq.

>**1.21 HATRA:** general view of palace.

Situated between the Tigris and the Euphrates, Hatra's prosperity depended on control of one of the few oases in the northern Mesopotamian desert crossed by the east–west trade route. It was occupied by Arabs in the 1st century BCE and was the seat of a monarchy from c. 156 to 241. Culturally, at least, it was dependent on both the Romans and the Parthians though the former failed to take it and it remained largely independent of the latter. It fell to the 3rd-century Sasanian king Shapur I and was then abandoned.

>**1.22 PETRA:** general view with 'Palace Tomb' (left) and 'Corinthian Tomb' (left centre).

Petra was the capital of the Nabataeans, whose kingdom was extinguished by the Roman emperor Trajan in 106. Its wealth, based on controlling the trade routes between Syria and Arabia, is most tangibly recalled by the tombs carved into the red sandstone cliffs. They range from the representation of the tower type common in the east to the free superimposition of Classical building types reproduced in three dimensions. Here the rich mix includes the temple, the tempietto (and ciborium), and the scenae frons.

1.21

The domed cube of the fire temple scarcely invited conversion to Muslim congregational prayer space, ideally broad and expansive to accommodate numerous worshippers aligned laterally before the qibla wall. However, beyond the ordered forecourt it contributed a grand motif

1.22

for asserting the qibla – and enhancing the presence of the ruler as prayer leader. Moreover, it seems to have been extrapolated to provide the dominant type of Muslim tomb – though towers may not be overlooked in this regard.[1.18c] On the other hand the Christian martyrium, which inspired the Muslims in principle at least, had its origin in the late-Classical mausoleum with its moulded mass and space.[1.22, 1.23]

Sasanian vaulting had ancient Mesopotamian origins but acknowledged the inspiration of the Romans in scale and variety. Beyond the transmission of the Greek conception of order – of secondary importance to Sasanians, Byzantine Christians and Muslims even when reusing Orders pillaged from the sanctuaries of their predecessors – vaulted space on a grand scale and moulded with great variety in poured concrete was the major legacy of the Romans to the future of architecture. The temple may have been a simple cubicle in principle but the diversification of space and mass characterized the major imperial Roman secular types: the aisled and apsed basilica in which king or magistrate sat in state but especially the great bathing complexes with their stunning scenographic perspectives.

The basilica, adopted by the early Christians as the archetypical church, was hardly more suitable for the breadth of Muslim congregational prayer than the domed cube but it could be imposed on the hypostyle hall to distinguish the axis of prayer and it was retained by caliphs as the setting for court ceremonial. The baths – building type and purpose – were to be appreciated at least as much by Muslims as Christians in the west Asian provinces of Byzantium inherited from Rome and first to be overwhelmed by the Arabs.[1.24]

The Roman tradition had been taken to its apotheosis in the Christian church as the image of the City of God by the architects of Constantinople – the Byzantine cap-

1.23a

>1.23 ROMANO-CHRISTIAN TOMB TYPES: (a) Rome, Vatican Cemetery, Tomb of the Caetennii (2nd century); (b) Jerusalem, Church of the Holy Sepulchre on Golgotha (c. 326–36), 'Edicule' enshrining Christ's tomb (5th century?, model; Narbonne, Museum of Art and History).

The two proto-typical Classical tomb types, the cubical and the 'tempietto' – superimposed for the so-called Corinthian tomb at Petra, were widely represented in the Roman world singly or combined. Within, the recession housing the main patron's urn was distinguished by an aedicule. By the middle of the 2nd century aedicules had proliferated in a decorative band broken only by a great arched niche to distinguish the main one.

1.23b

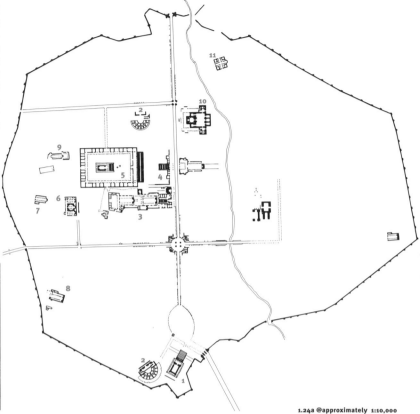

›1.24 LATE-ROMAN AND EARLY CHRISTIAN SPATIAL TYPES: (a) Gerasa, plan with (1) Temple of Zeus, (2) theatres, (3) complex of basilicas incorporating the so-called cathedral to the east and the church of S. Theodore, (4) elements of the sacred way leading to (5) the Temple of Artemis, (6) triple church complex of Ss. Cosmas and Damian, S. John the Baptist and S. George, (7) S. Genesius, (8) Ss. Peter and Paul, (9) 'synagogue', (10) North Baths, (11) cruciform basilica; (b–d) Qalb Lozeh, basilica plan, interior and view from the east.

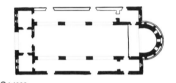

1.24b @ 1:1000

1.24c

1.24a @approximately 1:10,000

1.24d

ital which survived the fall of Rome by a thousand years.[1.25] Islam ultimately acquired the supreme example, converted it and applied its principles to comparable effect. Before their acquisition of the Anatolian provinces of Byzantium over the previous century and more, the Muslims had rarely invented cover for vast spaces beyond the trabeated or arcaded hall of repetitive bays – or canopies in the courtyard which sufficed in the Arabic heartlands. Beyond the simple domed cube, they did embrace the nine-square, five-domed building type known as 'quincunx': familiar to the Sasanians, at least in approximation,[1.20h] this highly rational but essentially restrictive formula was adopted by both Christians and

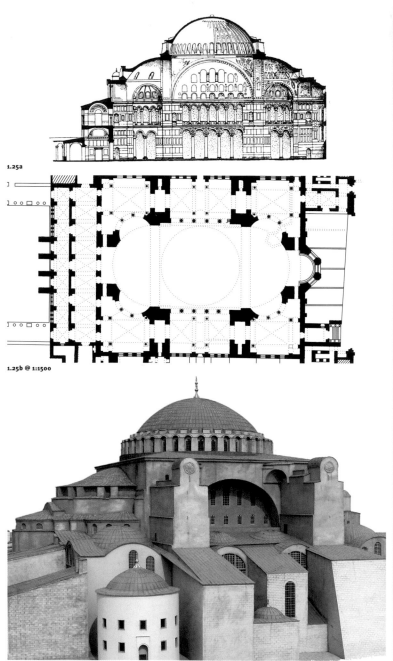

1.25a

1.25b @ 1:1500

1.25c

1.25d

Muslims for small communities of worshippers at about the same time: in so far as the accidents of survival testify (AICI, pages 800 ff.), that was little more than a century after the Islamic tradition had crossed the ageless hypostyle hall with the Romano-Christian basilica.

Beyond its spatial types, all three distinguishing features of the congregational mosque – minaret, mihrab and minbar – may be seen to have originated in the Graeco-Roman tradition adapted by the Christians. The mihrab descends from the basilican apse.**1.26a,b, 1.24c** The stepped pulpit derives from the Roman seat of judgement, like the bishop's chair in the apse of the Christian basilica, but it also fulfils the function of the ambo.**1.26c,d** The minaret was added, or kept from the church, to assert the presence of Islam with a landmark which ultimately eclipsed the Christian bell-tower in broadcasting the times of prayer: church towers, square in plan, were common in Syria.**1.24b,c** With obvious symbolic relevance, however, the Arabic term relates to 'lighthouse' – of which the Pharos of Alexandria was the most celebrated example.**1.26e**

The seat of Muslim political power – in principle indistinguishable from religious authority – also naturally

>**1.25 ISTANBUL, HAGIA SOPHIA,** 6th century CE: (a, b) section and plan of main volume, (c) model from south (Istanbul, Miniaturk), (d) apsidal and central vaulting with detail of mosaic embellishment.

1.26e

>**1.26 PRECEDENTS FOR MIHRAB, MINBAR AND MINAR:** (a) Baalbek, temenos of the Temple of Jupiter (1st century), niche; (b) Torah niche from Synagogue II, Dura Europos (3rd century CE); (c) apse from S. Agnese, Rome (625), apse; (d) ambo from the Church of the Virgin, Cairo (7th century); (e) the Pharos of Alexandria on a coin of Antoninus Pius, 138–61, after which most reconstructions place a polygonal lantern on an octagonal 'drum' above the high, battered rectangular base.

1.26d

1.26a

1.26b

1.26c

›1.27 THE ROMAN MILITARY COMPLEX: (a) Lambaesis (Algeria), late-1st-century camp; (b) Split, camp-palace of the emperor Diocletian (c. 300); (c) R'safah, 6th-century fortified town (Byzantine Sergiopolis): overview.

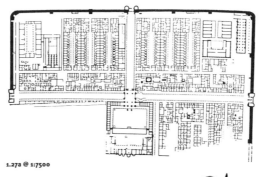

1.27a @ 1:7500

The camp of the Third Augustan Legion at Lambaesis, established c. 80 CE to protect the frontiers of the provinces of Africa and Numidia (in modern Algeria), was typical in facilitating the efficient deployment of the garrisons along the two main axes (*cardo* and *decumanus*) and a complete circuit of streets within the walls. The grid regimented the disposition of houses or tents in the quarters.

Like a camp, Split's rectangular compound had square towers at the corners and between the twin-towered gates on each of the three landward sides: on the sea front there was an open gallery above a water gate. The colonnaded *cardo* and *decumanus* crossed in the centre, to the south of the accommodation for the household and guests, to the north of the main palace buildings. On the central axis, continuing the route from the north which passes between the temple and mausoleum, a portico preceded a domed vestibule, the imperial place of appearance or epiphany. The form of portico with arch penetrating pediment is called fastigium. It symbolizes the canopy of heaven which first achieved apotheosis on the ziggurat of Ur-Nammu at Ur. Adapted to the tent of appearance, it became the ciborium or baldachino, the domical canopy carried over thrones and altars which prompted the arching of the entablature over the central bay and was typically echoed in the great niche above palace portals.

With its rational plan perpetuating the ideal of the Roman camp, R'safah was one of a string of fortified outposts on the Syrian frontier, founded by Emperor Justinian (527–65) and annexed by Islam. Typically the great square compound defended the establishments of church and state as well as providing housing and facilities for the garrison. Outside the walls are the remains of a nine-square tetraconch which has been identified from an inscription of c. 560 as the ceremonial hall of Justinian's Ghassanid tributary, al-Mundir.

1.27b

1.27c

acknowledges the Roman and Byzantine traditions of both the four-square fort and the expansive complex of courts and halls developed organically in town or countryside. Diocletian's retreat at Split and its more prosaic progenitors, often recalled at various scales by Justinian and his successors on the eastern frontier of the empire, are clearly relevant representatives of the former.**1.27** The

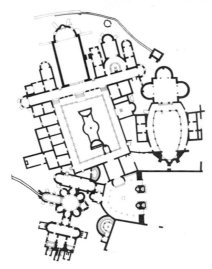

1.28a @ 1:2000

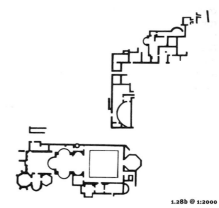

1.28b @ 1:2000

imperial palaces of Rome and Constantinople or the imperial villas at Tivoli and Piazza Armerina are the most prominent representatives of the more organic type: they are somewhat distant but there were doubtless comparable complexes in the rich provinces of west Asia and north Africa.[1.28] Of more immediate relevance is the proconsular palace, like the one at Apollonia in eastern Libya: the type recurs throughout the empire.[1.29]

>1.28. LATE-ROMAN IMPERIAL VILLAS: (a) Piazza Armerina (Sicily) villa (early 4th century), plan; (b) Desenzano (northern Italy) villa (4th century), plan; (c) mosaic pavement from a villa in the Province of Africa (Ifriqiya, modern Tunisia) but with ubiquitous 'grotesque' motif; (d) Qanawat (Syria, after 250 CE) portal with rampant vine motif of the type later to be called 'arabesque'.

The lavish villa at Piazza Armerina in Sicily represents the ultimate fruition of the organic tradition most expansively represented by the 2nd-century emperor Hadrian's villa at Tivoli – though the layout in whole and in main part is irregular rather than informal. It was not unique. Contemporary – or later – villas, comparable in

1.28c

1.28d

complexity and in the quality of their embellishment, remain incompletely excavated in many former Roman provinces – at Desanzano by Lake Garda, for example. Consistent is a succession of courts aligned on axis in the context of stricter regularity than appealed to the patron of Piazza Armerina, and the hemicycle proved enduringly popular for the distinction of main spaces.

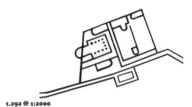

1.29a @ 1:2000

›1.29 APOLLONIA, PALACE REMAINS, 6th century: (a) plan, (b) view from the south-east.

Little of external significance survives but the major internal spaces are well represented: on a relatively modest scale, naturally, these follow the imperial example of a sequence of vestibules, flanked by apartments, culminating in a peristylar court before the seat of power in its basilica.

1.29b

The rooms of such villas– and most other buildings of any pretension – would have been plastered and frescoed and paved with mosaic tiles. Patterns ranged from the representational to the abstract but a special place was held by the stylized floral meander motif with anthropomorphic or zoomorphic figures sprouting irrationally from the sensuous vine.**1.28c** That motif ramped over architectural elements in elevation too, denying structural logic.**1.28d**

There is no clear line of development from either the formal or the organic plan type as survivals are limited: new rulers were usually peripatetic and, in any case, wanted new palaces hastily erected – inevitably with perishable materials pillaged in part, at least, from the complex of their predecessors. However, the widely scattered remains usually recall the age-old tripartite division into zones for the ruler's public audience and bureaucracy, private council and personal accommodation connected with the enclosed quarters of his women. A regular theme, too, is the twin-towered portal – the venerable place of appearance of the ruler as god or regent of god among men.**1.30b**

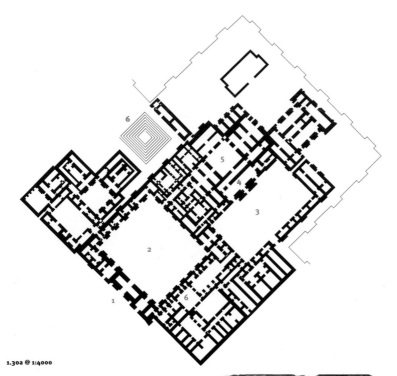

1.30a @ 1:4000

1.30b

Fortified as an assertion of power at least as much as for defence, the complex of palace, temple and ziggurat on the vast terrace at Dur-Sharrukin brought the Mesopotamian architectural tradition to its apogee. Three gatehouses (1) led straight through to the near-square outer court (2), where those seeking or summoned to audience presumably assembled. From this, the offset exit restricted access to the great audience court (3), which was dominated from the centre of its south-western side by the twin-towered portal of the throne room (4). Two further right-angle turns led slightly off axis to the king's apartment, centred on the court of private audience and its three flanking suites (5) beyond which was the ziggurat temple complex (6). The upper walls of courts and halls were largely embellished with images of the king and his courtiers over orthostat reliefs of hunting, military and religious subjects and massive stone human-headed winged bulls (*lamassu*) at the corners of the entrances.

Symbolic of royal prowess, the *lamassu* reinforced a venerable tradition. From at least the early 2nd millennium BCE, temples like the one dedicated to Ishtar-Kititum at Ischali in the ancient Iraqi domain of Eshnunna had a sequence of twin-towered portals to their major spaces. Presented with such assertive multiplicity in such a hallowed context, it is not hard to imagine how the arch flanked by towers became the symbol of epiphany: the place of appearance of the god among men in the divine image presented by the ruler as high priest. Annexing the temple to which it belonged, the ruler of Eshnunna appropriated the motif as the symbol of quasi-divine royal authority: the king in the tower-flanked portal of his garden in the relief from Nineveh clearly articulates the theme. The Parthian palace at Ashur[1.20a] and the Sasanian one at Ctesiphon[1.20e] sustain the tradition in the context of the scenae frons: early Muslim builders knew the latter, at least, and the motif was a standard royal symbol on coins.

A regularly varied theme is the celebration of water in court and garden. If foliage was allowed to ramp freely in decoration, the garden from which it derived was usually disciplined by regular geometry for containment, for access and especially for channelling the water. That is as old as the Egyptians though the square compound quartered by axial canals, which the Persians called *paridaeza* and which Xenophon translated into Greek as *paradeisos*, may be traced back at least to the Assyrians[1.30b] – if not to the Hebrews whose Biblical tradition of the garden of Paradise was ever of fundamental significance to Muslims and, of course, to Christians.

The substance of building in the world overtaken by Islam naturally varies from fine ashlar to mud-brick according to climate and resource. So does its ornament which ranges from fine stone carving, sometimes articulating structure, to moulded brickwork and mosaic tiling whose anti-anthropomorphic patterns ramp in lush disregard of structure. The Mediterranean littoral, where masonry construction and carving were perfected by the Greeks and diversified by the Romans, provided skills, example and, above all at first, ready-fashioned elements for reuse. But brick and glazed tile dominate in the central riverine plains of the Fertile Crescent and its dessicated peripheries, where urban civilization began and monumental building was initiated. And it was there that the builders of the new faith began to find their way towards idiosyncratic monumentality and its embellishment.

NOTE: a fuller account of the background may be found in *Architecture in Context I, Antiquity* (referred to as AIC1).

>**1.31 THE TRIUMPH OF ISLAM AT THE EPIPHANY PORTAL:** detail of mosaic revetment, Great Mosque, Damascus.

In the east, tradition attributed divinity – at least of inspiration – to the ruler who sustained his mandate in furthering prosperity and security: thus, in the place of the Hellenistic king, Roman emperors achieved apotheosis. Temples were dedicated to Rome and Augustus after the death of the latter – the first emperor – and many of his successors were similarly honoured. But the building type specifically designed to celebrate the apotheosis of imperial power was the triumphal arch (AIC1, pages 561ff.). Proclaiming the glory of the ruler, the gate in the urban limits was ideally extracted from that context to mark the Sacred Way of triumph to the Temple of Jupiter Capitolinus in cities all over the empire, as in Rome. With the apotheosis of the ruler on eastern lines, it assumed the Hellenized form of the ancient Mesopotamian twin-towered palace portal where divinity appeared before man through the agency of the king.

PART 1 DAR AL-ISLAM

1.1 ASCENDANCY OF THE CALIPHATE AND THE ASSERTION OF ORTHODOXY

1.32a

1 THE UMAYYADS OF DAMASCUS

The opprobrium heaped on the regime of Yasid, the successor of the Umayyad caliph Mu'awiya (661–80), was to undermine it but Umayyads reigned from Damascus – or the desert outpost of R'safah – for another seventy years. The most effective were Abd al-Malik (685–705), Abd al-Walid I (705–15) and Hisham (724–43) who completed the ordering of the administrative establishment. They assiduously sustained a professional army encamped in the manner inherited by Byzantium from the Romans: it was certainly not idle but under them there was a new peace in the old Fertile Crescent. With that peace there was prosperity furthered by the revival of agricultural estates sequestered by the new elite from the old Byzantine landed class. With the concomitant lucrative taxation and the rich booty of expanding conquest, the rulers disposed of great riches not only on their military ambitions and their army: determined to eclipse their predecessors – particularly the Christians – in the expression of their magnificence in building, they may be credited with the foundation of the monumental tradition of Islam. And as befits conquerors, they did this with thoroughgoing eclecticism.[1.31]

PREMIER MONUMENTS OF THE FAITH

Caliph Abd al-Malik was responsible for the faith's most sacred monument after the mosques of Mecca and Medina: the Dome of the Rock which dominates the holy city of Jerusalem from Mount Moriah, the elevated site accorded by tradition to Solomon's Temple where a rocky protruberance is believed to have provided Abraham with the altar for his intended sacrifice of Isaac and Muhammad with the platform for his ascent into heaven. It recalls the canopy type of martyrium derived by the Christians

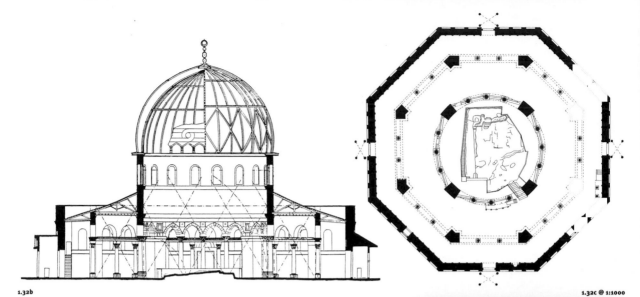

from the Antique heroon, but most particularly inspired by the Anastasis rotunda built by Emperor Constantine over Christ's sepulchre.[1.23b] Embellished with both Byzantine and Sasanian imperial symbols in the form of trophies, it was clearly conceived to celebrate the triumph of Islam.[1.32]

Dome of the Rock

Resplendent in blue and gold, the first monument of Islam is reached through arcaded screens at the head of six flights of stairs (probably added c. 900). It is entered through portals facing in the cardinal directions, the one facing Mecca to the south distinguished by a portico which was probably not part of the original design.

The octagonal canopy is supported by arches springing from antique columns alternating with piers. These form a double ambulatory for pilgrims to circulate around the holy rock: the outer arcade is octagonal like the perimeter walls, but the central one, below the double-skinned timber dome (20 metres in diameter, 25 metres high), hovers between circle and square. The arches are generally lightly pointed. Offering more resistance to the load bearing down upon it than the typically Roman semi-

1.32d

›1.32 JERUSALEM, DOME OF THE ROCK,
691: (a) distant view (early 19th-century lithograph by
David Roberts), (b, c) section and plan, (d, e) models,
(f–h) details of interior and mosaic representations of
Sasanian and Byzantine royal symbols in an arabesque
context.

1.32e

1.32g

1.32h

circular form – which tends to flatten out at the top – the pointed arch was
to be characteristic of Islamic architecture.

Contrary to normal Byzantine practice, the double-shell dome rises
high on its drum over the surrounding ambulatory roofs: its gilding
enhances the impact of Islam on the holy place of Jews and Christians.
The walls below were all originally covered with mosaics over a marble
dado but these were replaced with magnificent tiles by the Ottomans
from the 16th century. Inside, the original mosaics have fared better than
most of their contemporaries – though marble has replaced them in spandrels and the friezes below the 16th-century wooden ceilings of the
ambulatory. With the most prominent exception of the interior of the
dome itself, relined in 1818, the mosaics may be Byzantine in execution
and in the way they ramp freely in essentially un-Classical denial of the
integrity of structural forms, but not in their hybrid forms or eclectic mix
of Koranic calligraphy, denials of Christian dogma, Byzantine and Sasanian symbols of imperium and entirely non-figurative floral motifs of Persian as well as Hellenistic origin. The latter are clearly related to the
antique Roman 'grotesque':[1.28c] eschewing the anthropomorphic elements, however, they are defined as 'arabesque'.

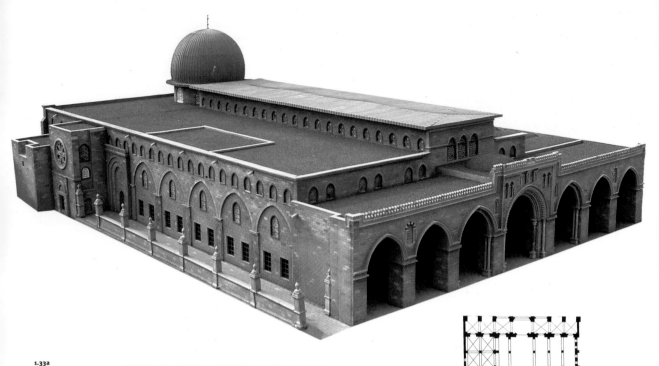

1.33a

THE MONUMENTAL UMAYYAD MOSQUE

Abd al-Malik's secure and prosperous successor, Abd al-Walid, provided Muslim posterity with three imperious precedents – at Damascus, Medina and Jerusalem – for translating the domestic court of the prototypical mosque – if the Prophet's establishment at Medina may be so described – into a monument conceived to rival the architectural glories of the Byzantine and Roman past. Accordingly, of course, the ruler was accommodated in an adjacent palace rather than in the mosque itself, but as the latter remained a social and political forum, as well as a place of worship, it usually retained the community's treasury.

Pretension went hand in hand with pragmatism: the caliph's architects solved the problem of covering large areas by recycling columns from redundant buildings to

›1.33 ECLECTICISM: (a, b) Jerusalem, Al-Aqsa Mosque (mid-7th-century foundation rebuilt in the late-7th century, expanded from 709, rebuilt mid-8th century, mid-11th century and extensively renovated on several subsequent occasions), model (Istanbul, Miniaturk) and plan; (c) Medina, Prophet's Mosque (707), plan.

In Jerusalem, a temporary structure of c. 640 was replaced under the caliph Abd al-Malik with a completely roofed building reusing Classical columns: as the whole of the Temple Mount was *haram*, the mosque needed no special precinct enclosure before its prayer hall. Under al-Walid the latter was expanded to the north beyond a wider, clerestory-lit nave perpendicular to the distinct qibla range: there were probably seven bays on each side, all covered with pitched roofs carried on columns but the greater height of the nave required walling over stout arcades as in the typical Christian basilica.[1.24b,c] First rebuilt at the very end of the Umayyad period after an earthquake in 747, the original scheme was reiterated but the qibla qubba dome was probably added at this time. The 11th-century campaign reduced the number of aisles but inserted a grander dome. The porch is 12th century.

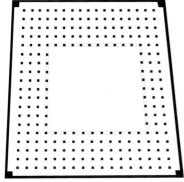

1.33c @ 1:2000

In Medina, against local opposition, the primitive foundation was demolished and replaced with a multi-bay structure framing an open court on a near-trapezoidal plan. Arcades masked the trabeation on all four court fronts and the embellishment – reputedly in part provided by the Byzantine emperor – was lavish. The new compound is reputed to have been endowed with four corner minarets – if so, they seem long to have remained unique. References to the qibla dome of this work are the earliest so far found in Umayyad annals.

>**1.35 DAMASCUS, GREAT UMAYYAD MOSQUE** (705–15): (a) detail of 'arabesque' motif, (b) court from north-east, (c) plan with (1) entrances, (2) prayer court, (3) treasury, (4) minarets, (5) prayer hall, (6) transept, (7) mihrab, (8) domed bay, (d) detail of court side of western entrance, (e) engraved detail of mosaic revetment and fenestration, (f) court from western entrance, (g) prayer hall interior.

1.35a

form hypostyle halls which could by expanded at will. Basra (665), Kufa (670), Fustat (673) and Wasit (702) were among the most important palatine mosques already endowed with hypostyle halls under Mu'awiyah or Abd al-Malik. There were doubtless many more of which few necessarily conformed to the imperial type with distinguished nave. And in the context of that type, at first at least, redundant Christian bell towers – not strictly necessary for announcing the times of prayer – were readily converted to the assertion of the dominance of Islam: representation was indeed seen as the primary consideration when the caliph himself was credited with ordering the prototype in unknown form for Basra in 665 but examples are extremely rare before the 9th century.

Work on al-Walid's greatest mosque was initiated in 705 on a long-sacred site beside the palace in his Syrian capital, Damascus. The city's complex past provided an impressive range of ingredients for the new eclecticism. Not the least of these is the mihrab niche, as the symbol of the Prophet's authority in the absence of anthropomorphic representation, but more spectacular is the domed nave adopted to assert the qibla and to distinguish the zone of the ruler in the age-old manner of the ciborium: only the date of the dome is unclear. The following year he began rebuilding at Medina, quadrupling the Prophet's court and surrounding it with riwaqs, and initiated work on a similar plan elsewhere, notably at San'a.[1.12] Before the end of the decade he founded the al-Aqsa mosque in Jerusalem. The latter and the premier mosque of Medina have been much altered. The Damascene work was devastated by fire in 1893 but its restoration, inaccurate in some respects, preserved much of the original.[1.33, 1.34]

1.34b

›ARCHITECTURE IN CONTEXT »DAR AL-ISLAM

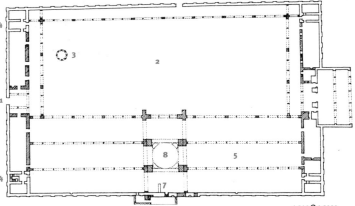

1.34c @ 1:2000

The Great Mosque of Damascus

The exercise is typical of Arab practice in old urban civilizations. There had been a cult centre on the site since time immemorial: under the emperor Theodosius I (379–95) the last temple of the Roman era was converted into the church of S. John the Baptist – it contained his head, as does the mosque. Determined to supersede the old beliefs, the Muslims demolished the former temple but kept the precinct (157 by 100 metres) and tripled the colonnade on the south (the side of Mecca) to form the prayer hall: innovatively, the qibla was asserted by a nave perpendicular to the three aisles. The origin of the maqsura – the place reserved for the royal patron's prayers – has been located here.

No longer the result of ad hoc growth, the plan of the mosque is ordered by the regular geometry of temple and basilica, as the temenos was adapted for the prayer court and the reused columns ordered the elevation of prayer hall and cloister. More specifically, similarity has been seen between the court façade and the representation of a Byzantine palace in Theodoric's church of S. Apollinare Nuovo at Ravenna (AIC1, page 690). In both, the central frontispiece derives from the Roman fastigium – the monumental propylaeum of temple and palace which was particularly prominent in Syria (AIC1, page 600). There was such a propylaeum to the east.

There are four entrances – the principal one in place of the Roman propylaeum to the east, a secondary one at the western end of the cross-axis, a minor one in the north range unaligned with the central entrance from court to nave, and the former caliph's private one beside the central

1.34d

1.34e

1.34f

1.348

mihrab in the qibla wall to the south. Al-Walid's builders were responsible for the piers, originally alternating with columns, which form the cloisters. Unlike the earlier pointed ones in the Dome of the Rock, the arches are generally semi-circular in the Roman and Byzantine manner. The Romano-Christian precinct provided the bases of the southern minarets: the south-eastern one was reputedly the bell tower of the Christian cathedral; the northern one, resplendent in its mosaic revetment, is credited in origin to al-Walid but was replaced in the late-12th century. The domed octagon raised on columns towards the west end of the court was the treasury.

The revetment was opulent in the extreme. Marble panels of exquisite quality originally provided a high dado around the main walls and marble grills in alternating geometric patterns screened the windows. Above the marble, most exposed surfaces were covered with mosaics traditionally attributed to artists from Constantinople – like all the most opulent works of early Islamic builders. Even after the fire which devastated the mosque in 1893, some of their work survives on the central frontispiece and western portico. The motifs are largely floral: direct is the derivation of the 'arabesque' motif from Hagia Sophia.[1.25] Elsewhere realism prevails for trees and enigmatic buildings – the natural world and the cities of the Umayyad caliphate, the City of God and His Eden? – but not people or animals. The window grills are geometrical in pattern – in anticipation of another major Muslim motif.

Inside, the triple colonnade of the prayer hall may have been inspired by the typical basilica, Roman or Christian, with its nave and side aisles, but here all three parts are equal in width. At the head of the nave which cuts through these colonnades, the main mihrab is the earliest known, though it was probably anticipated in al-Walid's rebuilding of the Prophet's mosque at Medina. Two other mihrabs were subsequently arranged in near symmetry with it in the qibla wall, while a fourth, just to the west of the central one, dates from after the fire of 1893.

The present dome is an unhappy reconstruction on 11th-century foundations after the late-19th-century fire. The original dome was inserted at an unknown date, probably closer to the mihrab following the example set under al-Walid at Medina: dome and 'nave' are the major innovations attributed to his architects.

1.35a

1.35b

›1.35 QASR AL-HAYR AL-SHARQI (east Syrian desert), dated to 728/9 from an inscription of Caliph Hisham): (a, b) entrance and general view, (c, d) plans of main and secondary enclosures.

Standing at a major intersection of the trade routes from Damascus to the Jazira and Aleppo to the lower Euphrates, there are two enclosures in the eastern complex: the larger one is clearly residential, the smaller one auxiliary. Paired apartments were typical of Umayyad domestic building. Here particularly grand examples flank all four sides of the square court of the main fortified enclosure, while small utilitarian ones surround the secondary enclosure which doubtless provided stabling and grain storage.

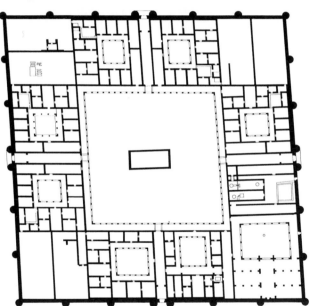

1.35c @ 1:1000

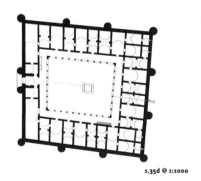

1.35d @ 1:1000

CAMPS AND PALACES

The principal urban seats of the Damascene Umayyads have fared badly over time and tumult but several provincial establishments remain and there is a series of well-preserved, if enigmatic, walled compounds in the Syrian desert. Doubtless garrisoned centres of rural economy or outposts of trade, they accommodated peripatetic Arab rulers out hunting or campaigning or simply escaping

1.36a

›**1.36 QASR AL-HAYR AL-GHARBI** (west Syrian desert), c. 730: (a) detail of figurative fresco, (b) entrance front.

1.36b

from the alien city with sobriety yet rather more comfort than they had previously known. And, of course, they also proclaimed the triumph of Islam – the more so because their defences were often primarily symbolic, despite the origin of their typical form.

After the model of the Roman fort and its successor, the Byzantine command post like the one at R'safah,**1.27c** the Umayyad camps were usually rectangular, their stone-clad walls punctuated with circular or polygonal rubble-filled towers and the twin-towered portals of age-old royal potency.**1.35, 1.36** There was a full complement of four of these, backed by axial corridors, at Syrian Qasr al-Hayr al-Sharqi, north-east of Palmyra, but three were subsequently sealed. There were two on the east–west axis at Qasr al-Hayr al-Gharbi, south-west of Palmyra, and only one at the smaller, tauter Qasr Kharana in Jordan. The purpose of the exercise in all these cases is obscure. However, the larger of the al-Hayr structures has been defined by the excavators as a medina (town) though it can hardly have accommodated more than an elite in the apartments (bayts) of the two-storey ranges which frame its colonnaded or arcaded court: the smaller one may be the earliest-known caravanserai.

In so far as the accidents of survival testify, the urban seat of power was an extended complex of several courts, housing the ruler, his entourage and the administration in the Sasanian manner – at least in part – but not without reference to the Roman basilica. At the several extra-urban sites, of which the most significant are Mshatta south of Amman and Khirbat al-Mafjar near Jericho, Caliph al-Walid II provided himself with luxurious retreats: eclectic in their lavish ornament, they recall both eastern and west-

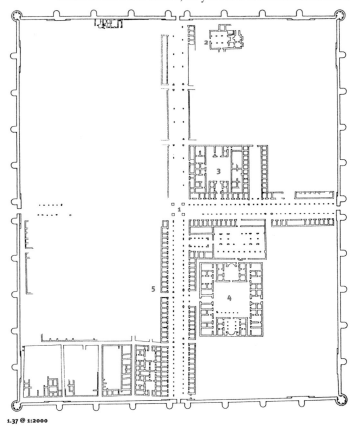

1.37 @ 1:2000

>**1.37 ANJAR, CAMP-CITY,** early 8th century?: plan with (1) tetrapylon at the intersection of the shop-lined *cardo* and *decumanus*, (2) audience hall with attached bath house, (3) administration building (dar al-imara), (4) palace, (5) houses.

ern prototypes on a scale apparently conceived to accommodate most of the court and the administration. No less richly decorated, there were also smaller desert establishments consisting of a reception hall associated with a bath house incorporating varied spaces for the various facilities of a provincial Roman thermal complex: the most notable of the latter survives alone at Qasr Amra.[1.37–1.42]

›1.38 KUFA, VICE-REGAL PALACE, 638–70 and perhaps later: plan.

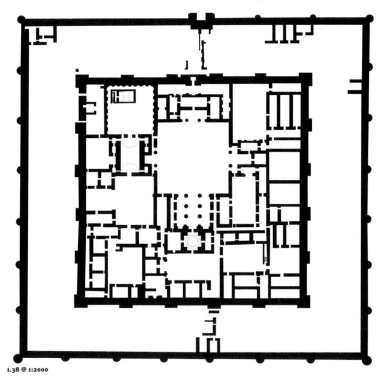

1.38 @ 1:2000

Umayyad seats

It is not clear from the remains how much of a garrison was quartered at Anjar, but the general distribution recalls Roman frontier cities like Timgad or, more particularly, the purely military camps like Lambaesis from which Timgad was founded.[1.27a] The form was sustained by the Byzantine emperors, as at R'safah.

The dar al-imara (domain of government, including an administration block and palace), in the south-eastern quarter south of the mosque, is

1.39a

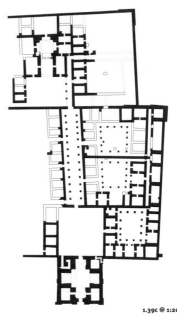

1.39c @ 1:2000

1.39b

›1.39 AMMAN, UMAYYAD GOVERNOR'S PALACE, c. 735: (a, b) southern ceremonial palace, exterior and interior, (c) plan.

centred on an open court like those at other Umayyad sites, but strictly regular. Like the audience hall associated with the bath house near the northern gate, the main reception rooms on the north–south axis of the palace are enclosed basilicas with apsidal ends. To either side of the court are matched paired apartments. The arrangement is reflected on a smaller scale and without the symmetry in the houses of the south-west quarter.

Naturally the governors of newly conquered Mesopotamia preferred the traditional eastern model directly descended from four-iwan Parthian palace buildings through Sasanian Firozabad and Ctesiphon. The earliest example was begun at Kufa by the conqueror and viceroy Sa'd bin Abd al-Waqqas within a year of Islam's triumph in the area: condemned by the caliph Omar for its monarchical pretensions, it was destroyed but rebuilt by Ziyad ibn Abihi who was governor of Kufa in the 670s. It is therefore older than Anjar at least in its conception but whether that ran to the basilican hall interpolated between the court and the qubba at the head of the principal axis is a matter for conjecture.

At Amman, the governor's extensive palace had three distinct parts. Bayts are aligned in the central zone to the east of an axial route linking ceremonial buildings: perhaps a complementary range was projected to the west as well. To the north is a court and hall of audience on the Firoz-abad model but without the entrance range. To the south, the best-preserved element of the three is a square building with four iwans dependent on a central square space which may have once been domed: the place of royal epiphany was usually a domed entrance pavilion in Roman, Hellenistic and ancient Mesopotamian palaces, and contemporary descriptions affirm that the significance of the dome of heaven was not lost on the Umayyads. Ornamental fragments preserved at the site combine anthropomorphic and stylized floral motifs in circular frames incorporating Hellenistic mouldings.

Umayyad retreats

Far grander than the palaces of Amman or Anjar, the vast enclosure at Mshatta was unfinished at the end of the brief reign of its probable patron, Abd al-Walid II (743–44). Nowhere – except perhaps at Qasr al-Hayr al-Gharbi – is the transition from defence to ceremonial better illustrated than on the resplendent façade of the palatine compound with its rosettes superimposed on filigree panels in a strictly triangular framework. Within

1.40a

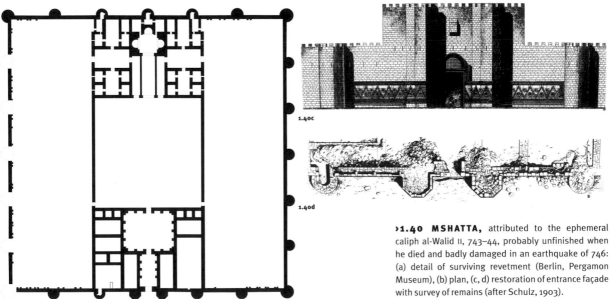

1.40b @ 1:2000

1.40c

1.40d

>**1.40 MSHATTA,** attributed to the ephemeral caliph al-Walid II, 743–44, probably unfinished when he died and badly damaged in an earthquake of 746: (a) detail of surviving revetment (Berlin, Pergamon Museum), (b) plan, (c, d) restoration of entrance façade with survey of remains (after Schulz, 1903).

there were the three zones typical of an oriental palace from time immemorial. Along the main axis was the ceremonial core with guard house, central court and basilican hall of audience. At the entrance to the last the caliph could appear – as in epiphany – before his subjects assembled for public audience in the great court: the entire scheme here responds to the waxing of formal court ceremonial along hallowed monarchical lines quite contrary to the original ideal of the caliphate but already apparent in the Kufa palace condemned by the caliph Omar. At the culmination of the axis was a triapsidal domed throne room with frescoes and stucco work of great vigour: precedents for the triconch may be found in the type of palace represented by the imperial villa at Piazza Armerina or, more immediately, in al-Mundir's tetraconch palace pavilion outside the walls at R'safah. For audience with subject rulers, ambassadors, ministers and other dignitaries, the apsidal hall was doubtless flanked by the ruler's withdrawing rooms. These must have been assigned in part to his wives pending the completion of a harem zone. This and the service zone on the other side evidently were never developed.

In adapting the ancient Mesopotamian tradition, something of the core ceremonial grandeur of the imperial palace at Constantinople – in its long-obscured post-Justinian form – was translated from town to country at Mshatta. Khirbat al-Mafjar, on the other hand, is less regular and its main formal elements are juxtaposed with a degree of formality which did not depend on axial routes. Moreover, these elements conform only in part to the main eastern or western palace prototypes followed elsewhere under the Umayyads. Approach, from the south, is via a terrace with an octagonal pavilion enclosing a fountain. To the south of this, the eastern entrance to the Qasr-like court is aligned with twin chambers in the centre of the west range but these hardly constitute an iwan and nor does the apsidal chamber to the south. There are no bayts of the typical Umayyad courtyard type. A passage leads from the north-west corner of the court, across a terrace on a semi-diagonal to the south-west corner of the detached, multi-apsidal, hypostyle throne hall which was backed by a thermal range: a precedent for the nine-square scheme may be found in the R'safah tetraconch attributed to the Ghassanids.[1.27c] The main entrance to this detached complex, through a richly embellished domed

1.41a

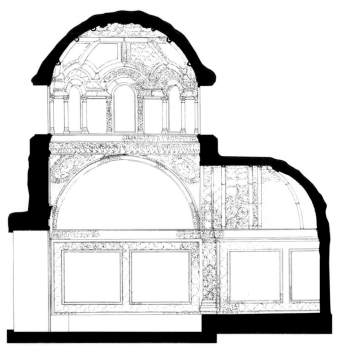

1.41d

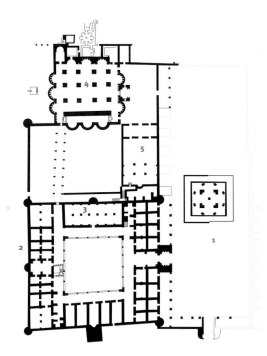

1.41b @ 1:3000

1.41e

1.41c

›1.41 KHIRBAT AL-MAFJAR, built for the caliph Hisham, 723–43, or his successor, al-Walid II: (a) roundel from the dome of a minor thermal chamber, (b) plan with (1) terrace and fountain pavilion, (2) qasr, (3) throne hall, (4) bath complex, (5) mosque, (c) restoration of qasr façade and octagonal fountain pavilion, (d, e) reconstruction of thermal hall and its apse mosaic.

In addition to the representational, the naturalistic and the abstract, it will be noted that the ornament embraces even the 'grotesque' combination of stylized flora and human heads foreign to the 'arabesque'.

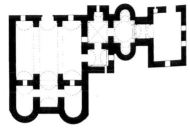

›1.42 QASR AMRA, attributed to the caliph Al-Walid I on the basis of an inscribed image of that caliph receiving homage: (a) plan, (b) detail of vaulting in tripartite main hall.

    The purpose of this small complex of formally disposed and luxuriously decorated rooms in an irregular compound was clearly not to accommodate an extensive entourage for extended periods. The outstanding element is a bath house with vaulted cold, warm and hot rooms beside a great hall with barrel vaulting between transverse arches.

1.42b

portal aligned with the most lavishly decorated apse, is again from the east and perpendicular to the qibla of the mosque to its south.

    In the lavish decoration too, fresco and mosaic inspired by Roman and Byzantine work – of which there were plentiful survivals – occasionally achieve the exotic aspect of a woven carpet – as at Khirbat al-Mafjar. And, whether stylized or naturalistic – as at Amman – stone or stucco work may be florid in the refined Palmyran manner or it may be figural after Sasanian models but forthright in naivety. In general, ornament may be contained in a tectonic frame but is not usually subordinate to architecture.

2 THE EARLY ABBASIDS

By the end of the reign of Abd al-Walid 1 the empire was over-extended. Advance was checked at Poitiers in central-western France in 732, at Kashgar in central Asia in 736 – and before the walls of Constantinople in 717, as on several other occasions. The later Umayyad caliphs could not always rely on their armies, as their progenitors had done, and needed a civil establishment which it was beyond the Arabs to supply. Indeed, rapid expansion meant traumatically rapid change for Arab tribesmen encouraged to settle in newly conquered lands, often well-established urban civilizations with a strong sense of individual identity even when they were provinces of empires. And, of course, there was always the religious divide between Sunnis and Shi'ites.

ADVENT TO APOGEE

The problems of holding the various fractious elements together were enormous. In the late-740s an unusually well-organized rebellion in the east was provoked by a revolutionary Shi'ite faction which preached the injustice and infidelity of the regime and the coming of a saviour (*mahdi*). This movement had been harnessed by descendants of Muhammad's cousin al-Abbas (566–652), who claimed primacy in Islam on the death of Ali's male heirs and succeeded to the imamate – though his motivation was anti-Umayyad in essence rather than anti-orthodox. Iranian Khorasan was won over for the Abassid *imam* Ibrahim (succeeded 743) by a former Kufan slave known as Abu Muslim. Under the Mahadist black banner, the latter led an army of mainly Yemeni Shi'ite Arabs to secure Iraq for the Abassids. Yemenis throughout the empire rose in support and most of the Shi'ites rallied to the cause, believing it consistent with their loyalty to Ali as the blood relative of the Prophet.

Abu'l Abbas, who inherited the imamate on the death of his brother Ibrahim early in 749, was proclaimed caliph in the wake of Abu Muslim's successes and assumed the title of as-Saffah – precursor of the *mahdi*. Seemingly invincible, his forces engaged those of Caliph al-Marwan II at Busir in August 750 and prevailed. The Umayyads were decimated. One of their number, Abd al-Rahman ibn Mu'awiya, escaped to Spain and founded a kingdom at Cordoba. Claiming their own back from the Abbasids, his successors assumed the title of Caliph in the 10th century.

Abu'l Abbas was confronted with turmoil as his disparate champions had been unified solely in the cause of eliminating the Umayyads. His successor, his brother Abu Ja'far (754–75) who assumed the title of al-Mansour ('the divinely ordained'), was challenged on various fronts and resorted to Abu Muslim for help. However, the latter's success and enhanced prestige were so great that the alarmed caliph had him eliminated. Bitterly disaffected by this, the most fanatical Shi'ites disclaimed al-Mansour's legitimacy: the rebels were suppressed in the cause of orthodoxy.

To celebrate his dynasty's triumph – and the better to watch the Shi'ites – al-Mansour founded a new city at Baghdad, on the Tigris opposite Sasanian Ctesiphon. Baghdad was central to the great bulk of the west Asian empire but also in the orbit of Iran. With both the Mesopotamian and Persian traditions of imperial government to draw on, the Abbasids approached the apogee of their power and prosperity under al-Mansour and fully achieved it under Harun al-Rashid (786–809).**1.44**

Disintegration began within a decade of Harun's death. His successor, al-Amin (809–13), was challenged by his brother al-Ma'mun, governor of Khorasan in the east: in the service of the latter, an army led by the Persian general Tahir bin Husayn captured Baghdad, killed al-Amin and secured al-Ma'mun's control over the Arab heartland. Sent back to deal with insurrection in the east, Tahir was rewarded with the governorship of Khorasan in 820: there his heirs constituted a quasi-independent dynasty.

ADVENT OF THE TURKS

From the mid-6th century the essentially nomadic Turkik tribes of eastern Siberia and Mongolia, divided into eastern and western khanates and a perennial nuisance to the Chinese, were on the move against the Hephalite Huns: so too were the Sasanians. Victory led to division of the spoils: the Turks received Soghdiana, the Sasanians Bactria. Coveting the latter too, the khan turned on his former allies and entered into alliance with Byzantium which lasted until his successor was ready to invade Byzantine territories around the Black Sea.

Two thousand metres in diameter, al-Mansour's 'City of Peace' (Medinet as-Salam) was ringed by a massive wall. The four twin-towered gates had domed chambers on the first floor in accordance with the imperial tradition descending through Byzantium and Rome from the capitals of the Hellenistic world and, ultimately, ancient Ur. From the gates, four barrel-vaulted shopping arcades (souks) cut through rings of houses in blocks served by concentric streets and radial alleys. In the vast central area were the official buildings, the palace and the mosque. The palace, known only from contemporary descriptions, is not uncontroversially reconstructed with a central court and domed chamber from which four halls (iwans on the axes of the gates) lead to the nuclear courts of the residential and administrative blocks: a horse and armed rider reputedly crowned the central dome – the conceptual centre of the world ruled by the warrior caliph – but otherwise Sasanian derivation is usually postulated.

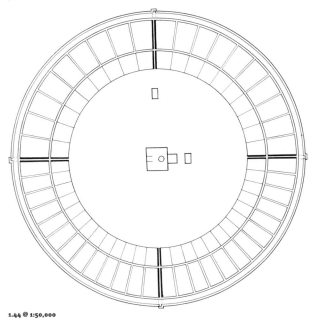

1.44 @ 1:50,000

The putative Turkish empire disintegrated in the late-7th century at the instigation of the powerful early rulers of the Tang dynasty but after the Chinese were routed by the Arabs in eastern Khorasan in the middle of the 8th century, two Turkish kingdoms were established on the Syr Darya (Jaxartes): the Qarluk on the upper reaches, the Oghuz to the north. Involved with the Arabs – if usually in conflict – many Turks were converted to Islam.

As aggressive for Islam as they had been for pasture, Turks organized themselves into bands of 'Fighters for the Faith' (*ghazis*) dedicated to a peripatetic existence in ceaseless conflict with the infidel. Some – lost to conflict with Caucasian powers or the Byzantine emperors, or the Rus who were establishing themselves in the vast territory which would take their name – were acquired as slaves (*mamluks*) by caliphs and other rulers to fill regiments of guards.

In constant conflict with Byzantium, al-Ma'mun's successor, al-Mu'tasim (833–42), found himself dependent on his Turkish mercenaries. Successful in war and influential in politics, the Turkish leaders soon aroused hostility in Baghdad and the caliph founded a new capital upriver at Samarra where luxurious retreat seduced his successors.**1.46**

NEW CAPITALS

The expansion of Islam and the growth in the number of converts naturally inflated demand for Muslim buildings and extended the scale of secular ones too well beyond the Umayyad norm. As the centre of political gravity shifted east from Damascus to Baghdad and eastward, expansion reached into lands largely foreign to the Graeco-Roman tradition – or indebted to it only superficially – vernacular approaches to structure and decoration were drawn upon by the builders of the faith and a new architectural synthesis emerged to meet both new and old purposes. In general the Classical components of style, increasingly debased the further they penetrated east, were dispensed with in favour of essentially Mesopotamian or Iranian ones and the brick-built secular vernacular untainted by unwelcome religious associations.

From the outset, Abbasid rulers ceded little to the ancient Assyrian kings in their will to move their seats to new sites or in the vast scale of their operations. Caliph al-Mansour's new palatine and administrative enclosure at Baghdad was circular. Occupied by the palace of the caliph – rather than the palatine mosque – the centre of the Muslim world is seen as the navel of the universe but Classicism was not yet forgotten: the ideal was Vitruvian though the immediate inspiration was provided by the first Sasanian ruler, Ardashir I (224–41), at Firozabad. There the gates

1.45a

had faced the cardinal directions: here they were evidently equidistant from the Mecca gate of the qibla. Beyond the circle were barracks and markets which provided hubs for organic domestic and industrial development.[1.44]

Before rationalism resorted definitively to the rectangle of the typical Roman camp at the close of the 8th century, other circular or semi-circular cities were conceived in the Fertile Crescent but never fully realized. Pragmatism overcame the ideal even at Baghdad, where the contrivance of the centre soon ceded to the nature of its surroundings. Nothing remains of al-Mansour's palace or mosque, but descriptions give the latter a hypostyle hall on the qibla side of a cloistered court in the tradition established by the Umayyads, and the former a court and an arched recession before domed chambers in the Sasanian manner.

As we have seen, the palaces of the Umayyads at Damascus have disappeared, but extensive remains elsewhere indicate that Umayyad builders capitalized on the Sasanian legacy. The Abbasids could hardly have avoided doing so in their turn when they established themselves at Baghdad, in the sphere of the venerable Mesopotamian and vital Persian cultural traditions.

If nothing remains of al-Mansour's Baghdad – or indeed of much later caliphate work there – the ruins of his strictly rectangular desert retreat at Ukhaydir (begun c. 780) and of Samarra, the capital founded by al-Mu'tasim in 836 to escape the uncontrollable Turkish guard, clearly reveal the influence of the Sasanians. So too, naturally, did the Muslim conquerors of Iran at Merv – according, at least, to the descriptions of the palace built there by the Abbasid champion, Abu Muslim, c. 750. Beyond the nuclear court and iwan, caliphate planners sustained the ubiquitous Asian formula for palace planning, with its tripartite division into zones of public appearance, private audience and harem enclosure for the royal women.[1.45, 1.46]

1.45b

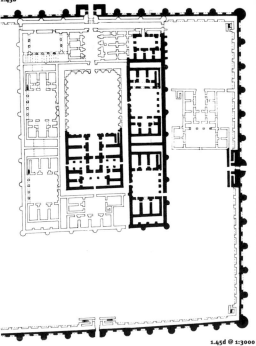

1.45d @ 1:3000

1.45e

›1.45 UKHAYDIR, PALACE, c. 780: (a)
north/west front, (b, c) entrance wing, court front and
interior, (d) plan, (e , f) corridor separating ceremonial
and residential apartments and interior enfilade, (g)
private court with horseshoe-shaped arch/interior, (h)
view from north, with main court and iwan foreground.

Ukhaydir

The great palace at Ukhaydir (193 kilometres south-west of Baghdad) is a fortified compound in the desert clearly inspired by Roman and Byzantine outposts, like Qasr al-Hayr al-Sharqi and other Umayyad secular works, but greatly amplified on Sasanian lines.[1.20, 1.27c, 1.36] Independent of the city rather than its hub – effective and symbolic – its context remains obscure. So does the purpose of the irregular space between the rectangular palace proper and the outer enclosure – though a broad analogy has been made with the arrangement at al-Mansour's Baghdad. Surviving to roof height in several areas, the rubble and brick structure was restored in the 1980s.

The outer enclosure (175 by 169 metres) – is pierced with gates facing the cardinal directions, the main one to the north in a rectangular projection, the others flanked by round towers. Within, Sasanian symmetry is disrupted only by the placing of a mosque to the west of the vaulted entrance hall and guard room. The great iwan on the southern side of the court, higher than the flanking arcades and set in a frontispiece, has been seen as a precursor of the pishtaq which was to play such an important part in the later Iranian tradition. Obviously the place of public appearance, it leads to a similarly vaulted square chamber flanked and backed by columned halls. If the square room was another public audience hall, private audience would doubtless have been held in the great chamber of the southernmost apartment on the central axis. The twin sets of harem apartments to either side recall the Umayyad bayt but more closely follow the example set at Qasr-i Shirin in the Imrat-i Kusraw: twin iwans address their courts, the northern ones with interpolated vestibules on the cross-axis; cavernous corridors isolate them from the ceremonial elements. Blind arcading, some carried on semi-circular piers, recalls the articulation of Sasanian court façades.

1.45e

1.45f

1.45g

1.45h

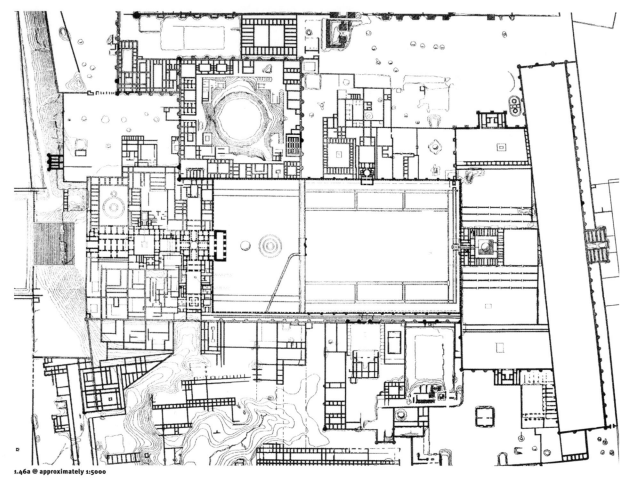

1.46a @ approximately 1:5000

Samarra

Occupied for less than fifty years after its foundation by al-Mutasim in 836, but constantly augmented, Samarra (ultimately extending some 50 kilometres along the Tigris from its original centre about 100 kilometres north of Baghdad) was a city of palaces apparently unwalled despite its military and administrative importance. In so far as the limited excavation indicates, the residential areas were laid out on a grid cut by the main axial artery. Flanked by grand courtyard houses, this led to the palace district. Contrary to precedent, the main mosque was located in the popular market zone rather than beside the main palace.

>1.46 SAMARRA, ABBASID PALACES: (a) Jusaq al-Khaqani (Dar al-Khilafa, c. 840), plan; (b) Balkuwara (c. 850), plan; (c–e) decorative stucco panels from private houses showing the advance from realism (Style A,[1.43]) to abstraction and the elimination of secondary framework within the main field (Style B,[1.46c] Style C,[1.46d, 1.46e] the last with cusped niche); (f) Qasr al-Ashiq (c. 880), exterior showing cusped arches.

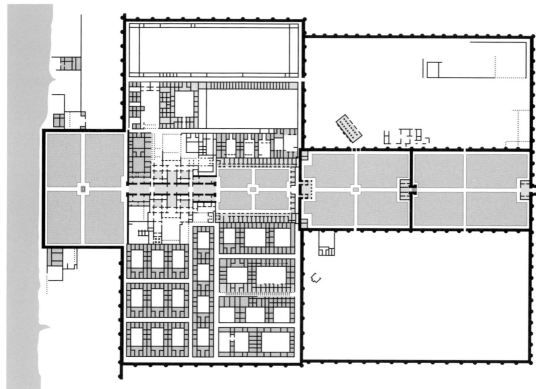

1.46b @ approximately 1:5000

Most of the twenty-one vast walled palaces so far identified at the site were built hastily of pise or mud brick and are far less well-preserved than Ukhaydir. Excavation is far from complete but enough has been recovered to indicate that the planning and massing were loose and off axis in the Jusaq al-Khaqani, rather tauter overall in the Balkuwara – as at Ukhaydir but on a vaster scale. The axis of audience is always rigorous, however: particularly notable is the succession of portals which dignified progression from the triple-arched triumphal entrance – derived from the grandest form of Roman triumphal arch or fastigium via R'safah[1.27c] – through the atria and vast forecourts to the caliph on his epiphany platform. Beyond that, a basilical hall led to the domed chamber of private audience from which three identical halls led sideways to the subsidiary courts – as, probably, at Baghdad – and on along the main axis to the corridor-enclosed harem zone – though that is conjectural.

A distinct square walled enclosure contiguous with the Jusaq epiphany court may have been a caravanserai for important visitors and their entourages. It seems to have enclosed a garden and there was a garden terrace between it and the central palace block, overlooking an escarpment. Samarra was celebrated for its gardens and the sophisticated hydraulic devices that kept them alive in the midst of the desert: indebtedness for both is most immediately to the Romans, ultimately to the Assyrians.[1.30b] It is also celebrated for the rich variety of its foliated stucco work: realistic or stylized, arabesque or abstract, within regular geometric frames – as at Mshatta – or ramping in abstract repetition with new freedom, the plants of the garden are clearly to be enjoyed not in their natural habitat alone.[1.43, 1.46c, d]

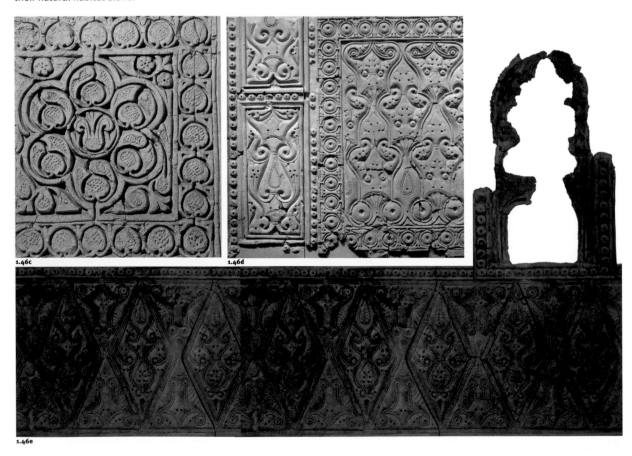

1.46c

1.46d

1.46e

1.46f

In Syria the Umayyads built primarily of stone supplemented by brick. In Iraq the Abbasids, like the Sasanians, relied on plastered rubble instead of stone and perpetuated the ancient Mesopotamian tradition of mud-brick which they protected with plaster, mosaic or, occasionally, elaborately patterned baked brickwork (hazarbaf). The richest materials and the decorative treatment of the revetment were confined to the remotest interiors of palaces, hidden – as the caliph was to become – from the eyes of common man.

Abbasid buildings were predominantly arcuate: like the Sasanians, they drew considerable effect from arches springing low from stumpy columns but they did not articulate their mural structures in the sub-Classical way the Parthians and Sasanians had derived from the Roman scenae frons. From c. 770 at Raqqa, Ukhaydir and Samarra, however, semi-circular or four-centred arches appear in portals and vaults: some are slightly pointed in the Sasanian manner,[1.20] some incurved at the base like a horseshoe as in early Christian Armenia or Visigothic Spain (AIC1, page 741). Arched niches are often fringed with semi-circular projections.[1.46e, f] Multiple small-scale projections of this kind are cusps, fewer and larger they are lobes: if the latter suggest combined horseshoes, the former seem to derive from the Roman scallop-shell niche.[1.26a]

Within severe external walls, quasi-military in their buttressed strength like their ancient Mesopotamian predecessors, multiple arcades covered the largest areas of Abbasid buildings – apart from primitive trabeation which limited height. The most prominent examples are the great mosque of Caliph al-Mutawakkil at Samarra and the smaller exercise from the same reign at Abu Dulaf. The larger work was a conventional hypostyle mosque in all but scale, but with piers instead of columns. The smaller one was innovative in the directional disposition of piers whose

1.47a

1.47b

width lent new gravitas to the court fronts and whose potential for extra elevation enhanced the distinction of the nave and the qibla range. The extra width of the latter distinguished it as a transept perpendicular to the nave: as

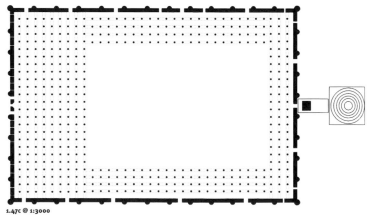

1.47c @ 1:3000

›1.47 **SAMARRA, MOSQUES:** (a–c) al-Mutawakkil (c. 850), exterior with spiral minaret, prayer court, plan; (d, e) Abu Dulaf (c. 860), minaret, plan.

The vast double-walled compound, the restored inner one (240 by 156 metres) punctuated by round towers as at Ukhaydir, enclosed a hypostyle hall and riwaqs framing the largest-known prayer court. Stout octagonal piers with attached columns define the nine by twenty-five bays of the prayer hall before the qibla wall (south) and riwaqs (four bays deep on the eastern and western sides, three bays deep to the north). The roof was doubtless flat and wooden. Decoration appears to have been sparse, except for the distiction of the huge mihrab in marble and mosaic. The extraordinary minaret, on axis with the mihrab, spirals to 52 metres outside the inner compound.

The Abu Dulaf Mosque, also with double enclosure and spiral minaret, is smaller (the partially preserved inner wall was 213 by 135 metres, the hall was seventeen by seven bays). The arcades of the prayer hall, widened in the centre to form a nave, were carried on

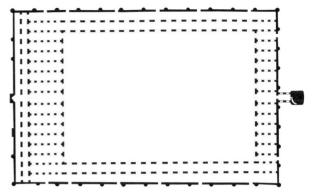

1.47e @ 1:3000

1.47d
varied piers, T-shaped in the first and sixth ranges (and the court front of the entrance riwaqs), rectangular in the intermediate ones and perpendicular to the qibla wall except for the innermost seventh range which is set in parallel to form a double transept.

we have implied, the 'T' junction of wider bay ranges may have been initiated in the al-Aqsa Mosque at Jerusalem.

The introduction of perpendicular nave and transept imposed a hierarchical order on the plan of large-scale works, of course. It is probable that the nave provided exclusive space (maqsura) for the ruler's prayers: his entourage may then have been accommodated in the transept. That is conjectural. Certainly not without controversy, too, the other exceptional feature of these mosques, the spiral minaret, may be seen as descending from the ancient ziggurat (AIC1, page 89) – perhaps via the Parthians and Sasanians who are known to have had Zoroastrian fire towers with external spiral ramps. The antique association would specifically have capitalized on the conversion of the tower of Babel – the Biblical monument to the folly of man in ceding the unity of his dominion to linguistic discord – into a base for the proclamation of the one true faith by the one true voice.[1.47]

3 TURKS IN EGYPT AND IFRIQIYA

The most able Turks in service to the caliph at Samarra were elevated to government. One such was Ibrahim ibn al-Aghlab who was sent c. 800 to govern the western-most province of Ifriqiya (modern Tunisia). Beset with troubles, the ephemeral caliph al-Amin allowed Ibrahim to appoint his own successor: in consequence, his Agh-labid dynasty asserted virtual independence and went on to extend its rule to much of central North Africa and Sicily. The situation was similar in Egypt at the instiga-tion of the Turkish governor, Ahmad ibn Tulun (c. 868–905): he repudiated his master in 872 after extending

1.48a
>**1.48 FUSTAT (CAIRO), MOSQUE OF AMR,** 641–827, extensively renovated c. 1270, qibla rebuilt 1401: (a) court and prayer hall, (b) plan.

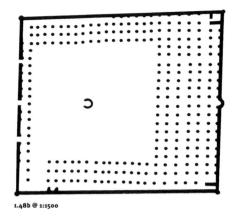

1.48b @ 1:1500

his regime to Syria. With Syria eclipsed by Baghdad, outside Iraq it is in North Africa under the rule of these Turks that the most important works from the early Abbasid period are to be found.

The premier mosque of the Egyptian capital Fustat was built immediately after the conquest of the lower Nile valley in 640–41 by Amr ibn al-As. It was expanded in 673 on the order of the caliph Mu'awiya into a hypostyle hall, dependent on pillaged antique columns, and endowed with four square corner towers: as the towers of the Great Mosque in Damascus were converted from their Christian purpose and the situation at Medina is unclear, these are the first known to be specifically built for Islam and doubtless followed the Damascene example. Extended in 711, the complex was doubled in 827 (at the expense of the original enclosure and its towers) on the order of the caliph al-Ma'mun by his governor, Abd Allah ibn Tahir.[1.48]

Ahmad ibn Tulun, a soldier of *mamluk* descent but formed in Samarra and favoured by the caliph al-Ma'mun because of his exceptional promise, was sent to Fustat as governor in 868. He found the city too small for his Turkish troops and the latter too large for his continued subservience to Baghdad: he founded the suburb of al-Qata'l in 870 and by the middle of the decade was celebrating his independence with the foundation of a new mosque – required, in any case, by the considerable expansion of the city's population. The T-shaped plan, piers carrying pointed arches, domed mihrab bay and spiral minaret were translated from Samarra. Apart from allowing greater height, the substitution of piers for pillaged columns promoted a new order in mosque design. The piers of prayer hall and cloisters have attached colonnettes – also derived from Samarra – below pointed arches incurved at the impost and delicately incised.[1.49]

1.49a

1.49b

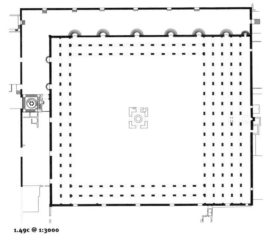

1.49c @ 1:3000

›1.49 FUSTAT (CAIRO), MOSQUE OF IBN TULUN, 870s: (a) overview, (b) outer precinct, (c) plan, (d) court with fountain pavilion and minaret, (e, f) details of prayer hall arcading.

Built beside the lavish palace (long lost) with which the governor asserted his autonomy, the mosque of Tulun's new quarter (called al-Qata'I after its subdivisions) emulates developments at the centre of the caliphate. A square compound (c. 160 metres per side) encloses a rectangular complex (122 by 140 metres) with broad bands of communication space between them, as in the Ptolemaic Temple of Horus at Edfu (AIC1 pages 29–31). The inner square court (c. 92 metres per side) is surrounded by doubled arcades and three additional arcades project the prayer hall into a rectangle at the expense of the outer channel of communication space to the south-east (qibla). An ablution fountain occupied the centre of the court. The spiral minaret replaced an earlier one in the 14th century.

The pointed arches, consistent throughout the interior of the prayer hall, spring through a slight incurve from columns inset into the corners of rectangular brick piers. The stucco rendering is delicately incised with stylized floral motifs designed primarily to relieve the piers at base and to outline the arcuate structure.

1.49d

1.49e

1.49f

1.50a

1.50b @ 1:3000

›1.50 KAIROUAN (QAIRAWAN), GREAT
MOSQUE, founded 665, enlarged 772, 836, 862 and 875, restored 13th century and many times later: (a) court and minaret, (b) plan, (c, d) prayer hall front and interior, (e) outer bays of Abu Ibrahim.

Before the qibla wall (south-east), the enlarged rectangular compound – extended eastwards from Yazid's work to 135 by 80 metres – has an arcaded prayer hall nine bays deep and sixteen wide, the wider, higher central nave leading to a domed mihrab chamber where it is joined at right angles by transepts of similar dimensions. The outer two bays with their central dome, added by Abu Ibrahim Ahmad (*amir* 856–63), are continued around the other sides of the court as cloisters. The columns supporting the arcades are mainly recycled from the province's rich heritage of Roman buildings and are screened from the court by arches on piers with attached colonnettes. Of particular importance in the richly decorated mihrab qubba is the octagonal zone of transition from square to circle with its scallop-shell squinches supporting the ribbed dome across the corners and matching cusped arches to the sides: structure is actually elucidated by the detail in the dome, if not on the mihrab wall, and the origin of the cusped arch in the Classical scallop-shell-headed niche could hardly be more clearly revealed than here in the transition zone.

The hypostyle formula, developed at Fustat, Kufa and Basra in the 670s, reached Ifriqiya a century later. Uqba ibn Nafi, the conqueror of the province, founded his seat at Kairouan in 665. His primitive mosque was rebuilt in 772 by Yazid ibn Hatim, the Abbasid governor, with multiple colonnades parallel to the qibla. These were incorporated

1.50c

1.50d

The minaret projects from the eastern arcade of the court, opposite – but out of alignment with – the nave and its mihrab dome. Hardly less arresting than its spiral counterpart at Samarra, if somewhat less plausibly related to the ziggurat, the base of this great tiered structure is unlikely to preserve the only substantial remains of the earlier mosque as some maintain: it would have been beyond the north-eastern perimeter even of Yazid's complex. The upper two storeys postdate Ziyadat Allah but the three-tier form, which may have been essential to the original conception, was that of the Pharos.

1.50e

into the present mosque, the enlargement of which was begun in self-aggrandizement by Ziyadat Allah (817–38), the Abbasids' Aghlabid viceroy who was asserting autonomy at the time – and defending it against Byzantium with impressive sea-walls until he greatly enhanced his prestige by overwhelming imperial Sicily.

Ziyadat's builders at Kairouan amplified the T-shaped plan – implicit at Damascus, asserted at Samarra – and distinguished the nave from parallel aisles somewhat more lucidly than at Samarra. A screen of horseshoe arches masks the prayer hall from the court but reused columns support its roof; the splendidly embellished mihrab bay is domed as at Damascus. A second dome over the central courtyard bay, introducing the nave, confronts the massive stepped minaret. The latter reminds most commentators of the Pharos of Alexandria.**1.50, 1.26e**

1.52a

1.52b

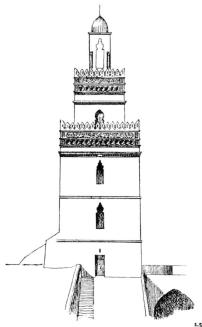

1.51

›1.51 SFAX. c. 850: minaret.
The contemporary example attached to Sousse's fortified barracks of defenders of the Faith (ribat), which incorporates a mosque also finished in the middle of the 9th century, is square at base and cylindrical above.

›1.52 TUNIS, GREAT MOSQUE, founded 732, enlarged 864, nave dome 991: (a) court, (b) prayer hall.

›1.53 TRIPOLI, MOSQUE OF AL-NAQAH, mid-8th century and later: (a) exterior with minaret, (b) prayer hall interior.

The mosque builders elsewhere in Ifriqiya, notably at Tunis, followed the Kairouan precedent on a smaller scale and without a similar minaret. However, variations on the latter distinguish Sfax and Sousse, in particular.[1.51] They were furthered in neighbouring Libya at the al-Naqah Mosque in Tripoli. That grand work was founded in the mid-7th century by Amr ibn al-As, who extended his conquests into the area from Egypt in 643: like its neighbour at Kairouan, however, it was largely reworked at some stage in the century after the emergence of Ziyadat Allah to primacy in Ifriqiya.[1.52, 1.53]

1.53a

1.53b

The minaret of the Sousse ribat actually served as a lighthouse – as the ones at Sfax and Tripoli could well have done. Lighthouses apart, the Aghlabid regime is celebrated for outstanding waterworks. Drawing on the old province's rich Classical inheritance, the new state's hydraulic engineers provided the principal cities with

›1.54 KAIROUAN, AGHLABID CISTERN, second half of the 9th century.

The complex included at least two exposed circular pools (131 and 37.5 metres in diameter) and an underground reservoir: water from dams on seasonal watercourses was fed into the smaller pool where sediment was allowed to settle before it was transferred to the larger pool by shallow sluice and then, further filtered,

fed into the underground reservoir to supplement water still brought by the Roman aqueduct from the Djebel Cherichera (38 kilometres away).

extensive collection, filtration, conservation and distribution plants – none was more impressive than the reservoirs and filtration plant in the northern suburbs of Kairouan which both guaranteed the supply of water to the palace and provided the ruler with a theatre for the display of aquatic spectacle.[1.54]

1.2 DECADENCE OF THE CALIPHATE: SHI'ITE CHALLENGE

1.55a

4 IRANIANS

Turkish influence had extended to Samarra by the reign of al-Mutawakkil (847–61) but Turks were not alone in asserting quasi-independent authority in the provinces. The Aghlabids sustained themselves in Ifriqiya until 909 but were then supplanted by heterodox Arabs who called themselves Fatimids, as we shall see. In the face of Fatimid challenge the caliphate reasserted control in Egypt at the expense of Ahmad ibn Tulun's successor but another Turkish general took advantage of confusion in Baghdad to establish his Ikhshidid dynasty in Cairo (935–69). In Khorasan, on the other hand, the successive contenders for power were Persian: the Tahirids were dispossessed by the Saffarids of Seistan (c. 870) and they, in turn, were overtaken (c. 900) by the Samanids of Balkh who, as the effective rulers of all the caliphate's eastern provinces, moved their seat to Bukhara.**1.55**

DISCORD AND DIVISION

Caliph al-Mut'amid (870–92), who endorsed the first Samanid governor of Transoxiana (the region between the Amu Darya – Greek Oxus – and Syr Darya – Greek Yaxartes – Rivers) in 875, moved back to Baghdad to escape the overweening power of his aides. Turkish soldiers apart, the caliph's administration was dependent on heterodox Iran, with its own vital imperial tradition, and Iranians had begun to eclipse Arabs in Baghdad early in the 9th century. The cultural division between Arab and Iranian was, of course, manifest most dramatically in the opposition of Sunni and Shi'ite. The five pillars of Islam were unassailable, but the sects were divided between and among themselves by differences over much else.

Strands of rationalism and emotionalism – characteristic of Sunnis and Shi'ites respectively but not exclusive to either and complementing one another on the intellectual and popular levels – lead back to the 7th century when Islam first encountered Greek philosophy on the one hand, Christian mysticism on the other. Muhammad himself followed the ascetic into the wilderness, was impressed with the ideal of the hermit and was certainly not inimical to mysticism.

Over the first two centuries in which his faith spread to areas with strong theosophic traditions, popular mysticism – and disgust with conflict and corruption among worldly leaders – produced many saints from ascetic holy men (*sufis*). Akin to the hermits and mendicants of both Buddhism and Christianity, their intercession was sought for personal salvation.[1.56] On the demise of its occupant, the hermit's cell was developed into a mortuary 'place of witness' (mashhad). Orders of dervishes housed in khanqahs developed in association with the most venerable mashhads: there were to be many, distinguished by variations in rule and ritual – the latter most famously inducing

>1.55 IRANIAN EMBELLISHMENT, 10th century: (a) stucco wall panel from Nishapur (New York, Metropolitan Museum of Art); (b) armed horseman (earthenware dish, north-eastern Iran; Berlin, Museum of Islamic Art).

It is tempting to see the armed rider as Samanid – if not Turkish.

catalepsy through incessant chanting and whirling. Naturally unorthodox, mystical in their motive, the Turkish *ghazis* were among the most significant devotees to *sufi* cults though they served the orthodox cause.

On the intellectual level, the influence of neo-Platonism was profound: scholars bent on elaborating the metaphysics of Sufism and converting Islamic theology to mysticism were certainly not uninfluenced by Dionysius the pseudo-Areopagite in particular (see AICI, page 679f.). It can be no coincidence that the ordering of the *sufi* movement with rules of conduct and devotion imparted to the novice by his mentor, predicated an ascending order of purgations to be achieved before contemplation could lead to intuitive experience of God. On the other hand, the most significant of the intellectuals included the Mu'tazilites (separatists), who denied the orthodox belief that the Koran was uncreated, asserted human responsibility in general, and challenged faith with reason.

Mu'tazilitism won the approbation of the caliphs in the first half of the 9th century, and though it was renounced by al-Mutawakkil (847–61), who persecuted its adherents as vigorously as he persecuted Shi'ites, its intellectual rationalism remained potent in opposition to the heterodoxies of both Shi'ism and Sufism. By this time the Hanafi and Maliki schools of law had emerged dominant from a plethora of contenders and, bent on reconciling their differences, the jurists Shafi'i and Hanbali founded two more from the systematic analysis of the Koran, the *hadith*, pre-Islamic convention and common practice analogous to Koranic prescription.

In the following century Abu'l-Hasan al-Ash'ari, a prominent Mu'tazilite who had reverted to orthodoxy, developed a systematic theology from the application of reason to the interpretation of faith. This failed to attract general approbation, inevitably, but inspired the founding of theological colleges in Sunni centres whose influence was to be pervasive: on graduation, the learned (*ulema*) constituted a priestly body whose legalistic principles moulded Muslim government – beyond the Shi'ite domains, of course – primarily as the defenders of orthodox law (*muftis*) and the judges who administered it (*cadis*).

The imperial bond of orthodoxy was not long to remain fast. Cocooned in the enervating luxury of exclusive palaces, the caliphate was decadent before the 10th century was far advanced and its Sunni clients were in terminal decline. The Shi'ite heterodoxy, forged by perceived Abbasid betrayal into a messianic force opposed to all Sunni authority, was evolving under its successive *imams*: the twelfth of these disappeared c. 873 under mysterious

THE FORCES OF ALI ASSAULT A FORTRESS (watercolour miniature, Herat, 1415; Istanbul, Topkapi Library).

circumstances which prompted the time-defying mysticism of his anticipated reappearance. As we have already noted, that was heralded in Ifriqiya in 909 by the emergence of the Fatimids.

While the Fatimids were recovering from their first reverse in Egypt c. 920, the main force of the party of Ali began flooding forth from the Elrbuz mountains of northwest Iran, to which they had been reduced under Harun al-Rashid.[1.57] They were led by the sons of a Shi'ite servant of the Samanids named Buya. One of these, Ahmad Mu'izz al-Daulah (932–62) took Baghdad in 946. He deposed the caliph but retained the caliphate: the Abbasids subsisted as religious figureheads under Ahmad's Buyid line until the latter were undermined by Turkish infiltration in the middle of the 11th century.

The Buyids established a regime on traditional Iranian monarchical principles and introduced heterodox mourning cults, derived from pre-Islamic royal ritual, for the Shiite *imams*. Following ancient practice too, they left the provinces to their relatives as quasi-independent potentates. This had the time-honoured consequence politically when the centre passed to a weak figure. However, it had great significance intellectually as the provincial courts attracted the foremost thinkers of the age – such as the philosopher- astronomer al-Biruni (973–1048), who found his way to the Ghaznavid court, or his contemporary, the outstanding polymath Ibn Sina of Bukhara (Avicenna) whose treatise on medicine was not supplanted for more than half a millennium.

The unity of Islam, long tenuous even in western Asia, was lost to the Buyids. Fragmentation in the east apart, Iranian powers behind the caliph's throne had little appeal in the west. Much there had long been quasi-independent or well beyond the Abbasid writ anyway – such as Umayyad Spain and Morocco, as we shall see.

EARLY IRANIAN MOSQUES

Little is left from Islam's first century in the Iranian world of either secular or religious building. However, excavation at 8th-century Susa and 9th-century Siraf have revealed hypostyle prayer halls of no great extent and square-bay arcading assertive of neither axis. The contemporary great mosques of Bukhara, Nishapur, Qumm, Shiraz and Yazd are known from written records and occasional foundation material.

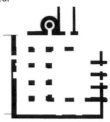

›1.58 FAHRAJ, JAMI-MASJID, c. 900?: plan
The five aisles perpendicular to the qibla are all tunnel vaulted.

1.58 @ 1:1000

›1.59 DAMGHAN, TARIK KHANA, c. 900?: (a) arcade, (b) plan.
The three-bay prayer hall and single-bay cloisters frame a square court in the conventional manner. Flattened arches on plain piers address the court all round but the arcades framing the individually vaulted bays of the interior are parabolic. The minarets, in patterned brickwork, are cylindrical.

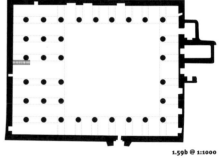

1.59b @ 1:1000

1.59a

Apart from fragments of a palace at Nishapur[1.55] and traces of fortified country seats not unrelated to those of the Umayyads, the late-9th or early 10th centuries offer more substance: notably the Tarik Khana at Damghan and the Jami-masjids of Nayin and Fahraj. In the absence of all but a few bays at Abu Dulaf, the general effect of early Abbasid prayer-hall arcading may be gained at the much-reduced scale of these works: pointed arches rise through shallow curves, as at Samarra, but instead of timber roofs the Iranian arcades carry vaults. Ungainly as the forest of supports might be, they allowed greater elevation than

c. 900 and later:
(a) plan, (b) prayer hall interior, (c) overview of court
with entrance range left.

Carried on a variety of piers and circular or polygonal
columns, rather than the consistently cylindrical ones
of the wider arcade at Damghan, the flattened arches of
the prayer hall are extended as riwaqs framing the
court – four bays to the north-west, three to the south-
east and one to the north-east. The half columns of patterned brick between the arches may date from a
late-10th-century renovation. The central bays of the
nave form a T with the inner qibla range though this is
partly obscured by an interpolated screen at the junction. The nave arches are raised higher than the others
– anticipating the insertion of the iwan – and so too is
the opposite bay in the entrance front. Domes distinguish the central mihrab bay and its neighbours: most
of the other bays have individual tunnel vaults, pointed
in profile. The stucco embellishment is confined to the
central qibla bays. The mihrab is a niche framed by
recessed arches in a rectangular screen: the formula
was long to endure, not only in Iran.

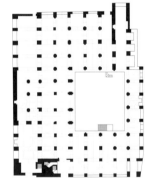

1.60a @ 1:1000

1.60b

traditional trabeation provided. At Damghan and Nayin,
moreover, the parapets are raised to distinguish the central qibla arcade: the evolution of the court frontispiece
(pishtaq) – to which Iranians were particularly dedicated
– begins in works like these.**1.58–1.60**

The fine brickwork of Nayin, accented with geometrical patterns, was to be typical of Iranian Muslim architecture but the embellishment of the interior in stucco was to
remain comparatively rare. Carved or moulded stucco
revetment, with predominantly stylized floral motifs confined in geometric frames or ramping within the main

1.60c

lines of the structure, is characteristic of early Abbasid palaces in Iraq but the limited evidence suggests that the mosques there relied for their effect primarily on the play of architectural forms, particularly the scenographic vistas through multiple arcades. This approach was to be advanced in Iran well before the end of the 10th century but, in so far as its dilapidation testifies, the Tarik Khana – in contrast to the work at Nayin – already demonstrated its potential.

The mosques of Samarra were probably the inspiration for the earliest work on the Jami-masjid of Isfahan. From its foundation in the 9th century that work was exceptional in scale and its hall seems to have been crossed by a nave on the qibla – but the several important phases of later work, beginning under the Buyids in the 10th century, have obscured the original form. Several notable smaller works of obscure date depart from the hypostyle tradition in

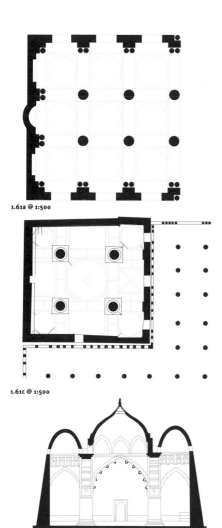

1.61a @ 1:500

1.61c @ 1:500

1.61d

›1.61 THE 9TH-CENTURY IRANIAN QUIN-CUNX: (a, b) Balkh, Masjid-i Nuh Gunbad, plan and view of ruins; (c, d) Hazara, Masjid-i Diggarun, plan and section.

1.61b

favour of a square with a central dome carried on four piers: the nine-domed ones at Samanid Balkh and Tirmidh are perhaps the most substantial, the one at Hazara near Bukhara, to which the Samanids had moved their seat, is a simple quincunx. The source may have been the Ghassanid R'safah quincunx – or its source – recalled by the Umayyads at Khirbat al-Mafjar: as the Byzantine ecclesiastical permutation was in its early infancy, the native fire temple was doubtless basic to the concept.**[1.61, 1.20, 1.41]**

Various motifs relieve the varied planes of prominent exterior elements, particularly the portal in its progress to distinction as a self-assertive pishtaq. The Buyids promoted this development at the Jami-masjid in Isfahan and in works like the enigmatic Jurjir portal there. Typically, offset rectangular bricks are arranged in geometric patterns – zig-zag, diamond and cruciform. In the Jurjir work, which stands as an early landmark in the Muslim realization of the decorative potential of brick, blind cusps fringe the main arch and within it fragments of a semi-dome are assertively framed and filled with the rectilinear stylization of flora which begins to assimilate itself to Kufic script. Colour was generally provided in paint but little of

this has survived: indeed, its failings prompted experiments with more durable media which led to the chief glory of later Iran – the glazed tile.**1.62**

THE DEVELOPMENT OF THE MAUSOLEUM

Something of the presumed severity of al-Mutawakkil's great works at Samarra may be gained from the restoration there of the near-contemporary Qubba al-Sulaybiya. Inspired by the Dome of the Rock,**1.32** this enigmatic building may be identified with the tomb documented as

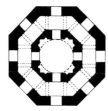

1.63a @ 1:1000

1.63b

1.63c

>**1.63 SAMARRA, QUBBA AL-SULAYBIYA,** c. 862: (a, b) plan and section, (c) exterior (restored).

The earliest building of the octagonal canopy tomb type to survive, it integrates square and octagon in development of the plan of the Dome of the Rock. The outer arcades of the latter were blind: here the single octagonal ambulatory is unwalled to all sides.

having been built for the caliph al-Muntasir (who reigned for six months in 862), but is possibly a Shi'ite martyrium (mashhad). Be that as it may, it provided one of the two basic prototypes for the Muslim tomb: the canopy form carried on open arches to conform conceptually (at least) with *hadith* stricture that the Muslim grave must be open to the sky.[1.63]

The alternative prototype is the freestanding qubba, with open arches to all four sides, which emerged in the Iranian world of the Zoroastrian chahar-taq.[1.20g] That connection is somewhat controversial due to functional disparity but the Classical martyria seems even more remote. Popular in Iran – naturally, if the chahar-taq was in fact the model – it recalled the primitive canopies which had been erected over the graves of the principal Shi'ite martyrs – Ali and his son Husayn at Najaf and Karbala – and was exported to the west by Shi'ites as the prototypical funerary building. Most significantly, moreover, the dome stood for heaven which alone should canopy the orthodox grave.

The prime examples of the qubba type, both 10th century, are the Arab-ata at Tim near Samarkand and the

1.64c

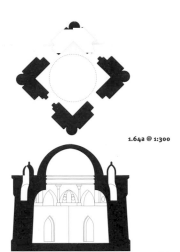

1.64a @ 1:300

1.64b

> **1.64 BUKHARA, SAMANID TOMB,** c. 940: (a, b) plan and section, (c, d) exterior and interior.

Traditionally associated with Ismail Samanid (892–907) – the supplanter of the Saffavids – but probably a dynastic tomb built by Nasr (914–43), the cube – 10 metres square – is a stoutly battered mass of patterned brickwork, relieved by a galleried parapet above and cylindrical corner piers surmounted by tiny stilted domes – the piers are purely decorative but light is admitted to the interior through the galleries. To support the main dome over the cubical interior, squinches effect transition from square to octagon, colonnettes from octagon to sixteen-sided polygon. Unusually, the interpolation of a cross-rib in the squinches allows the penetration of light from the gallery at the corners. The corner 'turrets' may be seen as putative engaged minarets.

Not unrelated in its cylindrical form and its dependence for effect on patterned brickwork – though the motifs are different – is the stump of the freestanding structure known as Manarat Mujda near Ukhaydir in Iraq: its date and purpose are unknown but the cylindrical form in patterned brick was to have a great future in the minarets of Iran.

1.64d

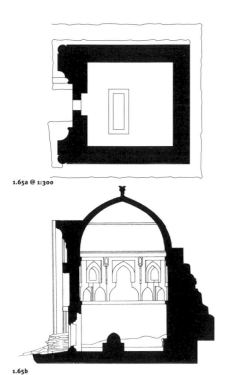

1.65a @ 1:300

1.65b

›1.65 TIM, ARAB-ATA TOMB, c. 977: (a–c) plan, section and elevation.

Extending the square plan (5.6 metres per internal side, 8 by 8.7 metres externally), the pishtaq incorporates an arch, surmounted by three cusped niches, framed by projecting bands of basket-weave brickwork and Kufic script. The horizontal band at the top, raised higher than the main mass by the windows, masks the dome. The relief on the front is not matched on the sides – as it was in the Samanid work at Bukhara.

Inside, instead of one arch and semi-dome across each corner, forming an octagon over a square, a trilobed form in plan and elevation consists of fragments of a lower, broader semi-dome, springing from the corners but decapitated and doubly recessed through rectangle and semi-circle, supporting a taller, narrower semi-dome. The elevation is repeated as blind arcading on the intermediate sides. Minute squinches, rising from colonettes, assist transition from eight to sixteen sides. There is a related work, identified as the tomb of Baba Khatum, near Bukhara.

1.65c

tomb at Bukhara attributed to the Samanids of Khorasan. The cubical mass of the latter, with its four identical façades, suggests a setting in a four-square garden (chahar-bagh) – the Persian image of paradise, the context of most later tombs of the Persianized world.**1.64, 1.65**

In stark contrast to the Samarran work, all the walls of the Samanid mausoleum and the front at Tim are richly relieved with abstract patterns – basket-weave dominates in the Bukhara work, geometry of the Jurjir kind at Tim – and, of course, the baked brick used throughout the Samanid work lent durability to the art. Planar recession is more vigorous in the Isfahani work than in the one at Tim but the latter furthers the development of the pishtaq as a screen distinguished in height and embellishment from the body of the building. Further, the division of the semi-dome in the Jurjir portal to admit light was anticipated pragmatically – less dramatically – in the squinches of the Samanid tomb.

The division of the internal elevation of a qubba into three zones is implicit in a form combining cubical and semi-spherical elements. After Bukhara the central zone of transition between the square of the base and the circle of the dome was to be enriched with experiments in the fragmentation and recombination of the squinches upon which that transition depends. The designer of the Arab-ata went further than his known predecessors and combined the segments into trilobes which, etched on the main walls at least, were essentially decorative rather than structural. Thereafter, the decorative manipulation of structural form, already apparent in the treatment of the arch in Abbasid secular building, was taken to an extreme: the squinch, extracted from its structural context and multiplied on a reduced scale, formed a honeycomb-like web of squinchlettes – known as muqarnas – which ultimately covered entire vaults.

By the beginning of the 11th century a third tomb type had emerged in Iran: the slender faceted tower. The origin is obscure: perhaps it develops the venerable antique tradition represented at Palmyra**1.18c** or the enigmatic tower at Naqsh-i Rustam; perhaps it descended from some lost native commemorative form, crossed with the tent; petrified and elevated, perhaps the latter stands for the former habitation of the deceased, under which inhumation was traditional. Be any of this as it may, form, not space, was the prime concern of its builder and his inspiration is most plausibly to be found in the essentially commemorative minaret. The most monumental example is the Gunbad-i Qabus near the Caspian Sea in north-east Iran: with ten triangular projections from a circular core, it is noted as much for its pristine brickwork, relieved only by narrow inscription bands, as for its scale.**1.66**

›1.66 IRAN, GUNBAD-I QABUS, 1006: general view.

Built for Qabus ibn Vashmgir of the Ziyarid line of governors who had asserted their independence of the Abbasids in north-east Iran, this is the earliest and largest surviving representative of the tower tomb type.

1.66

Reduced from the apogee of the Gunbad-i Qabus, the tower tomb has a long history. Early examples, restrained in their patterned brickwork, include the cylindrical one at Damghan dated to 1026 and the octagonal one at Abarquh of the next generation: both are relatively squat and domed; the earlier one is restrained in its patterned brickwork, the later one advanced in its development of a muqarnas cornice.**1.67** Most subsequent examples, of high-quality baked brick, have slightly pointed domical or conical roofs over lower inner domes: proportions are sometimes attenuated but the main line of development was to reduce the height of a polygonal 'drum' over a stout rectangular base.

Well before the end of the 11th century – when the mysticism of personal salvation prompted the proliferation of tombs in the orbit of *sufis* – the tomb-tower was being eclipsed in Iran and its north-eastern extension by the

>**1.67 ABARQUH, GUNBAD-I ALI,** 1056: general view.

The only relief to the rubble walls is provided by the elaboration of the muqarnas for the cornice: that is the earliest example of the accumulation of miniature squinches so far identified but it is implausible that the process began on a rugged outcrop of rock in southern Iran.

>**1.68 KHARRAQAN, MAUSOLEUMS** of 1067 (right) and 1093.

The later work here has the earliest double-shell dome so far identified in Iran.

1.67

1.68

1.69a

1.69b

›1.69 IMAM DUR, TOMB OF MUSLIM BIN QURAISH, 1085: (a) interior, (b) exterior.

Built by the local ruler for himself and related descendants of the fifth *imam*, this small cubic building, unusually closed to the sides, is remarkable for its superstructure of five tapering tiers of stucco muqarnas. Outside, the battered mass has circular corner piers or turrets, like the Samanid tomb at Bukhara,[1.64] but these project further like those of several Iranian tomb towers – the slightly later ones at Kharraqan, for instance. The type was reproduced numerous times in Iraq.

square or polygonal canopy type. Most often, perhaps, the canopy is carried on attenuated blind arcades, richly embellished with geometric relief: early examples, significantly built for Turks long familiar with the campaign tent, are the octagonal pair at Kharraqan from the second half of the 11th century.[1.68] Naturally, the types were crossed to produce hybrids and the process was enduringly popular. Perhaps the most extraordinary example is the qubba at Imam Dur in Shi'ite Iraq where the vault is composed entirely of muqarnas.[1.69]

1.70a

›1.70 FATIMID EMBELLISHMENT: (a) roundel centred on the name of Ali (from the portal of the Cairene al-Aqmar Mosque, 1125); (b) door panel with 'grotesque' motif (c. 1060; New York, Metropolitan Museum of Art).

1.70b

5 THE FATIMIDS

A clandestine network of Shi'ite subversion had been developed throughout the caliphate by the end of the 9th century: it surfaced then, when the Abbasids were evidently losing their grip – especially in the west. Called al-Shi'i, one Abu Abdullah al-Husayn was a Syrian agent of heterodoxy in Arabia where he was persuaded by itinerant Berbers to take his cause to North Africa. Promising the advent of a *mahdi*, he managed to assert enough authority to concern the Aghlabid ruler Ibrahim in Kairouan until dissent among the Berbers seemed to nullify the threat. However, disputed succession on Ibrahim's demise in 902 gave al-Shi'i a new chance: he established a territorial base and called on his Syrian co-sectarians to send the promised *mahdi*. The chosen figure, Ubayd Allah, claimed to be the great-grandson of Isma'il, great-grandson of Ali's second son Husayn: his following was styled Fatimid in virtue of this descent from the Prophet's daughter, Fatima.**1.70**

1.71a

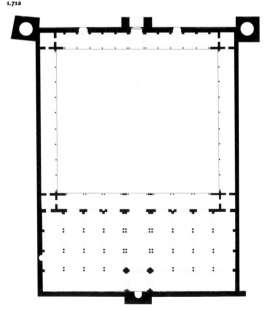

1.71b @ 1:1500

The gate is the central element in an innovative arcaded façade scheme terminating in projecting towers: the composition of the gate, with a central great arch flanked by niches all with horseshoe-shaped arches, introduced a motif which was to prove enduringly popular with the Fatimids.

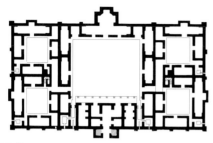

1.72a @ 1:1000

As elsewhere in early Islamic lands, the nucleus derives from the Roman camp, the entrance from the triumphal arch. However, the scheme as a whole recalls an imperial thermal complex with the cruciform audience hall projecting from the north front as the caldarium projected from Diocletian's great Roman exercise – or, more particularly, the great northern baths of Timgad. Common origin in that type explains the similarity with the north-central block of Umayyad Mshatta – the basilica there ceding to the court here and the audience hall renouncing the protection from the rear of enclosure in a range of service rooms. In both cases the adaptation of the model for domestic purposes incorporated 'bayts' in place of palaestras.

Probably an audience hall of the palace as developed when the Ifriqiyan capital had been relocated to Beni Hammad, the Manar pavilion encloses a square hall crowned with a dome and reached by a perimeter ramp from an arcaded basement. The exterior was articulated with blind arcading.

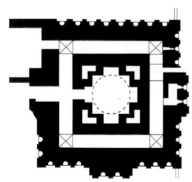

1.72b @ 1:500

MAHDIA AND ITS WESTERN OUTPOSTS

Under the *mahdi*'s banner, the Fatimids finally overcame the Aghlabids in 909: they established a new capital south of Kairouan called Mahdia and acknowledged their leader as caliph. The antique triumphal arch, with its age-old symbolism,[1.31] was adapted for the main gate in the doubled land walls protecting Mahdia's peninsula. The motif is echoed in the main portal of the city's much-restored principal mosque where it plays a central role in a near-symmetrical façade composition for which the most convincing precedents are to be found in the Arab fortified retreats of the Muslim heartland and their Roman predecessors.[1.71, 1.37] Access through that portal was direct. In the palace portal, on the other hand, approach is deflected off-axis to side passages to assert exclusiveness, if not to enhance security.

Beyond its portal, the Mahdia palace complex has largely disappeared but the principal ceremonial element of a secondary seat near Kairouan incorporated an iwan beyond an elongated hall. The remains of smaller contemporary complexes at Ashir and Beni Hammad in the Algerian Maghreb – the seats of Fatimid vassals – are more revealing. The latter is a citadel with numerous formal elements, palace buildings – notably a four-square domed ceremonial pavilion known as the Qasr al-Manar – and a mosque, informally disposed to the north of a huge rectangular tank – presumably inspired by Roman legend – and its axial adjuncts. The wholly rectangular complex at Ashir was entered through a portal of the Mahdia type: it opened the principal axis of an idealistically symmetrical scheme in which the ceremonial suite, opposite the entrance beyond a square court, again incorporated a laterally disposed hall but the throne room was cruciform.[1.72]

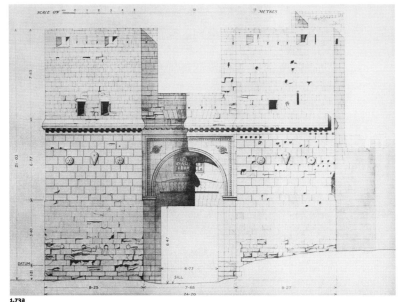

1.73a

The sections of the defences, transformed from brick to fine ashlar by Badr al-Jamali between 1087 and 1092, included three of the gates: the square towers flanking the semi-blind, semi-circular arch of the Bab al-Nasr recall the Golden Gate of Constantinople – if not Pharaonic pylons; the semi-circular ones of the Bab al-Futuh are equally persuasively Roman – and not foreign to Cairo itself. Stone is used throughout and the arches are resolutely semi-circular (AIC1, pages 30ff., 105, 559, 704).

1.73C

FROM IFRIQIYA TO EGYPT

Proceeding to penetrate west and east, early in the second quarter of the 10th century the Fatimids took Fez, capital of the independent Idrissid kingdom of Morocco founded by a refugee from the Abbasids towards the end of the 9th century. They were repulsed from Alexandria by Abbasid forces several times but, after a period of internal strife, they finally took Fustat in 969. Having established their camp outside the city, they named it al-Qahira ('Cairo') after their victory and developed their definitive new capital within the moated mud-brick walls of its square compound.

From al-Qahira, the capital after 972, the Fatimids consolidated their hold on Egypt, asserted their claim to the caliphate, crossed to the Hija and went on to overcome Syria. In the very year of their Egyptian triumph, however, a new threat manifested itself: ever bitter at the loss of the Holy Land, the forces of Byzantium retook Antioch under the banner of Christ and inspired later generations of

1.73b

1.73d

Christian Europeans to embark on their Crusades to recover Jerusalem.

The first two Fatimid reigns were prosperous. Power had passed to the army by the 1030s but the western provinces were lost to the Zirids, erstwhile vassals in Algeria, and to the Almoravids in Morocco. The failure of successive Nile floods in the 1060s was catastrophic for the regime: destabilized by social unrest in Egypt, its hold on Tunisia and Algeria failed and the Holy Land was lost to the Crusaders by the end of the century. However, the governor of Acre, an Armenian convert to Shi'ism, Badr al-Jamali, had assumed control in Egypt in 1074 and established a hereditary wazirate which – though marking the ascendancy of the official class at the expense of the caliph – sustained the Fatimids in al-Qahira for another century. The effort was expensive, not least for rebuilding exposed sections of the city's fortifications in stone against the Sunni Seljuk Turks from the east and the Crusaders from the west.**1.73**

CIVIL WORKS

Al-Qahira was developed within the nearly square compound defended by the walls and divided by a north–south axial artery which may still be traced. The great palaces of state in the centre and the suburban garden pavilions, to which the caliph resorted for relaxation, have disappeared but several houses datable to c. 1100 have been uncovered in old Fustat. Related to the palace as described by contemporaries – but naturally on a much smaller scale and ingeniously distributed on irregular plots – these are invariably centred on a courtyard and some have opposed iwans beyond lateral halls like the bayts of Samarra and the throne room of Mahdia. The type had doubtless been translated to Fustat at least as early as the Tulunid era.[1.74]

METROPOLITAN MOSQUES

The Fatimids renovated the several important mosques in the Holy Lands of their conquests, notably al-Aqsa in Jerusalem where they were responsible for the lavish mosaics of the mihrab bay. In Cairo three outstanding mosques survive from their era. Two of these were of imperial scale: al-Azhar, founded before the transfer of the capital in 972 and thereafter the collegiate centre of radical Shi'ite propaganda in the new empire, and the even larger al-Hakim built outside the north gate from c. 990 evidently to accommodate the retinues of caliph and vassals participating in the perennial ceremony of allegiance renewal.[1.75]

After the mid-11th-century crisis the regime lacked means and motive for grand projects. In contrast to self-assertive structures on distinct sites, mosque building was reduced to the intimate scale of local centres of prayer confined to restricted sites in the existing warren of streets: a prime example is the al-Aqmar Mosque of c. 1125. A generation later, the mosque of al-Salih Tala'i was able to impose regularity on its extra-mural commercial site.[1.76]

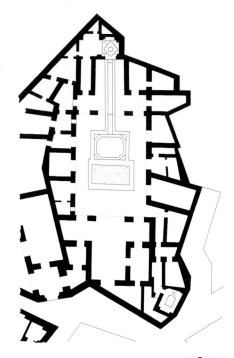

1.74 @ 1:500

›1.74 CAIRO, LATE-FATIMID HOUSE FROM AL-FUSTAT: plan.

1.75a

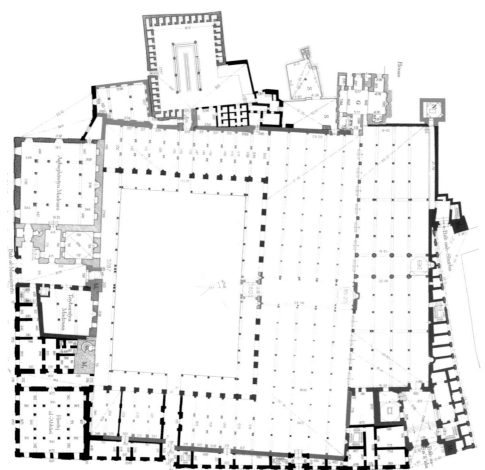

1.75b @ 1:3000

The quarters of heterodoxy

As we have seen, the Mosque of Ibn Tulun recalled the double-walled compound of the greatest Ptolemaic temples – in conception if not substance – but, unlike the Pharaonic hypostyle hall, the multiple arcades which form its aisles of prayer are cut by no dominant nave or transept. Borrowed by the Fatimids from Kairouan first for their mosque at Mahdia, these latter features – and the three domed bays of the qibla arcade – distinguished their main works in Egypt. And the form was exported to southern Arabia, then governed by a Shi'ite dynasty which acknowledged the suzerainty of the Fatimids.

›1.75 CAIRO, EARLY FATIMID MOSQUES: (a–d) al-Azhar (c. 970, remodelled mid-12th century), prayer hall from the court, plan (after Creswell), interior of prayer hall and mihrab; (e, f) al-Hakim (begun by Caliph al-Aziz c. 990 and completed under al-Hakim in 1013), axonometric reconstruction (after Farid Shafi'i) and detail of arcade.

1.75c

1.75d

Though thus more advanced in plan than the Mosque of Ibn Tulun, the hypostyle prayer hall of al-Azhar (85 by 69 metres) was more conservative in elevation, with recycled columns supporting arches. These survived the remodelling of the court façades, probably towards the middle of the 12th century, when the dome was built at the head of the nave and the minarets were added. The nave arcades and internal walls are of brick, stuccoed and incised with restrained calligraphic and floral relief: the former present doctrinal justification for the Fatimid claim to the caliphate.

Towards the end of the 10th century antique spoils were inadequate to meet the greatly expanded needs of al-Hakim's mosque: the plan formula is that of the earlier work, but tauter, and within the stone-walled compound (121 by 131 metres) brick piers stand in place of columns to support the timber roofs of the hall, the higher nave and the riwaqs. The main

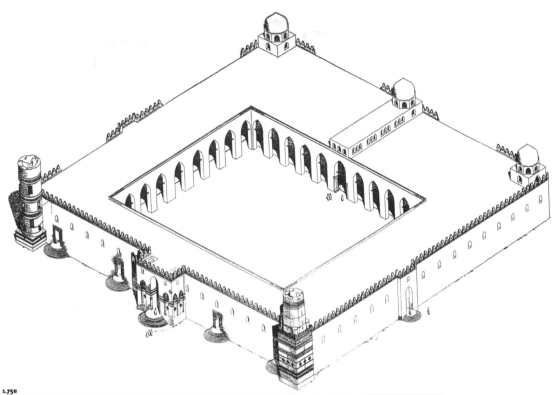

1.75e

1.75f

›ARCHITECTURE IN CONTEXT »DAR AL-ISLAM

›1.76 CAIRO, LATER FATIMID MOSQUES:
(a–c) al-Aqmar (built by the vizier Ma'mun al-Bata'ihi
from 1125), façades to street and prayer hall, plan;
(d, e) al-Salih Tala'i (1160), overview and plan.

external walls are of roughly dressed stone – brick was used only for
interior partitions – but the towers and gates are of fine ashlar with bands
of calligraphic, geometric and floral ornament carved in sharp relief from
the stone. The main gate, in the north-west wall, varies the triumphal arch
formula of Mahdia. The towers – one built over a circular plan, the other
square – were later encased in bastions double the elevation of the walls
resulting in a triple-height structure which reminds some commentators
of the Pharos of Alexandria – if through the intermediacy of Kairouan.
Minarets were contributed by the Sunni Ayyubids who also undertook the
substantial renovation of al-Azhar.

1.76b

1.76c @ 1:1000

1.76a

The smaller, later Mosque of al-Aqmar is built of fine masonry, especially richly carved for the portal but still clearly derived from the antique
triumphal arch like the earliest Fatimid work at Mahdiya: particularly
noteworthy are the grooved arch and niche heads, recalling Abbasid
Samarra in profile at least, and the muqarnas translated from later Iraq.
Ingenuity was required to effect the transition from the north–south
alignment of the façade on the street with the south-east axis of prayer.
Service rooms fill the triangle left between the square court and the
street corner: elsewhere such ancillary space was given over to revenue-
producing shops.

The Tala'i mosque was innovative for Cairo in being built over a shopping arcade now largely obliterated by the general rise in the ground

1.76d

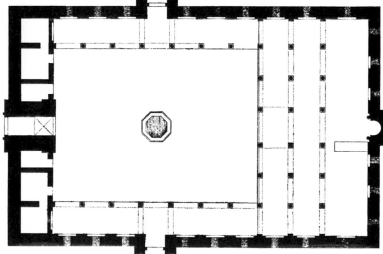

1.76e @ 1:1000

level. The portico of arcades carried on pillaged antique columns, stretching between projections at each end of the entrance front and once closed with a wooden screen (mashrabiya), is unique in Cairo but there are Iriqiyan precedents, for instance the Bu Fatata at Susa. The court seems not originally to have had riwaqs on the north-west (entrance) side but there were single ranges to the sides and triple ones formed the prayer hall on the south-east. Following the Fatimid fashion, the spandrels of the arches are relieved with medallions and bands of script.

The norm for Fatimid religious buildings is the pointed arch, usually stilted and often scalloped – as on the al-Aqmar façade where the muqarnas motif flanks it in complex variation. As there too, the geometric governed the vegetal yet, in timber panelling at least, the arabesque occasionally reapproximates the grotesque as the floral becomes the animal.[1.70b] Above all, however, surfaces are carved with assiduous didactic purpose: calligraphy was of particular importance in the period and achieved unsurpassed monumentality on façades.[1.70a] This was the corollary of the Fatimid revival of the venerable Egyptian art of finely dressed masonry for exteriors: their builders had acquired the expertise in Ifriqiya where stone was also the traditional material. Brick and stucco may have persisted in interiors and carved woodwork was a special feature of Egyptian furnishing but stone – varied in consistency and colour, inscribed in the manner which had long appealed to Egyptians or carved with restraint and contrasted in tone in the fine chromatic manner of Syria, overlaid or inlaid with marble for special effect – was to be the dominant material in all the central Muslim lands, from Egypt to Turkey.

MONUMENTS TO THE DEAD

Heterodox, the Fatimids dedicated themselves not to building grandiose royal memorials but to commemorating the interment of holy men – particularly descendants of Ali, among whom they counted themselves. The Muslim dead had long been interred in a great cemetery to the south of Fustat and at least as early as the 9th century mashhads had appeared there. By the middle of the 10th century, when the Fatimids were well established, the norm was the domed 'canopy' with open arcades to all sides, like the Qubba al-Subabiya at Sumarra but square like the contemporary Samanid tomb at Bukhara. Survivors of the type from the first Fatimid century are sparse but there are numerous examples from early thereafter, notably at Aswan: these are attributable not to rulers but to bourgeois patrons.**1.77**

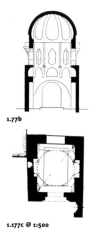

1.77b

1.177c @ 1:500

1.77a

By the middle of the 11th century the mashhad had gained a new complexity in response to the patronage of rulers and their viziers: not surprisingly, the Mesopotamian muqarnas motif first appears in Egypt in this context. The Fatimids themselves built a mausoleum incorporating a mashhad dedicated to Ali's martyred son, Husayn, but only the latter survived Ayyubid antipathy to their heterodox predecessors. The enigmatic 'al-Juyushi Masjid' built by Badr al-Jamali in 1085 fared better: identified as a mashhad in an inscription but without a tomb and perched on an elevated site beyond the Southern Cemetery, it consists of a domed qubba with mihrab preceded by a vestibule, a court and an entrance hall under a

›**1.77 ASWAN, LATE-11TH-CENTURY COMMEMORATIVE BUILDINGS:** (a) tombs; (b, c) mausoleum 24, plan and section; (d, e) mashhad, plan and section (after Creswell)

Open to one, two, three or (rarely) four sides, the majority of the mausoleums at the site are domed qubbas but several have tunnel-vaulted extensions east and west. Whitewashed plaster over brick or rubble is the norm for them all. The octagonal zone of transition from cube to dome is usually of the single squinch type but there are occasional pendentives. In the contemporary mashhad at the same site, the zone of transition incorporates tripartite squinches – putative muqarnas

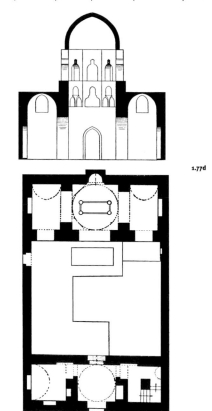

1.77d

1.77e @ 1:500

of the Tim type – with mini-pendentives supporting the uppermost unit and without the frame. External splayed spurs, like inverted buttresses between the arched windows, are peculiar to the Aswan mausoleums.

›1.78 CAIRO, THE FATIMID MASHHAD:
(a–c) the al-Juyushi complex (1085), section, plan (both after Creswell) and view; (d–f) the complex of Sayyidah Ruqayyah (1133), exterior and interior views.

The walls of such complexes were usually of rough-cast masonry, the domes of brick.

minaret of the Kairouan type but with a muqarnas cornice supporting the balcony. No doubt surrounds the other notable Cairene complex of the type with domed qubba and ancilliary spaces, the mashhad built for Sayyidah Ruqayyah in 1133.**1.78**

1.78d

1.78e

1.78b @ 1:500

1.78c

1.78f

1.3 SUNNI REACTION: CALIPHATE AND SULTANATE

1.79

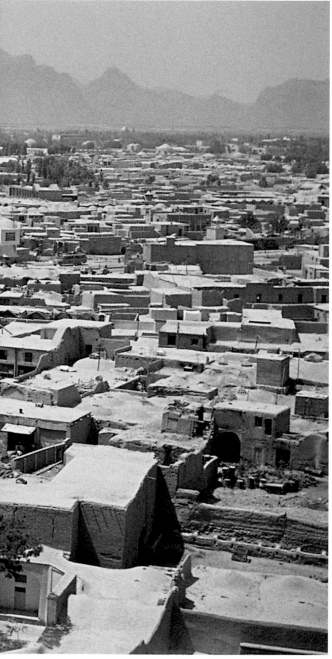

1.81a, b

6 THE GREAT SELJUKS AND IRAN

The far west was a foreign caliphate. A Shi'ite rival to the orthodox Abbasid caliph had extended his sway from Ifriqiya to Egypt, advanced into Palestine and went on to seize the Holy Cities of the Hijaz. In their central domains of ancient Mesopotamia and Iran the decadent Abbasids were in thrall to the mayors of their palace, the Shi'ite Buyids and, therefore, impotent. Beyond Baghdad, to the east, as we have seen, power had passed to the provinces. In Iran and neighbouring areas, many of these had been unsettled by the infiltration of Turks.

As in the centre of the caliphate itself, when a weak ruler acceded and his provincial relatives asserted themselves in contention, the *mamluk* officers secured control. One such, appointed by the Samanids to govern Ghazni, successfully challenged his master and handed the province to his son: the latter was succeeded by one of his *mamluks* who then took Khorasan and handed both provinces on to his son Mahmud.

THE GHAZNAVID EAST

The first ruler of note to emerge from *mamluk* lineage – the first of many in the Iranian world and the heartlands of Islam – Mahmud of Ghazni (998–1030) extended his rule over much of modern Afghanistan and led a series of booty raids on the major religious centres of northern

1.80c @ 1:2000

India but was not bent on the acquisition of territory there. He marked his triumph and the consequent extension of Islam with ceremonial minarets and wielded power from the four-iwan courts of the palaces at Ghazni and Lashkari Bazaar.**1.80**

›1.79 ISFAHAN: view south from the Jami-masjid.

›1.80 LASHKARI BAZAAR: (a, b) Great or South Palace of Mahmud of Ghazni (998–1030), plan and reconstruction of entrance block, (c) garden pavilion plan.

Lashkari Bazaar

The southern palace is one of several in a series of walled enclosures on the bank of the Helmand River. In a rectangular compound – 100 by 250 metres – the distribution clearly recalls Samarra and Ukhaydir and beyond them Sasanian Firozabad and Parthian Assur.**1.20a–c** The Abbasid seat is also recalled in the cusped and pointed horseshoe-arch form which the Ghaznavids liberally employed. These appear in the context of variations on the Iranian repertoire of decorative themes, most notably muqarnas and exceptionally vigorous calligraphy. The structure is largely of mud bricks – reinforced with baked brick or stone at salient points.

The entrance hall (cruciform like several of the halls of Samarra) leads to a court with four iwans – as at Assur but precociously in the palaces of Islam. As at Firozabad and Ukhaydir, the main one opposite the entrance leads to a domed room, a vestibule and a huge hall overlooking the river and notable for its figural murals in addition to geometric patterns and Koranic script in moulded stucco. To either side of this ceremonial core are four private suites – recalling Ukhaydir and the Umayyad paired apartments (bayts) – each with its own nuclear court and four iwans. The northern pair, accessible from the great hall, appear to have been the ruler's quarters. The one to the west of the main iwan, communicating with smaller courts and rooms added later to the west of the main court but with restricted access from it, was doubtless the harem. All the living quarters were supplied with running water from a reservoir fed from the river.

Gardens and views of the river were essential featurs of all the palaces in the complex. The one to the east of the central palace is overlooked by a square pavilion with a square central room, four iwans and four square corner rooms: the particularly important Persian garden pavilion type known as hasht behisht is an octagonal variant of the form.

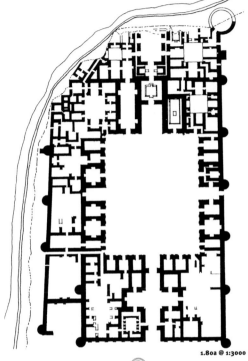

1.80a @ 1:3000

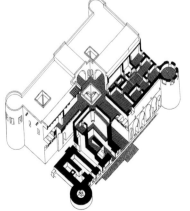

1.80b

›1.81 SELJUK RULERS AT COURT AND PLAY
(early 13th-century miniatures on vellum and ceramics;
Boston, Museum of Fine Art and Berlin, Museum for
Islamic Art).

1.81c

ADVENT OF THE SELJUKS

In the last quarter of the 10th century an Oghuz Turkik
tribal chief called Seljuk entered his followers in the service of the Samanids as soldiers, settled them near Bukhara
and converted to orthodox Islam – as did the Turkish infil-
trators in general. Challenged by the Turks of Ghazni, who
dispatched the Samanids in 1005 and espoused the anti-
Buyid Sunni cause with fanaticism, Seljuk's two grandsons
won control of Khorasan. Chaghri Beg consolidated his
hold there with the main Turkoman force. Tughril Beg set
out with a new army formed of *mamluks* to exterminate
the Shi'ite Buyids, who still controlled the Abbasid caliph:
he invaded Baghdad in 1055, received the submission of
the last Buyid and was given the title of sultan by the

grateful caliph – in lieu of the legitimacy which came with Arabic descent from the Prophet. Thus installed, the Seljuks accommodated themselves to the predominantly Iranian civilization in which they found themselves: rather than spoiling it, indeed, they emerged as its protectors.

Many Turkomen followed the path of the Seljuks. Forging a successful army from unruly tribesmen was expected of a great chief. Forging a sound administration from the same material, with effective control over hosts of other intruders, was beyond even Tughril Beg. And immediate opposition from other Turks, particularly those who had served the Buyids as generals, received Fatimid support. Baghdad was lost, then won again with help from Khorasan, and a working partnership was forged between sultan and caliph: the latter providing religious authority, the former power.

The caliph remained in Baghdad. The better to control dissident Shi'ite Iran, the sultan moved his seat to Hamadan. He went on to take the central city of Isfahan in 1050 and was buried at Rayy (Teheran), the ancient metropolis from which much of eastern Iran had traditionally been governed. These were secondary capitals: Rayy was devastated by strife between Shi'tes and Sunnis in the 12th century and obliterated by the Mongols a century later; Isfahan retains its glories.**1.79**

Tughril Beg was succeeded by Chaghri Beg's son Alp Arslan in 1063: the suppression of dissent and the construction of a regime capable of sustaining unity were the challenges facing him. The main immediate threat came from continued destabilizing Turkoman infiltration, especially in the region known as the Jazira – the 'island' between the upper reaches of the Tigris and Euphrates – and eastern Anatolia. To control the tribal chiefs and deflect them from Syria, as much as to expand his territory, Alp Arslan galvanized the disparate forces into attack on the remaining provinces of the Byzantine empire in eastern Anatolia and ultimately defeated the emperor decisively at Manzikert in 1071. However, as he had more pressing problems to deal with elsewhere and died the next year, the legatees were the Turkoman tribal chiefs who were left to rivalry for dominance – the various contenders assisted by calls for help from rival claimants to the Byzantine throne.

To address the problems of consolidating power and confronting the Shi'ite challenge – issued particularly from Fatimid al-Azhar in Cairo – Alp Arslan retained as grand vizier the Khorasani Nizam al-Mulk (died 1092). They launched an extensive programme of mosque building: much of their monumental achievement endures, most notably at Isfahan, Ardistan and Qazvin; much else has been lost or obscured by later development, notably at Kerman, Rayy, Shiraz and Yazd – as also further afield at Bukhara, Herat, Khiva and Merv to name only a few of the major provincial or princely seats. Even more significantly, perhaps, they launched a programme of orthodox Sunni education: teaching colleges were built, mosques reformed or extended to incorporate them, and numerous splendid ceremonial minarets, sometimes paired at the entrance to the mosque, always richly inscribed in the context of patterned brickwork, were raised in affirmation of allegiance to orthodoxy – and to counter it.[1.80]

The caliphate's administration was reformed along the network of familial lines laid down by the Buyid: each province was given to a Seljuk prince and divided into fiefs with military governors (*atabegs*). The enfiefed lands supported the soldiers in return for the protection of farmers or traders from rival Turkomen intruders. The grand vizier Nizam al-Mulk was retained and his work furthered under Alp Arslan's son Malik-shah (1072–92). He was constantly on campaigns to consolidate his power from Syria,

1.82a

where he sent his brother as governor, to Ferghana where he himself was active from his base, Sultan Kala at newly fortified Merv. However, on his early death his gains were largely lost to ambitious *atabegs* and rivalry among contenders for the sultanate which, naturally, involved the princely provincial governors. The dissension favoured the Shi'ites, the Turkomen intruders and the fief-holders in the forts controlling local arable land or trade routes.**1.82**

Khorasan was an exception. There the late sultan's son Sanjar maintained control as governor for his older brothers, who succeeded one another at the centre. Sultan himself from 1118 to 1157, Sanjar restored control and revived

the Abbasid caliphate. The Seljuk *atabegs* of Mosul had regained Syria before the end of Sanjar's reign and, subsequently independent, went on to terminate the ambitions of the Crusaders in the Holy Land – as we shall see.

The gains of Sanjar and his contemporaries had been lost to Turkoman rivalry and the Seljuk regime was succumbing to tribal revolt by the end of the 12th century. By the middle of the next century Seljuks, Abbasids and almost everyone else were at the mercy of the Mongol hordes unleashed across Asia by the devastating Ghengis Khan (1206–27): Baghdad and its caliphate fell to them in 1258 – as we shall recall in due course (see page 368).

1.82b

1.82c

›**1.82 BAM:** (a, b) general views from the south towards the citadel and of the town from the citadel with the governor's palace court centre and the caravanserai below it, (c) citadel entrance.

Bam, controlling a route skirting the Dasht-i Lut Desert, was fortified as a centre of local power at least from Sasanian times: the citadel is integrated with the town defences in the north-west sector. Naturally, mud-brick building needs constant renovation and, though it was generally considered the most medieval of Iranian towns in essence, much that survived until the earthquake of 2004 was substantially Safavid (16th–17th centuries).

1.83

›**1.83 BAHLA (OMAN):** general view of mud-brick fort.

The site was fortified before Islam reached the east coast of Arabia c. 630. The defences were developed by the Nabahina rulers of inland Oman from the 12th century – ostensibly and not without the influence of European trading powers after the 16th century, when the Portuguese arrived.

FORT AND PALACE

The dissolution of the central Abbasid authority, undermining pan-Islamic security, had prompted the construction of local defences throughout the heartlands of the caliphate and many great citadels and forts survive there, at least in part. Bam provided an unrivalled image of the fortified town which approached its definitive form as an *atabeg* seat in the late-Seljuk era. The type recurs wherever the mud-brick or adobe tradition thrives in the oases of desiccated tracts: a splendid example – one drawn from many – is at Bahla across the Straits of Hormuz in Oman.**1.82, 1.83**

The citadel was the seat of power, the palace of king or governor – or *atabeg* – but palaces tend to be built for the immediate gratification of pretension rather than for durability. Brick was the usual material in Seljuk Iran and neighbouring areas and brick is perishable unless it is baked, tightly massed and constantly maintained. Baked brick, usual for the major religious buildings and tombs, was too expensive for extensive secular work and stucco was the normal revetment inside. After Samarra and Ukhaydir, the vicissitudes of power and consequent vagaries of maintenance – let alone wayward construction and wilful destruction – have left little trace of the courtyard complexes of the Abbasids and their Seljuk protectors. Yet they were built to eclipse Ctesiphon – enough of which still stands in testimony to their failure (AICI, pages 652–653). The ubiquitous iwan, which cannot have failed to dominate their courts, may be represented by timeless domestic examples.[1.86]

The walled city, citadel and palace have been traced at Sanjar's Merv: the principal palace building is symmetrically planned about a court with four iwans – as might well be expected if even the Mamluk rulers of an eastern province were building magnificently to that formula.[1.84,] [1.80] Bam's palace was a reduced version of the type. Still smaller, simpler pavilions in the area are of the type known as kiosk: beyond Merv, examples include the adjunct to the main court in the so-called Regent's Palace on the Oxus at Tirmidh.[1.85]

CARAVANSERAI

The Seljuks controlled much of the territory first amassed by the Achaemenids. That great domain was bound together by the best roads the world had yet seen and over succeeding centuries imperial messengers and armies had shared them with the caravans of traders, not least those

1.84a

>**1.84 SELJUK PALACE REMAINS,** early 12th century: (a) stucco figure; (b) Merv, plan.

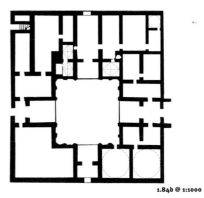

1.84b @ 1:1000

Though modest in comparison with the palaces of the caliph – its exterior is c. 45 by 40 metres and the court is 16 metres square – the ceremonial Shahriyar block of the palace at Merv dominated a fortified enclosure (the Sultan Qal'a) which contained numerous other facilities. If not defended by the citadel walls within the town defences, palaces of the predominant Seljuk type would have walled compounds of their own in which formally planned kiosks were distributed informally.

>**1.85 TIRMIDH, KIRK-KIZ,** date unknown: plan.

The site was a Samanid centre and therefore the introverted labyrinthine palace block there has been dated to as early as the 9th century: others place it as

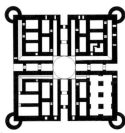

1.85 @ 1:1000

late as the 12th century. The iwans are reduced to corridors defining three multi-vaulted apartments and a mosque. Certainly 12th century, the so-called Regent's Palace at the same site (incompletely excavated) has a much simpler kiosk – with four iwans radiating from a domical centre – attached to the outer wall of the main courtyard complex.

1.86

>**1.86 MOSUL, TRADITIONAL HOUSE:** court and iwan.

Relatively modern, such houses may nevertheless be taken as representative of a long tradition. It was in this context that the teaching college developed.

>**1.87 EARLY CARAVANSERAI PLAN TYPES:** (a) Ribat-i Sharaf; (b) Akcha Qal'a.

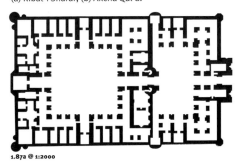

1.87a @ 1:2000

who plied the so-called Silk Road to China. Between the towns, at intervals of a day's journey, these were accommodated in hostels (caravanserai). Defensible quadrangles related to both the Roman fort and the Mesopotamian palace in type, several of these date from the Seljuk period. And in the towns which prospered on trade, apart from communal facilities such as baths – and, of course, mosques – there were commodity exchanges for the wholesale distribution of goods and covered shopping streets (souks) for the retailers which extended like arteries through the cellular corpus of courtyard houses.[1.79]

The size varied with multiplicity of purpose: there was staging-post accommodation for traders with facilities for communication and interchange as well as barracks for soldiers and, perhaps, proponents of the Faith – the latter two as the designation 'ribat' implies. Most common was the stoutly walled single courtyard with central fountain entered through a pishtaq: the Ribat-i Sharaf in the northwest of Iran represents the type. The splendid complex with a forecourt on the Nishapur–Merv road given the princely style 'Sharaf' was inscribed c. 1154 with reference to Sultan Sanjar but probably dates in main part from at least a generation earlier. Also near Merv, Akcha Qal'a is usually dated to c. 1100 but is rare for that date in having two complete courtyards.[1.87]

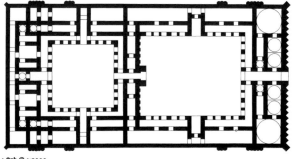

1.87b @ 1:2000

THE MOSQUE AND THE FOUR-IWAN PLAN

Court and hypostyle hall with rectangular or cylindrical brick piers or pillars – rather than columns – carrying tunnel or domical brick vaults are the norm in early Muslim Iran, as we have seen.**1.58–1.60** The pier eclipses the pillar as the 11th century progresses: the corollary is increased flat surface and the development of a rectangular grid to order façades. Stucco persists, especially in interiors, above all in mihrabs, but patterned brickwork achieves a high degree of finesse in arabesque or geometric panels and calligraphic bands deployed to elucidate structure no less than to provide selective emphasis: both these roles are already also occasionally played by tile, the glory of the future.

As the traditional place of epiphany, the iwan first asserted itself as the dominant element on the qibla – interrupting the grid in plan and elevation – in central Iranian mosques both as entrance to the compound and entrance to the sanctuary – developments elsewhere are sadly obscure. The motif had made a tentative appearance in the raising of the height of the central qibla bays of both the eastern and western court ranges in the late-9th-century

1.88

>**1.88 GULPAYAGAN, JAMI-MASJID,** rebuilt from 1104: domed sanctuary.

This represents the so-called kiosk type of mosque which has been identified as a qubba adapted from the chahar-taq of the Sasanian fire temple by sealing the arch in the side facing Mecca with a mihrab but leaving the other three open to a precinct. In the zone of transition, clearly contributed by the rebuilders, the squinch is a polylobed arch with three tires of muqarnas. In the absence of archaeological evidence to substantiate literary accounts, some scholars dispute the origin of the Iranian qubba in the chahar-taq.

>**1.89 ZAVAREH, JAMI-MASJID,** 1136: (a) overview of court, (b) plan.

The four-iwan formula appeared for the first time with qubba in the jami-masjid at Zavareh – which is also sometimes identified as a kiosk mosque in origin. The main sanctuary iwan is as yet distinguished only by its size. The façades to either side are symmetrical and behind them tunnel vaulting is perpendicular to the qibla.

1.89a

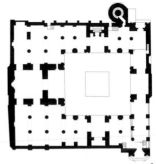

1.89b @ 1:1000

mosque at Nayin.[1.60] A century later at Niriz, it alone formed the sanctuary but elsewhere sanctuaries incorporated domed qubbas.[1.88] These may derive from the Sasanian fire temple, not without knowledge of the western precedents, but the combination of iwan and qubba had secular antecedents fully appreciated by Islamic builders.[1.20, 1.80]

By 1136, at Zavareh, the foundation scheme for the mosque is the earliest known to have incorporated four iwans of which the tallest asserted the qibla in association with a domed sanctuary.[1.89] The reason for the development is inconclusively debated: certainly it promoted aesthetic unity without denying the authority of the qibla. A generation later the formula had achieved superb monumentality in the conversion of the hypostyle mosque at Ardistan with two storeys of arcades between the four iwans and a domed sanctuary.[1.90] At Isfahan, during these same years, four iwans were inserted in the Buyid Jami-masjid and minarets further distinguished the frontispiece of the largest one, on the qibla before the grandest of domed sanctuaries.[1.91]

1.90a

1.90b

1.90c

1.90d

›1.90 ARDISTAN, JAMI-MASJID, mid-12th century (restored): (a) exterior from north-west, (b) court seen from sanctuary iwan, (c) detail of applied stucco revetment in south-west iwan, (d) mihrab bay.

The precinct of a magnificent kiosk mosque, rebuilt between 1072 and 1092 on the site of a fire temple, was transformed into a court with four iwans. The mihrab is decorated in painted stucco, with florid, but symmetrical, arabesque motifs in contrasting scales on the areas framed and framing – the latter, indeed, calligraphic in its intricacy. In contrast, the stucco panels in the southwest iwan are applied as a tapestry or carpet, in selfassertive revetment.

›1.91 ISFAHAN, JAMI-MASJID: (a) plan with (1, grey area) 10th-century Buyid court, hypostyle hall and arcades probably extended into the court of an earlier Abbasid foundation (c. 140 by 90 metres) – by one bay all round, (2) public entrances, (3) qubba of Nizam al-Mulk (dedicated c. 1086), (4) qubba with attributory inscription of Taj al-Mulk (1088, rebuilt after the fire of 1122), (5) sanctuary iwan, (6) winter prayer hall, (b) prayer hall bays to the east of the qibla and south of the entrance passage, (c) interior of northern qubba (1088), (d) interior of north-east iwan, (e) court to south-west with qibla iwan left.

Isfahan Jami-masjid

The original Abbasid mosque seems to have had a hypostyle prayer hall with a distinct central nave asserting the qibla. To all four sides of the rectangular court, the Buyids added an arcade carried on decorated brick cylindrical piers. In the interior of the prayer hall's eastern section, the combination of massive square and circular brick piers, plain or relieved with virile zig-zag patterns, also accords with Buyid practice. They were doubtless always stout but must have needed even greater girth when the original wooden roof was destroyed by fire in 1122 and replaced with domical vaulting carried on squinches framed by four-centre arches. Echoed in later extensions to the prayer hall here and elsewhere, the multiple miniature domes are notable for their variety and many are supported on muqarnas squinches. For special emphasis, particularly in the mihrab niche, brick was masked by stucco carved into prominently relieved, highly stylized, sinuous and sensual floral patterns – as at Ardistan.

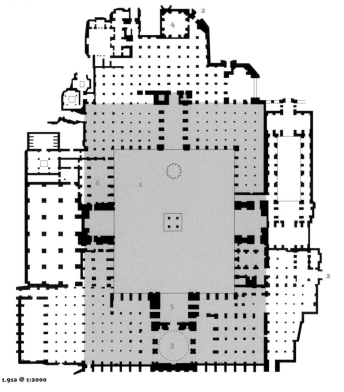

1.91a @ 1:2000

1.91b

1.91c

The most radical transformation of the hypostyle hall was effected with the interpolation of an exceptionally grand domed qubba, five bays square, in front of the central mihrab at the south-western end of the main axis: probably built as a maqsura detached from the prayer hall bays which frame it, it immeasurably enhances the qibla. Datable to c. 1086, a dedicatory inscription in the name of Sultan Malik-shah – who had visited Damascus where the Great Mosque had just received a new dome – identifies Nizam al-Mulk as the builder. According to another inscription of 1088, the slightly smaller qubba at the north-eastern end was added by the Nizam al-Mulk's rival Taj al-Mulk: apparently originally freestanding, it was probably the ceremonial entrance in the tradition of the domed ciborium. On the completion of these two qubbas, the main axis extended to 150 metres.

In both the great qubbas – as elsewhere by the late-11th century – the internal elevation is tripartite. Above the basic cube, the zone of transition to the dome runs through eight to sixteen arched sides, eight of them shallow squinches. In the main squinches, which develop the muqarnas theme first known to have been stated at Tim, the trilobes of fragmentary vaulting are raised from the main walls of the cubical space by miniature façade elements in which paired bays are framed by colonnettes supporting the fragments of vault, seeming to transmit the residual thrust of their arched profiles to a firm base. Inset in the massive walls, blind arches support the colonnettes at the confluences of the segments within each squinch. Between the squinches and the shallow side bays

1.91e

the colonnettes continue to the ground. The precision of the patterned brickwork is at its most impressive in the northern qubba. In the southern dome, ribs span straightforwardly between opposite corners of the octagon and the apexes of opposite arches, but the lattice of ribs forming a complex star in the northern dome demonstrates that the motif was decorative, not structural – though it may have been inspired by constructional procedure.

The date of the insertion of the iwans is obscure, at least in main part: according to an inscription on the portal behind the north-east iwan, building began there after the fire of 1122: that work is traditional in its elongation whereas the other three are square. The process of inserting the latter doubtless continued into the second half of the century. If so, the earliest recorded example of twin minarets applied to an iwan front, in the Imam Hasan Mosque at Ardistan (1158), is roughly contemporary. The north-east entrance, though a putative pishtaq, has no flanking minarets.

Muqarnas vaults appear in iwans by the 1130s at Sin and elsewhere but the earliest here, those of the south iwan, were not inserted until the second half of the 14th century and were reworked a century later. To supplement the decoration implicit in the brickwork, tile was inserted to enhance script or to articulate structural lines. Faience tiles solely in turquoise first appear to serve these purposes from the 11th century – at Damghan, for instance – but coverage in multi-coloured tiles is a phenomenon developed from the late-14th century which, at first still disciplined by the lines of the structure, would ultimately obviate an architectonic approach to decoration.

The great precedent set in the Isfahan Jami-masjid by the Nizam al-Mulk was first followed on a comparable scale at Qazvin under Malik-shah. Thereafter – and following the initial steps we have already traced – qubba-backed iwans proliferated. The four-iwan scheme proliferated too – though, of course, it was not invariable. And the relatively new-found sanctity of court and iwan did not obviate secular variants in a culture that accepted no bounds to religion.

›1.92 TERRACOTTA EMBELLISHMENT: (a) Bukhara, mosque of Maghak-i Attari (founded 10th century), façade with unglazed monochrome tiles (late-12th/early 13th century); (b) Kashan, Maidan mosque mihrab with lustre-painted tiles (1226; Berlin, Museum of Islamic Art).

The use of monochrome terracotta revetment was widespread by the 13th century – the precise date of the Bukhara work is unknown.

Kashan, the centre of the production of lustre-painted terracotta wares by the second quarter of the 13th century, was the widely exploited source of tiles for mural embellishment (hence *kashi* as a contraction of Kashani as the generic Iranian term for tiles). Within several rectangular frames, the principal ones with Koranic inscriptions assembled from square or rectangular units, the *kashi* mihrab is usually composed of superimposed triangulated arches delineating spandrels and tympana richly embossed with arabesques: the articulating colour is generally blue.

1.92a

1.92b

There was a wide variety of detail, especially in the form of the squinch, the elaboration of the muqarnas motif, the configuration of the ribs in domes and the patterns in the bonding of the brickwork. Zig-zag patterns were most popular, mortar courses might be thick and recessed for deep shadow lines or filled with carved stucco. Blanket stucco is not typical of the high Seljuk period in Iran: it is usually applied to significant surfaces in calligraphic bands or panels with differentiated patterns – like the framed and framing elements of a mihrab or pishtaq, for example.**1.90c, d** The same is true of tiles and terracotta panels which provided a more durable alternative – especially, of course, on exteriors.**1.91e, 1.92**

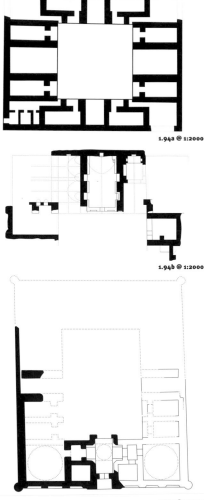

1.94a @ 1:2000

1.94b @ 1:2000

1.94c @ 1:2000

THE FOUR-IWAN PLAN AND THE MADRASA

Determined to reassert orthodoxy in the face of the Shi'ite challenge issued by the Fatimids, the Abbasids' Seljuk champions recognized the popular craving for spiritual release spectacularly met by the veneration at the shrines of Ali and his heirs. They endorsed the promotion of Sunni mystic cults through the endowment of *sufi* shrine complexes. With accommodation for a teacher (*shaikh*) and his disciples, the type (khanqah) is first known in eastern Iran in the 10th century but Seljuk amirs promoted its proliferation throughout their provinces. The centre of pilgrimage, the khanqah naturally developed into a centre of public welfare.

Teaching was always the prerogative of the mosque, but the school was often the house of the teacher – especially when a measure of discussion was admitted to supplement rote learning.**1.93** Piety and missionary zeal prompted private patrons to sponsor the development of the special collegiate complex (madrasa) in Iran from the end of the 9th century: one from that era, the first of several, was recorded

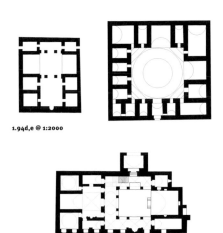

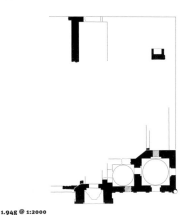

›1.94 THE ORIGIN OF THE MADRASA IN PLAN: (a, b) Khargird and Rayy, fragmentary plans of buildings with inscriptions relating to the Nizam al-Mulk; (c) Samarkand, the foundation associated with Ibrahim I Karakhanid; (d) Bosra, foundation of Abu Mohammad Gumushtegin; (e) Tokat, Cukur; (f) Diyarbakr, Mas'udiye; (g) Garjistan, Shah-i Mashhad; (h) Zuzan, foundation of Qiwam al-Din Mu'ayyad al-Mulk.

at Nishapur. Iwans accommodating the various classes doubtless interrupted cells accommodating the students around a quadrangle but, as with the khanqah, consistency of form is hardly likely. The inclusion of a small mosque would have dictated orientation, but pre-Mongol remains are too sparse to reveal any formal ordering of the characteristic domestic arrangement.

Official sponsorship of orthodox colleges with accommodation for one or more teachers and their pupils was vigorously espoused by central and local authorities in areas where heterodox cults seemed unduly popular or where Islam was newly established. The great vizier Nizam al-Mulk adopted the idea on an imperial scale: to confront the Shi'ites officially, in 1068 he inaugurated – or perhaps endorsed – a wide-ranging campaign of collegiate building to promote traditional Sunni doctrine, canon law and augment the body of orthodox clerics (*ulema*).

The early madrasa

Neither remains nor descriptions of the Nizamiyas founded by the Nizam al-Mulk indicate how far the evolution of the collegiate type was taken before the end of the 11th century: bureaucratic standardization might well be assumed, however, given the extent of the exercise. Inscriptions relating to the Nizam al-Mulk have been found on much dilapidated complexes at Khargird and Rayy (Teheran) but neither is uncontroversially identified as a madrasa.[1.94a, b] To these may be added a foundation in Samarkand attributed to the Nizam al-Mulk's slightly earlier contemporary, Ibrahim I Karakhanid (1052–68).[1.94c]

Though the type seems to have originated in the east, the earliest securely dated madrasa (1113) is attached to the mosque at Urfa (Edessa) in the upper Euphrates valley – where Alp Arslan had asserted control over the marauding Turkomen forces. The earliest independent example (from 1136) seems to be at Bosra in southern Syria[1.94d] where Malik-shah's brother, Tutush, had been sent to build a buffer against the Fatimids: contrary to the assumed foreign prototype, its court may have been vaulted.

In Seljuk Asia Minor the earliest examples date from c. 1150[1.94e] and the Mas'udiye (1194) at Diyarbakr in the neighbouring Jazira is the earliest example so far identified as possibly catering for all four schools of law.[1.94f] In the eastern Seljuk orbit – in modern Afghanistan – the earliest survival inscribed as a madrasa is the Shah-i Mashhad, dated to 117.[1.94g] After that, the next significant example, at Zurzan in north-east Iran, is dated to 1218.[1.94h]

All four schools of law were not necessarily catered for in the earliest madrasas identified so far but the remains of our eastern examples and even the small structure at Bosra seem to indicate a court with four iwans – of which the qibla one was doubtless for teaching as well as prayer and the other for entrance. The Anatolian ones do not have the complete complement – even the one at Diyarbakr had only two – but all four schools could have been accommodated in the side chambers opening from the central colonnaded court. A similar deduction could, in fact, be made from the Bosran plan – though only the sanctuary iwan could have accommodated a class of any size. Be that as it may, the general diversity of form naturally suggests diversity of purpose and patronage: with or without residential facilities, madrasas were certainly commissioned by both public and private patrons to cater for one or more orthodox schools but they also served *sufi* cults which may, or may not, have attracted official patronage.

The existence of four schools of Sunni law imposed its own discipline, of course, and an obviously relevant prototype for formal order was ready to hand in the four-iwan palace building inherited by the caliphate from the Parthians. The earliest madrasa-builders of eastern Iran may well have found another model in the Buddhist vihara – commonly a cell-bordered court dominated by a larger cell for the holy image (AIC2, pages 52ff.). Buddhism had risen to dominance in the area under the patronage of the Kushanas and following in the footsteps of the Parthians the Kushanas were themselves no strangers to the four-iwan palace plan.

›1.95   BAGHDAD,   MUSTANSIRIYA MADRASA, 1233: (a) plan, (b) view within court.

This extensive rectangular building – 106 by 48 metres – with student cells on two storeys and communal facilities around a court (62 by 26 metres) was built in emulation of the works of the great Nizam al-Mulk, who had served as vizier to al-Mustansir's ancestor 150 years earlier. Accommodating 300 students, it exceeded its model.

The axial space in the southern range, opening through three arches, is a mosque. The triple motif is echoed on the northern side opposite: the entrance iwan, obviously unsuited to teaching as the mosque may well have been, is flanked by two chambers which were doubtless used for schools instead. There are several other possible interpretations of a plan not matched by the articulation of the façades.

The earliest madrasa undoubtedly designed with four recesses – three iwans and an oratory – specifically for the four schools of Sunni law is the Mustansiriya of Baghdad, built by the penultimate Abbasid caliph, al-Mustansir, in 1233.**1.95** That was a moment of brief revival in the fortunes of the caliphate – and of Baghdad's Iraqi orbit. Long before that, the centre of cultural gravity had shifted to Iran and the four-iwan plan had been adopted for mosques. The reasons remain obscure but it is likely that the type was also collegiate. Shi'ite intransigence apart, otherwise it is difficult to explain the dearth of identified madrasas from the pre-14th-century repertory of Iranian survivals though they were common elsewhere.

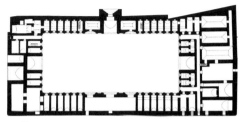

1.95a @ 1:2000

1.95b

MINARETS AND MAUSOLEUMS

Apart from the minarets attached to the sanctuary frontispieces of Jami-masjids – as at Isfahan – Iran and its central-Asian extension are well equipped with freestanding minarets: there are important attenuated conical examples at Isfahan, Damghan and Bukhara.**1.80, 1.96** Not necessarily part of a mosque complex, their purpose is somewhat obscure but was probably multiple. Those near a Jami-

›1.96 **THE MONUMENTAL MINARET IN AFGHANISTAN:** (a) of Mas'ud III at Ghazni (early 12th century, 19th-century engraved view); (b) of Ghiyath al-Din at Jam, near Firuzkuh (late-12th century).

The earlier work, built near Mas'ud's palace of the Lashkari type, was originally some 44 metres high but lost its top section in an earthquake in 1902: the stellate remaining section, of brick and terracotta, is richly

1.96a

1.96b

embroidered with geometric patterns and Kufic script – as was the palace. The 'telescopic' shaft of the later work originally rose to 60 metres: the three tiers are separated by balconies on muqarnas corbels and the terracotta revetment is lavishly embossed within a serpentine framework.

›1.97 BUKHARA, KALAYAN MINARET, 1127.

Of exceptionally fine patterned brickwork, but far less slender than the Seljuk norm in Iran, this great work (some 47 metres high) was built by Sultan Arslan Shah of the Karakhanid dynasty. Muqarnas corbels support the upper gallery – as elsewhere they support balconies.

1.97

masjid were doubtless used to broadcast the times of prayer – but, as with the earliest manifestation of the minaret (see page 40), this alone does not explain their magnificence. As landmarks visible to the traveller from afar, announcing oases, they were monuments to the triumph of Islam above all – and to the glory of their patron. The tradition was taken to unprecedented heights and decorative splendour by the Ghurid successors of the Ghaznavids: ruling from Herat and Firuzkuh, they entered India with much more determined purpose than their predecessors – as we shall see in due course.**1.97**

Well before the end of the 11th century – when the mysticism of personal salvation prompted the proliferation of tombs in the orbit of *sufis* and their mashhads – the tower type of tomb, faceted or otherwise, endured but was being eclipsed in Iran and its north-eastern extension by the cubical, cylindrical or polygonal canopy type. From a cross between the tower type and works like the pair at Kharraqan, the main lines of development over the following century – in north-western Iran, at least – are represented by the Gunbad-i Surkh (1147) and Gunbad-i Qabud (1197) at Maragha: the former is square in plan with a shallow dome rising through an octagonal drum; the latter is octagonal throughout and richly embellished with geometric relief; both are of stone in the main and both have crypts.**1.98** Naturally, more radical hybrids were enduringly popular: in particular, the extraordinarily confection at Imam Dur was often emulated – notably in the nine-tier structure of c. 1150 at Baghdad known as the Tomb of Zubayda.

On the orthodox hand, however, the outstanding mid-12th-century survivor is the qubba tomb of Sultan Sanjar at Merv which, adjacent to the palace, doubled as a mosque: it indeed derived from the qibla qubba of the typical Iranian mosque but, beyond that, continued a venerable tradition perhaps best represented at Split.**1.99, 1.27b** As generally hitherto in the Iranian sphere, Sanjar's dome was appreciable primarily from within, despite its lost blue tiles and the double shell which would later allow the envelope to soar over drum and parapet. The pishtaq, whose origin we have noted at Tim, did not recommend itself to Sanjar's architect but elsewhere in nearby central Asia to the east of the Caspian – notably at Urgench and Uzgend – the 12th century saw the motif emerge as an elaborate screen masking all but the dome behind it. In the case of the tomb of the Khorezmshah Sultan Tekesh at Urgench, that was a qubba-tower hybrid with a conical tent-like roof.**1.100, 1.101, 1.65**

1.98

›**1.98 MARAGHA, GUNBAD-I QABUD,** 1197: view from the south-east.

›**1.99 MERV, TOMB OF SULTAN SANJAR,** 1157: (a, b) views before and after restoration, (c) section.

1.99b

1.99a

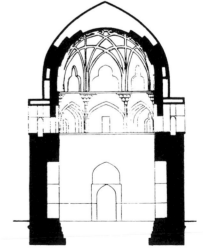

1.99c

The qubba, 17 metres square with massive walls rising to 14 metres of unrelieved brickwork, was covered by a semi-circular vault over which was a separate helmet-shaped dome – an early example of double-shell masonry, doubtless following a timber prototype, anticipated in one of the octagonal canopy tombs at Kharraqan (1093). The double-dome system was naturally more resistant to earthquakes than a rigid single shell – particularly if timber was used for the internal supports. Lost except for the lower courses of brickwork but now restored, the outer shell was covered with blue-glazed tiles.

The remains sugggest a drum but originally the dome was stilted over the arcaded gallery which – as in the Samanid tomb at Bukhara – surmounts the main mass outside: in respect of architectonics by no means universal in the period, patterned brickwork is confined to the relief of the corner piers. At this level inside – the zone of transition – single-arched squinches enclosed rectangular windows with trilobed frames, and the trilobed pattern was echoed in the lower zone of the vault. The inner shell of the dome is relieved to aesthetic effect – and its construction facilitated – by a network of ribs running between every second and every fourth pier where they are supported – visually, at least – by muqarnas 'pendentives'.

>1.100 UZGEND, KARAKHANID MAUSOLEUMS, 11th and 12th centuries: (a, b) views before and after restoration.

The central tomb is associated with Nasr bin Ali and dated to 1012; the one to the left (south) is ascribed to Jalal al-Din Hussain and dates from 1152; the northern one, unascribed, is dated to 1186. In both the later examples the Tim precedent for distinguishing front from sides is elaborated with the incorporation of an increasing number of varied mouldings.

>1.101 URGENCH, TOMB OF SULTAN TEKESH (1172–1200): view from the south-east.

1.100a

1.100b

1.101

1.106d

7 SERVANTS OF THE SELJUKS: ZENGIDS AND AYYUBIDS

THE JAZIRA AND SYRIA

As we have seen, Alp Arslan asserted his authority over the Turks rampaging through the Jazira and their defeat of the Byzantine forces at Manzikert in 1071 opened Asia Minor to Islam: the great Seljuk had little option but to let the *Ghazi*'s Turkish vanguard loose in Anatolia in the attempt to deflect them from Syria – to which he himself would have turned had he not been called to Transoxiana and to his death there in 1072. On the way from Iran, through Iraq, these forces encountered a rich diversity of cultures in the great towns of the tripartite region: notably Mosul on the middle reach of the Tigris (Diyar Rabi'a), Raqqa and Edessa on the upper Euphrates (Diyar Mudar) and Diyarbakr near the source of the Tigris in the mountains of south-east Anatolia (Diyar

›1.102 ALEPPO, GREAT MOSQUE: minaret.

›1.103 MOSUL, GREAT MOSQUE: minaret.

Bakr). They pressed on, maintaining a presence in these and many other Jazira towns, leaving the rest to local contenders whose monuments, naturally, betray wide-ranging influences.

Syria was neglected after the Abbasids moved the centre of political gravity to Iraq and fell to the Fatimids early in the 10th century. The retaking of the province and reassertion of orthodoxy there were prime objectives of the Seljuks. Alp Arslan's death left the region prey to the Turks – despite his endeavour to deflect them to Anatolia – and one of their chiefs took Damascus in 1076: Alp Arslan's son, Malik-shah's brother Tutush, was sent to confront this situation and counter the Fatimid response. He was responsible for restoring several of the most important mosques and beginning Aleppo's splendid minaret.**1.102**

After the deaths of Malik-shah in 1092 and Tutush three years later, rivalry for the succesion sapped Seljuk power, as we have noted. One of Tutush's sons took Aleppo, another Damascus and Diyarbakr but their heirs were displaced by their *atabegs* under threat from the Crusaders. In the third decade of the new century, the sultan's authority was restored by Sanjar – Malik-shah's fourth son – through the agency of his Mosul *atabegs*, Zengi (died 1146) and his son Nur al-Din (died 1174): the former consolidated his master's hold on Aleppo and ejected the Crusaders from Edessa; the latter extended his rule to Damascus – which had eluded the Crusaders when coastal Syria and Palestine fell to them. Having reunified Syria, Nur al-Din ruled independently under the sultan's ineffective successors.

THE ZENGID PHASE

Zengi and his followers resumed Tutush's orthodox works, building or rebuilding many mosques and madrasas – and shrines to Biblical patriarchs as well as latter-day *sufis* –

1.104a

from Mosul to Raqqa. Little new building of importance survives from the previous era – the great exception is the Aleppo minaret, on which the work was furthered. In Mosul the minaret is all that remains of Zengi's great mosque: not surprisingly, its elaborate brickwork betrays the influence of Seljuk Iran.[1.103] So too do the scanty remains of the palace founded by Zengi and developed by his successors but, minarets apart, the major legacy of a contentious age is a spectacular series of forts.[1.104a]

1.104b

1.104c

›1.104 DIYARBAKR: (a) fort (11th century and later over older foundations) viewed over Tigris and Seljuk bridge; (b, c) mosque, model and view of western façade (date obscure, probably early 11th century on earlier foundations).

›1.105 DUNAYSIR, GREAT MOSQUE, 1204: (a, b) elevation and plan.

As at Diyarbakr, beyond the court is a hypostyle hall with lateral aisles cut by the qibla transept, as in Damascus.

The outstanding monuments of post-Zengid Jazira are the mosques at Diyarbakr and Dunaysir, early 12th and early 13th century respectively. With its Damascene plan, its 'scenae frons' with debased Roman columns, its mixture of pointed arches and trabeated bays, and the vigour of Seljuk ornament translated from brick, the former is quite the most hybrid of the surviving works of an area where stone was the ubiquitous building material and where Hellenization was not forgotten despite centuries of vigorous Christian activity.**1.104b, c** The Great Mosque at Dunaysir, near the conjunction of all three of the Jazira regions, is also unsurprisingly highly eclectic with its cusped and foliate arches, multiplied in recession for the central bay of the main façade, its native tunnel vaulting, its sanctuary dome of Iranian grandeur, its muqarnas squinches and its Roman scallop-shell mihrab niche.**1.105**

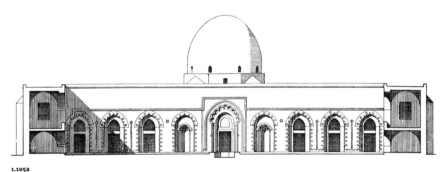

1.105a

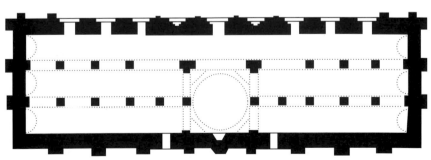

1.105b @ 1:750

In Syria and Palestine, Zengi's Sunni regime restored the venerable mosques, after the intrusion of the Christians, and provided new ones – usually of the old hypostyle type – where new urban expansion attended the prosperity regained with stability. Of course, too, they sponsored the proliferation of madrasas – mainly small, rarely catering for all four schools of law – and endowed numerous hospitals on the plan of court and iwan: several examples, in the fine ashlar perfected at Aleppo, survived the depradations of the Mongols.

Nur al-Din's most notable Damascene work is his own four-iwan Nuriyya funerary complex, founded in 1168, which initiated the important combination of madrasa and tomb. With its central fountain court and elongated prayer hall in place of the sanctuary iwan, the madrasa bears little relationship to the earlier Bosran example. Surprisingly, perhaps, his tomb follows the precedent set at Imam Dur.**1.106** Unsurprisingly, that form was popular

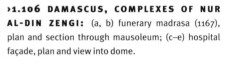

>**1.106 DAMASCUS, COMPLEXES OF NUR AL-DIN ZENGI:** (a, b) funerary madrasa (1167), plan and section through mausoleum; (c–e) hospital façade, plan and view into dome.

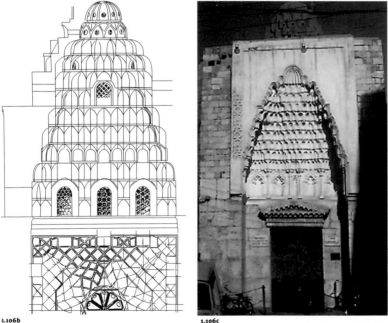

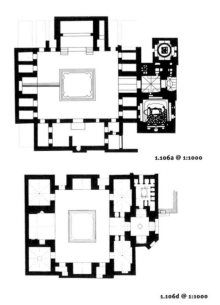

1.106a @ 1:1000

1.106d @ 1:1000

1.106b

1.106c

in Iraq after the waning of Seljuk power: the most prominent example is the mid-13th-century mashhad of Awn al-Din in Mosul, built barely a decade before the descent of the Mongols.

THE AYYUBIDS: FROM DAMASCUS TO CAIRO

Nur al-Din Zengi's troops were often commanded by Kurds. The most notable of these were Ayyub Shadhy of Ajdanakan, governor of Damascus from 1154, and his son Salah al-Din – known to his European adversaries as Saladin. The latter was despatched with his uncle to eliminate the threat to Nur al-Din's domain from Egypt and restore orthodoxy there. The threat was posed primarily by the Crusaders who launched four Egyptian expeditions in the five years to 1169: Salah al-Din emerged victorious in Nur al-Din's name. On the latter's death in 1174, his vassals renounced allegiance to his heir: Salah al-Din came to his assistance but rapidly displaced him. Having consolidated his hold over Syria and the Jazira, as well as Egypt, he decisively defeated the Crusaders and took the Latin kingdom of Jerusalem in 1187 which he held despite the impressive recovery of the Christians at the beginning of the next decade.

Salah al-Din's victory over the Crusaders in Egypt was rewarded by the Fatimid caliph with the wazirate. However, on the death of his patron two years later he terminated the Fatimid regime, promoted the replacement of the Shi'ite vassal regime in the Yemen with a Sunni one and restored the name of the Abbasid caliph to Friday prayers. After his death in 1193, his Syrian domains disintegrated and Mosul passed to its *atabeg*. However, his heirs (known as Ayyubids after Salah al-Din's father) held Egypt – which was left unscathed by the Mongols if not by the passage of time – until 1260.

1.107a

Beyond additions to the walls of Damascus and Jerusalem, the greatest work of Salah al-Din's followers was the early 13th-century citadel in the centre of Aleppo, from which the ruler could survey his seat in security. It was naturally the principal object of Mongol depredation despite its formidable glacis but much survived for restoration later in the century, including the palace.**1.107**

Aleppo citadel

Occupied since neo-Hittite times and a Muslim royal residence from the 10th century at least, Aleppo's present fortifications were conceived by Sultan al-Zahir Ghazi (1186–1216) and rebuilt by the Mamluks following the depredations of the Mongols in 1260. Ringing the conical mound, whose steep slopes formed an unscalable glacis, the walls punctuated by particularly stout bastions are unrivalled in magnificence but typical in general form. The idea of projecting a major inhabitable mass over the gate, aggressively confronting the approach to the weakest point – and commanding the settlement beyond – was to be further developed by both Muslim and Christian military engineers. Projection of the machicolations in box-hoods provided for the uninhibited patrol of sentries around the enclosed wall-walks. This too became standard practice in later defences throughout the Muslim and Christian worlds.

In the centre of the compound on the plateau, more than usual survives of the palace of al-Zahir Ghazi's successor, Sultan al-Malik al-Aziz Muhammad. The complex is asymmetrical in general distribution, formal in its nucleus. A high portal, with muqarnas and boldly contrasted quoins, led from the outer court to a circuitous passage which, in turn, led to the principal reception area. This consisted of a square atrium in the form of a roofed fountain court, with iwans to all four sides – the main one opposite the point of access.

Throughout the remains of the complex, as in the other significant Ayyubid Syrian works, the fine masonry was left unrelieved – except at structurally significant points, lintels or important arched portals. Usual is the calligraphic band as frieze or stringcourse. Extraordinary is the serpentine motif rimming the arch in the main gate. Colour contrasts are

1.107b

›1.107 ALEPPO, CITADEL, early 13th century, restored: (a) walls and main gate, (b–d) Palace of Sultan al'Malik al'Aziz Muhammad (1216–37) portal, plan and court.

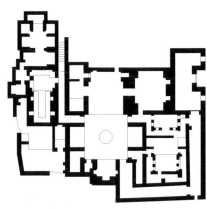

1.107c @ approximately 1:1000

1.107d

used for rare but striking effect, as on the portal of the palace, but austerity cedes to luxury only with the introduction of the muqarnas in the tympanum.

The Ayyubids continued the restoration of the mosques and completed the Aleppo minaret.[1.102] They also contributed several funerary complexes in which the mausoleum is given pride of place before a khanqah or madrasa. The most prominent example of the former is the al-Farafra foundation in Aleppo: one iwan dominates a court surrounded by cells on two levels. The typical

1.108a

madrasa, too, has a court with one major iwan for one school: there is often also an elongated prayer hall vaulted in a variety of ways. The incorporation of a tomb in a madrasa complex was to be the norm in Syria but the Ayyubid examples, usually built by amirs rather than sultans, did not conform to a generally accepted official prototype as seems to have been the case elsewhere: diversity in plan and scale doubtless responded to unofficial patronage of diverse cults which did not necessarily require accommodation for students. Exceptional is Aleppo's superb Firdaws complex, founded by an Ayyubid princess in 1235.**1.108**

Salah al-Din and his Ayyubid followers continued to

›**1.108 ALEPPO, FIRDAWS MADRASA,** 1235: (a) court and iwan, (b) mihrab, (c) interior detail, (d) plan.

The complex may have served the community for communal prayers as well as providing facilities for teaching: the incorporation of a distinct mosque, however small, is by no means uncommon in the Syrian madrasa complex. The court is unusual – in this context at least – in recalling the Classical colonnaded peristyle – except for the pointed arches carried on the columns. Elsewhere, stone vaulting required stout stone piers or walls: embellishment was minimal.

The mosque, on the southern side of the court opposite the iwan, is a triple-domed hall. The iwan addressing the court is backed by another facing north and now unenclosed. Flanking the latter are two small courts, each with at least two iwans. The plan is a near-

1.108b

1.108c

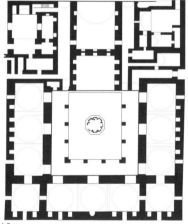

1.108d @ 1:1000

symmetrical variant on the theme stated in the Zahiriyya of al-Malik al-Zahir Ghazi also in Aleppo.

work on the walls of Cairo, extending them to incorporate a citadel built to protect a new seat of power on an eminence to the south-east of Fatimid al-Qahira: the latter is notable for its stout semi-circular towers.[1.109a,b] Except for this, the legacy of the relatively shortlived regime is small but significant. This includes at least one palace closely related in plan to the royal residence in the citadel at Aleppo.[1.109c] Houses of the affluent continue to follow the west-Asian form of square fountain court, covered or open and addressed by an iwan from one or two opposing sides – introduced under the Tulunids and favoured under the Fatimids.[1.74]

Dedicated to promoting orthodoxy, contrary to their Fatimid predecessors, the Ayyubids introduced the madrasa to Cairo. On the other hand, unable to suppress the popular devotion to saints, which was characteristic of Shi'ites, they sponsored the parallel development of the

1.109a

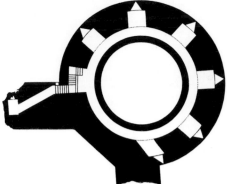

1.109b

1.109c @ approximately 1:1000

›1.109 CAIRO, AYUBBID SECULAR WORKS: (a, b) walls of Salah al-Din, tower at Darb al-Mahruq, section and plan (after Creswell); (c) Roda Island, Palace of Sultan Salih Najim al-Din Ayyub (c. 1241), plan.

sufi khanqah – as we have seen, both were domestic in origin. The regime exported the orthodox form, at least, to their Sunni vassals in the Yemen.

On his accession Salah al-Din himself founded the first Egyptian madrasa beside the grave of the great Sunni jurist al-Shafi in the Southern Cemetery of Cairo: in the second decade of the new century, Sultan al-Malik al-Kamal surpassed Fatimid precedent in enshrining al-Shafi's cenotaph in a domed qubba which ranks among the largest in all Islam. Conceived by the sultan to double as his own dynastic mausoleum – and to justify it in the face of strict orthodoxy – the tomb survives, much renovated, but the madrasa has been lost.**1.110a, b**

Little survives of the dynasty's later works but, with the notable exception of the muqarnas in the zone of transition, the evidence is of sustained sobriety: the muqarnas ramp through that zone but not beyond it and otherwise ornament is disciplined by the frames of door, window or

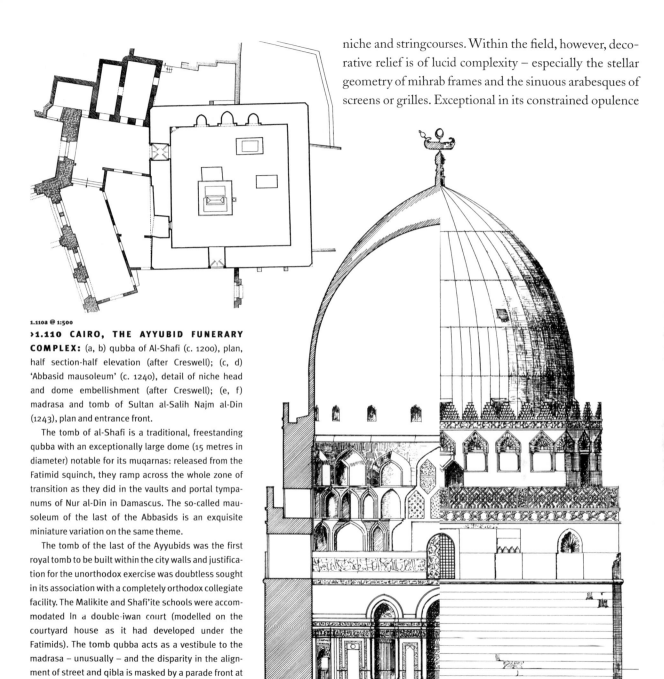

niche and stringcourses. Within the field, however, decorative relief is of lucid complexity – especially the stellar geometry of mihrab frames and the sinuous arabesques of screens or grilles. Exceptional in its constrained opulence

1.110a @ 1:500

›1.110 CAIRO, THE AYYUBID FUNERARY COMPLEX: (a, b) qubba of Al-Shafi (c. 1200), plan, half section-half elevation (after Creswell); (c, d) 'Abbasid mausoleum' (c. 1240), detail of niche head and dome embellishment (after Creswell); (e, f) madrasa and tomb of Sultan al-Salih Najm al-Din (1243), plan and entrance front.

The tomb of al-Shafi is a traditional, freestanding qubba with an exceptionally large dome (15 metres in diameter) notable for its muqarnas: released from the Fatimid squinch, they ramp across the whole zone of transition as they did in the vaults and portal tympanums of Nur al-Din in Damascus. The so-called mausoleum of the last of the Abbasids is an exquisite miniature variation on the same theme.

The tomb of the last of the Ayyubids was the first royal tomb to be built within the city walls and justification for the unorthodox exercise was doubtless sought in its association with a completely orthodox collegiate facility. The Malikite and Shafi'ite schools were accommodated in a double-iwan court (modelled on the courtyard house as it had developed under the Fatimids). The tomb qubba acts as a vestibule to the madrasa – unusually – and the disparity in the alignment of street and qibla is masked by a parade front at an acute angle to the qubba.

1.110b

1.110c

1.110d

is the enigmatic qubba, later assigned to the interment of the last Abbasid caliphs. It is much smaller than al-Malik's work but even richer in its internal embellishment.**1.110c, d**

Innovative, and adroit in its planning, is the near contemporary complex founded by Sultan al-Salih Najm al-

Across a small street to the south was an apparently identical (but now largely lost) double-iwan court for the Hanafites and Hanbalites. Both courts were flanked by cells on two storeys for the students, and a minaret crowns the entrance to both sides of the complex at the head of the intermediate street.

In refinement of the Fatimid adaptation of the Pharos model, by the end of the Ayyubid era the minaret was usually of two storeys, the lower one square in plan and supporting a balcony, the upper one octagonal and crowned by a ribbed cupola.

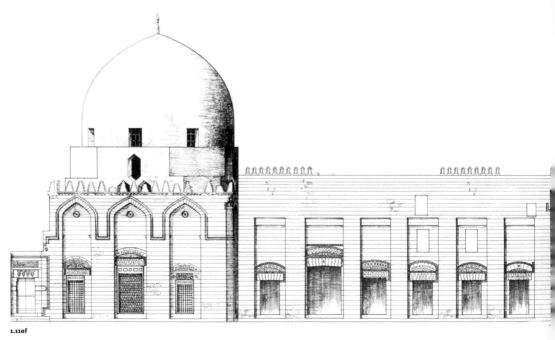

1.110f

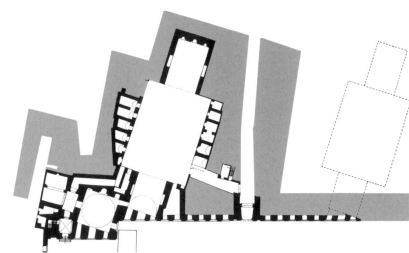

1.110e @ 1:1500

Din Ayyub (1240–49) on the site of the Fatimid eastern palace in Cairo: consisting of two courts, each with twin iwans opposed on the qibla, it was the first in Egypt to cater for all four schools of law and it set an important precedent in incorporating the tomb of its royal founder, domed in brick and far more austere than the so-called Abbasid tomb: it was also exemplary in the development of an extended façade to mask disjointed orientation.**1.110e, f**

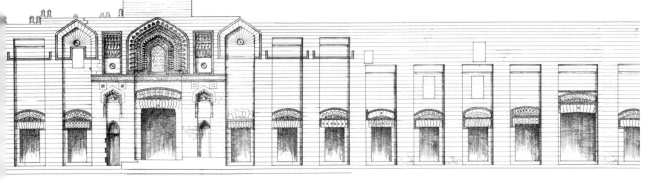

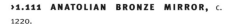

8 THE SELJUKS OF RUM

The leaders of the Turkish *ghazis* deflected into the frontier zone of Anatolia by Alp Arslan had established several principalities there by the beginning of the 12th century: the most notable were centred on Kayseri, Sivas, Erzurum, Divrigi and Konya. However, from the outset the main force was led by Suleyman Qutalmish: Seljuk but antipathetic to the great Seljuk sultan, he occupied Cilicia and expanded his own sultanate on rewards for support of rival claimants to the Byzantine throne. By the end of the century the putative central-Anatolian realm had been inherited by Suleyman's son, Kilij Arslan, who had eluded Malik-shah after many vicissitudes but lost the southern coast to the Crusaders, Cilicia to Armenians, the northeast to rival Danishmend Turks and was confronted in the west by the new Comnene rulers of Byzantium.

Victorious against the Christians in 1101, Kilij Arslan turned his attention to displacing the main line of Seljuk sultans, currently weakened by internal dissent. He lost and his sons, who succeeded him as Malik-shah (1107–16) and Mas'ud I (1116–55), were confined again to central Anatolia where they developed their sultanate in isolation from the rest of Islam. Surrounded by Christians except to the south-east, their polyglot dominion included at least as many Byzantine Greeks and Armenians as Turks. Thus their culture was eclectic and the institutions of their state were formed under the influence of both imperial Byzantium and the greater Seljuk sultanate. Naturally, the rulers were orthodox, like their Great Seljuk cousins, though *ghazi* devotion to *sufi* cults and their dervishes did not go unpatronized.

Mas'ud had established his capital at Konya and his long reign was one of consolidation. His son, Kilij Arslan II (1155–92), expanded the sultanate at the expense of its contentious neighbours – particularly the Danishmends of Sivas and Kayseri, which fell to him in 1168, but not the Mangujak principality of Divrigi. Rivalry for the succession weakened the state until the emergence of Kaikhosrau, the late sultan's youngest son, in alliance with the Greeks against the Crusaders who had sacked Constantinople in 1204.

Kaikaus (1211–19) took the independent Greek state of Trebizond, and its Black Sea coast. His son, Ala al-Din Kayqubad (1219–34), took the sultanate to its apogee, annexing the last of the Turkish principalities, Erzurum, and extending his rule as far as Seleucia and the Cilician coast, but his ambitions in northern Syria were thwarted by the Ayyubids. His patricidal successor's empire was badly mauled by the Mongols in 1243 and eastern Anatolia was lost to attempted retaliation in 1277. Over the following half century the rump disintegrated into principalities again.

ANATOLIAN ECLECTICISM

Prosperity grew with the triumph of the Seljuks of Rum. Commerce revived with the extension of the great trade routes – the old Silk Road and its tributaries – from northern Mesopotamia and Syria. Naturally unification, regular commerce in ideas and wealthy patrons helped to promote the development of some consistency of architectural style. However, there was no clear break in the Anatolian tradition with the forging of the Rum sultanate

1.112a

1.112b

›1.112 THE ANATOLIAN CARAVANSERAI: (a, b) Agzikara Han (c. 1230), court and mosque pavilion; (c, d) Sultan Han (1232), plan and model (Istanbul, Miniaturk).

Located about 30 kilometres apart (one day's journey), the caravanserai of Anatolia are noted for their grand scale and fine masonry. The simplest are tunnel-vaulted basilican halls without court. Derived from Syria, the courtyard form – rectangular with monumental portals and arcaded galleries – recurs frequently after the early 13th century. The grandest examples, like the Sultan and Agzikara hans, combine the two basic types: a monumental portal leads to a court centred on a mosque over a water tank and surrounded by stables, guestrooms, storerooms and baths; a second portal leads further into a basilican exchange hall with raised lantern and conical cap.

1.112C

1.112d @ 1:1000

over much of the 12th century and there was no clear break after its defeat by the Mongols either, for it subsisted in vassalage. Essentially eclectic, the successive Turkish factions introduced new ingredients – or reinvented old ones – to enrich the prevailing synthesis. By far the most important of these were the various methods of covering space.

In the secular field, monumental stone caravanserai were a highly characteristic product of the new commercial prosperity: some were entirely covered with tunnel vaults over elongated bays; some had central courts framed by tunnel-vaulted bays; inevitably, some combined both forms and incorporated both domical and tunnel vaults. There are Iranian precedents for both the court type and hybrid types, of course, but the monumentality is native to the Anatolian masonry tradition. Of enduring utility as well as substance, many survive.**1.112**

The remains of the royal palaces are sparse. Like peoples of nomadic origin from time immemorial, the Seljuks moved with camps and when the sultans settled on Konya – never exclusively – their tents became kiosks within a fortified compound away from town. Such a complex was, naturally, among the first to suffer on dynastic reverse but the type may be represented by the remains of the retreat laid out c. 1224 for Sultan Ala al-Din Kayqubad by Lake Beysehir. In contrast, warrens of courts and halls in two detached blocks, celebrated for their tile revetment and surrounded by gardens, distinguish Kayqubad's slightly later palace at Kubadabad.**1.113**

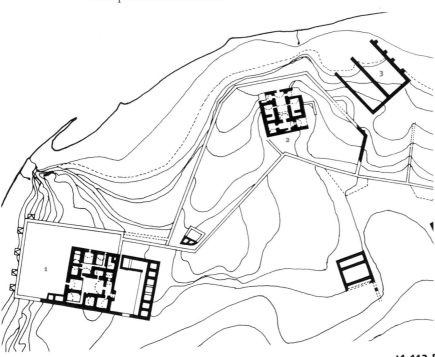

1.113a @ 1:2500

Religious buildings have, of course, fared better than most of their non-commercial secular contemporaries. New mosques were needed in lands newly conquered for Islam. Madrasas were built assiduously in this assertively

›1.113 PALACE AND TOWN IN SELJUK ANATOLIA: (a) Kubadabad (Beysehir), Palace of Ala'al-din Kayqubad (c. 1235), plan with informal distribution of (1) Great Palace with audience court and throne hall, (2) Lesser Palace with private audience hall (?), (3) harem remains (?); (b) Mardin, model showing the

organic agglomeration of religious and secular buildings (Istanbul, Miniaturk).

The asymmetry of Kayqubad's ceremonial block
contrasts paradoxically with the symmetry of the presumably more private 'Lesser Palace' and the lack of
any formal route to or between the units is notable.

Sunni period and common is the type of complex known
as kulliye in Turkey: typically Zengid in concept – if eclectic in style and often organic in development about a
reduced court – they usually incorporate mosque and
madrasa in association with a range of public utilities and
the tomb of the patron.

Derived from the Iranian canopy and tower form, the tomb (turbe) usually incorporated a burial vault in a rectangular basement and a cenotaph chamber in a truncated polygonal tower with conical cap. With rare exception, the type prevails in the plethora of 13th-century survivors. Plans are circular or polygonal, often over a battered square podium with stairs to the elevated entrance. Proportions also differ but Iranian elevation was not generally emulated. Indeed, recalling the tent less equivocally than the earliest Iranian examples, the cylinder with its conical top is typical and has been related to the Armenian church tower – at least as much for the handling of the material as for the origin of the form.**1.114**

Mosques and madrasas – and their combination – survive in considerable numbers from before and after the Mongols mauled the Rum Sultanate. Naturally the corpus is dominated by metropolitan foundations but the wide distribution of varied forms suggests popular demand as well as official patronage. The builders were experimental in planning to meet the demands of the climate for exten-

›**1.114 THE ANATOLIAN TOMB:** (a) Erzurum, necropolis with the tomb of Amir Saltuq (late-12th century) foreground; (b, c) Kayseri, Cifte Kumbad (c. 1270) and Doner Kumbed (c. 1275) model (Istanbul, Miniaturk) and exterior view.

1.114b

1.114a

1.114c

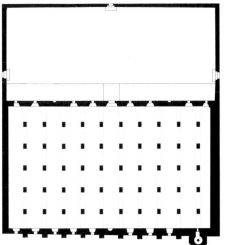

1.115 @ 1:1000

›1.115 SIVAS, GREAT MOSQUE, 1197: plan.
Stone piers support the flat timber roof.

›1.116 KONYA, ALA AL-DIN MOSQUE,
1156–1235: (a) plan, (b) model (Istanbul, Miniaturk).
The hypostyle hall reuses Hellenistic and Byzantine
columns to support groin and domical vaulting. The complex was beside the palace and incorporated twin royal
tombs: the decagon of Sultan Kilic Arslan II (1156–92) was
of a select royal type.

sive covered space and the several principalities founded
by Alp Arslan's followers produced ideosyncratic variations on themes developed by their Byzantine predecessors – and by fellow Turks elsewhere. As in the secular field,
tunnel, groin and domical vaulting – as well as flat roofs –
are all to be found and zones of transition incorporate the
squinch, the muqarnas and the pendentive.

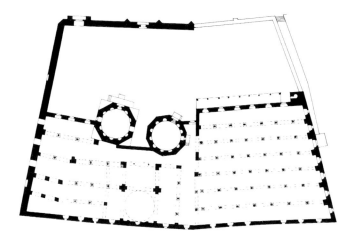

1.116a @ 1:1000

1.1b

In the 12th century the mosque usually had a hypostyle prayer hall preceded by an open court or the court might disappear under an extended forest of posts supporting a flat ceiling or various types of vault: internal posts were occasionally of timber but stone was the norm and the Seljuks promoted the development of domical vaulting in response to the climate.**1.115–1.118** The type persisted into the 13th century, as in the Ala ad-Din mosque at Nigde and, with wider domical bays to stress the qibla, in the complex at Divrigi. As there, most of the wall surface was left unadorned but portals and mihrabs were often

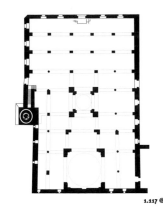

1.117 @ 1:1000

›1.117 KAYSERI, ULU CAMI, 1140: plan.

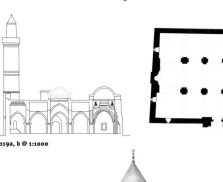

1.119a, b @ 1:1000

1.118 @ 1:1000

›1.118 DIVRIGI, KALE MOSQUE, 1180: plan.

›1.119 NIGDE, ALA AD-DIN CAMI, 1223: (a–c) section, plan and model (Istanbul, Miniaturk).

Built under its namesake, Sultan Ala ad-Din Kaiquabad I (1219–37), this work is distinguished by the disparity of entrance axis and qibla. The former is given a particularly assertive pishtaq. As the three bays of the qibla range are all domed, the mihrab is unaided in its specific assertion of the axis of prayer. Stout in its proportions, the minaret rises from a base and socle which seem to have been extrapolated from the contemporary tomb type.

1.119c

1.120a

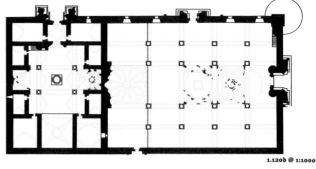

1.120b @ 1:1000

1.120c

›1.120 DIVRIGI, GREAT MOSQUE AND HOSPITAL, 1228: (a) frontispiece, (b, c) plan and section, (d) model (Istanbul, Miniaturk).

The complex at Divrigi consists of a basilican mosque with nave and doubled aisles, variously vaulted and accented with an octagon raised over the central nave bay and a pyramidal roof further elevating the mihrab bay. Beyond the mosque, the complex includes a hospital and the octagonal tomb of the local ruler, Ahmad Shah Mangujak. The form derives from the most traditional type of Christian church on the periphery of the Byzantine empire.

1.120d

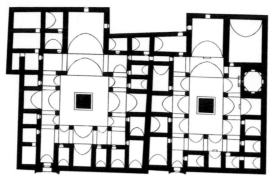

1.121a @ 1:1000

›1.121 KAYSERI, THE CHARITABLE COM-
PLEX (KULLIYE): (a) Cifte madrasa and hospital
(early 13th century), plan; (b) Khuand Khatun mosque
and madrasa (1237–38), plan.

The Cifte madrasa – the earliest securely dated
Seljuk one – is doubled to provide a hospital though
the difference of function is scarcely revealed by the
planning. The Khuand Khatun kulliye – dedicated in the
name of the widow of Sultan Ala'al-Din Kayqubad II –
consists of a basilican mosque with a small open court
in the centre, a tomb in the north-east corner and an
open court madrasa with one dominant iwan opposite
the entrance.

exuberantly carved with bizarre combinations of foliate,
geometric and calligraphic motifs framing muqarnas.**1.119–1.123**

By the third decade of the 13th century the Iranian court
and iwan type – introduced directly and via Syria – was the
norm for the madrasa and it was occasionally used for

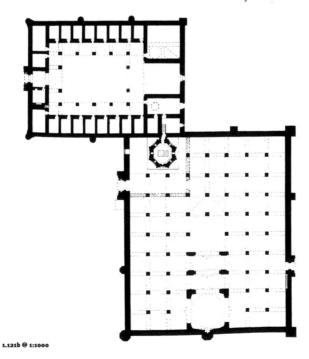

1.121b @ 1:1000

1.122a

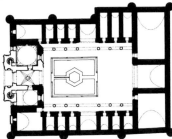

1.122b @ 1:500

›1.122 SIVAS: (a) Cifte Minare madrasa (1271), detail of entrance portal; (b–d) Gok madrasa (1271), plan, model (Istanbul, Miniaturk) and entrance façade.

Heavy stone piers define eleven aisles and support the flat timber roof of the prayer hall beyond the courtyard.

1.122c

1.122d

mosques, especially in the context of the kulliye. Representative examples range from the Cifte madrasa attached to a domed hypostyle mosque at Kayseri, the mosque and

1.123a

1.123c

›1.123 ERZURUM MADRASAS: (a–e) Cifte
Minare madrasa (dated 1253, but this date and the
building sequence are not without contention), model
from west (Istanbul, Miniaturk), plan, detail of
entrance, court to entrance, model from south (Istanbul, Miniaturk); (f) Yakutiye (1310), plan.

An open court is dominated by four iwans in the
Mesopotamian manner and surrounded by cells on two
storeys. The qibla iwan is wider than the others to
accommodate the mosque. Beyond this is a tomb: in
the much-extended earlier work, Amir Saltuq (late-12th
century) is given a cylinder articulated with blind
arcades supporting the conical roof in the typical

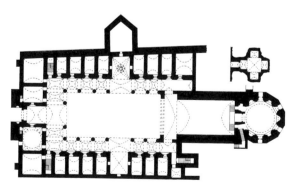

1.123b @ 1:1000

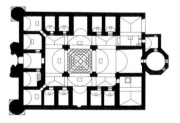

1.123f @ 1:1000

Anatolian Seljuk tent-like manner. More attention is paid to the exterior than was normal in other regions where usually the entrance alone was embellished: the Cifte Minare madrasa is one of the earliest in Anatolia to follow the Iranian Seljuk precedent of incorporating two minarets in a pishtaq frontispiece.

1.123d

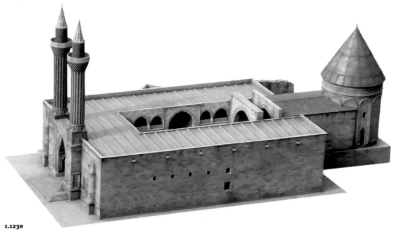

1.123e

1.124a

1.124b

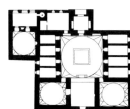

1.124c @ 1:1000

1.124d

1.124f

1.124e

›**1.124 KONYA:** (a–e) Ince Minare (c. 1260), view towards entrance, model (Istanbul, Miniaturk), plan, details of frontispiece and interior; (f) Beyhekim (c. 1260), mihrab (Berlin, Museum of Islamic Art); (g–i) Karatay (1252), detail of façade, model (Istanbul, Miniaturk) and plan.

The domed hall recalls the domed bema of the typical Byzantine church, while the single iwan flanked by domed chambers occupies the place of the sanctuary and its flanking pastophoria.

Instead of the façade display provided by the Iranian

madrasa of the Khuand Khatun kulliye also at Kayseri, the Gok madrasa at Sivas and the Cifte Minareli and Yakutiye madrasas at Erzurum.**1.121–1.123**

In the second half of the 13th century the development of covered space for both mosques and madrasas was furthered after the example of the pervasive Byzantine centralized domical church. The Karatay and Ince Minare at Konya and the Caca Bey at Kirsehir are outstanding examples in which the dome is of overriding importance: idiosyncratically, the great dome of Konya rises over a fan-shaped wedge of planes known as the 'Turkish triangle' rather than the squinches, muqarnas or pendentives of earlier works. Inside, it is the space that impresses, of course; outside, it is the articulation of the elevation – at its most spectacular in a highly mannered denial of structural reality.**1.124**

A single minaret rises in three stages beside the main domed building of the Ince Minare madrasa: the elongated central zone terminates in a balcony with muqarnas corbels. Elsewhere twin minarets appear over pishtaqs with

1.124g

1.124h

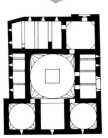

1.124i @ 1:1000

pishtaq, Konya's magnificent entrance portals are embellished in colouristic masonry in the Syrian manner and/or highly mannered, anti-architectural stone-cut relief of varied depth with stylized floral and geometric motifs: especially striking are the knotted fillets and interlaced bands of thulth script of the Ince Minare complex.

Tiles make their appearance inside 13th-century foundations. The Anatolians used them for rather more comprehensive coverage of zones of transition, even walls, than was usual elsewhere but especially, of course, for mihrabs. The ultimate source was Iran for both the medium and the muqarnas motif in the mihrab, though the latter may have come via Syria and tiles were produced locally with less brilliance than was typical of Kashan.

›**1.125 KIRSEHIR, CACA BAY,** 1272: plan.

1.125 @ 1:1000

iwans richly embellished with muqarnas, as at Erzurum and Sivas – and in Iran. And as in Iran the minaret is occasionally a freestanding monument.**1.126, 1.122, 1.123**

Stone was the usual building material in Anatolia, as in Armenia – but not, of course, in Iran – and, naturally, there were regional differences of type. Apart from structural technique, it lent itself to colouristic patterning, as on the tomb of Amir Saltuq at Erzurum or the Karatay at Konya. More significantly, it prompted bold, exuberant, high-relief sculpture as on the Doner Kumbad at Kayseri and at Sivas, Divrigi and Erzerum. The main ornamental motifs – calligraphic, geometric and arabesque – have their equivalents in Iranian patterned brickwork. However, most characteristic are the chunky Armenian anthropomorphic and heraldic animal ones set within a light, even whimsical, architectonic frame and usually offset against extensive void. The result may best be called 'grotesque' in the sense the later Italian Mannerists were to give that word in designating the bizarre combination of stylized structural, vegetal and even animal motifs discovered in the cave-like remains of imperial Roman interiors. And some commentators canvas a connection with contemporary work in Romanesque Europe – which had sent out the Crusaders.[1.79]

1.126

>1.126 ANTALYA, YIVLI MINARET, early 13th century.

PART 2 BEYOND THE WESTERN PALE

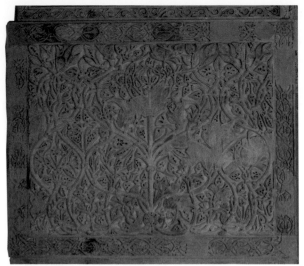

1 CORDOBAN CALIPHATE

In the extreme west of the Muslim world – al-Andalus –
the Umayyads of Cordoba had prospered after Abd al-
Rahman ibn Mu'awiya had established himself as an independent power with the support of the refugees who
acccompanied him from Syria. A succession of able rulers
culminated in Abd al-Rahman III (912–61): building on
the base developed by Abd al-Rahman II (833–52) and certainly not ignorant of Syrian or Samarran developments,
he presided over one of the most sophisticated and cul-
tured courts in the world. He claimed back the title of
Caliph in 929 and assumed the title Nasir al-Din Allah
(Defender of the Law of God). He took advantage of
Fatimid problems in the east to extend his power to troubled Morocco.

Islam had been taken to the Moroccan shores of the
Atlantic – the Maghrib al-Aqsa, 'furthest west' – from
Ifriqiya by Uqba ibn Nafi in 683. Uqba met his death there
at the hands of the local Berbers and a second Islamic wave
had unspectacular success until the arrival in 788 of Idris
bin Abdullah, a great-grandson of the caliph Ali in flight

from the Abbasids: under circumstances which remain obscure he was proclaimed king by Berber chiefs who had been won to the cause. His forceful personality had great appeal in an era of political and spiritual uncertainty and he consolidated such a hold over the tribes of the Maghrib al-Aqsa that he attracted the enmity of the caliph, Haroun al-Rashid, who purportedly had him poisoned: enshrined in his base, Moulay Idris near the ancient Roman town of Volubilis, he was the object of enduring veneration.**2.18** His infant son, who miraculously survived his minority to rule for more than twenty years from his foundation at Fez, proved extremely effective in consolidating and extending the gains of his father but the new kingdom was divided between his several sons on his death in 828. Such unity as his Idrisid dynasty was to sustain thereafter had been undermined by unruly Berbers by the time Abd al-Rahman III was taking Cordoba to its apogee.

Abd al-Rahman's son al-Hakam (961–76) sustained the glory and decline was postponed under the weak Hisham II (976–1009) by the able vizier al-Mansur, but it was rapid thereafter. The advance of the Christian reconquistadors from the north was steady and the infiltration of Berbers from North Africa unsettled the regime. It collapsed in 1031. Spain shattered into petty states whose rivalries favoured the Christians bent on reversing the tide of Islam throughout Iberia.

THE INCEPTION OF THE WESTERN TRADITION

The western Umayyad rivals of the Abbasids and Fatimids ceded to none of their contemporaries as patrons of an original school of Muslim architecture – indeed, the Great Mosque of Cordoba is one of the chief glories of Islam. Protection from the harsh winters even of southern Spain required the forest of columns supporting tiers of arches and a timber ceiling, which first appeared in 784. This was extended and vaulted to cover much of the enclosure over the next two centuries – longitudinally in all but the last phase when the proximity of the river required lateral development.**2.2**

2.2a

The Great Mosque of Cordoba

Abd al-Rahman I's foundation was roughly 75 metres square. Slightly more than half the superficial area was covered by a prayer hall of eleven aisles defined by two-tiered arcades carried on antique columns: the latter were aligned north-east/south-west, in inaccurate accord with the qibla, and the two central ones were set further apart than the others (8 metres rather than 7) to distinguish the aisle – or nave – before the mihrab.

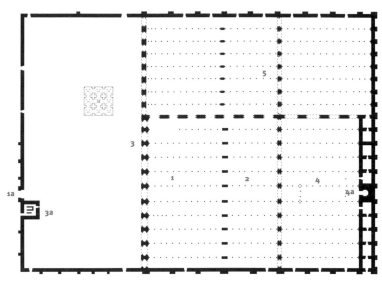

2.2b @ 1:2000

›2.2 CORDOBA, UMAYYAD MOSQUE: (a) western entrance to extension of al-Hakim, (b) plan of compound with the stages of development from (1) the foundation of Abd al-Rahman I c. 784, including the surviving Bab al-Wuzara (1a), to (2) the extension of the prayer hall begun under Abd Al-Rahman II in 836, (3) the extension of the court, with cloisters and minaret (3a), begun under Abd al-Rahman III c. 951, (4) the first maqsura chamber and further extension of the prayer hall, including a new three-bay maqsura before the definitive mihrab bay (4a), under al-Hakim II of 976, and (5) the lateral extension of the whole complex begun under Hisham – the last Umayyad caliph of Cordoba – by the vizier al-Mansur c. 987 (achieving overall dimensions of 190 by 140 metres), (c, d) colonnades of 784 and 987, (e–h) central bay of maqsura, external arcades, interior with mihrab and vault, (i, j) side-bay of maqsura, vault.

There were three major campaigns of extension: under Abd al-Rahman II, who added eight bays beyond the original qibla wall; under Abd al-Rahman III, who extended the court to embrace a new minaret and his son al-Hakam (961–76), who added a further twelve bays beyond the qibla; under al-Hisham, who extended the whole complex laterally by eight bays at the expense of the original symmetry. Of the great compound in its final form (190 by 140 metres) one-third is a cloistered court, the rest a vast hypostyle hall of nineteen bays brutally interrupted by the 16th-century Christian cathedral.

There are some eleven portals in the restored peripheral walls. The western entrances, including the original Bab al-Wuzara, are dazzling confections of stylized floral motifs and horseshoe-shaped arches – the main ones with alternately carved and plain voussoirs within a raised rectangular frame, the side ones trilobed and the upper ones interlocking. As we have seen, there are Syrian – or Palestinian – precedents for all these features but the horseshoe arch had been extensively used in Iberia by the Umayyads' Visigothic predecessors.

The standard early Muslim practice of reusing Roman columns as supports for a forest of arches sustaining the extensive roof was transformed from the outset by the spectacular device of a second tier of boldly

2.2c

accented voussoir arches springing from suspended piers: the columns available were too small to serve unaugmented. Perhaps suggested by a Roman aqueduct, this certainly achieved a more satisfactory relationship between height and breadth than the available columns allowed. The incurvature of the imposts – most apparent in the one surviving portal – and the alternation of brick and stone voussoirs set a dramatic precedent developed in the 10th-century arcades.

Apart from the unique forest of the final form, the mosque's most dazzling features are the domed chamber added by al-Hakam beyond the central qibla bay (possibly originally intended as a maqsura for the caliph's personal use, now the Villaviciosa chapel), and the three domed chambers of a second screened maqsura before the new mihrab with its horseshoe arch in a rectangular frame. These are also composed of superimposed arches but of interpenetrating cusped and horseshoe forms in three tiers. The vaults are variations on the theme of interlocking ribs: paired in a grid over a rectangle to form a square central compartment, but cut by ribs linking the centres of adjacent sides to form another square on the diagonal in the earlier maqsura; paired between opposite

2.2d

sides of an octagon to form an eight-pointed star and an octagonal central compartment in the two side bays of the later triple maqsura; overlapping across the oblique angles between each pair of adjacent sides of
an octagon to form an octagonal central compartment in the central bay
before the mihrab. In none of these was the potential of the rib to lighten
structure – rather than to facilitate construction – realized and analyses
confirm that the prime motive of displaying them was decorative.

The later maqsura enclosure is screened with interlaced cusped
arches. Maximum use is made of cusped and horseshoe arches for
clerestory windows and squinches, the scalloped semi-domes behind the
horseshoe squinches of the two subsidiary domes flanking the mihrab
bay in the qibla range again demonstrating the origin of the cusped arch
– but on the horizontal rather than the vertical plane. The vaults rely on
the play of varied lighting on their cannelled compartments and inset

2.2g

2.2h

floral domelettes; the vault of the central mihrab bay, finely chased with stylized floral motifs and Koranic calligraphy, is covered in resplendent mosaic. The mihrab itself, no mere niche but a small heptagonal room of marble and stucco, displays a sumptous confection of cusped horseshoe arches with differentiated voussoirs and glowing inscriptions. It is entered through an intricately incised horseshoe arch whose exaggerated incurvature within a rectangular frame emblazoned with Koranic script reflects the form of the main gate to the court, as though marking the final stage in the progression to grace.

2.2i

2.2j

Abd al-Rahman III's extensions involved the demolition of the primitive minaret and its replacement with a splendid tower which was to provide future imperial builders with an inescapable model. His son al-Hakam II, calling on the emperor for Byzantine craftsmen able to emulate the work of his ancestors in Damascus, set an equally persuasive example in concentrating the most elaborate embellishment on the definition of special areas of prayer.

Mosaics were novel in the west. The treatment of the arch was of more particular significance: certainly it had begun to lose its purely structural form at Ukhaydir and the tendency was furthered in the Arab-ata, as we have seen.[1.65] However, at Cordoba it became purely decorative in the incurved cusped and interlaced style which came to be called Moorish though, indeed, the fragmentation and recombination of arcuate elements were to be the most characteristic features of the style of al-Andalus. By virtue of this obsession with the arcuate and the subordination of surface ornament to it, ironically, the Cordoban approach to decoration may be seen as essentially architectonic – at least in religious building.

The great mosque was to be turned into a cathedral by the Christian conquistadores, later involving the regrettable insertion of a high vaulted nave and choir. Naturally, many lesser mosques were also converted. Of the rare survivors from the late-Umayyad period, the most notable is the church of El Cristo de la Luz in Toledo – originally the Bab al-Mardum. It echoes the main motifs of the great Cordoban work on a tiny scale.[2.3]

Little of the caliphate palace survives in Cordoba: it was superseded after Abd al-Rahman III declared himself caliph in 929 and found it inadequate for his new dignity. Within his first decade, instead, he resorted to a new site on the nearby slopes of the Sierra de Cordoba – or, rather, to one once graced by Roman villas. There he embarked

2.3a

2.3b

›2.3 TOLEDO, BAB AL-MARDUM (El Cristo de la Luz), c. 1000: (a) exterior, (b) interior.

The tiny brick building (8 metres square) is elevated over a nine-square plan: by the end of the 10th century that formula was well established in Byzantine lands and even in the Carolingian West (which extended to northern Spain) but Muslim precedents seem too remote[1.61] or obscure. Perhaps in distant homage to the superimposed arcades of Cordoba, the north front has interpenetrating blind arches on corbels over the three variously cusped and horseshoe entrances. In clear recollection of Cordoba, the domed compartments have flying ribs arranged in various stellar patterns which increase in complexity in the bays nearest the mihrab.

on a vast project for a new palace and administrative centre which he called Medina al-Zahra after his favourite wife. Excavation has revealed terraces drawn from the contours of the site and little of axial rigidity in the distribution of the accommodation: basilican ceremonial halls on rectangular terraces and apartments surrounding formal courts, often informally related, incorporated belvederes (miradors), distant views or overlooked gardens, at least one of which was a rectangle crossed by axial canals.**2.1, 2.4**

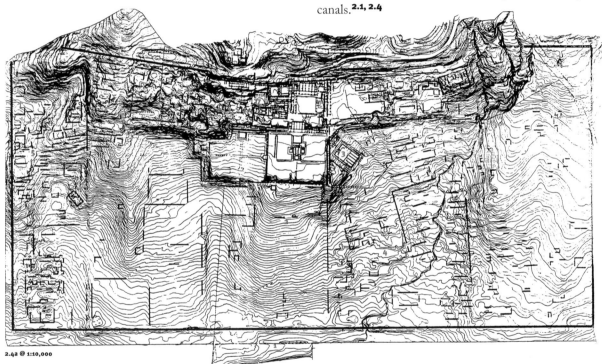

2.4a @ 1:10,000

Medina al-Zahra

A contemporary court chronicler records the name of the architect, Maslama ben Abdullah, and credits him with knowledge of Byzantium. He also wrote of expansive views over gardens, many-columned pavilions, and fountains of bronze and marble. Substantiating much of this, the incomplete excavation reveals an informal grouping of palace buildings in

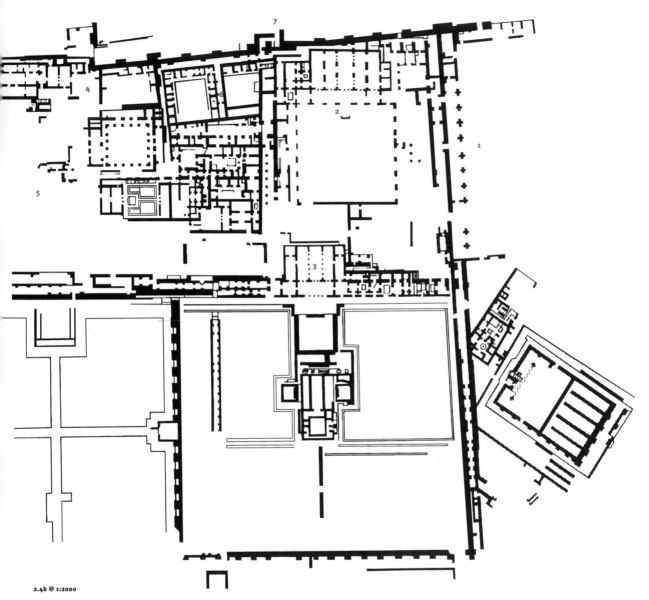

2.4b @ 1:2000

the north-centre of a roughly rectangular compound (some 1500 by 800 metres), the central zone of which, at least, was protected by doubled walls of limestone. In that zone, the main palace pavilions were on the top terrace and gardens on the intermediate level: the eastern quarter is

›2.4 MEDINA AL-ZAHRA, PALACE CITY OF ABD AL-RAHMAN III, founded 936 and built throughout the reign: (a) site plan with (1) the southern gate to the outer town, Bab al-Qubba or Puerta de los Bovedas, (2) intermediate Bab Asudda to the palace zone, (3) mosque, (4) town, (5) cavalry barracks, (6) infantry barracks, (7) palace, (b) plan of excavations in the palace zone with (1) eastern ceremonial entrance, Bab al-Xam, (2) Dar al-Gharbi, principal audience hall, (3) Dar al-Mulk ('Salon Rico'), (4) caliph's private residential block, (5) administrative zone, (6) zone of private audience and vizier's quarters, (7) northern Bab al-Jebel or Puerta del Monte, (c) aerial view of excavations in palace zone, (d–h) Dar al-Gharbi, ceremonial entrance screen, overview and remains of basilica, architectural details of capital and base, (i–l) Dar al-Mulk, overview and details of interior of 'Salon Rico'.

2.4c

largely unexcavated and may never have been completed. The barracks and the town of palace dependants, dominated by the congregational mosque, was distributed across the lower slopes but here too excavation has barely begun – except for the mosque.

2.4d

2.4e

Contemporary chroniclers celebrate the dazzling marble (from local quarries) and gold-domed throne room – Majlis al-Khalifa – on the upper terrace (called al-Mumarrad, 'the Resplendent') with its vestibule pool of quicksilver whose darting lights eradicated mass. This has vanished except for traces of foundations: it was evidently the central element in a triad of audience halls aligned east–west. The eastern one, which may have served as a waiting room for those called to audience in the centre but was reputedly used by al-Hakam II for the reception of ambassadors, has also vanished. The western one, within its own walled compound on the eastern edge of the excavated area, is the partially restored Dar al-Gharbi: a double-aisled basilica, its inner aisles were separated from the nave by colonnades, the outer two were walled. To its south, dominating a projecting square patio, is the more completely restored marble-paved Dar al-Mulk which catered primarily for the confidential meetings of the council of state: that also has a nave flanked by a pair of colonnaded

2.4f

2.4g

2.4h

2.4i

2.4j

2.4k

aisles beyond which are walled withdrawing rooms and dependent offices. To the west, backing on to the north wall in an elevated walled compound, were the courts and halls of the caliph's residential quarters. Beyond these were the extensive quarters of the caliph's entourage and the imperial bureaucracy.

Many intricately carved marble capitals – recalling the Byzantine transformation of the Classical Composite Order in style, if not necessarily in detail – survive on site and elsewhere but the principal testament to the sumptousness of the complex is provided by substantial fragments of the local limestone revetment from the Dar al-Gharbi and, more completely, the restored Dar al-Mulk (or 'Salon Rico', 953) with its water court and vestibule: in marble or limestone, the dominant arabesque decoration is developed in variations of exceptional refinement on the theme of the 'Tree of Life': the stylized life of the garden was translated to the interior – in general preference to geometric patterns – as at Samarra but with less exuberance. The tectonic frame is pervasive but comprehensive coverage tends to deny the architectonic discipline which governed the embellishment of the great mosque.

2.4l

The four-square garden (chahar bagh) is the microcosm of paradise in accordance with the ancient Persian ideal of order to which the Koran's Eden is related: an enclosed square divided into quarters by four rivers flowing in the cardinal directions from the source of the waters of life in the centre. And in the Koranic tradition the gardens of heaven were set with pavilions built over water. Thus Abd al-Rahman III's palace may well have been the image of the earthly paradise – as the imperial palace in Constantinople and, doubtless, Samarra's Jawsaq al-Khaqani were before it.

The informal conjunction of formal elements on a vigorously contoured site recurs at the turn of the 11th century at Banu Hammad in the Algerian Maghrib but the relaxation feasible at the apogee of Cordoban power seems not to have been typical of the earliest palace remains in the west. These are sparse but, as in the heartlands of the Umayyad and Abbasid caliphates, they tend to be regular with a nuclear court and three distinct zones in a stoutly defended rectangular compound – like the remains of Algerian Ashir and their later relatives.[1.72]

Medina al-Zahra was destroyed by Berber insurgents in 1010. From the period of political fragmentation which followed the fall of the Cordoban caliphate two decades later, Iberia retains many fragmentary palaces. The only princely seat to survive largely intact is the Aljaferia of Zaragoza. The Cordoban style is sustained in the embellishment of the main hall and mosque here but in the arcades screening the private apartments the decorative manipulation of structural form exceeds even the extreme of late Cordoba and strays into unique anti-architectonic asymmetry.[2.5]

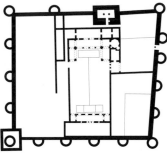

2.5a @ approximately 1:2000

›2.5 ZARAGOZA, ALJAFERIA PALACE, c. 1050: (a) plan, (b–d) exterior and details of north palace arcade.

The walled courtyard complex took its popular name – a contraction of al-Ja'fariyya – from its builder, the local princely ruler Abu Ja'far Ahmad ibn Suleyman al-Muqtadir (1049–83). An extramural castle, incorporating 9th-century remains in stout curtain walls with round towers, it conforms in general to the type descended from the Roman camp through the Umayyad qasr – as did the Almohad Alcazar in Seville.

In an incompletely rectangular compound, there are three main zones as usual in the palaces of Oriental potentates. The side courts and their projected accommodation, presumably for the guards and stores to the east, for the harem to the west, were never completed. The principal apartments overlooked the arcaded, canalized central court from the north and south: the laterally disposed main hall, presumably for public audience pending the construction of an alternative addressing the entrance court, is to the north where it is connected with an oratory. Both these rooms retain the Cordoban style of cusped and lobed arches with interlaced frames containing fields of intricate floral patterns incised in stucco. The parallel portico and hall to the south, relatively remote from the eastern entrance and partially screened with the most bizarre pattern of interlocking arch fragments, were probably for private audience. Here the screen of filigree valances in arches, whose trajectory goes beyond the frames, produces a bizarre asymmetry which was to remain unequalled until the 18th century.

The remains of the many other seats of devolved power in Iberia – varied in their substance – await scientific study.

2.5b

2.5c

2.5d

2.6

2 MOROCCAN SULTANATES

There was little stability in North-West Africa after the Berbers detected weakness in Umayyad rule early in the 11th century.**2.6** The nomadic Sanhaja ultimately emerged dominant. They had long been honing their arms in Sub-Saharan conquest, questing for the source of the legendary gold of Guinea: traded for salt from the mines of Sijilmasa and further south, on the edge of the Sahara, that gold had long excited the envy of North African rulers – Arab and otherwise.

ALMORAVIDS AND THE CHRISTIAN CHALLENGE

Having conquered and won converts to Islam as far as the Niger, the Sanhaja clan chief Yahya ibn Ibrahim turned to pilgrimage to Mecca. He returned to his Moroccan base fired with Sunni puritan zeal and quickly won a following. His successor, Yusuf ibn Tashufin, led the faithful to dominion. Yusuf overawed southern Morocco and took Marrakesh – conveniently placed to tax the gold exchange at Sijilmasa – as the capital of his Almoravid dynasty in

1062. In 1069 he took Fez, still pre-eminent among the cities founded by the Arab colonists even after the passing of the Idrisids and the domination of Cordoba. Pressing east into modern Algeria, he was to found Tlemcen in 1082. New mosques, or the comprehensive refurbishment of old ones, were ordered for each of these seats of power.

Meanwhile, the rivalry of the petty Arab and Berber states which had succeeded Cordoba in Spain had proved disastrous for Islam. Ferdinand I of Castile (1037–65) had reduced Zaragoza, Toledo and even Seville to vassalage. His successor Alphonso VI annexed Toledo in 1085. The next year, in response to appeals from the beleaguered Muslims, Yusuf ibn Tashufin crossed to Spain, made a bridgehead at Valencia and went on to secure much of Andalucia. He died in 1107. His fanatic energy died with him, but not before it had provoked the reaction of the Christians. However, the culture of the conquered conquered the conquerors and sapped the will of their champion's heir, Ali ibn Yusuf. By the end of his soft reign (1144), more Spanish Muslim states had been lost and the Moroccan tribes were restive again.

›2.6 MEKNES, GREAT MOSQUE, 14th–17th centuries: view into court.

›2.7 FEZ: (a) general view with the minaret of the Qarawiyin Mosque centre; (b–d) Qarawiyin Mosque (850s, 950s, 1130s), court (with 16th-century frontispiece), overview with minaret, plan.

The original mosque, founded in 857, was twelve bays wide and four deep with an interpolated T of wider nave and transept – as at Kairouan and, ultimately but less assertively, at Damascus. As at Kairouan, there was a minaret over the entrance to the court on axis with the mihrab: that was added by the 10th century. Contrary to the arrangement at Kairouan, the cutting of the transept through aisles parallel to the qibla wall follows the Damascene precedent but the placing of the

2.7b

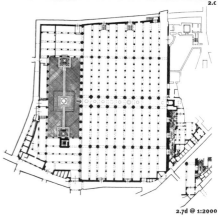

2.c

2.7d @ 1:2000

main entrance opposite the transept departs from both in favour of Cordoba.

Expansion for a growing population under the Umayyads in the middle of the 10th century included four new bays to either side, three new arcades to the north, displacing the old court and minaret, and a new court further north with a new minaret to its west, all in the style of contemporary Cordoba. Finally, in 1134 the Almoravids moved the qibla wall three arcades further south and enhanced the central axis with muqarnas vaulting, interpenetrating arches and cannellated domelettes in the late style of Cordoba – indeed, crafts-men were probably imported from Spain. Further Span-ish-style embellishment took place in the 16th century when the courtyard was endowed with end pavilions and a central frontispiece to the prayer hall.

ALMORAVID BUILDERS

Cordoba's cultural dominance was long felt in the far west: the emulation of Abbasid secular work, at least, was apparent at sites like Ashir as early as the mid-10th century, as we have noted, but the influence of Seljuk Iran was slow to filter through – especially with Shi'ite Fatimids in between. Fez was pre-eminent among Moroccan Arab towns, and pre-eminent among Moroccan mosques is Fez's Qarawiyin, founded in 857 by an Arab immigrant from Kairouan – whose name it perpetuates.[2.7]

The inspiration of the designer of the great mosque at Fez was drawn ultimately from the Umayyad mosque at Damascus but, quite contrary to the Levantine tradition and its Tunisian derivatives, it set the Maghribi precedent for reducing the court to relative insignificance before an expansive covered prayer hall. Under the domination of the caliph Abdul Rahman III by the mid-10th century, the mosque was renovated and expanded in the style of Cordoba. As there, a forest of columns was to be typical of the North African mosque from the Maghrib to Libya.

Under the spell of Andalucia, the Almoravid sultan Ali ibn Yusuf further extended the mosque at Fez in sympathy with the 10th-century Umayyad horseshoe arcades and built new Jami-masjids elsewhere – especially in fortified compounds on the frontiers (ribats). Most of his works have been rebuilt or ruined, but the additions at Fez, the restored ablution-tank canopy known as the Qubbat al-Barudiyin at Marrakesh and the filigree mihrab-bay vault at Tlemcen are the dynasty's most spectacular surviving buildings.

The Tlemcen work was conservative in plan, without a wide central nave as in the Jami-masjid in Algiers and its model at Kairouan: instead the qibla aisle was distinguished in the decorative treatment of the arches and opulent arabesque stucco work, as at Fez. In the Qubba

2.8a

2.8b

›**2.8 MARRAKESH, JAMI-MASJID OF ALI BEN YUSOF,** c. 1120: ablution-tank canopy (Qubbat al-Barudiyin): (a) interior of dome, (b) exterior.

Supported on cusped and pointed horseshoe arches and covered with a brick dome over a clerestory, the suspended canopy vault takes the decorative abstraction of once-structural forms to its dazzling conclusion. Transition from square within rectangle to cannellated dome within octagon is effected through eight overlapping arches springing between every second pier on adjacent sides, as in the mihrab bay at Cordoba. As there, cusped and pointed horseshoe arches play their elaborate part in the tiers of squinches and windows.

The identification of this unique structure as an ablution tank is not uncontroversial: no proposed function is generally accepted.

›**2.9 TLEMCEN, GREAT MOSQUE,** mihrab bay dome (early 12th century).

2.9

al-Barudiyn the arched rib has ceded to decreasing tiers of florid squinches. By the end of the era, squinches had been transmuted into muqarnas above arches wildly varied in profile: decorative manipulation of structural form in licentious stucco, characteristic of the Maghribi approach, cedes little to late Cordoba.**2.8, 2.9**

THE ALMOHADS AND CHRISTIAN TRIUMPH

Another puritan sect, Berber tribal enemies of the Almoravid Sanhajas, set out from their rugged Atlas lair to extirpate corruption. They were led by yet another *Mahdi*, Muhammad ibn Tumart, who returned from Mecca soon after Yusuf ibn Tashufin died and spent the rest of his life winning over other Berber tribesmen to unity with God. He died in 1130 but his equally zealous successor, Abd al-Mumin, took Marrakesh in 1141, Tlemcen in 1144, Fez in 1147 and assumed the title of caliph for his Almohad (unitarian) line. He then embarked on the conquest of Spain and the eastern Maghrib.

Abd al-Mumin's son Yusuf 1 (1163–84) established his court in Seville and devoted himself to scholarship and building. His son, Ya'qub al-Mansur (conqueror), preferred his new camp in northern Morocco, Rabat. A sound ruler and great builder who was indeed a fine warrior, he pushed the frontier with Christianity back further north and consolidated his hold on North Africa as far as Tunis. In the south, essentially, his forces overawed the trade route between the salt mines of the western Sahara and the gold mines of Guinea – the main source of wealth for all Moroccan rulers. By the time of his death in 1199, the Moroccan empire had reached its greatest extent and the apogee of its glory. Triumph was short: it ended on the frontier with Castile by the Christian victory over al-Mansur's successor at the battle of Las Navas de Tolosa in 1212.

2.10a

ALMOHAD BUILDERS

Puritanism is hardly the ethos most readily associated with prolixity yet profuse is the embellishment of the Almohad mosque at Tinmal, the lair from which their *mahdi* Muhammad ibn Tumart and his disciple Abd al-Mumin set out. The selective cusping of the prayer hall arches is unprecedented in convolution, effected in plaster, and there is extremely intricate muqarnas vaulting over the mihrab bay, the first of its kind in the Maghrib. In its translation from the east – and from stone to licentious plaster – the muqarnas motif lost any semblance of structural reality.**2.10**

>2.10 TINMAL, JAMI-MASJID, 1153: (a) prayer hall arcade, (b, c) mihrab bay and muqarnas vault, (d) plan.

The prayer hall has four arcades, nine bays wide, and the outer two bays extend as cloisters to each side of the court. The outermost ranges are wider than the others, commensurate with the qibla range which spans between them. Forming a nave, the central bay is wider still and, as at Kairouan for instance,**1.50** it joins the qibla range or transept at right angles immediately in front of the mihrab. As at Cordoba, the mihrab projects beyond the qibla wall as a miniature chamber (octagonal rather than heptagonal). The arches are either of pointed horseshoe or extremely elaborate cusped forms: elaboration increases with the significance of space. Beneath its muqarnas dome, the innov-

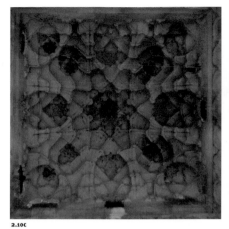

2.10c

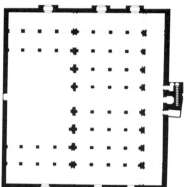

2.10d @ 1:1000

ative mihrab is somewhat surprisingly surrounded by geometric patterns rather than eccentric variations on the cusped arch – like the contemporary screens of Zaragoza.

2.10b

The later rulers of the line reduced the floridity and surpassed the Almoravids' Marrakesh mosque in scale. In particular, they asserted a nave and transept in their Kutubiya mosque begun soon after they took the enemy's seat in 1147. However, they retained their predecessors' convolution of the qibla arcades and added muqarnas domes at the termination of nave and transept. In this, as in their main approach to surface relief, they sustained the anti-architectonic treatment of essentially structural forms which had delighted the Muslim west at least since the second century of Cordoba.

Following the Almoravid precedent at Fez, itself following the Cordoban model, the Almohads commissioned a series of minarets to mark their triumph in the old Moroccan capital, in the new capital of Spain and in the camp from which the empire was taken to its greatest extent – bold geometry accompanied the intricacy of Tinmal and neither geometry nor the arabesque nor

2.11b

2.11a

›2.11 MARRAKESH: (a) Kutubiya Mosque, minaret (1158); (b) Bab Agnaou (c. 1160).

Work on the great minaret of Marrakesh seems to have begun at the end of the previous reign as part of the extension of the Almoravid mosque in the last year of Yusuf's reign. The windows on stepped levels at Marrakesh are framed in blind arches of varied profile, cusped and interlaced at the top.

›2.12 RABAT: (a) Hassan Mosque (1196), prayer hall ruins and minaret; (b) Oudaiah Kasba (c. 1195), gate.

The mosque was laid out with twenty-one aisles defined by columns, a transept three aisles deep along the qibla wall, a small outer court and two inner courts. The minaret was aligned with the qibla, as at Kairouan.

2.12b

2.12a

2.13

Commissioned in 1172 by Yusuf I in emulation of the Almoravid foundation in Marrakesh, the mosque in Seville consisted of a relatively long, shallow court preceded by a seventeen-bay prayer hall (now incorporated into the structure of one of the world's largest cathedrals). The motif of the interlaced arch is reduced to a delicate scale – producing a two-dimensional version of muqarnas – and extended in triple panels through most of the tower's height. The top storey is Christian.

script were dispensed with by Maghribi decorators: the Marrakesh Kutubiya minaret is the most prominent example of the style's early post-Tinmal phase and the Bab Agnaou nearby represents its bolder military mode.**2.11b** Ever more intricacy of blind foliate arches in panels relieved the Koutoubia minaret – like the Bab and the minarets of Marrakesh, Seville and Rabat. The latter belongs to a mosque conceived to eclipse all others known to its founder. He died soon after work was begun and, ambition having exceeded resource, the complex was never completed: stunted columns in serried ranks stand sentinel like decapitated soldiers before the huge bulk of the minaret with its incongruously delicate pattern of interlaced arches.**2.11–2.13**

The defences of the Rabat kasbah itself fared better, however, and al-Mansur's ceremonial Oudaiah gate set the pattern for the ceremonial portal in Morocco and Muslim Spain. In the valance ringing the voussoir and the frieze, the motifs of the lobed and cusped arch – blind, small-scale and out of structural context again – are varied in profile as at Tinmal, and meshed as on the minaret of the great mosque. Stylized floral motifs and scallop shells fill the spandrels within the frame of Kufic script. Thus the whole repertory of Islamic decorative forms is present, if geometry is admitted as the generator of the meshed lobed arches.**1.110b**

THE MARINIDS, THEIR CONTEMPORARIES AND FOLLOWERS

The Almohad empire in North Africa disintegrated quickly after the debacle of 1212. The Hafsid provincial governor of Ifriqiya had asserted his independence in 1235. Fired by the quest for new pastures rather than religious zeal, hardy desert clans of Berbers were advancing on Fez

›2.14 BERBER FORTIFICATIONS IN THE ANTE-ATLAS DADÈS RIVER VALLEY.

and Tlemcen at the same time: the Zayyanid branch took the latter in 1236; the Zenata clan took Fez in 1248 and made it the capital of their Marinid dynasty thirty years later, after they had laid out a new suburb. Many other tribes were won over by vigour again. Marrakesh and the last of the Almohads fell in 1269. An expedition to Spain failed to win again the old caliphate there, but close relations were forged with Granada. Tlemcen was retaken in 1336, but not Ifriqiya, and Berber vassals established a chain of fortified lairs along the trans-Atlas frontier.[2.14]

The trans-Atlas forts are splendid adobe vernacular structures. Even more splendid is the series of fortified trading posts which lined the routes between the polar sources of salt and gold in western Africa. There had, of course, been important changes in the structure of power there too. The Gulf of Guinea had been dominated by Ghana until the end of the 11th century: its wealth from the trade in gold and slaves was legendary – and confirmed by Arab travellers. From the several successor states, predominantly Muslim, Mali had emerged as an imperial

2.14b

2.14a

2.15a

power with the conquest of Songhai on the middle reaches of the Niger by the third decade of the 13th century: straddling the major artery of communication and proselytization in the region, Songhai had control of all the sources of gold. Further north, from their main seat at Timbuktu, the rulers of Mali challenged Moroccan con-

›2.15 THE SUB-SAHARAN ADOBE VERNAC-ULAR: (a) the Djinguereber Mosque at Timbuktu; (b) typical trading post village on the upper reaches of the Niger.

2.15b

trol of the salt mines in the Taghaza region – half-way between the rival centres of power. Naturally, Mali and Morocco exchanged embassies – until the Moroccans were irritated enough to attempt conquest again in the second half of the 16th century.[2.15]

Orthodox Sunni, and enlightened in their concern for public welfare, the new dynasties of the Maghrib promoted canonical education to counter the heterodox radicalism and sufism which the zeal of their predecessors had encouraged – though they built and restored mosques in a style derived from the Almohads. Most significantly, the Hafsids introduced the madrasa to Ifriqiya within a decade of their advent to power and the form, derived from Mamluk Egypt, was soon the chief focus of architectural activity in the domain of the Marinids – as much to foil the destabilizing popular *sufi* movement as to counter the heterodoxy of the Almohads.

BUILDINGS OF THE MARINID ERA

The 13th century was not a great age of building in Morocco. Almohad ambitions ended with the death of al-Mansur in 1199. His inadequate successors were preoccupied with unsuccessful war in Spain and at home and the limited building activity of the period was largely furthered by governors asserting independence – as, for, example the Hafsids of Tunis.

The Marinids, based on Fez from mid-century, had built Fez al-Jadid (new Fez) by 1276 and provided it with an unexceptional Jami-masjid. Their most elaborate work was the extension of the congregational mosque in Taza, a town of strategic importance for advance on Tlemcen. That proceeded at the end of the century when the warrior sultan Abu Ya'qub (1286–1307) returned to the scene with plans for a mosque which emulated al-Mansur's work at Rabat no more conclusively. Thereafter three prolific royal patrons – Abu Sa'id Uthman, Abu'l Hasan Ali and Abu Inan Faris – spanned the half-century from 1310 to 1359: they augmented many mosques, favouring novel embellishment with tiles, and inaugurated their great campaign of madrasa building at Fez with the translation of the iwan into Moroccan terms.

Tombs are rare in the Maghrib – at least until Abu Ya'qub's burial ground at Chellah, outside Rabat, was developed as a necropolis by his successors and Abu Inan built a mausoleum at Tlemcen in 1353. Even to provide the just context for a funerary memorial, moreover, the predecessors of the Marinids had not been notable madrasa builders: the radical Almohads were not interested in encouraging the promotion of orthodox doctrine and the Almoravids left education to the masters of the ribats. Under the Marinids, on the other hand, madrasas were built in all the major towns of the kingdom but the capital, naturally, was endowed with the greatest number. The survivors there range from the Saffarin, built in 1271 by Sultan Abu Yusof for thirty students, the Attarin, built in 1323 by Sultan Abu Sa'id Uthman for eleven students, to the Bu 'Inaniya built in 1350 by Abu Inan Faris for one hundred students.**2.16**

2.16a @ 1:1000

›2.16 FEZ, MARINID MADRASAS: (a) Saffarin (1271), plan; (b, c) Attarin (1323), plan and view towards qibla; (d) Bu 'Inaniya (1350), prayer-hall façade.

The Marinid madrasa

Ingeniously fitted into restricted urban sites, most Marinid madrasa are small as they catered solely for the Maliki school of law and, therefore, dispensed with the four-iwan plan: the Bu 'Inaniya is an apparent exception in its size and its lateral arches distinguishing a pair of lecture halls. All have tiled open courts serving a prayer hall, as clearly related to the axis of the entrance as the site permits, and flanked by cells over screened galleries or lecture rooms – if the prayer hall did not double for the purpose. The integration of wood, stone, tile and plaster provided the basis for the profuse geometric, floral and calligraphic embellishment of madrasa-court façades for centuries to come.

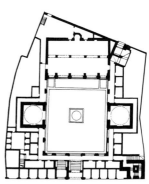

2.16b @ 1:1000

2.16c

The early Saffarin exercise is peculiarly disjointed, not merely in virtue of its deflected entrance but mainly because the breadth of site dictated the disposition of the court at an acute angle to the qibla. The Attarin court is rectangular, with the dog-leg entrance and square prayer hall on the short southern and northern sides respectively. This means that the mihrab marking the qibla is off-axis in the hall's right-hand wall. Of the other iwans, the southern one leads from the dog-leg passage (a typical domestic ploy to preserve privacy), but those on the eastern and western sides merely accent the arcades of shallow cloisters that flank the court throughout its length. Over a dado of coloured tiles set in simple geometric patterns, pilasters, walls and the screens that fill the arches above the northern and southern cloisters are covered with ornament incised in wood and stucco. The cusped-arch motif still plays a dominant role, but now it is repeated through several planes to resemble muqarnas – mirror-imaged to form a diaper pattern – or interlaced with such convolution that it is hardly to be distinguished from stylized floral ornament. Floral ornament has its role too, as does script.

As elsewhere by the mid-14th century, the madrasa doubles as a mosque in the great Bu 'Inaniya complex. The site was about half-way between the Qarawiyin Mosque in the centre of the old town and the new Marinid seat of Fez al-Jedid (founded 1276). Pending the construction of a new congregational mosque in the new town, the Bu 'Inaniya served the purpose and was endowed with the city's tallest minaret. Shops line the entrance front. The portal, court and mosque are aligned canonically on the qibla: the mosque has an inner arcade dividing it into two aisles, unequal in width, and supporting timber ceilings. The iwans on the other two sides open into teaching halls with wooden domes. Two storeys of cells for up to one hundred students are served by corridors in the corners, except to the north-east, and shops mask the exterior to either side of the central entrance (where a water clock measures the time for prayer). The complex was exceeded in size only by the Misbahiya, with its 117 cells grouped around two subsidiary courts.

2.16d

2.17a

2.17b

2.17c @ 1:1000

›2.17 RABAT, CHELLAH: (a) general view, (b) gate;, (c) necropolis plan, (d) detail of Hasan tomb exterior, (e) minaret.

Converted from the remains of a Roman fort into a ribat – a citadel of the Faith – Chellah was developed as the royal necropolis of the Marinid sultans Abu Sa'id and Abu'l Hasan, who built the compound wall in military style. In addition to the tombs, there was a mosque and a *sufi* hospice. The twin-towered gate, minaret and the surviving revetment of the Hasan tomb all still clearly sustain the Almohad style.

The last Marinid century – from the death of Abu Inan Faris in 1359 – was one of retrenchment, decline and disputed succession: it was not a great age of building. Troubled times turned popular devotion to *sufi* mysticism and from Rabat to Tunis the era is, perhaps, remembered as much for flight from strict orthodoxy in khanqahs as for the promotion of orthodoxy itself in madrasas.**2.17** There were to be many variants on awkward sites in the tight context of Morocco's cities but all Marinid works tend to be plain on the outside, profusely ornamented around the court, and plain again inside except for the vault and mihrab of the mosque.

2.17d

2.17e

2.18

SA'DI AND ALAWI

The source of Marinid wealth from the gold and slave trades across Sub-Saharan Africa was interrupted by the followers of a descendant of the Prophet known as Sharif al-Sa'di. They had taken Marrakesh by 1511 and went on to extend their rule over most of the south – from where they were ultimately to attempt the conquest of Songhai to eliminate the threat to the Sub-Saharan salt mines and secure control of the Guinea trade. In Morocco, at least, they were assisted by a *sufi* brotherhood dedicated to perpetuating the works of the Berber saint Sidi'l-Jazuli – whose prestige on his death in 1465 testifies to the revival of sufism under the late Marinids. The remnants of Marinid power in the north was extinguished by a *sharif* of the Alawi Berbers, Moulay Rashid (1667–72). He was succeeded by his brother, Moulay Ismail (1672–1727) who abandoned Fez for a new capital at Meknes and developed the shrine of Islam's progenitor in Morocca, Moulay Idris, in the hilltop town which bears his name.[2.18]

The Sa'dis, conservative in mosque planning, extended the madrasa type and style to Marrakesh with all the ingenuity required for awkward city sites. The sole significant survivor, built in the 1560s in emulation of the Fez Bu 'Inaniya but exceeding it in size, is called after the adjacent Almoravid mosque of Ali ibn Yusuf which its founder, 'Abdallah al-Ghalib (1557–74), had restored.[2.19]

The Sa'dis excelled both in the refinement of ornament, though infinite reduction of Marinid motifs is somewhat mechanical. Apart from the extant madrasa, this is nowhere better illustrated than in their necropolis, founded in association with the tomb of Sidi'l-Jazuli and the school of his followers: the first notable royal mausoleum in the Maghrib, this was sited in an Almohad burial ground beside the Kasba mosque. Moulay Ismail emulated this but surpassed it in opulence.[2.20, 2.21a, b]

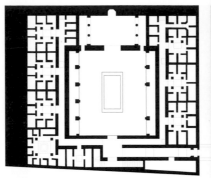

2.19b @ 1:1000

2.19b

›2.18 **MOULAY IDRIS:** general view with mosque and shrine centre.

Morocco's major pilgrimage destination, the shrine of the first Muslim king of the Maghrib achieved its definitive form under Moulay Ismail towards the end of the 17th century.

›2.19 **MARRAKESH MADRASAS:** (a) Bu 'Inaniya, plan; (b–e) Ibn Yusuf, 1562: mihrab, court, inner court gallery and cell.

More regular in disposition than was the norm – indeed near-symmetrical in a nearly square compound – the square court, with a triple-aisled mosque on the quibla axis and cloisters on the sides, is flanked by cells for well over one hundred students. A corridor leading from the prolifically ornamented entrance doubles back on itself to serve the stairs leading to the cells grouped in fours between seven galleried lightwells on the upper floor: the lightwells serve a similar arrangement of cells on the main level to either side of the central court. All the internal façades are chased with filigree lace-like arabesques in plaster over a tiled dado and under a huge valance of intricately carved timber.

2.19c

2.19d

2.19e

2.20b

>2.20 MARRAKESH, SA'DI NECROPOLIS,
16th century: (a) entrance, (b) tomb of Ahmad al-
Mansur (1590), interior.

The saint's complex was centred on the grave to
which his body was translated c. 1520 by the first Sa'di
ruler, Ahmad al-A'raj: it was served by a small oratory
and incorporated a lecture room and hospice. The first
royal tomb was built to a relatively simple cubical formula by al-A'raj (died 1557). From the 1590s, when he
buried his mother there, Ahmad al-Mansur initiated the
process of expansion and embellishment which culminated in a new mosque and his own colonnaded cenotaph chamber.

2.21a

2.21b

2.21C

Some 14th-century utilitarian work survives in the capital of Hafsid Ifriqiya, notably the Suq al-Attarin, but little remains of Hafsid, Marinid or even Sa'di palaces: contemporary descriptions and surveys of sites near Tunis, Tlemcen, Fez and especially in the garden of the Sa'dian Badi'a Palace in Marrakesh, reveal unsurprising similarities in plan to contemporary work in Spain – to which Marinid decorative detail is also closely related though carved more from wood than marble. Something of their opulence, of their integration of nature real and ideal, is doubtless conveyed by the remains of the triple palace complex of Moulay Ismail at Meknes. **2.21c, d** Much earlier, however, the clearest image is projected from Spain.

›**2.21 MEKNES:** (a, b) Tomb of Moulay Ismail, mosque gate and interior; (c) Bab al-Mansur; (d, e) ruins of the granaries and hall of Moulay Ismail's palace (later 17th century)

There were three main palaces in the royal complex: Dar al-Kabira (Grand Palace), the earliest of c. 1679, contained a congregational mosque, the sultan's tomb, the court and hall of public audience and more private accommodation round inner courts. The distribution of individually formal elements was not informal in this outer palace: the second, on the other hand, was a formal complex of garden courts surrounded by cells for the royal female entourage. Adjacent to this harem compound, the sultan's own quarters and halls of private audience are also related to formal enclosures, the largest of which was addressed by the hall of private audience.

2.21d

Much of the palace was destroyed in the conflict between rivals for the throne, though work was continued by al-Mansur's victorious son Moulay Abdallah, Some of the interior decoration has endured – most notably star-crossed wooden ceilings. The entrance to the outer palace, the Bab al-Mansur completed by Abdallah, displays a somewhat uncomfortable mixture of bombastic scale and intricately mechanical ornament: the latter is essentially conservative except in the extent to which it incorporates green and white ceramic tiles.

2.21e

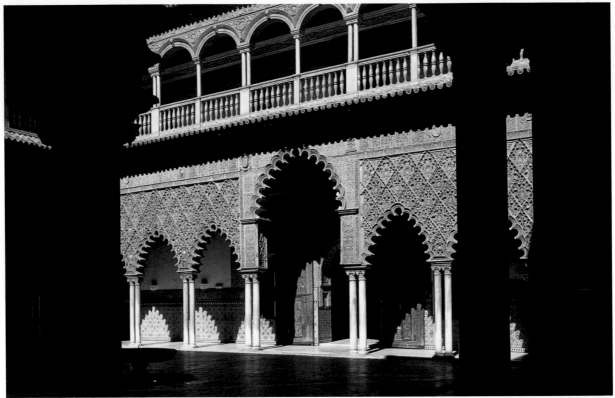

2.22a

3 ANDALUSIAN ENCLAVES

Las Navas de Tolosa (1212) was the gate to Iberia for the Christians. Cordoba was theirs in 1236, and Seville by 1248. By 1260 only the Nasrids Granada remained: that had been founded c. 1230 by a descendant of the last ruling prince of Zaragoza and survived as a tributary of the king of Castile because of the vital revenue. Its era came to a close with the complete triumph of the Catholic monarchs – Ferdinand of Aragon and Isabella of Castile – in 1492.

Surprisingly, perhaps, the new-found intolerance with which the Christians confronted the once-zealous Almohads did not extend to the so-called Moorish style –

2.22b

2.22c

›2.22 SEVILLE, ALCAZAR, 12th-century nucleus expanded from the mid-14th century: (a, b) outer and inner courts, (c, d) throne room and ceiling, (e) garden.

An extensive Moorish palace complex survives in the Seville Alcazar, but much of it was rebuilt (or at least redecorated) by the Christian king Pedro the Cruel in the second half of the 14th century. The extent to which the nucleus represents the Almohads is controversial, but the central Yeso court – with an iwan in the variegated cusped style of Tinmal and later Almohad structures – is usually accepted and the disposition of the rooms around the Court of the Maidens may well prefigure, rather than follow, the Alhambra. The throne room has a splendid ceiling patterned with intricate inlaid and overlaid wooden beams and panels. The type, called artesonado, was popular with Moorish patrons.

The garden perpetuates the four-square Persian type known as chahar bagh.

2.22d

indeed, they furthered it in Seville's Alcazar. The nucleus there may be dated to the 12th century but the rest of the Almohad palace was largely lost to rebuilding and expansion under Pedro the Cruel from 1365: the Muslim style appropriated by the Christians in exercises of this kind is known as Mudejar.**2.22**

2.22e

›ARCHITECTURE IN CONTEXT »BEYOND THE WESTERN PALE

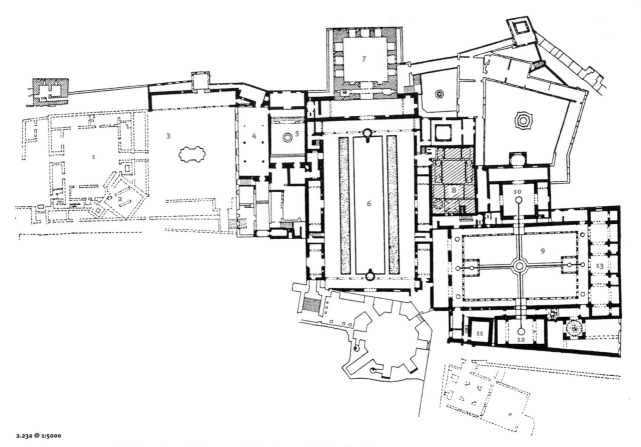

2.23a @ 1:5000

Under the sufferance of Castile until the fateful year
1492, the sultans of Granada luxuriated in the extreme
prolixity of their particular fortified paradise known from
the reddish hue of its masonry as the 'Red Fort' – qal'at
al-hamra, 'Alhambra'. On its splendid site, in its stoutly
defended compound, beyond the extreme beauty of its
courts and terraces, this legendary work is of prime
importance not least because of the extent of its preser-
vation due to the longevity of its beleaguered sovereigns
and the pre-occupation of its conquerors with centres of
gravity elsewhere.[2.23]

›2.23 GRANADA, ALHAMBRA: (a) plan with (1) outer court, (2) mosque, (3) Court of Machuca, (4) Mexuar (amir's private audience room), (5) Cuarto Dorado (Golden Room) and its court, (6) Patio de los Arrayanes (Court of the Myrtles), (7) Sala de los Embajadores (Hall of the Ambassadors), (8) baths, (9) Patio de los Leones (Court of the Lions), (10) Sala de la Dos Hermanas (Hall of the Two Sisters), (11) Sala de los Abencerrajes (the family murdered here in the 15th century), (12) Puerta de la Justicia (Gate of Justice), (13) Sala de los Reyes (Hall of the Kings or Muqarnas), (b) Puerta de la Justicia, (c) Mexuar interior, (d) Cuarto Dorado, (e) Patio de los Arrayanes, (f, g) Patio de los Leons, (h) Sala de la Dos Hermanas, muqarnas vault; (i) Sala de los Abencerrajes, (j) corner of the Torre de los Infantes, (k) Partal and water garden, (l–p) Generalife gardens, general view, canals, enclosures and view from belvedere back to the Alhambra.

2.23b

The Alhambra

The site was occupied in Roman times. The 9th-century foundations, overlaying the Roman ones, are themselves overlaid by the remains of the palace built in the middle of the 11th century by a Jewish vizier. Fortifications dependent on a massive keep on the western point of the eminence (the Alcazaba) and services (particularly an aqueduct) were built by the first Nasrid sultan to occupy the site, Muhammad I (1232–72). Under Muhammad II (1272–1302) several towers were converted to provide sumptuous accommodation and work was carried out on the outer courts: however, little remains from the 13th century. Over several generations

2.23c

thereafter, the palace was developed along the northern edge of the site. In the packed confines of a citadel, the succession of courts is typical of the Islamic palace but the traditional tripartite division is far from dogmatic – there is, indeed, nothing dogmatic about this fantasy palace.

The first major campaign of surviving work was undertaken by Yusuf I (1334–54). He built the Porta de la Justicia which now forms the main entrance. Recalling the venerable place of appearance of rulers from ancient Mesopotamia to Rome and Byzantium, this precedes a ceremonial entrance known as the Puerta del Vino which is usually attributed to Muhammad v (1354–91), though it incorporated earlier work. Presumably the missing outer court, immediately beyond the Puerta del Vino, was for public audience – or at least for public assembly in attendance on the ruler. Beyond, parallel to the northern wall, the first two courts of the private quarters – one once addressed by an oratory – survive only in ruin: they preceded the Mexuar, the original hall of private audience. This is generally attributed to Yusuf I, as is the succeeding Cuarto Dorado,

though its main southern façade was inscribed by Muhammad V. Over-looked by rooms for the women, the court provided private retreat from the Mexuar and its hall is one of the main outward-looking belve-deres; the twin doors led left into the harem and right (circuitously) into the Patio de los Arrayanes (myrtles) or Alberca (pool). This is dominated by the massive Torre de Comares, which gives this part of the palace its

2.23e

›ARCHITECTURE IN CONTEXT »BEYOND THE WESTERN PALE

2.23f

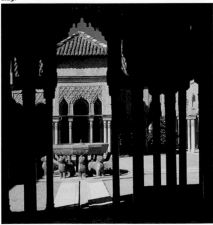

2.23g

name and into which the sultan's principal hall of audience, the Sala de los Embajadores, was installed: an inscription in the intricate plaster work identifies Yusuf I as the builder.

A door towards the south-east corner of the Patio de los Arrayanes, beyond the Baths of Yusuf I, leads to the Patio de los Leones, the nucleus of the new private apartments of Muhammad V. Rectangular and arcaded on all sides with lace-like intricacy, this celebrated work is centred on the lion-borne fountain at the crossing of axial canals: the long one, north-west/south-east, links the portico known as the Sala de los Mozarabes with the Sala de los Reyes but is curtailed before them by projecting porticoes descended from Medina al-Zahra; the short one, north-east/south-west, is extended into the splendid Sala de los Abencerrajes

2.23h

›ARCHITECTURE IN CONTEXT »BEYOND THE WESTERN PALE

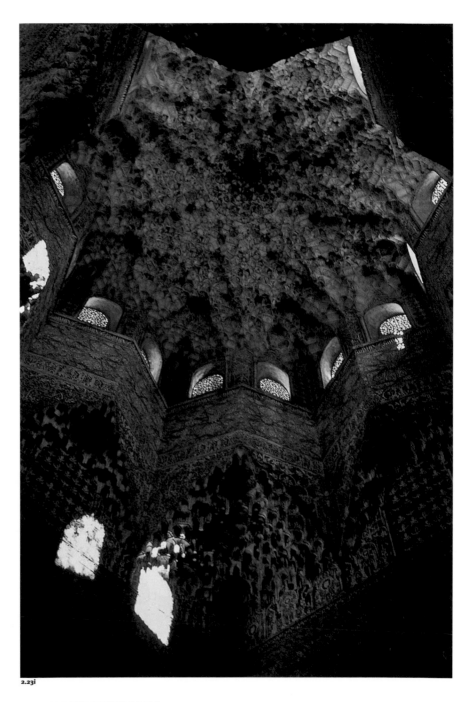

2.23i

2.23j

and, opposite it, the Sala de las Dos Hermanas – penetrated by the canals, these recall the 'rooms where brooks do flow' of the Koran's paradise. Beyond the Sala de las Dos Hermanas is the Mirador de Daraxa which overlooks the cloistered Patio de Lindaraja. Little survives beyond the Sala de los Reyes except the Partal which incorporates the 13th-century Torre de los Damas: the elegant loggia addressing the pool was probably built by Muhammad III (1302–09) but the complex seems to have been developed into a new palace (now lost) by Yusuf III (1408–17).

Throughout the complex, the great rooms – often converted from defensive towers – are flanked by smaller dependencies in no regular pattern but clear hierarchy. Under Yusuf I the grandest halls were covered with pyramidal roofs and suspended wooden ceilings, nowhere more elaborate than in the stars and sunbursts of the Sala de los Embajadores, but in general the palace buildings were trabeated, in the tradition of the Mexuar: like the beams there, arches and galleries are usually carried on columns. Yusuf I also introduced muqarnas and promoted greater complexity in the design of tile mosaic on the traditional dado. On upper surfaces, ornamental panels follow textile designs. Under Muhammad V the development of more sumptuous privacy prompted the refinement of the full repertory of motifs inherited from the Almohads and ultimately the Umayyads of Cordoba – in the Patio de los Leones the rhythmic grouping of the columns is at its most sophisticated and, indeed, the muqarnas ceilings of the lateral halls know no equal in their exquisite, empyraean intricacy. Decorative lines are curvilinear as well as geometric and Kufic script achieves its greatest splendour in the Sala de las Dos Hermanas but – as well as the sculpted lions in the court – there is also resplendent figural painting in the Sala de los Reyes.

The builders of the Alhambra were ultimately indebted to their ancestors who worked at Medina al-Zahra but the

2.23k

262 ›ARCHITECTURE IN CONTEXT »BEYOND THE WESTERN PALE

2.23l

2.23m

2.23n

2.230

immediate precedents for the Nasrid complex and its Marinid predecessors – which are known from literary accounts to have been similar, if grander – were set by the Almohads in Seville. The Almohads doubtless followed the now-lost example of the metropolitan palace of the Cordoban caliphs. Somewhat later and considerably further east, in north-east Algeria as we have noted, the early 12th-century Qasr al-Mulk of the Banu Hammad similarly combines major formal courtyard complexes, related in plan to various Umayyad and Abbasid precedents, in informal agglomeration – recalling the sensitivity to site contours of Hadrian's villa at Tivoli and, presumably, the imperial palace in Constantinople.

At Tivoli – and to a lesser extent at Constantinople – the site permitted the loose devolution of intrinsically formal units. At Granada, the tightly packed confines of an acropolis on the one hand, its splendid elevation on the other, inspired a *cantilena* of expansive outlook played in counterpoint over a ground base of intense introversion. And it is in contemplating the most seductive Court of the Lions that the full meaning of the exercise is revealed. With its central fountain and crossed canals, it is an image of Eden's lost paradise regained. At first the rectangle seems to deny this, for the ancient Persian *paradaieza*, from which Eden springs, is a square divided by the rivers of life into the four quarters of creation. But the arms of the canals are in fact co-extensive and their penetration through the iwans of the axial pavilions – projecting into the court east and west, receding from it north and south – is the literal interpretation of the Koranic paradise as a garden set with pavilions beneath which water flows. The *cantilena* takes up the theme and varies it with infinite resource in the Alhambra's harem and across the valley in the Generalife.

2.23p

PART 3 DAR AL-ISLAM DIVIDED

3.1b

PROLOGUE

The various Turko-Mongol nomads who roamed the dessicated area north of the Gobi had been forged into a powerful fighting force towards the end of the 12th century: unleashed on the vast span of Eurasia 'like devils from Tartarus' according to a contemporary chronicler, they came to be known in the West as 'Tartars' in grim homage to the dominant Tatar clan. The formidable personality responsible was the Mongol chief Temüjin – better known to history as Genghis Khan after he was proclaimed ruler of the consolidated Mongol tribes by a general assembly of chiefs in 1206. Havoc wreaked on neighbouring civilizations by marauding east-central Asian nomads was nothing new: the range of Genghis and his heirs at the head of the unified Mongol nations was extraordinary due to the concurrent disintegration of China on the one hand, Dar al-Islam on the other.

Genghis first turned on China, sacked Beijing in 1215 but left it to his son to complete the conquest in 1235 – eight years after his death. Instead, in 1218, he had turned

›3.1 MONGOLS: (a) at the gates of Baghdad; (b) in battle.

west across the Syr Darya to confront the Persianized Turkik Khorezmshahs who had overcome Sultan Sanjar in 1156 and established an independent Islamic domain in Transoxiana between the Syr and Amu Darya based on Bukhara and Samarkand. He took Bukhara in 1220, laid it to waste and proceded to do the same to Samarkand. He crossed the Amu Darya the following year and overcame Khorasan, destroying its principal cities – Balkh, Merv and Nishapur. He then returned to Mongolia where he died in 1227 on campaign against his Tangut relatives.

As the Great Khan's eldest son, Jochi, also died in 1227, his second son Chagatay inherited Transoxiana and the territory east to the Gobi. The third son, Ogoday, master of most of Mongolia, was acclaimed as the new Great Khan in 1229 and proceeded with the conquest of China. He also sent a force west to overcome resistance to Chagatay's followers in Khorezm: that accomplished, the force went on through the Caucasus to demolish the Sultanate of Rum. Further, Genghis's grandson Batu laid the foundations of the khanate of the Golden Horde in penetrating beyond Kievan Russia into the Balkans.

There was turmoil in the Great Khanate in the mid-1240s when Ogoday and his heir died in quick succession and his clan was butchered by the followers of Ghinghiz's youngest son, Toloy, whose son Mangu took the supreme position. Mangu sent his brother Hulagu back across the Amu Darya in 1256 to reassert control in Iran. Annihilating all opposition, he summoned the caliph al-Musta'sim (acceded 1242) to present himself at his camp. The caliph refused. The Mongols marched on Baghdad, took it, sacked it and dispatched the caliph in 1258.**3.1** Two years later, in Syria, the invaders met their first serious reverse at the hands of the Turkish mamluk general Baybars in the service of the decaying Ayyubid sultanate based on Cairo.**3.2**

3.2

›ARCHITECTURE IN CONTEXT »DAR AL-ISLAM DIVIDED

3.1 THE AXIS OF THE TURKS

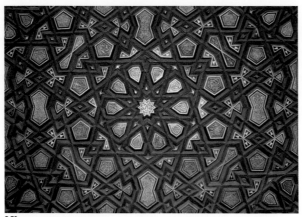

3.70

1 THE MAMLUKS OF EGYPT AND SYRIA

THE MAMLUKS: FROM CAIRO TO DAMASCUS

Constantly in dispute with the Christians in the Levant, Saleh's heirs accepted the help of an army of Qipchaq Turkish slaves (mamluks) to confront the Crusaders in Syria and Egypt: housed in barrracks on an island in the Nile, they were to be known as Bahri ('River') Mamluks. The effort seriously weakend the Ayyubids but strengthened the commanders (amirs) of their mamluk forces.

After the death of Sultan Salih Najm al-Din Ayyub in 1249 and the assassination of his unpopular son, Egypt was subject to a regency. Insecure, the regime succcumbed to the spectacular success of the late sultan's mamluk general, Baybars, against the Mongols at 'Ayn Jalut in Syria in 1260 to the relief of Egypt. The brother of the late caliph was accorded sanctuary in Cairo and confirmed in the title: attempting to return to reclaim Baghdad, he was killed in 1262 and succeeded by a cousin who inaugurated the wholly ineffective last phase of the Abbasid caliphate confined to the Egyptian capital.

The Mongol threat having been eliminated – at least in

›3.2 CAIRO, CITADEL, 1271–82 and later: view across the 'City of the Dead' with the mosque of Muhammad Ali Pasha left and the domes and minarets of the neighbouring al-Rifa'i and Hasan complexes right.

On its 67-metre eminence, dominating the vast cemetery to the east of the Fatimid city and probably fortified by the Romans, the citadel was refounded by Saleh al-Din as the key element in an extensive fortification programme involving the construction of walls around Fustat (the 'Entrenchment', the original Arab encampment around which the first Muslim capital developed) and al-Qahirah (the 'Vanquisher', the foundation of the Fatimid conquerors as their new capital). The military zone to the north-west preserves much of the original ramparts, with their covered wall-walk and regular sequence of round towers. The residential zone to the south-west has been much enlarged. The palace, which reached its greatest extent under Sultan al-Nasir Muhammad in the early 14th century, consisted of many courts and pavilions, including a throne chamber with a timber muqarnas vault preceded by a many-columned portico commanding the magnificent view of the city below. It was the best representative of many generations of Cairene palaces until blown up in 1824, to be replaced by the mosque of Muhammad Ali Pasha.

Ayyubid domains – Baybars went on to terminate the Christian hold on the Holy Land: he took their castles (among the greatest ever built anywhere, as we shall see in due course) and restored the fortifications of the Syrian cities breached by the Monguls. Meanwhile his initial triumph had carried him all the way to the sultanate in the Cairo citadel – which he developed for the protection of his new-found power.

The new regime moved the mamluk barracks to the citadel and initiated a new phase of architectural patronage in Cairo which was furthered elsewhere after the Mongols finally destroyed Dar al-Islam. In place of legitimately constituted rulers, they were self-made adventurers and to perpetuate their names they built lavish funerary complexes incorporating mosques, madrasas, mausoleums and a wide range of public utilities after the example set by Sultan al-Saleh Najm al-Din Ayyub. Baybars began the series but he died and was buried in Damascus, contrary to his Egyptian pretensions.**3.3, 3.4**

›3.3 DAMASCUS, MAUSOLEUM OF SULTAN BAYBARS, c. 1280: interior.

The surviving tomb chamber near the Great Mosque is remarkable for its polychrome marble dado, intricately inlaid in geometric and floral patterns around the mihrab, and glass-mosaic frieze which, like the surviving Umayyad work in the mosque, combines enigmatic architectural motifs with realistic and stylized plants.

3.4a @ 1:1000

3.4b

›3.4 CAIRO, BAYN AL-QASRAYN: (a) plan with (1) Madrasa of Sultan al-Salih Ayyub, (2) remains of the complex of Baybars, (3) Madrasa of Sultan Qala'un, (4) Tomb of Sultan Qala'un, (5) Madrasa of Sultan al-Nasir Muhammad, (6) Madrasa of Sultan Barquq, (b) view from Bab Zuwaylah.

Baybars I's immediate successors were elected from the company of mamluk amirs, and that in principle was to be the dynastic rule. Naturally this incited chronic dissent and dissaffection, especially as wealth passed to heirs was usually at the mercy of rival factions – unless it was tied to a pious endowment – as we shall see. The system proved unworkable almost at once. On the death of Baybars I's ultimate successor, Qala'un (1280–90) who had been another of the late Ayyubid sultan's aides, two of his sons succeded by default as the factions could not agree on a candidate from the ranks of the amirs: the second heir, al-Nasir Muhammad, was deposed in 1295 by one of his father's amirs, was returned to the throne in 1299 as a figurehead for another amir, lost and recovered it again and then reigned effectively for more than thirty years (1309–41). Nasir was succeeded by no less than seven sons, most for little more than months until the rapacity of the last, Hasan, alienated all the factions. He was assassinated in 1361.

Twenty years of chaos was terminated by Sultan Barquq Anas, a Circassian Turk who emerged from the ranks of the Burji ('Citadel') Mamluks. The internecine strife was particularly disastrous for Syria, delaying recovery from the devastation of the Mongols. And, of course, decades of turmoil, punctuated by the horrors of the Black Death in the middle of the 14th century, undermined the economy of Egypt too. But contention did not inhibit the extension of Mamluk rule from Egypt to Arabia and from Syria to eastern Anatolia at the expense of the post-Seljuk rulers there. Trade had begun to revive in northern Syria before Barquq's accession and the relative stability of his reign saw it vigorous enough again to finance the re-inauguration of grand building schemes in Damascus, Aleppo and, above all, in Cairo – Islam's largest city at the time.

After Barquq's death in 1399 the Mamluk system of succession by patronage, rather than heredity, was reinstated. The result was turbulence as before. Nevertheless, monumental building activity continued in Egypt for several generations, absorbing a rich range of influences from the far-flung provinces and neighbours of the empire. Syrian developments were cut short: hardly recovered from the Mongol onslaught, at the outset of the new century it was devastated again by the Turkish firebrand Timur – of whom we shall hear a great deal more.

BAHRI BUILDINGS

Sultan Baybars 1 – who alone of his line devoted much patronage to Syria – inaugurated the Mamluk era in Egypt with the foundation of the suburb of al-Husayniya beyond the Bab al-Futuh in the north wall of Fatimid Cairo and commissioned for it an enormous congregational mosque

›3.5 CAIRO, THE BAHRI MAMLUK MOSQUE: (a–c) al-Husayniya, elevation, plan and section (after the Napoleonic *Description de l' Egypte*); (d, e) Nasiriya, court and detail of mihrab bay; (f–h) Maridaniya, court, detail of hall, wooden mashrabiya which screens the hall from the court.

Al-Husayniya had larger arches than its model, under raised roofs on the main axes and a great qubba before the mihrab, as in Seljuk Iran but domed in wood rather than brick. The roof, also wooden, was supported by stone and brick arcades; the outer walls were of stone, embellished after the early 12th-century Fatimid style of al-Aqmar Mosque.

The mosques of al-Nasir and al-Maridani are both smaller than Baybars' fountain; both have huge mihrab chambers domed in wood, but are rich in materials pillaged from Christian and antique buildings. Al-Maridani's mihrab is a splendid exercise in the colouristic use of materials – including a variety of coloured stone as well as coloured glass and mother-of-pearl – which owes not a little to the regime's connection with Syria.

By al-Maridani's time the Cairene minaret had achieved its canonical form: a square base, at least two octagonal storeys variously embellished between balconies on muqarnas corbels and surmounted by a colonnaded tempietto with a bulbous cap.

modelled on the Fatimid al-Hakem. His successors built an unusual number of new congregational mosques in Egypt to meet the needs of a population whose growth, uniquely in the central Islamic world, was not arrested by Mongol decimation. They sustained the hallowed tradition of the courtyard surrounded by riwaqs deepened to form the prayer hall in the south-eastern range. The most notable Bahri examples are those of Sultan al-Nasir Muhammad (c. 1320) and Amir Altınbugha al-Maridani (c. 1339).**3.5**

3.5a

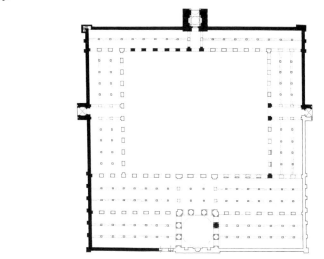

3.5b @ 1:2000

3.5c

3.5e

3.5d

3.5f

3.58

3.5h

The most spectacular contribution of the Mamluks and their amirs was the development of the funerary complex on the lines laid down by their predecessors but the scale and magnificence of their exercises exceeded all precedents. So, too, did the incentive: the insecurity of family legacy, inherent in the mamluk system, encouraged rulers and amirs to invest their fortunes in inviolable charitable trusts dedicated to the endowment of religious institutions or hallowed public utilities incorporated in funerary complexes which were to be maintained by – and maintain – their families as trustees. Economy was not a consideration. Cairene building in the Mamluk age was unrivalled in splendour: from myriad examples, the most outstanding survivors include the several royal foundations prestigiously sited on Cairo's main artery (the Qasaba) which led from the Bab al-Futuh to the foot of the Bab Zuwayla.

Redeveloped, the Qasaba sites were usually irregular and, as the north–south alignment of the street was off-qibla (Mecca is to the south-east of Cairo), considerable ingenuity was required in distributing the elements behind the façade screen, as in al-Salih Ayyub's complex.**1.110e, f** As the prime purpose was in fact commemorative, the mausoleum qubba was invariably the dominant mass and, though disparate in alignment, the requisite mosque was best adjacent to it and to the charitable foundation which was the official excuse for the exercise. However, if inventive planning was characteristic of Cairene builders, innovations in style were largely elaborative.

Often cannelated and stilted over cylindrical and/or polygonal drums, raising them to the view of the street, Cairene domes were of brick or wood for most of the Bahri period and intricate woodwork was the norm for ceilings and doors. In the main, however, the Mamluks maintained the fine ashlar arcuate tradition inherited by the Ayyubids from the Fatimids but further enriched it with muqarnas portals, multiple squinches in the zone of transition from cube to dome, ever-more-intricately carved screens and panels in stone or marble – especially for the mihrab. The colouristic alternation of light and dark stone in voussoirs and mosaic inlay, characteristic of Syria, made its mark in Cairo but rich revetment materials were ready to hand there: the early Mamluk sultans, at least, despoiled Ptolemaic and Roman buildings as well as Christian churches; the later sultans despoiled their predecessors.**3.6**

The Bahri Mamluk funerary foundation

At the outset Baybars effected a synthesis of Egyptian and Syrian elements. Like his former Ayyubid master, he proclaimed his pretensions in ostentatiously redeveloping part of the site of the Fatimid palace to the eastern side of the Qasaba for his funerary madrasa complex: devolved around a single court with four iwans, rather than two parallel courts, it marked the introduction of the muqarnas portal to Cairo from Syria and made much of striped masonry but little remains beyond part of the façade as the sultan was buried in Damascus.

3.6a

3.6b

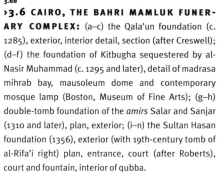

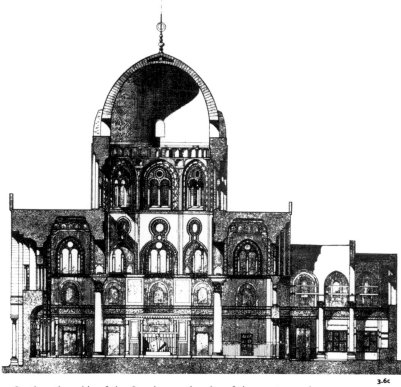

3.6c

›3.6 CAIRO, THE BAHRI MAMLUK FUNER-ARY COMPLEX: (a–c) the Qala'un foundation (c. 1285), exterior, interior detail, section (after Creswell); (d–f) the foundation of Kitbugha sequestered by al-Nasir Muhammad (c. 1295 and later), detail of madrasa mihrab bay, mausoleum dome and contemporary mosque lamp (Boston, Museum of Fine Arts); (g–h) double-tomb foundation of the *amirs* Salar and Sanjar (1310 and later), plan, exterior; (i–n) the Sultan Hasan foundation (1356), exterior (with 19th-century tomb of al-Rifa'i right) plan, entrance, court (after Roberts), court and fountain, interior of qubba.

On the other side of the Qasaba, on the site of the western palace which had housed the Fatimid heirs, the main surviving part of Qala'un's complex is penetrated by a long corridor to either side of which are the mausoleum and the madrasa court lined with cells between the single great iwan and the mosque – the corridor led on to the court of a hospital but that has largely disappeared. The eclecticism is imperial: antique columns, trophies from the pagan and Christian past, support pointed arches sometimes horseshoe-shaped like those of the Umayyads, east and west; the Ptolemaic granite columns supporting the wooden dome are arranged octagonally within an ambulatory in recollection of the Dome of the Rock; dadoes are formed of polychrome marble, as in the Umayyad mosque in Damascus, and the main mihrab is further enriched in the Syrian manner with glass and mother-of-pearl mosaic; the stucco work is unsurpassed in the crisp intricacy of its arabesque elaboration but recalls the finest motifs carved in stone in the Jazira or Anatolia.

3.6d

3.6e

3.6f

Several of the amirs who pretended to power during the minority of Qala'un's son al-Nasir Muhammad built significant complexes. The amir Salar, whose passing was the condition for al-Nasir's final return, initiated building on rising ground remote from the Qasaba and the project was developed by the amir Sanjar later in the reign: including a khanqah as well as a madrasa, it is notable for its ingenious planning, its tiered structure, its Syrian masonry domes and its splendid minaret with muqarnas corbels supporting the upper-storey balconies.

The earlier usurper of al-Nasir's throne, the amir Kitbugha (1295–97), took the more important site near Qala'un's complex on the Qasaba and

3.6g @ 1:1000

3.6h

set the Cairene precedent for the four-iwan-court scheme devised to accommodate all four schools of law: on his final restoration, al-Nasir sequestered and completed the complex (with a dome resting on brick muqarnas) for his mother and son but he himself was interred with his father. The eclecticism of the work ranges from the portal pillaged from a Crusader church at Acre (in the pointed-arch style later to be called gothic) to the exceptionally rich stucco work of the madrasa mihrab which clearly acknowledges familiarity with Persian work.

3.6i

The four-iwan type was developed on a grandiose scale by Sultan Hasan, the last of al-Nasir's sons to occupy the throne: the masterpiece of the era, it incorporated a vast domed tomb, a mosque, a madrasa, a hospital, an orphanage, a bazaar, a fountain and baths. The nuclear court and its iwans served the mosque in the qibla iwan – the plan type is Iranian but the inspiration probably came through Syria from Anatolia with which the Mamluks were directly involved. As in the Jami-masjid at Isfahan, the qibla iwan leads to a domed chamber: there it was a maqsura for the prince at prayer, here it is his tomb. The four schools of orthodox law were accommodated in courts in the corners, surrounded by several storeys of cells for the students. Still smaller courts served the other facilities in the northern part of the peninsula site.

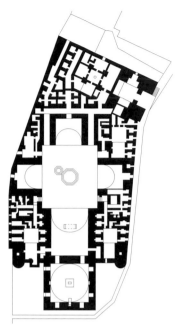

3.6j @ 1:2000

3.6l

3.6k

The eclectic opulence of Hasan's decoration surpasses even Qala'un's seminal work though there is far less intricate stucco. Within the iwans of both entrance and court (the former originally conceived as a frontispiece with paired minarets) muqarnas vaulting dominates. Panelled revetment and voussoirs in marbles of contrasting colours are surmounted by a frieze of bold Kufic script as in Qala'un's complex. Over marble revetment and a gilded Kufic frieze, the bulbous wooden dome of the mausoleum, the largest of its kind in Cairo, is carried on complex wooden muqarnas.

The earliest surviving bulbous domes in Cairo – some ribbed, some plain like the one over the fountain in the court of Hasan's complex – pre-date the earliest surviving examples in Iran. That may nevertheless be the source but the form is a resounding echo of the horseshoe-shaped arch, familiar throughout North Africa. The dome is a marker.

As the funerary complex is usually absorbed by its labyrinthine context, necessarily even more assertive is the minaret. The Pharos inspiration has yet to fade completely: Qal'un's composition retains the rectilinear intermediate block of the model but, instead, there is an elegant octagonal drum for the crowning lantern of the complex of Salar and Sanjar with a corresponding proliferation of balconies. By Hasan's time the 'pepper-pot' cupola has achieved its definitive bulbous form.

3.6m

3.6n

3.7a

3.7b

3.7d

BURJI BUILDINGS

The impact of Hasan's great work endured: the final complement to it was paid at the outset of the 20th century in the mosque of al-Rifa'i opposite. Hasan's Circassian successors – the Burji Mamluks – emulated, but never equalled, his achievement. Most significantly, however, the potential of the four-iwan scheme to serve mosque and madrasa simultaneously in their crowded metropolis was not lost on them. Barquq was the last to command a unified site on the Qasaba – near the complex sequestered by al-Nasir a century earlier – where he built a funerary complex in which the main element was a mosque-madrasa: Hasan's influence is clear in the nucleus of the plan and in the major elevations but masonry prevails over scarce timber in the construction of the mausoleum dome, if not in the magnificent ceiling of the qibla iwan.**3.7a–d**

›**3.7 CAIRO, BURJI FUNERARY FOUNDA-
TIONS:** (a–d) the Barquq foundation (c. 1390),
entrance (with minarets of Sultans al-Nasir, right, and
Qala'un), court, main qibla iwan, tomb vault; (e–h) the
double-tomb Faraj foundation (c. 1405), court with
mosque centre, interior of the princes' tomb, plan with
(1) mosque, (2) princes' tomb, (3) ladies' tomb, (4)
fountain and entrance pavilions with teaching and
other facilities, detail of mihrab; (i) the double tomb
courtyard mosque of Sultan al-Mu'ayyad Shaykh and
his women (c. 1420), overview; (j–m) the funerary complex of Sultan Qa'it Bay in the Northern Cemetery, (c.
1474), general view (after Roberts), crossing dome,
plan, interior of tomb.

Richness and the four-iwan mosque-madrasa plan
are sustained by Qa'it Bay but the tomb is now the
largest single element.

3.7c

Barquq was interred in his Qasaba complex but he had
willed his burial in the northern cemetery near a *sufi*
shrine. His son Faraj (1399–1412) complied with a vast
complex incorporating a mosque, a madrasa, a khanqah
for devotions to the *sufi* and two domed tombs built
entirely of masonry, one for himself and the other to
receive his father's translated remains.**3.7e–h** Most of the
Burjis followed the precedent, primarily in developing
cemetery sites associated with *sufis* but also in the last great
urban mosque built to the traditional plan with riwaqs to
all four sides by Sultan al-Mu'ayyad Shaykh.**3.7i**

Stone domes were the norm by the time the Burjis
replaced the Bahris, even on a large scale: by Faraj's time
cannelation had ceded to chevron patterns, as chevrons
would later cede to geometric webs woven with stars, as in
Qa'it Bay's great work. In emulating Faraj's work,

3.7e

3.7g

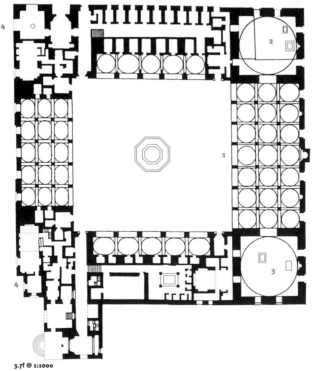

3.7f @ 1:1000

3.7h

3.7i

Mu'ayyad Sheikh's builders erected a masonry dome over the sultan's tomb to the north but not over the women's tomb to the south: the qibla wall between is unexcelled in the richness of its coloured marble and stucco revetment but most of the rest of the enclosure has been rebuilt.

3.7j

3.7k

3.7l @ 1:1000

Despite incessant internecine strife, repeated outbreaks of plague and economic recession following the eclipse of the overland eastern trade routes by Portuguese seafarers, magnificent building exercises were sustained until the Ottoman Turks destroyed the Mamluk regime in 1517. The last sultan, Qansuh al-Ghawri (1501–17) – who added the tallest minaret to al-Azhar Mosque **1.75** – returned to the Qasaba but had to build the mosque and madrasa on one side, the mausoleum, khanqah and public facilities on the

3.7m

other. The workmanship was rough, the style refined. In the latter it followed the final masterpiece of the era, the complex of the last great Mamluk sultan, Qa'it Bay (1468–96) – who also worked extensively at al-Azhar. His exquisitely embellished funerary foundation represents the culmination of work in Cairo's Northern Cemetery: the four-iwan mosque-madrasa plan is sustained together with the usual range of facilities but the tomb is now the largest element. **3.7j–m**

3.8a

The defences of all the empire's major cities were restored and the regime widely promoted the proliferation of public utilities ranging from hospitals and caravanserai to bridges, canals and public water dispensaries. Some of these civil facilities – within and without funerary complexes – survive though many have been rebuilt or superseded.**3.8a,b** Mamluk palaces in Egypt and Syria have not fared much better than those of the remoter past. The main palace in Cairo, on the citadel hill, was replaced by the

›3.8 CAIRO, SECULAR WORKS OF THE LATE AND POST-MAMLUK ERA: (a) Wikalah Bazar'ah (17th century), caravanserai court; (b) Sh' al-Mu'izz II, sabil-kuttab (school with a public fountain) in the Mamluk style (rebuilt in 1774, restored 1984); (c, d) Qa'it Bay's palace (1485), elevation and plan.

The court was ubiquitous, of course, but the similarity of the northern façade of the palace with its loggia to the haram façade of the Ashrafia Madrasa in Jerusalem is striking – if hardly surprising as both were built by the same sultan at the same time and for a similar purpose of royal display.

3.8b

mosque of Muhammad Ali after 1824, as we have noted, but part of Qa'it Bay's preferred residence survives in plan and elevation.**3.8c, d** The same architect clearly worked for the sultan on extensions to the Masjid al-Ashrafiya in Jerusalem.**3.9**

Cairo was most favoured by Burji builders, as it had been under their Bahri predecessors. Their *amirs* in Syria were not inactive as founders of funerary complexes of limited scale but building there was not extensive until after the depredations of Timur. Outside Egypt, the sultans directed their patronage mainly to Jerusalem but Qa'it Bay's long reign saw the restoration of the major mosques of all the great cities of the empire – Mecca, Medina and Jerusalem as well as Cairo, Damascus and Aleppo.

Having erected madrasas within the sacred precinct of Mecca and Medina, Qa'it Bay commissioned the extension of the courtyard complex founded to the west of the Dome of the Rock by his predecessor, Sultan Kushqadam,

3.8d @ 1:1000

3.8c

›3.9 JERUSALEM, MASJID AL-
ASHRAFIYA: (a) reconstruction of eastern
façade (after Walls, *Islamic Jerusalem*), (b) plan.

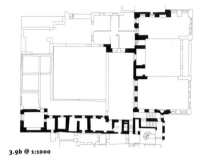

3.9b @ 1:1000

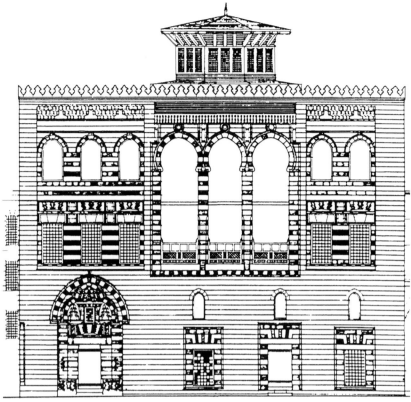

3.9a

in 1465. The earlier work was built up against the arcade which lined the site's western perimeter: the new work was based on the eastern range of this structure but projected well beyond the arcade into the harem towards the venerable dome. The ground floor of the block thus formed was divided between an entrance portico, stairs, a pair of mortuary chambers and a hall in which the original arcade piers were retained to support the upper floor. That was devoted to the madrasa's teaching space which was divided into elongated halls to the north and south of a nuclear square, an iwan niche to the west and a loggia overlooking the harem to the east. Accommodation was provided over the southern and western ranges of the original court.

3.10a

›ARCHITECTURE IN CONTEXT »DAR AL-ISLAM DIVIDED

3.10b

›3.10 **DAMASCUS, PALACE OF THE AL-AZEM FAMILY,** mid-18th century: (a) entrance, (b) fountain court.

In conformity with the Oriental norm, the compound is divided into three zones: an open court area with freestanding reception pavilions, a block of apartments for the male members of the family and the enclosed harem. The latter is wholly traditional and the style of the accessible elements is Syrian but the informal distribution of regularly planned pavilions is consistent with Turkish practice.

In Damascus the remains of the citadel palace do not extend much beyond the Ayyubid nucleus. However, for some idea of what the palaces of post-Timurid Syria were like, one may (with care) look into the 18th century and extrapolate. Virtually complete, the splendid palace of the al-Azem family has all the traditional features known from literary descriptions: convoluted entrance, fountain court and the ceremonial iwan of time immemorial.**3.10**

2 ANATOLIA AND THE ADVENT OF THE OTTOMANS

POST-SELJUK FRAGMENTATION

When it was again divided between jostling principalities (beyliks), Anatolia was not a scene of major building in the century after the demise of the Seljuks. As with beleaguered powers everywhere, most of the princes who took local power from the remnants of Rum resorted to tent-like kiosks of the Seljuk type in stoutly defended citadels dominating their power base from elevated ground: this is well demonstrated by the substantial legacy of the Shirvanshahis at Baku on the north-eastern edge of the Seljuk conquests: established at Shirvan prior to the late-11th-century Seljuk invasion and clients thereafter, the dynasty re-established itself at Baku when their eponymous seat fell to the Turkish tribe known as Qaraqoyunlu ('Black Sheep') – of whom we shall hear more in due course.**3.11**

The central beyliks continued to prefer the domed court type of madrasa developed in Konya. The open-court type with two or four iwans subsists elsewhere – usually with

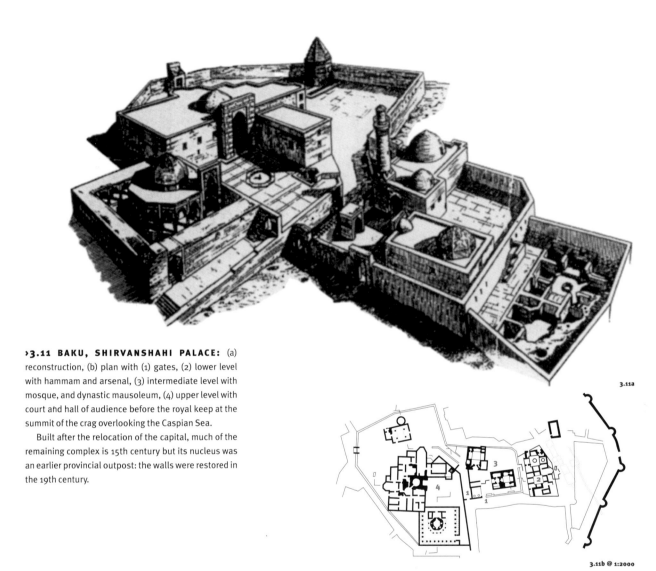

›3.11 BAKU, SHIRVANSHAHI PALACE: (a) reconstruction, (b) plan with (1) gates, (2) lower level with hammam and arsenal, (3) intermediate level with mosque, and dynastic mausoleum, (4) upper level with court and hall of audience before the royal keep at the summit of the crag overlooking the Caspian Sea.

Built after the relocation of the capital, much of the remaining complex is 15th century but its nucleus was an earlier provincial outpost: the walls were restored in the 19th century.

3.11a

3.11b @ 1:2000

twin minaret portals and incorporating the circular or polygonal tomb-tower of the patron, as in the Cifte Minare Madrasa at Erzurum, for example.[1.123]

On the other hand, the domed cube had emerged from the madrasa complex towards the end of the Seljuk sultanate to stand alone as a mosque. The form rapidly achieved dominance throughout Anatolia and proliferated as the Ottoman successors to the Seljuks expanded their empire from their Anatolian base. Squinches sometimes bridged the corner of the square to support the circle but more usual was the faceted 'Turkish triangle' adopted in Konya in place of the pendentive. Porches with groined or domical bays amplified the more important examples. The Sircali or the Hoca Hasan at Konya are representative, the Nebi at Diyarbakr is typical.**3.12**

The late Rum Sultanate, founded on Sunni orthodoxy like its relatives elsewhere, was certainly not devoid of devotees to esoteric *sufi* cults and nor were the beyliks into which the sultanate disintegrated. In particular, official patronage was most favourable to the guilds of artisans and craftsmen involved in the building trade and devoted to the Ahi sect of dervishes (the Brotherhood of Virtue). Their rites involved ritual feasts and entrancing dancing held in domed meeting houses which included accommodation for itinerants (zaviye = khanqah in Turkey). In general, however, as there was no bar for an otherwise orthodox Sunni to acknowledge a *sufi* shaikh as master, the zaviye provided much-needed orthodox teaching facilities and accommodation while catering for the esoteric. The domed cube was the nucleus of the typical zaviye – when its domestic origin in the home of the shaikh was superseded and a more formal version disseminated.**3.13**

Basilicas and hypostyle halls, with or without naves, were still built throughout Anatolia as congregational mosques: the latter might still be roofed in wood but more often both types were vaulted in a variety of ways. The most celebrated example, recalling the venerable model provided by the Umayyads in Damascus and transmitted to Anatolia through the Jazira, is the Isa Bey Mosque at Seljuk (near Ephesos) but its more sophisticated contemporary at Manisa was to mark the way ahead.**3.14–3.16**

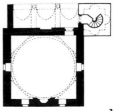

3.12a @ 1:500

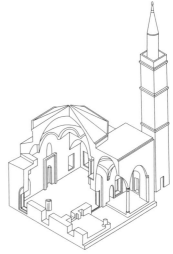

3.12b

›**3.12 THE SINGLE-DOMED PRAYER-HALL:**
(a) Konya, Hoca Hasan Mosque (late-13th, early 14th century), plan; (b) Diyarbakr, Nebi Mosque, cut-away axonometric.

3.13 @ 1:500

›**3.13 TOKAT, KHANQAH OF SUNBUL BABA,**
1291: plan.

BEYSEHIR, ESREFOGLU MOSQUE,
1299: (a) interior, (b) plan.

The venerable timber hypostyle hall, with nave and six aisles perpendicular to the qibla wall, is retained though the building dates from long after the area was familiar with masonry vaulting of various forms.

3.14a

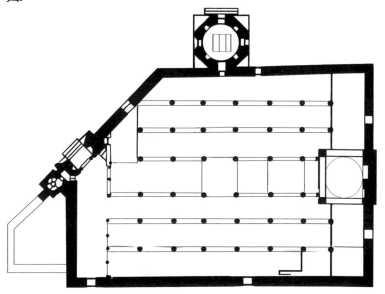

3.14b @ 1:500

3.15a

3.15b

3.15c

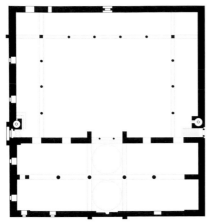

3.15d @ 1:1000

›3.15 SELJUK, MOSQUE OF ISA BEY, 1374:
(a) overview, (b) model (Istanbul, Mimiaturk), (c) portal, (d) plan.

In the work at Seljuk, as in the Great Mosque of Damascus, the aisles are parallel to the qibla wall and cut by a nave – with two domes rather than one. Instead of an iwan, the qibla is marked by a tripartite portal at the head of the court. This was originally surrounded by arcades incorporating columns pillaged from Classical Ephesos and integrated with the prayer-hall façade. The entrances at the junction between court colonnade and prayer hall were marked by minarets: the western portal is outstanding in virtue of its embellishment with abstract geometical pattern in two-toned marble which suggest derivation from Syrian works like the Fidaws madrasa at Aleppo.

›3.16 MANISA, GREAT MOSQUE AND ZAVIYE, 1376: plan.

The near contemporary of Seljuk's Isa Bey Cami, the Manisa work is rather more sophisticated in its plan: one dome covers the nine central bays of a twenty-eight-bay hall (seven bays wide, four deep) and the paired side bays are extended to integrate the court which is virtually commensurate with the prayer hall. The combination of a congregational mosque and a madrasa is far from uncommon but, as Manisa was a dervish stronghold, the extension to the west here was probably a zaviye.

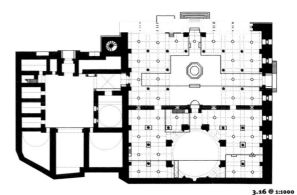

3.16 @ 1:1000

THE OSMANLI BEYLIK AND ITS EXPANSION

An Oghuz *ghazi* band in the service of the Seljuks in Anatolia, themselves hard-pressed at the time by the Mongols, was settled on a *beylik* in north-western Anatolia – on the frontiers of the Byzantine empire. Their chief, Ertughrul Ghazi, was succeeded in 1281 by his son Osman who became a tributary of the Ikhanid Mongols in 1308. The latter held eastern Anatolia until towards the middle of the 14th century, when their regime succumbed to internal dissension and the ambition of provincial rulers: by the 1370s the area was divided between the Qaraqoyunlu and Aqqoyunlu Turks (the Black and the White Sheep). The Byzantine west was prey to the Oghuz forces who were known as Osmanlis – or Ottomans – after Osman had adopted the title of sultan lost to the Seljuks.

Like the late-Seljuks and their successors elsewhere in Anatolia, the Osmanlis had found affinity – in unorthodox religious affiliation, at least – with the guilds of artisans and craftsmen devoted to dervish sects – particularly the Ahi Brotherhood of Virtue. In accordance with their ethos – as well as greed for plunder – they constantly raided Christian lands and expanded their holdings, but if their *ghazi* zeal was irresistible, they were wholly unequipped to administer their gains. They relied on the guildsmen and on their dervishes whose sect mysticism was not entirely alien to the Christians they sought to convert.

Much credit both for expansion and the establishment of a provisional administration is due to the second sultan, Orhan Ghazi (1324–60). He had reduced the Byzantine empire to insignificance in Asia Minor by 1340 and established his capital at Bursa. He complemented the unruly *ghazi* cavalry with a standing infantry consisting solely of impressed Christian youths: the Janissaries (from *yeni cheri*, 'new troops') they were converted, trained in arms and regulated on ascetic lines of celibacy as a dervish sect.**3.17**

Called on for help by a pretender to the Byzantine throne, Orhan's forces effected a bridgehead to Europe and were entrenched on the western shore of the Dardanelles by 1353. Murad I (1362–89) captured Adrianople, which he used as a base for the acquisition of Thrace and penetration deep into the Balkans. His victories were consolidated by the settlement of Anatolian Muslims there. A warrior Turk with the mettle of his most vigorous ancestors, he was strongly inclined towards the dervishes and his most formidable fighting force was their elite corps of Janissaries. However, the very success of the radical dervish officials in providing provisional district administration prompted change: a great empire required a more orthodox form of government – as the *ulema*, to whom the main dervish sects were anathema, would certainly have been among the loudest to proclaim.

On Sultan Murad's death in victory against the Serbs at Kosovo, his son Bayezid (1389–1403) received the submission of Serbia. Religious zeal and incredible mobility sent his army to victory east and west. In 1396 a crusading force of allied European powers under the auspices of the pope was humiliated, Constantinople reduced to a tributary and Greece invaded. Two years earlier Bayezid had

3.17a

›3.17 JANISSARIES AND DERVISHES (16th-century Turkish miniatures).

3.17b

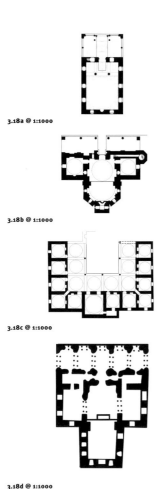

3.18a @ 1:1000

3.18b @ 1:1000

3.18c @ 1:1000

3.18d @ 1:1000

›3.18 EARLY OTTOMAN FOUNDATIONS, PLANS: (a) Iznik, Haci Ozbek Cami (1333); (b) Tire, Yesil Cami (1333); (c) Iznik, Suleyman Pasha Madrasa (c. 1335); (d) Bursa, Mosque of Orhan Ghazi (1339).

been recognized as successor to the old sultanate of Rum by the puppet Abbasid caliph in Cairo. However, progress in absorbing Anatolia led to a clash with the aggressive forces of the Central Asian predator Timur in 1402: the Ottomans were decisively defeated and the sultan taken prisoner. Bursa was burned. The capital was relocated across the sea at Edirne – as Adrianople is known to the Turks. The late-sultan's eldest son, Suleyman, succeeded to power there but he fell to his brother Mehmet who had taken Bursa: under Mehmet I (1413–21) and his son Murad II (1421–51) the empire was restored.

EARLY OTTOMAN BUILDING

If the architecture of the expanding Ottoman beylik differed from that elsewhere in Anatolia it was in its relative restraint and in its overwhelming preference for domed space on rational plans. The influence of Konya is crossed with the tradition of the west where Classical columns remained to be pillaged and Classical rationalism subsisted behind the shimmering veil of Christian mysticism.

The earliest Ottoman mosques consisted either of a single-domed prayer hall entered through a portico or a portico and court with iwans and several domed chambers.**3.18a, b** Madrasas, too, may have a domed nucleus or a cloistered court dominated by an iwan and domed sanctuary. The earliest surviving Ottoman example, built in Iznik by Orhan's son Suleyman, anticipates his line's obsession with the accretion of domed spaces.**3.18c**

Bursa's Orhan Ghazi Cami of 1339 is especially significant: the palatine oratory, it may be taken as introducing – or at least rationalizing – the zaviye type. It incorporates a hospice specifically for the accommodation of the Ahi dervishes patronized by the guilds which sustained Ottoman administration in the expanding empire.**3.18d**

The domed prayer hall is preceded by a similarly domed space in the place of the court and the latter is flanked by a pair of smaller domed transepts which might be used for teaching as well as for lodging (tabhane). This recalls the early Syrian form of single-school madrasa represented at Bosra[1.94d] and is hardly distinguishable from later works like the so-called Lala Sahin Pasha Madrasa at Bursa, except in its absolute symmetry. Moreover, similar planning was certainly not uncharacteristic of the late-Seljuk foundations at Konya and Kırsehir traditionally identified as madrasas.[1.124, 1.125] As we have noted, there was no consistency of type in the accommodation of instruction.

The earliest Ottoman metropolitan congregational mosque, in Bursa, was conservative in its hypostyle plan and even in its multiple domed bays: the culmination of a series extending from the early years of the Rum Seljuks, it was founded by Bayezid I at the end of the first Ottoman century – in 1396. Orhan Ghazi's 14th-century successors had preferred the zaviye of their palatine establishment – as they preferred its dervishes to the *ulema*. As in the Mamluk foundations, the palatine mosque also served – and was supported by – a complex of public utilities which included shops, hostels, food dispensaries and bath houses in addition to the invariable madrasa and hospital.

As in the realms of the Mamluks, again, the early Ottoman complex also usually served a tomb – or, indeed, a necropolis. However, unlike the Mamluks, the Ottomans placed comparatively minor emphasis on tombs, tending to revert to orthodoxy and limit them to canopies open to the sides. The progenitors of the line were provided with domed qubbas but the 15th century reverted to Seljuk precedents, substituting a dome for a cone over polygonal volumes, and escalating imperial pretension was served rather by change of scale than form.[3.19]

3.19a

3.19b

Royal Bursa

A palace dependency, the two-storey Hudavendigar Cami founded at Cekirge outside Bursa by Murad I in 1366 is a highly unusual variant of the T-shaped plan type developed for Orhan Ghazi: its architect admirably demonstrates the non-canonical nature of his craft. Doubtless to mollify the *ulema*, the zaviye formula was developed by his son on two levels: rooms for dervishes flanking iwans on either side of the fountain court below; a madrasa above with cells for the students opening on to a gallery overlooking the fountain court. Domed, the latter rises through the full height of the building on axis with the double-height mosque which, as elsewhere in Ottoman Turkey, projects to the south. The mosque and most of the other spaces are tunnel-vaulted. Byzantine *opus mixtum* is common in the period: layers of brick alternating with courses of stone; arches are

3.19e

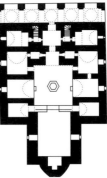

3.19c @ 1:1000

3.19d @ 1:1000

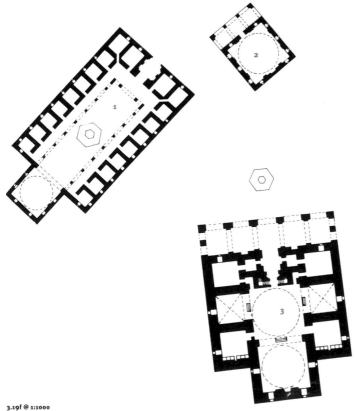

3.19f @ 1:1000

›3.19 BURSA: (a, b) Orhan Ghazi Cami (1339), interior of prayer hall and vestibule detail; (c) Hudavendigar (Cekirge), Cami of Murad I (1326–89), plans of ground and first floors; (d–j) Yıldırım Bayezid complex (1390), madrasa overview, plan with (1) cami, (2) madrasa, (3) turbe; cami portico and interior, shelving in southern side chamber, turbe exterior and interior; (k–o) Ulu Cami (Great Mosque of Bayezid I, c. 1400), model and plan, mihrab, interior and detail of vaulting; (p–u) Yesil Cami of Mehmet I (1413–21), interior, plan, section, royal box detail, general view with turbe left and detail of turbe tiling (page 304); (v–z) Muradiye complex (1421–51), mosque interior and tombs of Murad II and the younger sons of Mehmet I (1430) and of Mehmet II (1479).

3.19g

3.19j

3.19h

3.19i

3.19k

invariably of brick but this building has been much reworked after repeated earthquake damage.

Bayezid I built the twenty-bay Ulu Cami as an ex voto for his victory over Crusaders at Nicopolis in 1396: not without precedent, the central bay provides a fountain 'court' open to the sky through an oculus. In his palatine cami, which also served a charitable foundation, the sultan commissioned the return to the precedent set by his grandfather. However, unprecedented in grandeur and unexcelled for several generations is the magnificent five-bay portico, each bay distinctly framed partly in marble, which rises to the full height of the main spaces within. These, the 'court' and mosque, are separated by a low-slung arch rising from layers of muqarnas over deep niches: the form was henceforth to be identified with Bursa. Both court and mosque are domed but the zone of transition from square to circle is now treated not to octagonal arcading but to a staccato frieze of triangular forms resembling folded paper darts: the motif appears in the Yesil Cami at Iznik slightly earlier. Also noteworthy is the florid shelving (for water pots, perfume bottles, lamps, etc.) in the rooms flanking the iwans. The long, low madrasa is much altered as a clinic. The tomb, erected by the defeated sultan's son and comprehensively restored on several occasions, follows the qubba or mecit (small

3.19m

3.19l

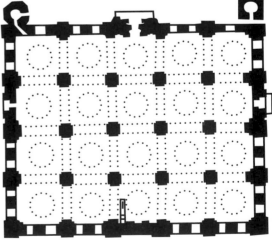

3.19n @ 1:500

3.19o

3.19p

domed prayer hall) precedent set by Orhan Ghazi for his father Osman when his remains were translated to Bursa.

On regaining Bursa after the disaster which had befallen his father, Mehmet I reiterated the domed zaviye associated with royal accommodation and administration offices in his celebrated Yesil complex. Beyond the vestibule, stairs lead up to the royal apartments which include a balcony tribune for the sultan's worship: a novel practical alternative to the maqsura in a quasi-palatial context, this was raised within the entrance iwan and sumptuously tiled. The extent to which tiles were used here was

3.19q

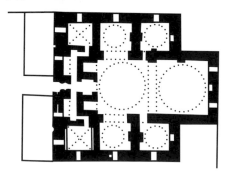

3.19r @ 1:500

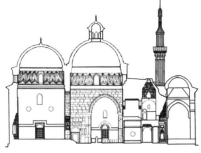

3.19s

3.19t

3.19u

unprecedented in Ottoman domains: the royal box apart, they form a high dado, and emblazon the mihrab with its muqarnas hood. The designer, sometimes identified as Naqqash Ali, is thought to have been taken to Samarkand in Timur's train – or originated there – where he would have seen tiles of both mosaic and panels combined as here. The zone of transition is triangulated.

Mehmet's Yesil complex also included a madrasa, public baths, kitchen and the sultan's octagonal tomb, built to the order of Mehmet's son, Murad II, in 1421. It was in this work that the masjid form adopted by the early Osmanlis was abandoned in favour of the Seljuk formula – distantly recalling the ancestral yurt and, more immediately, the tent in which the warrior sultans spent so much of their time. The splendid green tile revetment was destroyed in the earthquake of 1855 and replaced with some original pieces in a generally turquoise context. In his own tomb, Murad II's sarcophagus was covered by a dome on a ring of columns within an octagon: the motif, deriving ultimately from the Dome of the Rock in Jerusalem, had been adopted for the tomb of Murad I (died 1389) associated with the Hudavendigar at Cekirge and rebuilt after the 1855 earthquake.

3.19v

3.19w

3.19x

3.19y

3.20a

›3.20 EDIRNE: (a) Eski Cami (1403–14, much restored in the 18th and 20th centuries), interior; (b) Uc Serefeli Mosque (1440s), plan.

The Eski Cami was built to the nine-square formula, the central bay in the northern range providing the 'court', the corresponding one in the southern range accommodated the mihrab. Superseding it, Murad II's architect took domed space to the greatest extent yet achieved for his master's line: the sultan had retired temporarily to Manisa and there found the inspiration for that achievement. On a hexagonal arrangement of piers – rather than an octagon, as at Manisa – the dome

The last significant multi-domed mosque of the type perfected at Bursa by Bayezid I was the Eski Cami of Edirne begun c. 1403 by the late-sultan's son Suleyman and finished in 1414 by the latter's brother, Mehmet. However, the main line of development effected a synthesis between the zaviye, with its centralizing domed bay, and the multi-bay ulu form. The overriding object was the amplification of the prayer hall under the clear span of one great dome and its integration with the ancillary spaces.**3.20a**

A significant stage on the way to the realization of the ideal of the heavenly dome on a monumental scale was reached at Edirne in the Uc Serefeli mosque commissioned by Murad II (1421–51). At the beginning of his reign Murad had contributed a splendidly tiled zaviye to the second capital of his dynasty and now emulated Manisa by ordering accommodation for dervishes in the context of a congregational mosque. The integral court with domed arcades was adopted after the example set at Manisa too, but here it is refined and simplified. Integrated spatial elements were to be characteristic of later works but accommodation for dervishes was not. The esoteric sectarian guildsmen were soon to have had their day – as administrators, at least: then, shorn of the Uc Serefeli's tabhane bays, the great space centralized under the dome of heaven was to be the essence of the imperial mosque. **3.20**

Tiles played a key role in the Uc Serefeli mosque's decoration – though they are now depleted. Tiles prevailed

vaulted the most expansive unimpeded space of its time in Turkey at 24 metres: there had been a steady increase from c. 7.5 metres of the earliest Ottoman works to the 15 metres of the Ilyas Bey Cami at Balat of 1404. Instead of the self-contained adjunct at Marisa, the paired domed side bays, accessible from the narthex or the sides, provided accommodation for dervishes and/or students. The scale of the arcaded bays, which form a single cloister around the court, is varied to assert entrances and corners. With three balconies, the minarets at the junction of the narthex and prayer hall (recalling the arrangement at Seljuk) exceeded the highest of their predecessors to different extents. The tile work – originally extensive, now depleted – is in the 'Tabrizi' style introduced at Bursa.

›**3.21 CIVIL WORKS:** (a) Thessaloniki, Cifte Hamam of Murad II (c. 1444), overview; (b) Bursa, Bey Haman (c. 1360), plan; (c) bridge near Aspendos.

The essential features of the bathing complex were a domed hall, often with associated cold pools, a vaulted tepidarium and a cruciform caldarium. When doubled for men and women, the usual arrangement was in parallel suites, as in the 15th-century example from Thessaloniki.

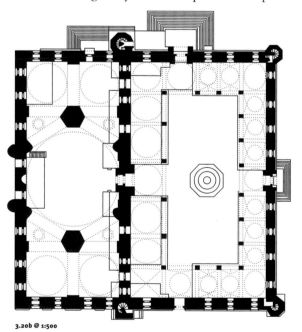

3.20b @ 1:500

3.21a

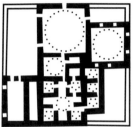

3.21b @ 1:500

over carved relief in the embellishment of the turbe in the precinct. The polygonal type persisted but the proportions were adjusted at the expense of the tower-like verticals and porches were added. The proportions of the minarets were also adjusted to the opposite effect: pencil-shaped, they mark the triumph of rationalism over necessity at the four corners of the court – as Uc Serefeli asserts. Henceforward, Ottoman builders invariably emulated their stout rectangular plinths with battered zone of transition to slender circular – or polygonal – shafts and attenuated conical caps. And, ultimately, four multi-storey minarets were to be essential articulating agents of the imperial mosque.

In or beyond the religious foundations, the most important Turkish civic buildings were bath houses and hans. The former, doubled for both sexes, retained all the facilities of the Romans. Roman aqueducts, restored by Ottoman

3.21c

3.22a

engineers, delivered the water. Roman roads still served but
the Ottomans needed many new ones and their engineers,
emulating the Seljuks, built some of the world's most beautiful bridges.

The Seljuk hans also still served. The Ottoman ones
were generally urban and associated with bazaars: the
courtyard, the inevitable nucleus of the former, was surrounded by accommodation for the merchants and their
stores on two levels; the latter usually had two parallel
ranges of domed bays. However, the early Ottomans are
remembered not primarily for their domesticity but for
their belligerence: the greatest monuments to that are the
forts on either side of the Bosphorus with which they
strangled Byzantium.**3.21, 3.22**

>**3.22 RUMELI HISAR,** 1452: (a, b) view and plan.

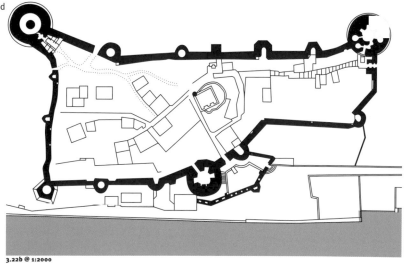

3.22b @ 1:2000

3.23a

Timurid manuscript and book illustration was a major source of inspiration to Ottoman artists not only in the same field but also in the embellishment of textiles and ceramics: the floral motifs were borrowed from the work of imported artists and Chinese ceramics which the Timurids especially prized. Mehmet II (the Conqueror) was personally interested in naturalistic Italian portraiture but his heirs, orthodox in their taste, avoided figural motifs in the decoration of textiles and ceramics: the traditional floral and calligraphic motifs prevailed. Early 16th-century conquests in Safavid domains led to an influx of Iranian artists – reinforcing Chinese influence – but the *saz* style, developed from their approach to floral ornament by local artists of the next generation, is distinctly Ottoman in its representation of composite flowers and elongated leaves on sinuous tendrils which usually cover entire, unbordered surfaces. Tiles painted in this way were a major medium of building revetment.

3.23b

3 OTTOMAN EMPIRE

The Ottomans had regained all their losses by 1420, at the expense of the beyliks whose petty rulers had been resuscitated by the Timurids. There were constant revolts in Europe and Asia, constant threats of invasion from west and east, but militancy and mobility rarely failed. Most of Greece was absorbed by 1446, Hungarian resistance was decisively dealt with at Kosovo in 1448 and Mehmet II (the Conqueror, 1451–81) was able to concentrate on the elimination of the Byzantines.**3.24**

FROM CONSTANTINOPLE TO CAIRO

Constantinople fell on 29 May 1453 and Hagia Sophia – the capital's principal church, the supreme monument of Emperor Justinian – was converted for congregational prayers on the following Friday.**1.25** Having taken the capital of the Eastern Empire, the Conqueror claimed all

Having taken the title of caliph from the last of the Abbasid puppets subsisting in the shadow of the sultan in Cairo, Selim I (1512–20) went on to assert his dominance in the Hijaz and assume the guardianship of Mecca and Medina. Representational tiles were, naturally, not the norm for the embellishment of large tracts of wall which was one of the principal glories of the Ottoman style as developed by Sinan, the architect of Suleyman (the Magnificent, 1520–66).

›3.24 MEHMET II (THE CONQUEROR),
1451–81.

its former territories as the heir of eastern Rome on the time-honoured principle of legitimacy by right of conquest. He and his son, Bayezid II (1481–1512), devoted themselves to consolidating their power over Anatolia and as much of the Balkans as they could reach – as far as Belgrade, in fact.

No longer a *ghazi* prince but a great emperor, the Conqueror could no longer depend on the provisional administrative service of heterodox dervishes. Developing the system of impressing the most able Christian youths to fill the ranks of the janissaries as professional soldiers, he established a college to train similarly impressed youths for civil service: a centralized empire would henceforth be run by a highly centralized professional administration – as it was expanded by a highly efficient professional army. As befitted a quasi-theocratic state in which religious authority was claimed by the orthodox *ulema* established in the capital, the days of dervish sectarian rule were over.

Shi'ism and Persia were the next objective of elimination. The Iranian shah was defeated by Selim I (1512-20) in 1514 – but not destroyed. Having taken most of Mesopotamia and the southern Caucasus, Selim turned on the Mamluks. Syria and Egypt had fallen to him by 1517 and he took the title of caliph from the last of the Abbasid puppets subsisting in the shadow of the sultan in Cairo. He went on to assert his dominance in the Hijaz and assume the guardianship of Mecca and Medina – as well as Jerusalem. But Selim relied on force, not purloined tradition, in his bid to reunite Islam. In this he was thwarted by death in 1520. If he pointed the Ottomans in the direction of their greatest power, he sowed the seeds of decline at his accession by buying the support of the Janissaries.

3.25a

3.25b

APOGEE AND ATTENUATION

Even more perniciously, Selim's successor Suleyman (the Magnificent, 1520–66) inaugurated the rule of the harem by acceding to his favourite wife and executing rivals to the succession of her son. But he took the empire to its apogee: he reached Vienna and forced recognition of his claims to Hungary from the Hapsburg emperor; he

›3.25 SULEYMAN THE MAGNIFICENT ON CAMPAIGN: (a, b) before the walls of Belgrade; (c) besieging Vienna (16th-century Ottoman miniatures).

3.25c

reached Tabriz and forced recognition of his claims to Mesopotamia from the Persian emperor. He forged a first-rate navy, and extended his rule across North Africa. The administration, manned largely by captured Christians specially trained for the service, also reached its peak during his reign. And Suleyman was one of history's great builders.**3.25**

3.26

3.27a

›**3.26 SELIM II** (1566–74) assisted in archery by the power behind the throne.

›**3.27 THE PRIVATE AND PUBLIC LIVES OF THE OTTOMAN SULTAN IN THE LATE-18TH CENTURY:** (a) the harem hamam (J.J.F. Lebarbier, 1785, private collection); (b) the audience court with Selim III (1789–1807) receiving the homage of the notables on a religious holiday (anonymous; Istanbul, Topkapi Museum).

3.27b

Decline began in the later 16th century as fortune favoured neither side consistently in renewed conflict with Austria on the one hand, Persia on the other. Victory no longer regular, the wealth of booty diminished. Wealth from trade diminished too with the opening of the sea route to India and the Persian Gulf. Characteristically, the principal imperial wife was the main power behind the throne during much of the reigns of Suleyman's successors Selim II, Murad III and his son Mehmet III – the last of the sultans to take personally to the battlefield, on the western front in 1596.**3.26** Yet the Ottoman tide was not turned until Murad IV was forced finally to retreat from the walls of Vienna in 1683. His successors retreated further into ritual and the harem: their protracted decadence ended with World War I.**3.27**

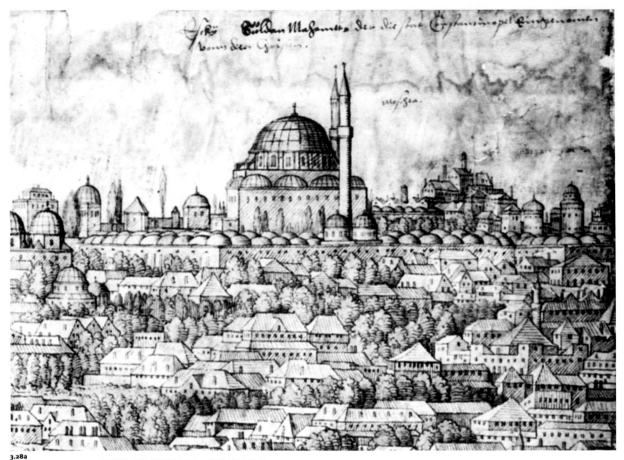

3.28a

THE IMPERIAL MOSQUE

After Mehmet the Conqueror had entered the imperial capital and converted the cathedral of Hagia Sophia, he ordered the construction of a mosque to celebrate his victory: it stood at the centre of a funerary, charitable and scholarly complex which, significantly, accommodated authorities on orthodox Sunni law but excluded *sufi* mystics. The complex was also dedicated to the sultan's interment: the site was that of the Church of the Holy Apostles, the second-most-important Byzantine church, which had been the imperial necropolis. Spectacular

›3.28 ISTANBUL, FATIH MOSQUE, 1463, rebuilt second half of the 18th century: (a) mid-16th century perspective (Melchior Lorichs, Leiden University Library), (b) plan.

Mehmet the Conqueror's funerary complex – with its victory mosque, tomb, madrasas, hospital, hospice, bath-house, food dispensary, caravanserai and bazaar but no khanqah – was built by an architect known as Sinan-i-Atik (the Elder) to distinguish him from his illustrious 16th-century namesake. The mosque was destroyed in the earthquake of 1766 and a similar work replaced it over the original foundations.

The architect extended the Uc Serefeli plan by one range of four bays towards the qibla, inserting the

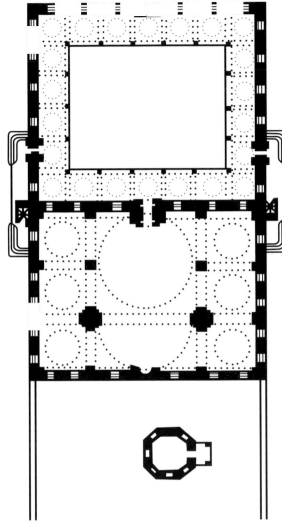

3.28b @ 1:1000

semi-dome in the central pair but leaving the main space open to abrupt transition from the cloister. Carried on pendentives over four piers (rather than the six of the Edirne work), the main dome (26 metres in diameter) was the largest to date in a Turkish mosque.

The madrasas sited to the east and the west of the mosque constituted the imperial college in which the new administrators were to be trained. There was a hospice but no accommodation for dervishes.

siting was to be characteristic of imperial Ottoman mosque builders from the Fatih exercise even beyond the sapping of will and resource for grandiose complexes in the later 17th century.

Furthering the development of the Anatolian qubba, already advanced by the Ottomans, the Fatih design pays homage not to its predecessor on the site but to Justinian's supreme achievement, Hagia Sophia – the inescapable precedent, incomparably sited, for covering the vast area needed for prayer on an imperial scale in an often inclement climate. However, instead of two semi-domes to buttress the central one on the axis of entry, his architect incorporated just one as an expanded bay to house the mihrab. The profile of the dome of heaven was one – inside and out, as in the great model – but the centralized plan was compromised to avoid contradicting the main motive of mosque design: to assert the qibla.**3.28**

After Fatih the splendid masonry revetment of Istanbul's soaring mosque elevations was to be more important than usual in the Islamic tradition which hitherto had favoured the embellishment of the interior. It surpassed the traditional Byzantine brick of the Greek model and the tiles used inside in conjunction with marble panels pillaged from the past were fine alternatives to the Christian mosaics. Marble revetment – supplemented with brilliant multi-coloured tiling – was to be a hallmark of the high Ottoman style.

The inadequacy of a centralized plan was further acknowledged by the beginning of the next century: the second semi-dome of the Justinian model restored the main axis in the mosque of Bayezid II (1481–1512). The original Fatih lost, this is the premier imperial Ottoman centre of worship, standing at the head of an astonishing series in which the subsidiary parts were increasingly clearly subordinated to the whole.**3.29**

3.29a

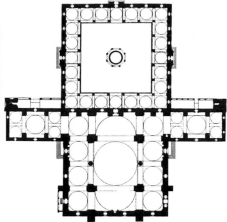

3.29b @ 1:1000

›3.29 ISTANBUL, MOSQUE OF BAYEZID II,
1501: (a) interior, (b) plan.

Built on the site of the old forum of Byzantium, in a district long in need of regeneration and repopulation, the new complex of mosque, schools and public utilities is due to the architect, Ya'qub Shah ibn Sultan Shah. Prayer hall and court are commensurate squares – the former resulting from the extension of the Fatih plan towards the court by one range of bays. Essential to this move was the restoration of the northern hemicycle to the Hagia Sophia formula, redressing the spatial balance and reinforcing the axis of prayer – but not indulging in the lateral differentiation of space so characteristic of Justinian's great work.

Carried on pendentives over L-shaped piers, the dome (17.5 metres in diameter) covers the central four squares. Carried on muqarnas, the semi-domes cover two bays each. The four domed bays to each side are spatially ambivalent: they are assimilated to one another longitudinally as aisles, yet without galleries to divide them in height they belong to a sixteen-part whole, and the middle pairs are screened from the centre dome only by a column. The residual thrust of the central dome is transmitted to piers projecting from the perimeter west, east and south but penetrating the interior to the north where they double as support for galleries.

Unlike his father's resolutely non-dervish Fatih Cami, Bayezid's mosques here and at Edirne (1485) have wings to east and west. At Edirne they were

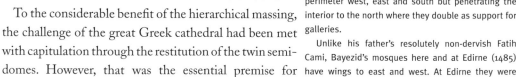

To the considerable benefit of the hierarchical massing, the challenge of the great Greek cathedral had been met with capitulation through the restitution of the twin semi-domes. However, that was the essential premise for

square with a cruciform hall and square rooms in all four corners – like a garden kiosk. Here they extend as tripartite domed halls to some confusion of the axial lines on entrance. In the earlier work the subsidiary spaces were for travellers, rather than dervishes. In the later one, whether or not they were originally partitioned as some maintain, they provided for the withdrawal of visitors from the main theatre of prayer.

›3.30 THE EMPYRAEAN MOSQUE AT ITS SIMPLEST: (a) Istanbul, Firuz Aga Cami (1490); (b) Skopje, community mosque (17th century), domed interior.

The simplest expression of the ideal has one main cubical volume lit by two tiers of windows and covered by a masonry dome carried on pendentives – like the typical Byzantine church dome – rather than the faceted 'Turkish triangle' of Konya. An arcaded portico carried on columns and a single minaret are the only other essentials.

The type was endlessly repeated throughout the empire. The variations are mainly confined to the number of bays in the portico – three, five, seven or nine unless it was extended to the sides of the main volume. More complex schemes, with subsidiary domed chambers, experimented with a variety of polygons in the arrangement of the central piers.

3.30a

advance through scores of metropolitan and provincial variations on the theme of the empyrean, representing the oneness of God.**3.30**

3.30b

The most important of those experiments were furthered by the great Greek architect known as Sinan. Taking the Ottoman tradition to its apogee – above all in his religious works but also in the secular field**3.32** – Sinan presided over the Corps of Court Architects. This was established within the imperial bureaucracy in 1520 to ensure uniformity of style, asserting universal sovereignty, in all metropolitan or provincial works initiated by the sultan or his entourage.

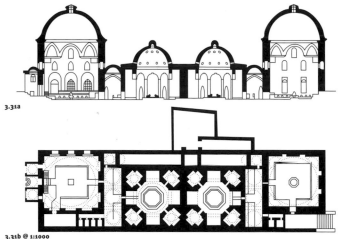

3.31a

3.31b @ 1:1000

3.31c

›3.31 ISTANBUL, HASEKI HURREM HAMAM, 1556: (a–c) section, plan and exterior.

The double formula is preserved but rationalized and the two suites are placed back to back as befits a complex forming the edge of a major public space.

The baths built for Suleyman the Magnificent by Sinan a century later in Istanbul – on the now-open site between Hagia Sophia and the Ahmediye complex – are unusual in their order, with the two suites joined end-to-end.

Despite standardized measurements, the ideal of uniformity was rarely achieved beyond the orbit of the capital. Though the chief architect was responsible for overseeing the projects at the design and construction stages in principal, in practice he had to delegate at least the latter to a subsidiary architect – from the Corps, if possible, but often from the distant building location. The degree of latitude allowed at site varied with distance but obviously the key to control was the dispatch of clearly articulated plans. Rare in Islam before the Ottomans came into their Greek inheritance, they were doubtless difficult for many to interpret and local traditions, developed in response to climate and resources, inevitably prevailed even when the official plans were faithfully followed. Regional variations are hardly negligible but, more even than usual in great empires, the Ottoman achievement is defined by the works of the capital and its vicinity.

The apogee in Istanbul (as Constantinople was named after the Ottoman conquest) is marked by two of the most spectacular mosques ever built: the Suleymaniye of Suleyman the Magnificent, crowning a dominant site in the centre, and the Ahmediye – the so-called Blue Mosque –

of Sultan Ahmed 1 (1603–17), which addresses Hagia Sophia from the other side of the ancient forum, on the site of the Byzantine imperial palace. The first of these is to be fully accounted for only in the light of the series of experiments inspired by the Uc Serefali Cami at Edirne – which Sinan himself furthered most notably in the Sehzade Cami in Istanbul, commissioned by Suleyman in memory of his dead heir (*sehzade*) Mehmed. He continued experimenting after the completion of the Suleymaniye and is supposed to have considered the Selimiye at Edirne his masterpiece: most commentators agree. The Ahmediye must be assessed in that light.**3.32–3.35**

3.32a

3.32b

3.32c

Sinan's legacy

Koca Sinan (1490–1588) was born in Karaman, probably to Greek parents, and was trained among captive youths for the Janissary corps, specializing in the science of building. From c. 1520 he served as an engineer in the armies of sultans Selim and Suleyman as far afield as the approach to Vienna before being appointed court architect in 1538. He spent the rest of his long life designing more than 300 mosques – and much else – for his imperial masters.

Sinan still considered himself an apprentice at work on the Sehzade in 1545. In this, his first major work, he replaced the ambivalent side bays of Bayezid II's mosque with two more semi-domes within a square (38 metres) – after the precedent established a generation earlier by Piri Mehmet Pasha, the last vizier of Selim I – though the centralized domical form had long been observed, especially by provincial mosque builders in Greece. The axis was vertical, from the square of earth to the dome of heaven, and the space was as open as the need for four sturdy piers allowed – in both respects unlike Hagia Sophia, where the axis of procession to grace is asserted horizontally as well as vertically and where sumptuous colonnades screen space in rich diversity for worshippers of varied status. After the pattern of Hagia Sophia, however, the main dome

3.32d

(a) exterior, (b) court, (c) detail of vaulting, (d) mihrab
hemicycle, (e) plan.

To the south of the Sehzade, beyond the qibla hemicycle, is an imperial necropolis – as in the Fatih complex; a madrasa and caravanserai occupy the eastern
section of the compound; the food dispensary shared a
separate site with a school. In the impressive terraced
precinct of the Suleymaniye, the distribution of the
usual facilities – including seven madrasas provided to
accommodate theological lawyers competent 'to
strengthen the mechanism of world sovereignty' – is
more symmetrical than in the Sehzade complex where
the mosque was west of centre.

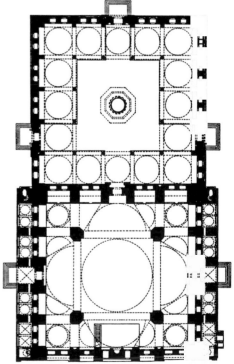

3.32e @ 1:1000

(19 metres in diameter, and nearly 38 metres high) was carried on pendentives, but the semi-domes rise over muqarnas and smaller semi-domes in the quadrants, which act as squinches: the resulting problem of reconciling arches of different heights over undifferentiated supports, real but not revealed in Hagia Sophia, was never to be resolved.

Cylindrical external buttresses simulating towers assist the four great quadrants in resisting the thrust exerted by the main dome. The residual stress is taken by more conventional pier buttresses on the perimeter: external and internal to the east and west where loggias relieve the façades, internal to the north where there are galleries, and external to the south to distinguish the qibla. Lightening the whole in both senses, inside and out the result was supreme in the clarity of its hierarchical ordering – stressed by the alternating red and grey simulated marble voussoirs. The Classical concern with exterior form – and the logic of the cruciform plan – extends to the novel endowment of the sides with colonnades. And furthering order through rational geometry, the court covers an area similar to that of the prayer hall – with which its riwaqs are fully integrated, as was now usual.

The formal perfection of the cross, of supreme significance to the Christian, naturally denied the dynamic of Muslim prayer. Having indulged a Classical will to pure form in his 'apprentice' work, Sinan restored a dominant axis, if not the singular dynamic of the qibla, in his major work for his master, the Suleymaniye. He was lost to confusion in the portico range of the forecourt arcade, where arches of different heights are carried at stepped levels from single columns, but in the main he clarified the relationship of the parts – mass and space – inherited from Hagia Sophia and its reinterpretation for Bayezid II. The central domed space is twice as high as it is wide (53 by 26.5 metres) and, of course, expands to twice its width on both the orthogonals and diagonals.

Building in stone and learning from the structural history of Hagia Sophia's brickwork, no doubt, Sinan obviated adventurous buttressing to achieve masterly concordance between volume and mass, aesthetics and structure, with a strictly limited repertory of autonomous but supportive semi-circular, semi-spherical and cubical forms. The walls to all four sides are punctuated by the massive pier buttresses upon which stability

primarily depends: those to the east and west, revealed inside and out, support external and internal galleries; to the north the great piers are wholly internal and support minor galleries to either side of the main door; to the south they are wholly external and the qibla wall relies on the mihrab and minbar for relief.

›3.33 ISTANBUL, SULEYMANIYE MOSQUE, 1556: (a) model (Istanbul, Miniaturk), (b) plan, (c) exterior view, (d) court, (e, f) interiors.

In its scale and splendid marble revetment outside, brilliant tiles penetrating up into the pendentives for the first time inside, Suleyman's turbe marks the apogee of the canopy type preferred by the Ottoman

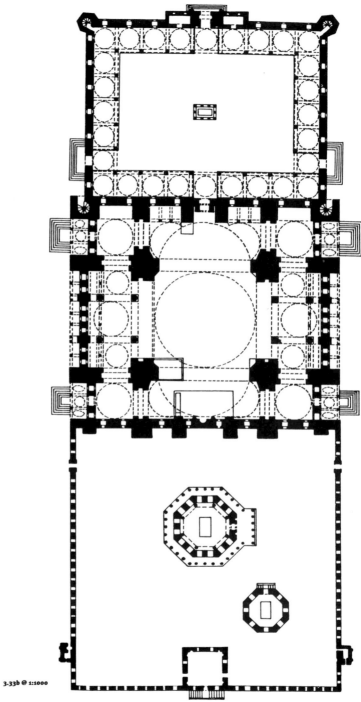

sultans – with specific reference to the Dome of the Rock in its interior distribution. As there, an arcade surrounds the main octagon: within, the double dome is supported on a circlet of columns. Entrance from the east was a departure from precedent followed by Suleyman's 16th-century successors and Ahmed I.

3.33b @ 1:1000

Clarity is enhanced by the exclusion of galleries from the square or semi-circular ancillary spaces but the problem caused by joining arches of different dimensions over single supports recurs in various guises here and disparity is enhanced where the muqarnas corbelling is invaded by the voussoirs of the larger arches. On the other hand, unity is stressed by the alternation of red and white imitation-marble blocks in the voussoirs of all the main arches above a grey dado. Within this architectonic scheme, moreover, the restrained use of tiles above and beside the mihrab sets a standard soon enough abandoned: the interior of the mosque of the vizier Rustam Pasha (1561), in which Sinan was inspired by Ss. Sergius and Bacchus, is almost entirely tiled.

3.33d

3.33e

3.33f

3.34a

3.34c

›3.34 SINAN AND THE PASHA'S MOSQUE:
(a–c) Rustem Pasha (1561), interior, portico, tile detail;
(d–i) Sokollu Mehmed Pasha (1571), vaulting, section,
plan, mihrab bay, exterior, detail of cubicle ceiling.

3.34b

3.34d

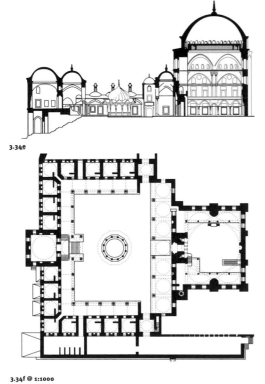

3.34e

3.34f @ 1:1000

3.34g

If the Suleymaniye was the masterpiece of its architect's middle ages, Sinan's career can be seen as culminating in the Selimiye at Edirne. Working on the Sokollu Mehmed Pasha Cami in Istanbul at the same time, he experimented with a return to the hexagonal arrangement of piers which characterizes the Uc Serefeli Cami in Edirne. There in the Selimiye, however, he reverts to the octagon to support a dome which finally rivalled that of Hagia Sophia in its dimensions: the eight great piers are pulled back to the perimeter on the qibla wall, almost to the perimeter on the other sides, to achieve the greatest expanse of uninterrupted space in any Ottoman mosque. The slivers of space between piers and wall east and west are undeveloped, except as corridors, but the shooting of the qibla through the southern pair of piers, opposite the entrance, restores the traditional Muslim dynamic: the mihrab is of marble and restrained tiling complements marble elsewhere in the interior. Outside, red sandstone – mainly in striped courses – relieves the otherwise golden ashlar.

3.35a

3.35b

3.35c

›3.35 EDIRNE, SELIMIYE MOSQUE, 1569: (a) model (Istanbul, Miniaturk), (b) courtyard with fountain, (c) general view from the west, (d) interior of dome, (e) plan, (f) interior.

The four minarets of the Suleymaniye marked the corners of the court. The Selimiye's exceptionally tall, slim minarets – 70 metres high – anchor the four corners of the hall's great canopy. A further subtlety is the grading of the height of the court arcade from the entrance to the portico: as a prelude to the ascending mass beyond, the central bay is the highest.

3-35d

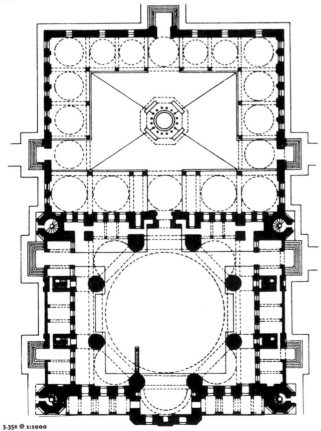

3-35e @ 1:1000

3-35f

›ARCHITECTURE IN CONTEXT »DAR AL-ISLAM DIVIDED

3.36a

›3.36 ISTANBUL, AHMEDIYE COMPLEX, 1609–17: (a) model (Istanbul, Miniaturk), (b) plan, (c) view from north, (d) court, (e) interior, (f) tomb.

The Ahmediye complex, irregular in disposition to cope with its environment, includes a bazaar to the south, a hospital and food dispensary to the west and the madrasa beside the tomb to the east. The turbe departs from the traditional octagonal formula with canopy roof in favour of a cube domed over an inner arcaded octagon and preceded by a three-bay portico in the manner of the smaller mosque type: the interior is lavishly tiled in accordance with the sultan's taste.

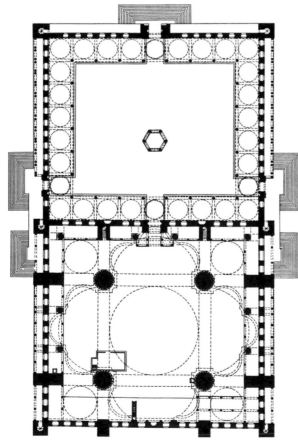

3.36b @ 1:1000

3.36c

3.36d

The Ahmediye, due to Sinan's sometime assistant and ultimate successor, Mehmet Aga (who was also a captured Christian), followed the precedent set by the master in the Sehzade but extended the essential rationalism of the plan to equal rectangles for prayer hall and court. Biaxial symmetry is renounced to a minimal extent to distinguish the qibla wall: that alone lacks a central exedra, galleries and the modulated light of planar variation. The four great piers supporting the dome (23.5 metres in diameter) are unfortunately greater than necessary, visually and structurally, and the imperial resources of the young patron stretched to the provision of six minarets – one at each corner of hall and court, perhaps two too many – but ran short of decorating the domes in a manner consistent with the quality of the dado of superb Iznic tiles, from which the mosque takes its popular name.

3.36e

Both the Suleymaniye and Ahmediye emulate Hagia Sophia in scale, but with different degrees of centralization, and harness the organic vitality exuded by its extraordinary mass over centuries of buttressing. Without sacrificing that vitality but channelling it through an ordered progression of similar forms expanding in scale but diminishing in number, Sinan's Suleymaniye echoed the great domed space and twin apses of his model – and several earlier mosques in the Ottoman capital. After the earlier example set by Sinan, Ahmed I's architect opted for the completely centrifugal aspiration of mass and space. On the horizontal plane of the qibla neither was appropriate for the traditional unidirectional focus of Muslim prayer, but in annexing the vertical plane of heaven they were increasingly successful in asserting the boundless expansion of Islamic faith. And instead of the dematerialized glory of Byzantine mosaic, emblazoned with the panoply of heaven, the garden of Islam's paradise is evoked by Ahmed Shah's celebrated revetment of blue tiles, the ethereal glory of the Ottoman tradition.

Tiles were rarely used on Ottoman exteriors: the revetment of the Dome of the Rock on Solomon's Temple Mount in Jerusalem, ordered with general refurbishment by the great Biblical ruler's namesake in 1545, is the most notable exception. Instead, in the metropolis complete tile

3.36f

coverage was confined to interiors and exteriors were enlivened with a range of imported and native masonry styles. Earliest and most notably, the bichrome masonry of Syria – popular in Mamluk Egypt too, as we have seen – may first have caught the Osmanli eye in the portal of the Isa Bey Mosque at Seljuk before Osman was far removed from his original beylik. Alternating dark and light stone, especially in voussoirs, recurs intermittently in Ottoman architecture: it is notable in the mosque of Murad I at Bursa, for instance, but never more assertive than in the work of Sinan after his return from supervising the construction of his Suleymaniye pilgrimage complex outside Damascus (1555). As a result it seems characteristically Ottoman.

3.37a

›3.37 ISTANBUL: (a) Fountain of Ahmed III (1728); (b) Nusretiye Mosque (c. 1750), (19th-century engravings).

As in France, whose early 18th-century Rococo style of interior decoration was especially appealing to Sultan Ahmed III, comfort and convenience were of prime importance to the affluent and it is hardly surprising that secular works set the general tone – or, rather, that the development seems less anomalous in the secular than in the religious field. The 'Tulip' period saw a proliferation of fountains and it is singularly appropriate that Sultan Ahmed is best remembered for his particularly florid contribution to the development of the genre – apart from some of the more intimate withdrawing rooms in the Topkapi harem.

›3.38 CAIRO, MUHAMMAD ALI MOSQUE, 1822–57: (a) vaulting, (b) view from court.

3.37b

3.38a

3.38b

After their triumph and the apogee of their architecture, the endless repetition of standard formulas in the 17th century was relieved by the introduction of European modes of ornament: as these were borrowed and applied out of context, with little impact on form other than obviating monumentality, the process naturally marked the decadence of the tradition and the first third of the 18th century is aptly dubbed the Tulip period after the favourite flower of Ahmed III (1703–30), whose patronage set a fashion which could only coarsen or atrophy.**3.37** The sequence and combination of styles which marked the age of European eclecticism in the late-18th and 19th centuries all had similar impact on the late-Ottomans, including the return to native traditions. Sinan was not spared: the era began with its most spectacular product, the Muhammad Ali Mosque on Cairo's citadel, whose progress, ironically, marked the loss of the sultanate's grip on Egypt.**3.38**

3.39a

›3.39 **DOGUBAYAZIT, 'PALACE OF ISHAK PASHA',** second half of the 18th century: (a) general view from the east, (b) model (Istanbul, Miniaturk).

Dominating the strategic pass through which the Silk Road entered Anatolia from Iran, opposite an ancient fortress, the palace was the seat of the Cildiroglu magnates, whose power base was in Georgia and who governed the eastern marches of Anatolia below Ararat as quasi-independent potentates. It was begun c. 1750 for Behlul Pasha and virtually completed c. 1790 by his son Ishak: an inscription on the door of the harem section is dated to 1784 (1199 H.). Dominated by the dome and minaret of a mosque, the complex has the usual three palace zones – public, private and harem – but the rectilinear distribution is rather more regular than the traditional hilltop citadels of the Anatolian *beyliks*. However, the main entrance portal descends directly from Seljuk Sivas or Erzerum.

3.39b

3.40a

THE IMPERIAL PALACE

Abandoning the old imperial complex, Mehmet the Conqueror began work on a new palace, the Topkapi, on the
peninsula between the Golden Horn and the Sea of Mar-
mara early in the 1460s. Following in the relaxed tradition
of courts and terraces sympathetically related to the contours of the site – inherited by the Byzantine emperors
from the Roman villa tradition – it grew organically, but
the familiar tripartite division into zones of public reception, private audience and harem prevails. The ubiquitous
enclosed harem apart, the organic development of compounds enclosing tent-like kiosks is the Turkish norm –
but it was not the invariable practice of Ottoman provincial magnates even in Anatolia.**3.39**

Within stout walls defending its exposed but isolated
site from sea and land, the Topkapi has in fact five main
courts – a sports ground, two for military parades and the
gradation of the public seeking audience, and two graded
in privacy – with many pavilions distributed informally
like tents in the camp which normally accommodated the
patron and his most impressive successors on campaigns.
The open spaces overwhelmingly dominate yet, largely
devoid of their original gardens (if not their water or their

superb views), they fail to impress as they must once have done. Little matches the charm of Granada's Alhambra. Indeed the complex's most outstanding asset is the horror of its harem. Entered past the cells of its guardian eunuchs, it is a warren of tight corridors leading to rooms and enclosed courts of varied scale for women of various ranks: gilded incarceration which left its victims with the opportunity for little but intrigue over the succession to the throne. Most Islamic dynasties ultimately succumbed to the debilitating effects of the harem's fetid atmosphere, but nowhere else in the world can one better see why.**3.40**

3.40b

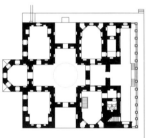

3.40c

3.40d @ 1:1000

Topkapi

To supplement a provisional town palace, Mehmet the Conqueror began his new palace (Yeni Saray) on the ancient Greek acropolis between the Golden Horn and the Bosphorus before the year of conquest was out. At first an encampment of summer pavilions overlooking the water and Asia beyond, it soon extended up the hilly promontory to include winter quarters which superseded the old town palace (Eski Saray) and accommodation for the administrative service. The initial campaign lasted for more than ten years but, of course, there were incessant changes and additions over centuries – not least to keep pace with the proliferation of bureaucrats in accordance with their nature everywhere.

Beyond the Conqueror's Bab-i Humayun, the main triumphal gate with its domed chamber echoing the Chalke of the Constantinian palace (AIC1, page 775), a succession of enclosures encapsulates and isolates the ultimate retreat of power: remote inapproachability was part of the terrible imperial ethos which, from time immemorial, wise councillors had warned their masters to avoid by holding regular public audience. In blatant pretension to world empire, pavilions in the Persian, Turkish and Greek style were built in the outer garden zone and another was projected to represent Italy. The only survivor is the first of these: dating from 1473, it is a hasht behisht with its Persian portico, iwan and revetment of blue, white and yellow tiles – after which it is called the Cinili (Tiled) Kiosk.

Clearly derived from the tent – like the palace pavilions of the Seljuks

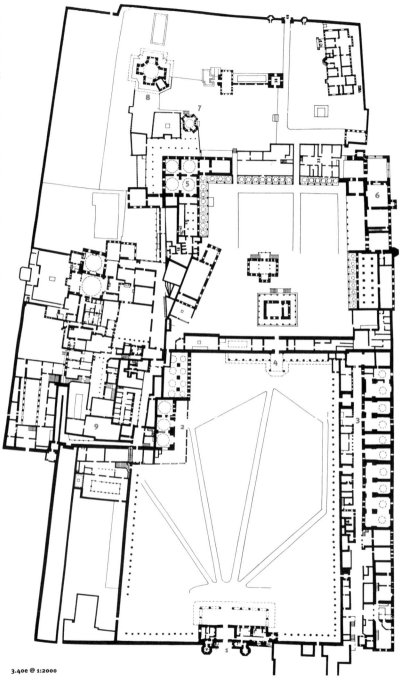

›3.40 ISTANBUL, TOPKAPI PALACE: (a) 17th-century overview, (b–d) Cinili Kiosk (1465–72, original wooden portico replaced in the 18th century), general view, section, plan, (e) plan with (1) Bab al-Salam (Gate of Peace) opening into the second court with the diwan (council hall) and outer treasury (2) on its north flank and kitchens (3) to its south, (4) Bab al-Sa'det (Gate of Felicity) to the third court with the free-standing throne kiosk of private audience (1585) and the Library of Ahmed III beyond, Reliquary of the Prophet (5) and inner treasury (6), (7, 8) Revan and Baghdad Kiosks (1635–38) in the fourth court, (9) harem, (e) second court with imperial portico right, (g, h) third court with kiosk of private audience left of centre and throne, (i) Baghdad Terrace colonnade, (j, k) Baghdad Kiosk, exterior and interior, (l–t) harem, entrance, internal corridor, double kiosk apartments, Hunkar Sofasi (Hall of the Emperor), prince's bedchamber, antechamber, dining room of Ahmed III, baths.

3.40e @ 1:2000

3.40f

3.40g

3.40h

3.40i

3.40j

3.40k

3.40l

3.40m

3.40n

3.40o

3.40p

and so many other Asian rulers since time immemorial – the most important structures in the second and third enclosures are the kiosks for
increasingly private audience: the outer one doubles as the gate between
the two enclosures; the inner one, the seat of one of the most powerful
rulers the world had ever seen, impressed not through grand scale but
lavish furniture and furnishings – especially the jewel-encrusted gold
throne. Most private of all, the third court to the north-east is disposed

for the view from its marble terraces. These are centred on the withdrawing pavilion built to commemorate the capture of Baghdad in 1638: a
variation on the theme of the hasht behisht, it is domed in wood and lavishly tiled.

The harem, straddling the boundary between the second and third
courts, to their north, developed from the Conqueror's early winter quarters: at its greatest it had more than two hundred rooms about forty-four
courts. The central core – if core can be detected in this presumably pre-
meditated labyrinth – accommodated the sultan secluded with his
women. There was a distinct apartment for the Queen Mother (Valide Sultan), who ruled here – as later she ruled rather more extensively. There
were the relatively opulent but painfully restricted chambers of the royal
offspring and their mothers. More painful still, of course, were the cubi-
cles of the host of the childless, hardly to be distinguished even by their
furnishing from the cells of the eunuchs who guarded the claustrophobic
establishment.

3.40r

3.40q

3.40s

3.40t

3.2 THE ORBIT OF IRAN

3.46a

3.41a, b

4 ILKHANIDS

By the middle of the 13th century, as we have noted, most of Asia was divided between the heirs of Ghingiz Khan: his grandson Hulagu had the Seljuk domains which he ruled as Ilkhan ('subsidiary *khan*', 1256–65). He and his followers sustained a nomadic existence, at least for part of the year, but they retained Baghdad as a winter seat. A generation later, Ghazan Khan (1295–1304) embraced Islam and renounced allegiance to the Great Khan: enlightened, his reforms and new-found stability fostered the recovery of the economy. Presiding over the resurgence of Iranian culture from summer seats in western Iran, notably Sultaniya, he and his successors, Oljeitu (1304–16) and Abu Sa'id (1316–35), took the dynasty to its apogee.**3.41**

The Ilkhanids' unruly subordinates were no more able to govern a vast, rapidly amassed empire than the Arabs before them, and equally rapidly they succumbed to it. Traditional tribal rivalries, not least over the succession, undermined unity and former vassals – in particular the Muzaffarids and the Jalayirids in the south and west respectively – asserted their independence. By 1353 the line was extinguished. A power vacuum supervened.

ILKHANID BUILDING

Destroyers and tent dwellers for much of their career, the Mongols have left a limited legacy of building even in early 14th-century Iran where disasters, natural and man-made, have not favoured survival. Converts to Islam, the great Ilkhanids naturally built or extended mosques and the stability of their regime encouraged renewed commerce which was served by new public utilities. However, the greatest memorial to their brief period as settled rulers is the mausoleum of Oljeitu at Sultaniya: rising from a complex of pious foundations – as was the Turkik norm – it is the supreme example of the octagonal type, galleried outside and in, unprecedented in grandeur.**3.42**

Work on the great Jami-masjid in Isfahan was taken up again by Oljeitu who espoused Shi'ism in 1309: its most notable product, the superb winter prayer hall to the north of the western iwan, marks a new interest in the development of an alternative to tunnel vaulting over rectangular spaces which obviated heavy walls and admitted light from the sides: depending on stout transverse arches, the system was also employed for the prayer hall of the madrasa added to the complex in 1366. On the other hand, the sombre later adjunct to the winter facilities has groin vaulting carried on oppressively low-slung arches: rising virtually from the floor, these were doubtless generated by a conception of structural necessity and approximate precedents may be sought in works as early as the Masjid-

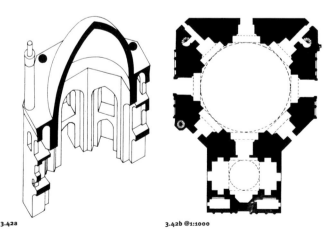

3.42a

3.42b @1:1000

The Seljuks embellished ceramics with a wide range of figurative images[1.81] and in the later stages of their era manuscript illustration was developed at Baghdad. The Ilkhanids furthered the latter practice with reference to Chinese scroll paintings and ceramics: in particular, a treatise on animate nature – including man – was copiously illustrated in c. 1295 for Sultan Ghazan as were several works devoted to recording the past, notably a world history commissioned by the vizier Rashid al-Din in the early 1300s and the *Shahnama* (recording the exploits of celebrated kings) of c. 1330. Formed under the inspiration of Chinese ceramics – among other media – the human, animal and floral motifs were retranslated from paper to ceramics by the artisans employed by the Ilkhanids themselves – artisans who thus played an important part in the design of the tiles used widely for the revetment of buildings for patrons whose eastern origins were alien to the anti-anthropomorphic prejudice of orthodox Arabic Islam.

›3.42 SULTANIYA, MAUSOLEUM OF OLJEITU, dedicated 1313: (a, b) section and plan, (c) exterior.

Following the precedent set by Ghazan Khan in his lost funerary complex at Tabriz, the foundation included a madrasa, khanqah, hospice and hospital grouped around the huge mausoleum (the domed chamber is 25 by 50 metres). Inspired by the domed chambers at Isfahan, Oljeitu's architect goes further than the great Seljuk tomb at Merv. The octagonal plan obviated the problem of effecting transition from square to circle – and the versatility shown by the Seljuks and their predecessors in designing squinches. Eight great arches support an 'entablature' in which the cornice consists of superimposed octagonal and circular rows of muqarnas, masking the disparity between obtuse angle and curve. Glazed brick in contrasting tones of blue is far more extensively used than previously, though painted plaster was still important.

An entrance screen extended the full width of the octagon, below the gallery, to form the north-eastern entrance front and its arcades are continued blind to the sides. The rectangular prayer hall with mihrab projects to the south-west. The blue-glazed dome rises from a shallow octagonal drum, invisible from below, within the ring of eight minarets crowning the gallery.

3.42c

›ARCHITECTURE IN CONTEXT »DAR AL-ISLAM DIVIDED

3.39a

3.39b

PRAYER HALL, c. 1350 or later: (a, b) interior and detail of mihrab (c. 1310?), (c) adjunct (mid-15th to mid-16th centuries).

Inserted to the north of the western iwan, the winter prayer hall was certainly not unprecedented in its roofing with a series of stout parallel transverse arches supporting pointed tunnel vaults. This technique for covering broad spaces in stone without intermediate piers, but allowing clerestory lighting, was familiar in Sasanian Iran and reappeared at Ukhaydir. The most spectacular example from the mid-14th century – perhaps contemporary with the Isfahan prayer hall – is the Han Ortmah/Khan al-Miran at Baghdad.

Arch within arch within rectangular frames, the form of the mihrab is traditional but the embellishment is exceptional. All the mouldings are crisp and similar motifs appear in similar context but their graded calibres distinguish each element: the frame has

3.43c

extremely elegant script superimposed on fleshy arabesques; the arabesques in the spandrels of the large arch are equally boldly cut; delicacy increases to extreme refinement in the tympanum; script dominates arabesque in the inner rectangular frame, then there is a panel of an abstract interlace pattern. Finally, there are arabesques graded from the delicate to the bold in the spandrels, arch and niche of the mihrab itself. The incorporation of the names of the twelve *imams* suggests the work was done after Oljeitu adopted Shi'ism.

i Diggarun at Hazara. They may well also have been inspired by ruins partially obscured by rising ground – as at Balkh**1.61a, b** but doubtless common enough in Iran after the depredations of the Mongols.**3.43**

The essentials for the future of the mosque in Iran had been defined with the introduction of the domed qubba and the four-iwan court by the Seljuks, as at Isfahan, and the formula ultimately found favour all over the Islamic world – as we have seen. The Ilkhanids furthered it in the traditional brick for mosques and madrasas – with important variants, of course. Assertion of the qibla axis was characteristically enhanced by exaggerating the scale of the main entrance and qubba iwans behind soaring pishtaqs lavishly embellished with tiles: the limited number of

3.44a

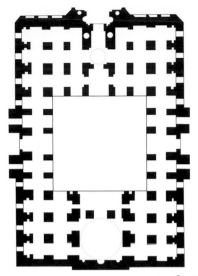

(a) detail of qubba vault, (b) entrance iwan, (c) plan.

3.44c @ 1:1000

3.44b

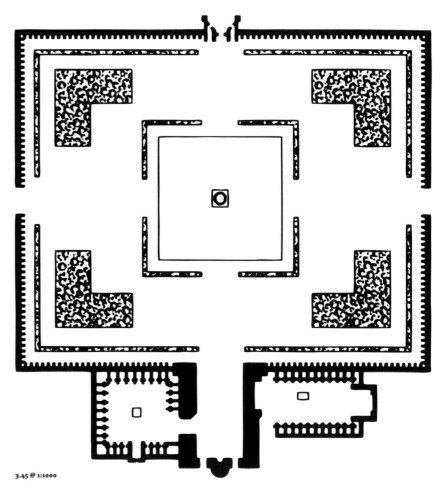

3.45 @ 1:1000

›3.45 TABRIZ, JAMI-MASJID, 1320: plan.

Built by the Taj al-Din Ali Shah Jilan Tabrizi, vizier to the Ilkhanid rulers Oljeitu and Abu Sa'id, this gargantuan exercise seems to return to the concept and scale of the Sasanian palace at Ctesiphon. Gigantism at Tabriz later also extended to experiments with domed spaces.

examples include the Jami-masjids at Varamin, Tabriz and Yazd. At the last site the entrance pishtaq still rises to unexcelled height, enhanced by twin minarets, and marks another shift in the interests of Ilkhanid architects: the spinning of essentially decorative webs of muqarnas over vaulting. It also marks the transition in tile work from the selective underlining of structure to delicate articulation in complete coverage.**3.44–3.46**

There are splended examples too on the smaller scale of the mosque and khanqah. Notable examples of the former

3.46b

A new mosque with a pair of prayer halls flanking the qibla iwan and qubba was begun c. 1330. The entrance pishtaq, between the old mosque and the new, is much restored presumably along the original lines: instead of the strips of rectangular tiles etched into the brick-work to provide a skeletal frame for bonding patterns, tiles were now cut for inlay into a blanket mosaic of floral or geometrical patterns and Kufic script. Naturally this required the traditional blue to be complemented by a range of new colours – black and white, violet, green and yellow.

3.46c @ approximately 1:1000

3.46d

3.46e

3-47a

include the Masjid-i Imami at Isfahan, with its three surviving iwans, and the four-iwan complex of Mir Shams al-
Din in Yazd. Of the khanqahs, the complex surrounding
the tomb of Sheikh Abd al-Samad at Natanz may well be
singled out.**3·47** Reflecting the organic development of the
great shrines of the *imams* at the major Shi'ite pilgrimage
centres, themselves largely rebuilt or re-embellished many
times over later centuries, the accretion of prayer, teaching
and hostel facilities around the tomb of a *sufi* saint was a
common phenomenon throughout the Sunni world – as
we have seen – and it naturally proliferated in Iran in the

**›3.47 NATANZ, KHANQAH OF SHEIKH ABD
AL-SAMAD,** 1304 and after: (a) entrance – mosque
with pyramidal tomb and minaret in the background,
(b) tomb interior, (c) plan.

Certainly not atypical of the Ilkhanid period, particularly at the great Shi'ite shrines, the mosque served as
a madrasa. The tomb of the *sufi* mystic, who had died in
1299, was his cell elevated into the traditional tower for
the purpose when the four-iwan mosque was built in
1304: the somewhat haphazard distribution of the
complex implies the constraint of existing building. The
hostel, now lost except for its richly tiled frontispiece
(restored), was added in 1317. The rich muqarnas are
repeated over the entire vault inside.

3.47b

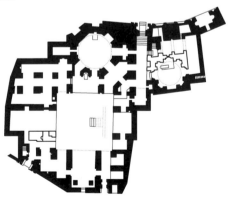

3.47c @ 1:1000

traumatic Mongol era. Tombs were also associated with madrasa complexes, of course. Freestanding tomb towers were still common.

All the rulers of the line lived in sumptuous tent palaces, with splendid audience marquees as well as accommodation for the harem pitched in gardens and private tents for the major members of the suite: they live on, of course, only in the descriptions of contemporaries. Permanent fixtures were rare, apart from extraordinary observatory complexes. However, Hulagu's son Abaqa (1265–82) resurrected a complex associated with the coronation of

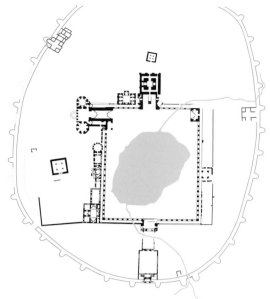

3.48 @ 1:5000

The accommodation, lavishly decorated with marble and tiles, is ranged around a four-iwan fountain court: beyond the northern iwan a domed qubba replaced a similar Sasanian structure – perhaps even incorporating its remains. That was doubtless the hall of public audience – though the Sasanian qubba is sometimes identified as a fire temple. The iwan in the western range – the ruler's private quarters – was displaced from the cross axis to the northern corner where it led to a more commodious hall flanked by octagonal rooms built on the foundations of its Sasanian predecessor.

›3.49 COMMERCIAL BUILDING: (a, b) Zavareh, overview with souk arteries and han (14th century), interior; (c) Yazd, souk interior.

Serving multiple purposes – exchange and public meeting place on festival days – the huge space at Zavareh is vaulted over a grid of stout piers rather than the transverse arches of structures like the winter prayer hall of the great Isfahani mosque,[1.91] or the mid-14th-century Khan Mirjan in Baghdad.

The Yazd souk is comparatively modern but is typical and well represents a tradition at least as old as brick vaulting.

Sasanian kings at a sacred site now known as Takht-i Sulayman. The plan, developed around a four-iwan court like the typical Sasanian palace, has emerged in part from the excavation of the ruin.[3.48]

More substantial are the remains of commercial buildings from the era of Ghazan's reforms and the revived trade which resulted from them: caravanserai, bazaars and hans. The caravanserai retained its traditional form and so too did the souk. Endless renovation and extension of most of these make it difficult to assign any one example to any one period; however, the vaulted shopping arteries and exchanges of the small Iranian town of Zavareh, developed in the first half of the 14th century, may be presented as illustrations of perennial types. The development of Yazd was also furthered in the Ilkhanid era, when the great mosque was rising, and illustrated as typical here too – with much more licence – is the interior of one of its souks.[3.49]

3.49a

3.49b

3.49c

385 ›ARCHITECTURE IN CONTEXT »DAR AL-ISLAM DIVIDED

3.50a

3.50b

5 THE TIMURIDS AND THEIR SUCCESSORS IN TRANSOXIANA

›**3.50 TIMUR:** (a, b) on destructive campaign and (c, d) in audience in his tent palace (16th-century miniatures).

The power vacuum left in central Asia and Iran by tribal rivalries and disputes over the Ilkhanid succession was filled by another firebrand of Turkish-Mongol descent whose passage through history was fully as devastating – if not quite as extensive – as that of his ancestor, Ghingiz Khan. Timur, the new scourge of establishments throughout western Asia, was surnamed Leng ('the Lame'), hence Tamerlane.**3.50**

3.50c

3.50d

TIMUR LENG

This extraordinary figure was born in 1336 of a supposed descendant of Genghis Khan and a Turkish mother at Kish (modern Shahr-i Sabz) near Samarkand in the region then known as Transoxiana. Many adventures and much duplicity led Timur to power at Samarkand in 1370. Proclaiming himself the restorer of the Mongol empire, he challenged the *khans* of the Golden Horde – which had taken Russia in the 1230s – and occupied Moscow in 1380. Constantly campaigning, he then turned on chaotic Iran. Khorasan and the other eastern provinces were his within two years, most of the rest by 1387. Pushing on through Mesopotamia, he destroyed Baghdad as a seat of rival power and was dominant in the Caucasus by 1395.

Much of what had survived the Mongols – preserved by their more civilized Ilkhanid descendants – was destroyed by Timur. Rebellions in Persia attracted particularly savage vengeance. So too did the Tughluq sultans of Delhi: Timur cut a swathe into India to destroy both city and sultanate in 1398. The Mamluks of Egypt and the Ottomans of Turkey were the next prey: the former were defeated at Damascus in 1400, the latter in Anatolia in 1402. Egypt and Byzantium offered submission and Timur turned towards China, but died on the way in 1405.

Meanwhile, in his Transoxianan heartland he invested fabulous booty in the commemoration of his imperial career by building on an unprecedented scale – and like Turks triumphant elsewhere he commemorated himelf in a grand funerary complex with madrasas and khanqah. He and his successors also retained a corps of chroniclers whose accounts – supplemented by less-flattering reports from outside – are invaluable for constructing images of much that has been lost.

Timur assigned Herat and eastern Persia to his son Shahrukh, Tabriz and the west to his son Miranshah, and Fars and the south to his grandson Pir Muhammad. Miranshah died in 1407 and Shahrukh managed to unite east and west after a protracted struggle. He fostered prosperity and his wife, Gawharshad, took Herat and Mashad to new brilliance in reparation of the waves of destruction visited on them by the Mongols and Timur – as on so much else. At Herat, Shahrukh groomed his grandson, Abd al-Latif, son of the learned Ulugh Beg who was the equally enlightened governor of Transoxiana and embellisher of Samarkand: his observatory there is perhaps his dynasty's most extraordinary legacy.[3.51] After Shahrukh's death in

›3.51 SAMARKAND, OBSERVATORY OF ULUGH BEG: c. 1429.

Originally cylindrical – in the most plausible reconstruction – the structure accommodated a sextant on the north–south diameter (48 metres) for the observation of the elevation of the stars. The superstructure was destroyed by the antipathetic *ulema*: the remains consist of the base of the cylinder imprinted with rooms of widely diverse shape and the great subterranean sextant inset with calibrated strips of polished stone.

1447, Ulugh Beg lasted for only two years before his assassination at the hands of Abd al-Latif, who was himself assassinated in 1450.

PALACES

The Timurids added to the stock of caravanserais and the usual civic amenities – some of which survive in part. However, little of substance survives of their most important secular works: apart from fabulous tent-palaces,**3.52** they too favoured transitory seats of reticent brickwork clothed in the opulence of carpets and canopies carried on

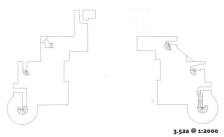

3.52a @ 1:2000

›3.52 THE SEAT OF POWER IN THE TIMURID ERA: (a–c) Shahr-i Sabz ('green town'), Akserai ('white') Palace, plan, remains of iwan and detail of revetment; (d, e) royal camp and ephemeral city palace.

Much of the site remains to be thoroughly examined and reconstructions of the plan depend on conflicting contemporary descriptions. Recalling the age-old portal of epiphany, the remaining structure (22 metres wide between round towers) may have been the main entrance or – more likely – the throne hall iwan pf the palace's main block. It was covered with glazed-brick and multi-coloured tile panels.

3.52b

3.52c

3.52d

3.52e

timber. Exceptionally, the Akserai palace at Timur's birth-place and designated capital, Kish, seems to have followed the four-iwan court tradition descending from the Parthians.[1.20] One of the iwans survives in part: huge, it is the earliest-known example flanked by minaret-like towers rising from the ground instead of perched on an applied frontispiece (pishtaq).**3.52b**

By contrast, the Bagh-i Maydan palace at Samarkand – the ultimate capital – seems to have consisted of pavilions in a succession of walled gardens divided by canals into four squares (chahar baghs): an image of the earthly paradise whose square plane is divided into quarters by four rivers flowing in the cardinal directions from the source of the waters of life in the centre, as we have seen. The Spanish ambassador to Timur's court, Gonzales de Clavijo, related the Bagh-i Maydan to the tent palaces of the monarch on his campaigns – which, of course, descend from the tent palaces of the Achaemenids (AICI, pages 209ff.).

The Timurid prince, Babur, later Emperor of India, describes the most celebrated element of the Bagh-i Maydan, the chihil sutun ('many-columned' pavilion), as square with corner towers and four two-storey portals which led to a cruciform central hall. This was a latter-day apadana derived from the ancient Achaemenid tradition. Babur also describes the Tareb Khana in the palace at Herat as having four subsidiary chambers on the diagonals in addition to vestibules on the main axes. This represents the garden-palace building type known as hasht behisht ('eight paradises'), no doubt because of the eight splendidly embellished chambers opening from the central octagon.

The earliest Timurid funerary complex of note was built by Timur for the *sufi* sheikh Ahmad Yasavi in Turkestan: the formal design, executed in accordance with a new imperial standard of measurement, provides rooms for prayer, teaching and accommodation to either side of the axis aligning the vast entrance iwan, a great domed central hall and the domed tomb chamber. This was nearing completion in 1399.

Early in the new century Timur began work on another complex associated with a khanqah at Samarkand and

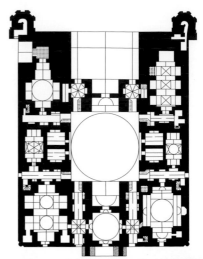

3.53a @ 1:1000

3.53b

›**3.53 YASI (TURKESTAN CITY), SHRINE OF AHMAD YASAVI,** c. 1395: (a) plan, (b) detail of interior.

Like the tomb, the rooms for preaching are beyond the iwan in each of the four sides of the central domed cube and a variety of halls for the accommodation of disciples (including a mosque) in the corners.

assigned it to his grandson, Muhammad Sultan, who died in 1402: finished towards the end of 1404, it received Timur himself less than three months later and then became the dynasty's mausoleum. The Shah-i Zinda developed around the martyrium associated with one of the Prophet's cousins, Qutham bin al-Abbas (reputedly killed here in 677), is another dynastic necropolis – particularly for the royal women. A further important funerary monument in Samarkand is the Ishrat Khana, attributed to Habiba Sultan, principal wife of the late Timurid ruler Abu Sa'id.**3.53–3.56**

›3.54 SAMARKAND, GUR-I MIR, 1404: (a, b) plan and section, (c) view from the south-east, (d, e) exterior and interior of the dome.

3.54a, b @ 1:1000

The Timurid dynastic mausoleum

The Gur-i Mir – as Timur's tomb is known – consists of iwan and domed chamber (qubba), octagonal outside, square inside with the arms of a Greek cross projecting through iwans from the square – a domed version of the courtyard of the funerary complex of Sultan Hasan in Cairo.**3.6i–n** Over the tomb chamber – rebuilt to a greater height than originally planned – a high drum with an exaggerated inner cavity raises the novel semi-bulbous ribbed outer dome way above the inner one. The addition of a madrasa to the north in 1434 altered the original front, but the minarets were detached from the iwan frontispiece and placed at the ends of screen walls. Much of the original brickwork survives on the other three unencumbered sides. Tiles – or rather glazed bricks – are used sparingly to form an irregular diagonal grid on the main walls. The drum has a huge Kufic inscription in multi-coloured tile panels and the dome is blue: glazed

3·54c

3.54d

3.54e

bricks or panels were cheaper than mosaic and practical for the revetment of walls but most curved surfaces required mosaic. Inside, a dado of hexagonal tiles in alabaster is surmounted by a band of script in jasper. The suspended vault is painted ostentatiously in blue and gold.

Exaggeratedly high drums and/or frontispieces were to be as characteristic of Timurid tombs as bulbous, cannellated domes. This is admirably illustrated in the Shah-i Zinda street of tombs on the outskirts of Samarkand. Addressing an artery in close proximity, most of the traditional qubba structures have spectacular pishtaqs decorated with blue-, white- and yellow-glazed tiles moulded to produce patterns in low relief. Square or octagonal, the sumptuously tiled cenotaph chambers are

3.55a

›ARCHITECTURE IN CONTEXT »DAR AL-ISLAM DIVIDED

3.55b

3.55c

›3.55 **AFRASIAB (SAMARKAND), SHAH-I ZINDA NECROPOLIS:** (a) central section of 'street' with tombs of Timur's sisters Chujuk and Shirin Bika (1380s) left and the Turkan-aka of Timur's niece (1372) right; (b) view from the south with portal of Ulugh Beg right foreground (c. 1434) and the tomb of unknown women formerly assigned to Ulugh Beg's astronomer Qadizada Rumi (1430s) left; (c) Chujuk Bika's façade; (d) plan with (1) south gate, (2) tomb of Timur's sisters, (3) Turkan-aka, (4) shrine of Qutham ibn Abbas; (e, f) general view and detail of pishtaq of late-14th-century tomb beside the shrine of Qutham ibn Abbas.

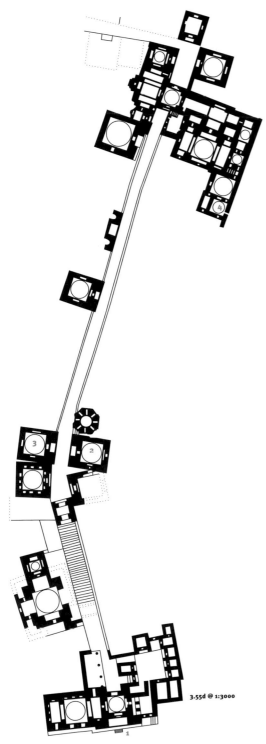

3.55d @ 1:3000

3.55e

3.55f

usually covered with semi-circular or octagonal domes: anticipating the Gur-i Mir, the early ones are cannelated; following it, the high drums of the later ones distance the inner and outer shells. Drum and dome often rise high enough over the pishtaq to impress the viewer in the 'street' and are therefore also sumptuous in their revetement. In general, tile work progresses from multi-coloured panels to mosaic.

The Ishrat Khana elsewhere in Samarkand was an extreme example of extended elevation, elaborate to an extreme beyond structural necessity in its crossed rib vaulting. The complex plan suggests the tomb was designed for numerous family members: the rectangular hall to the west may have been for obsequies, the central and subsidiary domed chambers would doubtless have contained cenotaphs, the actual burial sarcophagi would have been in the crypt. A further elaboration of the plan, providing oblong halls to all four sides of a square central space and square rooms in the corners, was devised for Abu Sa'id's son Ulugh Beg Miranshah, king of Kabul (1469–94).

The Ishrat Khana's saucer dome and the tall blind drum of the outer dome are carried on a lattice vault generated from the combination of square and Greek cross: the arches framing the outside and inside of each arm are echoed, amplified, across the main space between the imposts of their neighbours; to support the central dome a network of fragmentary arches connects the main ones forming a staccato series of triangular and lozenge-shaped squinches which echo the lower ones in the corners between the arms. The lattice of ribs diminishes the size of the central lantern vault: the superstructure is consequently lighter in weight and selected membranes between the ribs may be left void to admit light, dramatically.

The idea of the lattice vault may have developed from the transverse ribs supporting roofs over rectangular spaces like the winter prayer hall in the Jami-masjid at Isfahan. Responding to the cruciform plan, the motif seems to have been tested c. 1417 in the tomb chamber of Gauhar Shad's madrasa at Herat. This, in turn, developed a theme stated on a small scale in the side chambers of the Yasavi complex in Turkestan: the main domed chambers there, though also cruciform in plan, were covered with extremely intricate muqarnas.

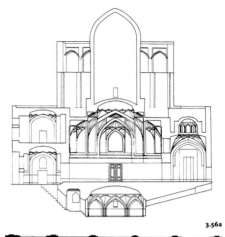

3.56a

3.56b @ 1:500

›3.56 SAMARKAND, ISHRAT KHANA, c. 1460: (a, b) section and plan.

3.57a

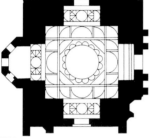
3.57b @ 1:1000

›**3.57 HERAT, GAUHAR SHAD MADRASA,** 1417–38: (a) interior of tomb vault, (b) plan.

›**3.58 SAMARKAND, BIBI KHANUM MOSQUE,** begun 1399: (a) plan, (b) overview; (c) remains from the south.

Bibi Khanum was Timur's mother-in-law, but the Spanish ambassador Gonzales de Clavijo's record implies that the mosque that bears her name was founded by Timur himself as the Jami-masjid of his capital. The current comprehensive restoration and rebuilding programme involves much retiling.

The ruins of the vast entrance iwan (18 metres wide and more than 30 metres high) still dominate much of Samarkand. The court (c. 75 by 65 metres) has four iwans, the main one on the qibla (the axis of prayer towards Mecca) only marginally smaller than the entrance and like it flanked by minarets rising from the ground, as was the Timurid norm. Clavijo records that Timur had it rebuilt because the original design was not high enough: rebuilding to an enhanced scale is suggested by the disparity between the qibla frontispiece and the sanctuary dome behind it. To either side of the qibla iwan, subsidiary iwans without pishtaqs lead to novel rectangular prayer halls with high ribbed domes.

MOSQUES AND MADRASAS

The depleted remains of the mosques and madrasas of the Timurids, built by architects and craftsmen pressed into Timur's service from all over his conquests, reveal the influence of their predecessors in distribution and form. The predominant four-iwan plan imposed a symmetry ubiquitous since the Seljuks, but the gigantic scale of the Bibi Khanum Mosque in Samarkand, like that of the palace at Kish, is Timur's own.**3.58** The later Timurids hardly matched the scale.

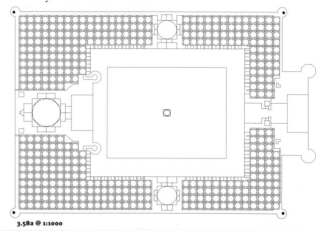
3.58a @ 1:1000

3.58b

3.58c

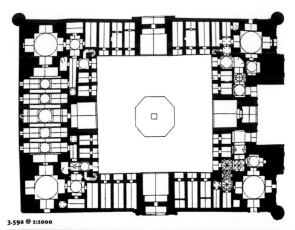

3.59a @ 1:1000

3.59b

begun c. 1417: (a) plan, (b) exterior.

In the manner now typical of the Timurids, the generous entrance iwan occupies most of the front of Ulugh Beg's madrasa, but the minarets are applied to all four outer corners rather than to the generous pish-taq (35 metres high). Smaller iwans, flanked by cells behind a single grand arcade, address the court (30 metres square) on its main axes. Beyond the qibla iwan, the mosque is an elongated hall communicating with a pair of cruciform domed chambers. Similar chambers fill the outer corners and these, at least, were probably meant to carry ribbed domes like the Shir Dar madrasa opposite.

Ulugh Beg founded the Bukhara madrasa – smaller but rigorously symmetrical about a two-iwan axis – at much the same time as his great Samarkand work.

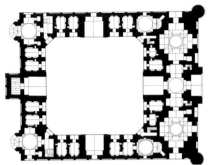

3.60b

›3.60 KIRGIRD, GHIYATHIYYA MADRASA,
1445: (a) plan, (b) detail of vault.

The shrine of Imam Reza in Mashhad was endowed with a mosque by Gauhar Shad (c. 1310) which was notable for its superbly tiled two-storey internal arcading – more like a madrasa than a mosque. Indeed, apart from the renovation of existing mosques, most of Timur's successors devoted themselves primarily to providing facilities for worship in the context of the madrasa or khanqah: the complex often embraced the patron's tomb – freestanding funerary monuments are rare in the period. Large scale was characteristic and rational planning about the four-iwan form was the norm but the madrasa formula allowed variation in the placing of the mosque and lecture halls. Corners were typically stressed with minarets. The most notable examples were built c. 1417 for Gauhar Shad at Herat and Ulugh Beg on the Registan at Samarkand and at Bukhara.**3.57–3.59**

As Ulugh Beg's building on the Samarkand Registan shows, mosques and madrasas are often difficult to distinguish until the interior is penetrated: then, of course, the complex prayer, teaching and residential requirements of the madrasa are apparent – as is the ingenuity of their planners in distributing their essential elements, particularly the collegiate mosque. Gauhar Shad's Herat complex is lost – except for her tomb – but Ulugh Beg's Registan work displays a new concern with symmetry in its precisely square court, its similar iwans, the centrality of its mosque behind the qibla iwan and its identical corner chambers. Later builders experimented with alternative means to the same end. The Ghiyathiyya madrasa in Kirgird (c. 1445) for instance, set a precedent for the complex development of the entrance range: the mosque was brought forward to the right wing and balanced on the left with a cruciform lecture hall which differs only in the design of its vaulting and the modulation of its light; moreover, the corners are canted and provide diagonal access to the chambers beyond.**3.60**

After the Bibi Khanum example, pishtaqs framing entrances generally screened most of the façade and were flanked by minarets rising from the ground. Domes tended to be bulbous and obscured by the pishtaq despite enhanced drums. Muqarnas proliferate in arches, in addition to interlaced ribs developing net-like zones of transition after the Ishrat Khana.**3.56** Far more surfaces than heretofore are covered with geometrical or floral patterns in predominantly blue-glazed tiles. Yet the decorative use of structural form notwithstanding, colour and pattern are increasingly subject to, and reinforce, structural lines – unlike the jagged pattern which ramps over the exposed surfaces of the Gur-i Mir.**3.54**

In western Iran the major monument surviving from the brief period of Qaraqoyunlu domination is the so-called Blue Mosque at Tabriz (1465). Like Timur's work for Ahmad Yasavi, the qibla is distinguished by a succession of domed spaces: an entrance vestibule within an iwan, the normally open court with putative iwans to all four sides and the cruciform prayer hall. The complex built by Uzun Hasan to surpass this work of his rivals has disappeared but some idea of its magnificence is conveyed by the extensive renovation of the mosques in his domain – most notably the Jami-masjid of Isfahan – and the Isfahani Darb-i Imam founded by the Qaraqoyunlu Jahanshah (1438–67).**3.61**

The great palace laid out at Isfahan for the Aqqoyunlu leader survives only in contemporary records: the description of one of its garden buildings as a domed chamber open to four rooms on axis and four in the corners identifies it as a hasht behisht like the Tareb Khana which the emperor Barbur saw at Herat. Another building of the type is the Cinili Kiosk in Istanbul: the plan form was doubtless taken to Anatolia and on to Istanbul by Turkomen craftsmen. Most significantly, the adaptation

›3.61 WORKS OF THE QARAQOYUNLU SULTAN JAHANSHAH: (a, b) Tabriz, Blue Mosque (Masjid-i Kabud, 1465), plan and detail of tiles; (c) Isfahan, Darb-i Imam (1453), portal.

The mosque originally served the Muzaffariya complex of khanqah and tomb built for the wife of the ruler Jahanshah (1438–67) who led the Qaraqoyunlu into the area: the date is given in an inscription over the portal. The central domed space (52 by 34 metres) – overwhelmingly dominant, unlike the central space in the domed mosques of Bursa – is enclosed in an ambulatory of small domed bays. The mosque takes its name primarily from the superb blue tiles, stencilled in gold, which clothed the prayer hall.

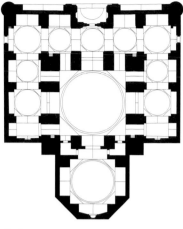

3.61a @ 1:1000

3.61b

3.61c

of the type for a tomb is represented by the once-richly embellished shrine of the *sufi* saint Khwaja Abu Nasr (died c. 1460) at Balkh.[3.62]

TURKOMEN RIVALRY RENEWED

After the assassination of Abd al-Latif, assassin of Ulugh Beg, confusion reigned in the Timurid domains for nearly two decades. The Timurid princes Ahmad bin Abu Sa'id and Husayn Baykara managed to retain Transoxiana and Khorasan respectively from 1469 but they were constantly menaced by yet another band of virile warriors, Uzbek Turks who claimed descent from Ghengis Khan through his oldest son Jochi's youngest son Shiban. Herat was sustained as the imperial capital, greatly augmented with religious and secular monuments, until Husayn Baykara was killed in battle with the Uzbeki Shibanids in 1506: war and earthquake have left only tantalizing fragments of the glory and even some of these were lost to the refabrication of the Jami-masjid in the mid-20th century.

Meanwhile Iran was the goal of the rival confederacies of Turkoman tribes known as the Black and White Sheep (Qaraqoyunlu and Aqqoyunlu), who had penetrated into

3.62a

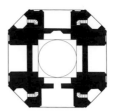

3.62b @ 1:1000

the area from Anatolia early in the 15th century. The Aqqoyunlu ultimately emerged predominant under Uzun Hasan (1453–78) but excited the opposition of the Ottomans and lost the empire to chaos in the west.

SHIBANIDS

While the Qaraqoyunlu and Aqqoyunlu were fighting over Iran, Transoxiana was left open to the Shibanids to establish their neo-Ilkhanid regime. Samarkand fell to them on the death of Sultan Ahmad in 1497 – despite the efforts of his nephew, Prince Babur, who went on to India instead. Herat was theirs in 1506. However, they ruled principally from Bukhara from about 1500 and maintained a subsidiary *khan* at Balkh. In about 1600 the Tuqay-Timuruds – similarly descended from Jochi's son Tuqay – assumed sovereignty and sustained it in unity or division for more than a century. Both lines of *khans* ruled through amirs, Mongol tribal elders, who led both the bureaucracy and the army.

Turkik and Sunni, the regime fostered orthodox scholarship and *sufi* mysticism. Hence, though splendid mosques were built to replace earlier losses, patronage primarily focused on the construction of madrasas and khanqahs, often in complexes incorporating earlier works: contrary to Ilkhanid and Timurid precedent, but as in contemporary Iran, grand mausoleums ceded to relatively modest tombs enveloped in saintly or scholarly *baraka*. And, as the regime benefitted from the revival of trans-Asian trade with prosperous Iran and emerging Russia, there was considerable wealth to lavish on that patronage in the central cities of the Silk Road and its tributaries – Bukhara, Samarkand and, later, Khiva.

>**3.63 BUKHARA, CITADEL (ARC):** (a) detail of Jami-masjid entrance, (b) entrance from the west.

3.63a

3.63b

›ARCHITECTURE IN CONTEXT »DAR AL-ISLAM DIVIDED

BUKHARA

The *khan* ruled from the citadel beyond the western wall of the roughly square inner city. Roughly perpendicular arteries, dividing the old town into quarters, drew development out in the cardinal directions – across the arm of the Zarafshan River to the south and well beyond its banks to the east and west. Under *khans* Ubaydallah (1512–40) and Abd' al-Aziz (1540–50), the sprawl was contained and the suburbs defended by a new ring of ramparts. The arteries of the old town were regularized as monumental building – religious and civic – made its impact in the second half of the 16th century and when suitable sites there were no longer available, new development provided nucleii of order in the suburbs. The first of these, beyond the outer walls of the citadel, was provided by a commercial forum and parade ground (registan) of the type represented by the old maidan near the Jami-masjid at Isfahan.**3.63**

Prosperity saw the proliferation of commercial buildings: caravanserai, offering the usual facilities with or without courts; warehouses (tim), of which the best examples are square with a domed central hall surrounded by smaller domed bays; bazaars, suites of domed bays with grand domed junctions where the richest products were

3.64a

3.64b

›**3.64 BUKHARA:** (a, b) souk and urban caravanserai (late-19th-century photographs); (c) Goldsmith's Dome; (d, e) merchant house, talar and court, reception room; (f) plan of central spine with (1) Kalyani-masjid, (2) Mir-i Arab Madrasa, (3) Ulugh Beg madrasa, (4) Abd al-Aziz Khan Madrasa, (5) Goldsmiths' Dome, (6) caravanserai, (7) Tim Abdullah Khan (exchange), (8) Hatsellers' Dome.

Around 1570 the main north–south artery of the bazaar was ordered for some 650 metres and punctuated with three central domed bays (chahar suq) for the goldsmiths, the hatters and the moneychangers.

In the most opulent merchant houses in Transoxiana, as in Iran, the court was addressed by a talar instead of an iwan.

3.64c

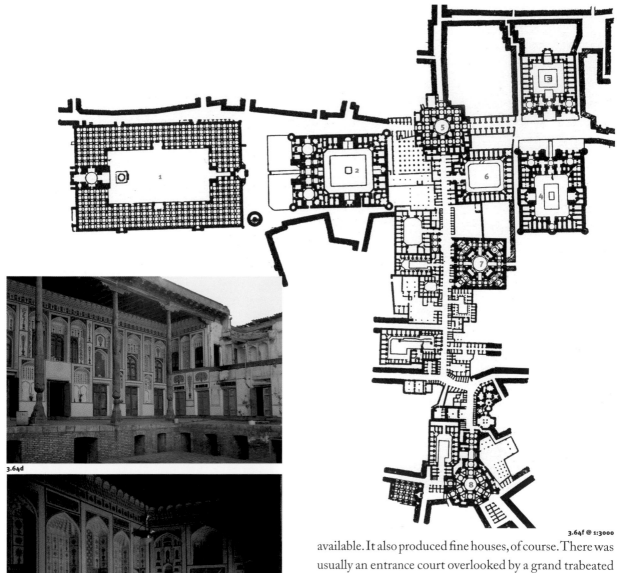

3.64f @ 1:3000

3.64d

3.64e

available. It also produced fine houses, of course. There was usually an entrance court overlooked by a grand trabeated portico (talar) before the reception rooms and a private court surrounded in part by accommodation on one or more levels, the main one including reception rooms to impress clients. The talar was ubiquitous: it was the major feature of both religious and secular buildings.**3.64**

3.65a

Stating his credentials in no uncertain manner at the
outset of his regime's career in the patronage of monumental buildings, Ubaydallah Khan renovated the great
Kalyani congregational mosque near the centre of the old
town on a scale to rival all but the most grandiose works
of Timur. Facing the mosque from the east on the important site at the perpendicular crossing of the two main arteries, the Mir-i Arab Madrasa was built for the *sufi shaikh*
Sayyid Mir Abdullah, towards the end of the reign. It was

›**3.65 BUKHARA, KALYANI MOSQUE,**
founded 1121 in association with the great minar, renovated from 1512: (a) court towards qibla, (b) entrance
pishtaq.

3.65b

the first in a series of such works: its most notable successors include those of Abdullah Khan and his mother (begun 1565), of the amir Qul Baba Kulkaltash (1569), of the amir Nadr Divanbegi Arlat's (1620) and – addressing the same tank – finally of Khan Abd al-Aziz (1652). There were numerous khanqahs in the city but Bukhara's most important *sufi* shrine was the Char Bakr beyond the new walls to the west.**3.65, 3.66**

The great works of Bukhara

The court of the great mosque (77 by 40 metres within a compound of 130 by 80 metres overall) is framed by single-storey arcades punctuated by four iwans of which the largest opens to the qibla qubba, as in the Isfahan Jami-masjid: in all 12,000 worshippers could be accommodated. The decoration is restrained: polished brick, with inset tiles outlining structure.

From the outset of their career as patrons in Bukhara, the Shibanids adopted both madrasa plan types introduced to the region by Ulugh Beg's architects: the two-iwan scheme of the complex in Bukhara itself and the grander four-iwan one on the Registan in Samarkand. The new

3.66a @ 1:1000

›3.66 BUKHARA, RELIGIOUS COMPLEXES: (a) Madar-i Khan and Abdullah Khan Madrasas (c. 1565 and c. 1585 respectively), plans; (b) Chahar Bagh-i Imam Abu Bakr ('Char Bakr', 1559–69), overview; (c) Mir-i Arab Madrasa, overview; (d) Qul Baba Kulkaltash madrasa court (1569); (e–g) the complex of Amir Nadr Divanbegi Arlat (Lab-i Khaus, 'tank-facing') and the adjacent Khan Abd al-Aziz, plan, tank fronts of Abd al-Aziz and Nadr Divanbegi Arlat.

3.66b

3.66c

regime, naturally, had a distinct preference for grandeur: the four-iwan scheme was followed across the period spanned by the Mir-i Arab, the Abdullah Khan and the Abd al-Aziz Madrasas; the simpler scheme is represented by Abdullah's Madar-i Khan and the contemporary work of his amir Qul Baba Kukaltash – though the latter with a court of 68 by 86 metres surrounded by cells for three hundred students is the region's largest. The Char Bakr complex of Imam Abu Bakr – whose garden at a noted *sufi* burial ground gives the site its popular name – is unique in having an open court flanked by the madrasa (south) and the mosque (north) linked by the khanqah range with a central iwan.

Corner towers, the front pair developed as minarets, and twin domes to either side of the recessed entrance portal were the norm for madrasas – respectively for the mosque to the right and a tomb or special meeting-

3.66d

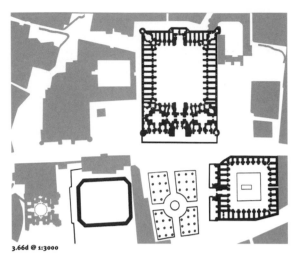

3.66d @ 1:3000

place to the left. In them all, the lavish tile revetment (often sadly depleted) relied heavily on floral motifs but in his main work Nadr Divan-begi preferred the symbolism of bizarre zoomorphic motifs.

In materials, form and style the Shibanids and their successors sustained the tradition inherited by the Timurids from the Ilkhanids – as befitted rulers claiming legitimacy in virtue of their ancestry. However, as there was exchange of ideas with trade between Bukhara and Isfahan – where, as we have seen, the Ilkhanid legacy was still potent – there is a genetic relationship between the schools of Safavids and their Uzbek contemporaries, though with no necessary equivalence in quality. The latter, like the former, avoided structural experiment and excelled at the theatrical but Uzbek stage effects, unsurpassed when applied to urban space, tended to be drawn from backdrops rather than the penetrating scenography and lighting which distinguished the greatest works of Isfahan. Repetitive, Bukharans relied primarily on dazzling tiling to astonish anew, especially the incorporation of bold figural motifs in the spandrels of major iwans, but the medium lost refinement as mosaic ceded to glazed panels or even glazed bricks.

3.66f

3.66g

3.67a

3.67b

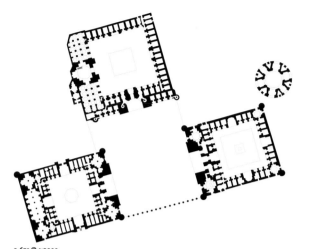

3.67c @ 1:3000

›3.67 SAMARKAND, REGISTAN: (a, b) Shir Dar ('Lion-possessing'), madrasa (1618–36), entrance front and court, (c) plan, (d) general view with the much-restored madrasas of Ulugh Beg (1417, left), Shir Dar (right) and Tila Kari ('Gilded', 1646–60, centre), (e) Tila Kari, interior of qibla qubba.

THE SAMARKAND REGISTAN

The centre of political gravity may have shifted to Bukhara under the Shibanids but Samarkand maintained its economic significance and was certainly in a position to lavish wealth on monuments. Under the Tuqay-Timurids it was the seat of an important amir as governor, Yalangtush Bi Alchin. In 1616 he set about the transformation of the Registan into one of the grandest urban complexes in the whole Islamic world: first, on the eastern site opposite the madrasa of Ulugh Beg, where the first Shibani had built a funerary complex now decayed, he founded the Shir Dar and completed it in 1636. Ten years later he founded the Tila Kari on the southern site where another funerary complex had been built under the early Shibanids. The formal association of the three buildings, governed by the geometry of their precinct and asserted in the similarity of their axial iwans, was complete in 1660.**3.67**

Rejistan

The madrasa of Ulugh Beg still dominated a roughly defined maidan from the west. In addition to the 16th-century Shibanid funerary madrasas to the east and south, khanqahs were developed in the early 17th century beside Ulugh Beg's great work and opposite it. As at Bukhara, such impressive clustering results from royal patrons rivalling their predecessors. Indeed, the scheme emulates the Lab-i Khaus complex in Bukhara, completed about the time Yalangtush's work was begun, and, about the time it was completed, to have been emulated at the shrine of Sheikh Abu Nasr Parsa at Balkh.

Like the façade of Ulugh Beg's madrasa opposite, Shir Dar's has minarets attached rather than freestanding, as was the norm elsewhere in the area, but the pair of side domes here are more assertive than in the earlier work: the spandrels of the great iwan are embellished with lions pursuing deer under an anthropomorphic sunburst. The qibla dictated the siting of the mosque in the western entrance wing, where it is balanced by a lecture room. Accommodation for students is arranged behind

3.67d

3.67e

two superimposed arcades. The qibla qubba dome of the final great work
of the series, the Tilakari mosque-madrasa, necessarily disrupts the symmetry of the scheme as a whole: the resplendent, but economical, interior
decoration of this latest work is in gilded stucco above a marble dado.

6 SAFAVID IRAN

In devastated Persia, underground resistance to the Aqqoyunlu intruders was fomented by *sufi* fraternities. The most radical, naturally, were Shi'ite. Of these, the Safavids – led by one Safi ud-Din, who claimed descent from Ali through the twelve *imams* – enrolled bands of Turkomans as soldiers in their cause. Caught up in the conflict between the Aqqoyunlu and the Qaraqoyunlu, the Safavids expanded their following and were led to their first great victory by Safi's descendant Ismail, who took Tabriz from the Aqqoyunlu in 1502.

Ismail proclaimed himself Shah and, promoting Ithna'ashariyya ('Twelver') Shi'ism, proceeded to absorb the western provinces of the former Timurid empire, left in chaos by the intruders.

After dispatching Husayn Baykara, the Sunni Shibanids of Transoxiana invaded Khorasan. Shah Ismail challenged them there and won the province. A vigorous Shi'ite in possession of the heartlands of the former Seljuk empire, he now excited the opposition of the staunchly Sunni Ottomans and lost northern Mesopotamia and north-western Iran, including his capital Tabriz, to the overwhelming forces of Selim I. The sultan was forced to withdraw by mutinous troops but the *shah* never recovered from the blow and died in 1524. He had moved to Isfahan – in central Iran, beyond the reach of the Ottomans – and maintained it as his base despite Selim's reverse. Preferring *baraka* to grandeur, however, he chose to be buried in a modest cylindrical tower tomb on a restricted site between the shrines of Sheikh Safi and his son at Ardabil: subsequently much embellished, the complex became a dynastic necropolis.

Reverse only stiffened Shi'ite resolve. Iran reasserted its cultural pre-eminence in central and southern Asia during the long reign of Ismail's son Tahmasp (1524–76).**3.69** However, recurrent conflict with their neighbours sapped

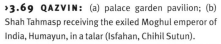

›3.69 QAZVIN: (a) palace garden pavilion; (b) Shah Tahmasp receiving the exiled Moghul emperor of India, Humayun, in a talar (Isfahan, Chihil Sutun).

3.69b

3.69a

(a) Najaf, Shrine of Imam Ali; (b) Kerbala, Shrine of Imam al-Husayn; (c) Samarra, Shrine of Imam Ali al-Hadi and his son Hasan al-Askari.

The sequence of building at these great sites is obscure: in general, a harem precinct had been defined and canopies erected over the graves of the martyrs by the end of the 7th century. The shrines were repeatedly destroyed and rebuilt in the 8th and 9th centuries under successive Abbasid caliphs. Mosques were added and major embellishments undertaken under the Buyids in the last quarter of the 10th century. Renovations after the depradations of the Mongols were delayed until the Ilkhanid grip was loosened in the last quarter of the 14th century: they then included gilding of domes and minarets. The Safavid Shah Ismail began a new phase of embellishment: halted by the loss of Mesopotamia to the Ottomans, it was continued by Abbas I and reversed in the fourth decade of the 17th century by the Ottoman sultan Murad IV – who whitewashed the domes. In the 18th century there was constant conflict between Turks and Persians but the relaxation of Ottoman control allowed various Persian rulers to maintain the sites and further their embellishment – notably Nadir Shah and the Qajar Aqa

Safavid strength and the Ottomans returned: the loss of the major Shi'ite shrines at Najaf, Kerbala and Samarra to them in the second decade of Tahmasp's reign undermined the *shah*'s standing as the defender of Shi'ism. An uneasy truce with the sultan had been reached by the time of Tahmasp's death, but then dynastic rivalry reduced Iran to chaos.

Emerging miraculously from the chaos – and relative obscurity – Shah Abbas I took the Safavids to their apogee in another long reign (1587–1629).[3.68] After a series of fresh reverses inflicted by both Ottomans and Uzbeks – who took Mashhad in 1589 – the *shah* availed himself of the expertise of envoys from Elizabethan England to replace inefficient and unruly tribal levies with a professional army. He won back Mashhad from the Shibanids at the beginning of the new century, ejected the Ottomans from Tabriz soon after and went on to regain most of the territory lost since the initial defeat of Shah Ismail: the recovery of the holy Shi'ite sites in Iraq led to the comprehensive refurbishment of the shrines of Ali and his sons, neglected under the Ottomans.[3.70]

3.70a

3.70b

3.70c

A great administrator and magnificent builder, Abbas I founded a new capital beside old Seljuk Isfahan and endowed it with several of the world's most superb mosques. There was disaster under his malevolent successor, but recovery and more splendid building under Abbas II (1642–66). The glory reflected on his successor, Shah Suleyman, but hid stagnation. Renewed conflict with the Ottomans and clashes with India over Kandahar and Russia over the Caucasus undermined the later Safavids, especially Shah Sultan Husayn (1696–1722), who was forced to abdicate by Afghan usurpers. His Zand governor asserted independence at Shiraz in the south. A nationalist revival led to chaos in the north until a Khorasanian adventurer seized the throne as Nadir Shah in 1736 and promoted the revival of Persian fortune.

Muhammad Shah who regilded the domes c. 1795. Sunni puritans of the Wahhabi sect wreaked havoc at the beginning of the 19th century but the Qajar Fath'ali Shah repaired the damage: the present appearance of the shrines dates largely from that time.

EARLY SAFAVID BUILDING

Little survives from the first Safavid reign – except the *shah*'s unexceptional tomb beside that of the dynasty's progenitor at Ardabil and the traditional four-iwan Masjid-i Ali in Isfahan. Shah Tahmasp moved back to the north-west after the Ottomans relinquished the area and established his capital at Qazvin: centre of limited architectural activity during the extended reign, its legacy was largely lost to earthquake. However, the remains of the garden palace demonstrate the subsistence of forms known to Timur's court, most notably the hasht behisht in addition to the talar in which Tahmasp receives Humayun – reputedly a chihil sutun or pavilion of forty columns, twenty of wood supporting the flat roof, twenty reflections of the same in the pool of the forecourt.**3.69** And these forms survive in the later Safavid palace of the new Isfahan inaugurated by Shah Abbas I in 1598 and completed by Shah Suleyman c. 1670.

Like all their predecessors, the Safavids built their religious monuments in brick but left not a course uncovered by tiles in the most ravishing of colours and patterns: their palaces made much more use of timber and plaster. Behind these scintillating veils to apparently conservative forms, considerable effort was spent on perfecting the innovative structural techniques of the late-Timurids – in particular the exploitation of the rib to lighten and enlighten structure. This marched with an increasing predilection for scenographic effects and it was that which prompted formal development – insofar as the traditional building types allowed.

The Safavids moved the centre of gravity from central Asia to central Persia, in particular to Isfahan, and there took the traditional Iranian building types to an apogee at once of theatricality and refinement. If they promoted an imperial style, it was not primarily because plans and artisans were sent out to the provinces from an authoritarian office of works in Isfahan – as they were from Istanbul – but because the craftsmen themselves were recruited from all parts of the realm – where variations in climate, materials and technology were far more limited than those of the Ottomans – and bent their native talents to effecting a synthesis in communion with their colleagues.

ISFAHAN AND SECULAR BUILDING

The exceptionally ordered plan of the town takes advantage of an open site to the south-west of the old centre, by the banks of the Zayandeh River. This had already been developed by Shah Ismail with a suburban garden retreat in the rectangular tradition of the earthly paradise. An elongated parade ground (maidan), framed with continuous shopping arcades and accommodating a market on specified days – like the one near the venerable Jami-masjid in the old city to the north – was laid out to the east of the latter: provision was made for a new congregational mosque to the south and a grand bazaar was extended into the new commercial district from the huge northern iwan.

The aristocracy apart, most town dwellers had courtyard houses which, naturally, responded in scale to rank and wealth. The grandest aristocratic residences were built to the west of the palace gardens, on either side of a splendid avenue laid out c. 1600 with a watercourse dividing it into two carriageways to channel traffic between the new town and the river crossing. To meet the needs of the expanding population in general – estimated to have reached well over half a million by 1600 – a second artery was developed from the river to the new maidan and beyond, along the tortuous street of the old bazaar, to the old maidan near the Jami-masjid.**3·71**

›3.71 SAFAVID ISFAHAN: (a) overview of palace; (b) plan with (1) Seljuk Jami-masjid, (2) souks, (3) Safavid maidan (parade and polo ground, 521 by 160 metres), (4) palace, (5) Lutfullah (palatine) mosque, (6) Masjid-i Shah (congregational mosque), (7) Garden Avenue (called Chahar Bagh after the four-square form of the gardens).

The maidan was laid out between 1590 and 1595 and had been framed with arcaded shops by 1602. The maidan scheme was followed elsewhere: the earliest was projected at much the same time by the governor of Kirman, Ganj Ali Khan.

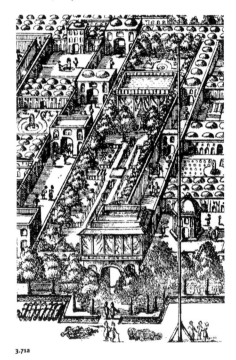

3.71a

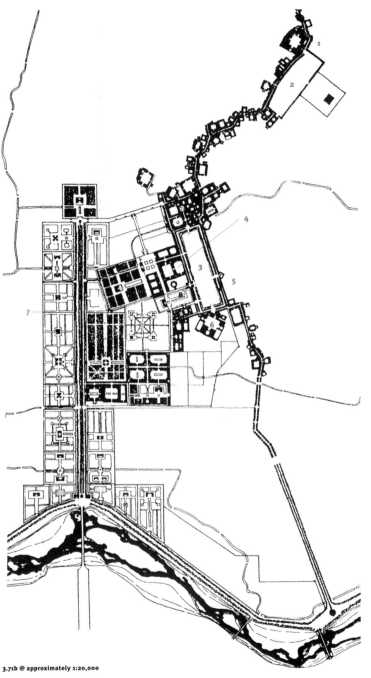

3.71b @ approximately 1:20,000

3.72a

The principal elements of the palace are the main gate
and place of appearance known as Ali Kapu, which overlooked the maidan from the west, and the main audience
hall known as Chihil Sutun. Both are columned porticoes
(talars) derived from the apadana. Both provided residential accommodation on several storeys behind the

3.72b

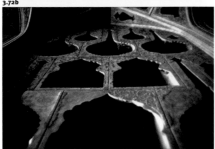
3.72c

>**3.72 ISFAHAN, PALACE:** (a–d) Ali Kapu (Lofty Gate) exterior, music-room vault and wall detail, section, (e–j) Chihil Sutun (Forty-Columned Hall) of Shah Abbas II (1647), view across tank, Shah Abbas I at a banquet (detail from a ceiling fresco), details of main iwan, plan, (k) cathedral (completed 1664), interior detail, (l–n), Hasht Behisht (Eight Paradises) of Shah Suleyman (1669), plan, section and central octagon vault, (o) damsel in a garden (faience panels; New York, Metropolitan Museum of Art).

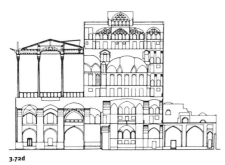
3.72d

columns. To the many other buildings which once enclosed courts and enjoyed the rectangular grid of chahar baghs, Shah Suleyman added a hasht behisht after the ancient model – but, unlike its predecessors, it survives in considerable splendour.**3.72**

Isfahan palace buildings

The Ali Kapu was in origin a gate to the garden palace of Shah Abbas I but it developed into a palace itself, with a superstructure of rooms behind a talar from which the ruler could review events in the maidan. Novel in its elevation and intensity, the talar surmounts a basement in which access to the palace from the maidan crosses the shopping arcade. Over two basement storeys are three more for the principal apartments, but much of the space is given to a grand double-height hall rising from the same level and to the same height as the portico. The joinery of the columned portico was gilded. The intricate interior of the top-floor music room, deeply recessed with vase-shaped niches as much to charm the ear as to divert the eye, was stuccoed and painted to resemble an extremely refined garden alive with birds.

Work on the Chihil Sutun complex seems to have begun under Shah Abbas I before the end of the 16th century. The audience hall with porticoes to north and south, iwans east and west, may date from the end of his reign but the central throne iwan, flanked by large rectangular chambers and the great portico, were due to Abbas II (and rebuilding after a fire in 1705). Fountains in the throne iwan and the columned portico fed a canal which ran on into the main pool – and just as water linked inside with out, so it doubled the portico by reflection ('chihil' may mean forty or many). The woodwork was gilded, with walls and vaults plastered and painted with stylized floral motifs, as usual. The exterior has aberrant murals in a pseudo-Western style; the main interior walls of the great hall follow Timurid precedent (recorded by Prince Babur), with murals representing episodes from the dynasty's history in an inflated indigenous style. Tile played a now-depleted part, but mirror mosaic remains the dominant element in the east-facing throne iwan behind the great columned portico: that reflective medium, veiling structural reality, was the final agent in the integration of the covered space and its external environment.

3.72e

3.72f

3.72g

3.72h

3.72i

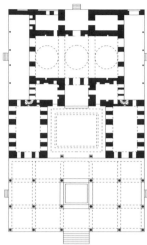

3.72j @ 1:1000

3.72k

3.72l

3.72m

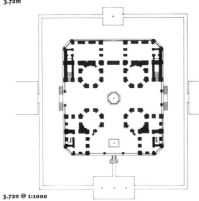

3.72n @ 1:1000

Inserted at the centre of the Nightingale Garden, laid out for Shah Abbas II, Shah Suleyman's garden pavilion presumably recalled its greater predecessors at Herat and Qazvin. The 'eight paradises' were the gorgeously decorated rooms on two levels in each of the four diagonal wings, flanking columned porticoes to south, west and east and an iwan to the north. The muqarnas retain some original florid plasterwork and mirror mosaic. Water channelled from the fountain in the centre of the octagon, reflecting light from several sources to the mirror mosaic ceiling, highlighted the unconstrained devolution of space from inside to out.

3.72o

3.73a

Flanked by raised walkways, the Si-o-sih pol (300 metres) is the longest of Safavid bridges. The later Khwaju pol (132 metres long) has three octagonal belvederes and two levels, the upper one for pedestrians, the lower one for wheeled traffic.

Nothing in Isfahan is a better measure of the prosperity which the stability of long reigns and lavish patronage were to bring than the splendid bridges which took the main arteries of the new town across the river: first the western avenue's Pol-i Si o Se ('Thirty-three arches'), then the eastern crossing's Khwaju pol of 1605.**3·73** The bridges were dams too – and recreational facilities. The water retained was used for irrigation, drinking water was provided by an extensive series of aqueducts. Other water conservation measures, instituted throughout the realm, included underground irrigation channels tapping subterranean water resources, domed cisterns and even ice houses. Agriculture flourished, the population had never been better fed and the *shah* promoted the construction of pigeon houses to supplement the popular diet.

Most Iranian cities benefited from Safavid patronage – as did the merchants of the age. Imperial arteries were

3.73b

3.74a

3.74b

›3.74 SAFAVID KHAN AT DIHBID ON THE YAZD–KERMAN ROAD: (a) overview, (b) detail of storage room, (c) view into court.

Devoid of ornament, the vast majority of Safavid caravanserai conformed to the traditional square plan: the corners were usually strengthened with round towers; the court usually had four iwans between which accommodation was ranged on two levels – stabling and storage below, guest rooms above. Some were fortified but Safavid roads were generally safe.

extended throughout the empire, often on foundations inherited from the Achaemenids: trade flourished; bazaars proliferated. The stock of commercial buildings was renovated and augmented everywhere. Particular attention was paid to lodgings for merchants (khans or caravanserai): the capital was endowed with at least one of imperial scale and a massive campaign ensured that the major trade routes were punctuated with full facilities at the intervals of a day's journey – about 20 kilometres. The four-iwan court within a rectangular perimeter was the norm, but there are rare formal octagonal variants and widely disparate climates prompted the development of wholly open-sided or wholly enclosed vaulted structures. **3.74**

3.74c

›**3.75 SULTANIYA, TOMB OF MULLAH HASAN,** 1530.

Earlier approximations to the hasht behisht form include the tomb of Khwaja Abu Nasir at Balkh (c. 1460), where the cross-in-square survives in plan but is converted to an octagon by squinches supporting the dome, and the chamfered sides of the exterior mass have deep niches on two levels between the four axial iwans.

›**3.76 QUMM, SHRINE OF FATIMA** (the 8th *imam* Reza's sister, who died in 816): general view.

Often sited in or beside the compound of a mosque or at least incorporating a prayer hall, the principal mausoleum (with its ambulatory for pilgrims) is the nucleus of an extensive complex which includes subsidiary tomb chambers for those fortunate enough to be buried in the orbit of grace emitted by the *imam* or his relative, a Koranic recitation room and facilities for propagating Shi'ite dogma.

›**3.77 ISFAHAN, SHRINE OF HARUN-I VILAYET,** early Safavid: screened sepulchre.

TOMBS, SHRINES AND MOSQUES

Square tombs were not uncommon in early Safavid Iran but an important alternative soon emerged. Instead of the square and cross of the main space – as in the Gur-i Mir or the Ishrat Khaneh – Safavid planners of works such as the tomb of Mullah Hasan at Sultaniya revised the octagonal form adopted for Khwaja Abu Nasr at Balkh, developed the subsidiary chambers on the diagonals and projected an arcade on to the exterior. The tomb became a hasht behisht – or rather the hasht behisht became a tomb – ideally set in the paradise of a chahar bagh.**3.72, 3.75**

A domed octagon was provided for the congregation of *sufi* disciples in the imperial necropolis at Ardabil by Shah Tahmasp and Shah Abbas I built another for the treasures with which he endowed the complex in conjunction with

3.76

3.77

his embellishment of the original reading room (dar al-huffaz). However, there were no grand imperial Safavid mausoleums. Instead, the Shi'ite great were buried in the aura of a holy man – or within a madrasa. Much money was lavished on the shrines of *imams* and Shi'ite saints, especially at Mashhad and Qumm after the Iraqi shrines had been lost. Regained by Shah Abbas 1 in 1623, work on the latter – neglected under the Ottomans – was furthered in the 1630s, as we have noted. **3.76, 3.77**

Splendid mosques and madrasas proliferated in the furthest corners of the empire, particularly in the cities of the Silk Road which could afford to rival the capital. However, the tradition of the four-iwan mosque, established at Isfahan under the Seljuks, was perfected there 500 years

3.78a

later under the Safavids. In the Masjid-i Lutfullah's singular aureole of unexcelled internal splendour on the one
hand, in the Masjid-i Shah's scenographic spectacle of
open and closed forms, consistent in shape and material,
ever changing in size, colour, light and pattern on the other,
the ancient Iranian kiosk and the four-iwan court mosque
types here achieve their apotheosis. Thereafter there was
some grandeur but the splendour was unsustainable.**3.7**⁸

›**3.78 ISFAHAN, IMPERIAL MOSQUES:** (a–c)
Sheikh Lutfullah Mosque (c. 1600), entrance from the
maidan, plan, interior; (d–i) Masjid-i Shah (begun c.
1611), overview, plan, portal, qibla qubba, qibla qubba
interior, view through southern prayer hall to mihrab in
qibla qubba; (j–m) Masjid-i Hakim (1656), plan, prayer-
hall front, interior with mihrab, interior of dome.

3.78b @ 1:1000

3.78c

The imperial Safavid mosque

Opposite the entrance to the palace, the domed Sheikh Lutfullah Mosque was the palatine oratory. At the southern end of the maidan, the Masjid-i Shah was the congregational mosque of the new capital. As the maidan and the qibla were at an acute angle to one another, considerable virtue was made of necessity in bending the line of access to the axis of prayer in each building: privacy was enhanced by the circuitous corridor to the Lutfullah's one great domed chamber. So too was drama – and withholding the impact of the Masjid-i Shah's sublime court until after penetration is a *coup de théâtre* of the first magnitude.

Entered from the centre of a recess in the cloister surrounding the maidan, the Lutfullah's corridor skirts the north-west and north-east sides of the domed qubba to the main portal on the qibla opposite the mihrab. The domed octagon – 76 metres square – is elementary in form but complex in surface pattern. Within and between the pointed arches, the squinches have simple grooved vaults (rather than muqarnas like the sumptuous front entrance iwan, for instance) but are inlaid with mosaic tiles in contrast to the painted tiles of dado and wall. The arches are rimmed with a spiral moulding in turquoise but their strength is reinforced by bands of deep blue with white inscriptions. Like the empyraean at the rising and setting of the sun, the dome dissolves in a cascade of blue and gold.

3.78d

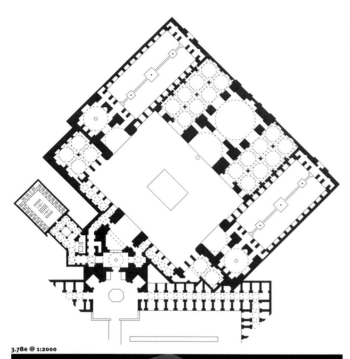

3.78e @ 1:2000

3.78f

3.78g

3.78h

North-facing and recessed beyond the line of the maidan cloisters, the Masjid-i Shah's entrance, with its pishtaq supporting paired minarets and framed with bands of Kufic script, leads to a small domed vestibule and then into the triangular apse of an iwan which effects alignment through 45 degrees with the qibla. Across the huge four-iwan court (70 metres square), the qibla qubba (52 metres high) and its majestic pishtaq – with twin minarets echoing those over the entrance – are flanked by a pair of smaller iwans, as in the Samarkand Bibi Khanum Mosque, leading to twin

3.78i

prayer halls of eight domed bays each. These in turn are flanked by twin (non-residential) madrasa courts.

Complexity of form is avoided in the spatial units of the great congregational mosque but not in their vaulting. An astonishing array of muqarnas enlivens the entrance, where the sun rarely illuminates the tilework, but elsewhere grooved semi-domes effect transition from square to circle – sometimes superimposed with decreasing depth to form lattice vaults. Above a continuous marble dado, every surface is revetted with painted tiles except for the domes and semi-domes, which have moulded mosaics. A wide range of colours is dominated by blue graded in depth to assert structure or dissolve void behind myriad floral patterns which form a truly celestial carpet in the great qubba.

The Lutfullah's portal is inscribed with a date corresponding to 1612 (presumably post-dating foundation by several years), the interior with another corresponding to 1618. The latter identifies the architect as the Isfahani *ustad* (master) Muhammad Riza ibn Ustad Husayn. An inscription on the portal of the Masjid-i Shah is dated with the equivalent of 1616 but work began up to five years earlier. Attributed to ustad Abu'l Qasim, Badi al-Zaman Tuni and the engineer Muhibb Ali Beg, the building seems to have taken nearly thirty years to complete, thanks in part to suspension of work for several years to allow for settlement prior to tiling. The Masjid-i Hakim is due to the next generation – that of Shah Abbas II – reputedly at the behest of a doctor who had made his fortune at the Mughal court in India: monumental in conception but somewhat mechanical in articulation, it was never finished.

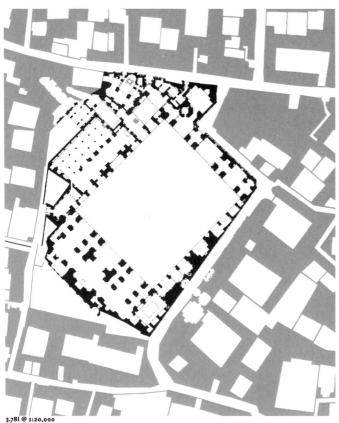

3.78l @ 1:20,000

3.78m

›ARCHITECTURE IN CONTEXT »DAR AL-ISLAM DIVIDED

3.78j

3.78k

Avoiding the rectangular junction of corridors between student cells, the Safavid madrasa develops a late-Timurid tendency to penetrate chamfered corners of the court on the diagonals and provide direct access to lecture rooms. The supreme example is the Isfahan Madrasa-yi Madar-i Shah.**3.79** There too, the collegiate mosque is dominant in the centre of the range defining the qibla. Precedents for both the diagonal penetration of the corners and the dominance of a centrally placed mosque may be found outside the Safavid domains in

›**3.79 ISFAHAN, MADRASA-YI MADAR-I SHAH,** 1706–15, (a) prayer court looking towards the qibla qubba, (b) interior, (c) qibla qubba and neighbouring cells.

The complex was founded by Shah Husayn I (1694–1722) for his mother and supported by the grand associated caravanserai.

3.79c

3.80a

Transoxiana: as we have seen the former appears in the early 16th-century Mir-i Arab Madrasa at Bukhara, the latter in the early 17th-century Tila Kari Madrasa on the Registan in Samarkand.

The Madrasa-yi Madar-i Shah marks the last flowering of an exceptionally rich tradition: by the time the complex was completed towards the end of the second decade of the 18th century, Isfahan's glorious age of building was

›3.80 SHIRAZ, MASJID-I VAKIL, 1766: (a) prayer court, (b) detail of tiling.

More traditional in plan than the great domed works of imperial Isfahan, the prayer hall is hypostyle and the court (60 metres square) has single-storey arcades between its two iwans. The tilework was heavily restored in the 19th century.

over. However, an extended epilogue unfolded in the south at the behest of Muhamad Karim Khan Zand, regent for the Safavids in Shiraz from 1750 to 1779. To the south of the old citadel (Arg), he laid out a maidan in emulation of the one in the imperial capital and, as there, the land to its south was assigned to a new congregational mosque – the Masjid-i Vakil.**3.80** To the east was a new bazaar. To the east of the citadel, where new apartments were installed, was an imperial talar: it became a post office. Such a fate for former glory was not unique but far more common was the atrophy of tired tradition, constantly reiterated by later builders of later dynasties – north and south – and the decadence underlying an icing of European ornament.

3.80b

PART 4 BEYOND THE EASTERN PALE

4.2

›ARCHITECTURE IN CONTEXT »BEYOND THE EASTERN PALE

1 AFGHANS, TURKS AND THEIR DELHI SULTANATE

The advent of Muhammad Ghuri and his Afghan forces into India (Hindustan to the Muslims) towards the end of the 12th century anticipated a triumph for Islam that would be matched only by the Ottoman conquest of Constantinople. The native Rajput rulers, who had divided the north-west of the Indian subcontinent in their incessant games of war with one another, were no match for the better-equipped, flexible, grimly determined Muslims. An extensive domain centred on the Chahamana Rajput seat of Rai Pithora (south-west of modern Delhi) was annexed to Ghuri in the early 1190s.

On Muhammad's assassination in 1206, his Mamluk commander in Delhi, Qutb ud-Din Aibek, seized the initiative and founded the so-called Slave Dynasty of

Delhi sultans: his base was the Lal Kot (Red Fort) which guarded Rai Pithora.**4.2** A signal display of proselytizing militancy – comparable only to that of the 7th-century Arabs in North Africa – carried them right across India to Bengal within a couple of years, reducing venerable Hindu kingdoms to provinces. The Rajputs checked their advance in Rajastan but failed to press success beyond the frontiers of parochial concern and dislodge the Turks from Delhi.

Though the new state was to be an Indian entity rather than an extension of Afghanistan, its rulers kept themselves aloof from the Indians. Muslims from Persia and Afghanistan, as well as the sultan's fellow Turks, filled the main offices – with a powerful body of Turkish Sunni theologians as their guiding force – or found lucrative careers in the armies. There was to be considerable rivalry among Muslim factions at the seats of power but all Muslims could look forward to privileged positions in the economic life of the regime. For centuries Arab traders had prospered in the ports of Gujarat and these were to be among the earliest centres of Islamic culture to flourish beyond the seats of the metropolitan power.

Qutb's successor, Iltutmish (1211–36), was relatively successful in consolidating his hold over north India and asserting his authority over the Turkish notables but his position was undermined by resurgent Rajputs and invading Mongols. Prey to internal dissent and decades of chaos, his Turkish successors lost the throne to the Afghan Khaljis. The greatest of their line, Ala-ud-din (1296–1316), held off the Mongols and took the sultanate to its peak with the conquest of the rich Hindu kingdoms of the Solanki west, the Malwan centre and Deccani south (AIC2, pages 175–179). He moved his seat to Siri, north-east of Lal Kot, but little survives there except the remains of a great talar.

›4.1 (PAGES 462–463) THE IDEAL GARDEN PALACE (Mughal school of Faizabad, c. 1765).

›4.2 DELHI, RAI PITHORA: aerial view with Quwwat al-Islam Mosque and Qutb Minar (left centre).

4.3a

QUWWAT AL-ISLAM

The Turks of Ghazni had marked their triumph with ceremonial minarets – as we have seen. When the Ghurids took Lal Kot and Qila Rai Pithora they marked the triumph of Islam in the subcontinent with the Quwwat al-Islam (Might of Islam) Mosque built of materials pillaged from twenty-seven Hindu temples and dominated by the greatest of all ceremonial minarets: the Qutb Minar marks the apogee of the Ghaznavid type.

The mosque (and a similar one at Ajmer) followed the plan of the first mosque of the Prophet. Apart from reusing Hindu materials, the Hindu masons impressed by the Muslim conquerors followed their own structural and decorative traditions, especially in the extensions undertaken by Iltutmish. To match his imperial pretensions, Ala-ud-din Khalji projected huge extensions but ambition outstripped resource. The main completed element, a cubic block of strikingly contrasted red sandstone and white marble which marks transition from indigenous to imported constructional techniques, was to prove highly influential.**4.3**

India's first imperial mosque

The extended platform of the main Hindu temple provides the court. In the improvisation of the hypostyle prayer hall and colonnades, the lavishly carved (and presumably plastered) Hindu columns were superimposed to raise the reused ceilings to greater height than they would have reached originally. A façade of five ogee arches was imposed to screen the trabeated prayer hall, but the qibla iwan rises higher than the superimposed piers behind. The Hindu masons, unfamiliar with the true voussoir arch, recall the corbelled forms of their ancient tradition and bands of progenitive lotus mouldings (padma), like those in the jambs of temple portals, are flanked by bands of Islamic calligraphy.

The Qutb Minar follows the specific precedents set at Ghazni and Jam, but also accords with a tradition in India that may be traced back to the

4.3b

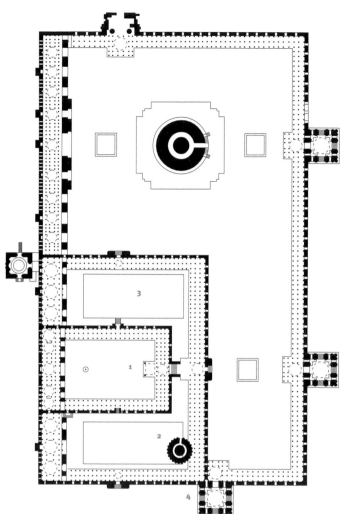

4.3c @ 1:1000

Mauryan pillars of the law. Qutb raised his great minar in commemoration of the triumph of his Muslim order. Of red sandstone and grey quartzose, this is circular in plan with a variety of circular and acute-angled projections. Originally there were three storeys marked by balconies on muqarnas and ringed by bands of Islamic calligraphy and Hindu foliage.

Iltutmish extended the prayer-hall screen by three bays on either end, enclosed the additional courts before them (the southern one incorporating the great minar), and projected his lavishly incised octagonal tomb

4.3d

>**4.3 DELHI, QUWWAT AL-ISLAM MOSQUE,**
1199 and later: (a) detail of reused Hindu column in prayer hall, (b) view from court to prayer hall, (c) plan with (1) original court and prayer hall, (2) Qutb Minar, (3) extensions of Iltutmish, (4) extensions of Ala ud-Din Khalji and Alai Darwaza, (d) Qutb Minar, (e) tomb of Iltutmish (c. 1230); (f) Alai Darwaza (1311).

4.3e

from the south-east corner. This is now a domeless qubba with eight corbelled ogee arches forming squinches on the diagonals or framing the mihrab and entrances on the main axes. Of fine red and grey sandstone, it depended on the skill of Indian stone carvers for its profuse low-relief ornament – though that is largely Islamic in motif.

Ala ud-Din Khalji's project – devised a century after Qutb's foundations were laid – involved the doubling of the prayer hall behind a taller arcade, the erection of new colonnades along the other three sides of a court nearly four times the area covered by Iltutmish, the provision of four

4.3f

monumental entrance pavilions and a minar twice the size of Qutb's. The minaret, which never rose beyond the first storey, is little more than a denuded stump. Of the rest, only the south-eastern entrance pavilion, the Alai Darwaza, reached any degree of completeness. Over a figured base into which steps are cut, this is a qubba, self-contained like its Zoroastrian or Roman triumphal antecedents despite its projected integration with the southern colonnade. Divided into two registers of screened arched windows and blind panels, the east, south and west façades are each dominated by a double-voussoir arch – novel in India – springing from colonnettes and relieved along the intrados by the spearhead valance that was to be so characteristic of the works of the later sultanate. The north façade is not articulated but its arch is treated to elaborately beaded mouldings. Interior and exterior are profusely ornamented with low-relief carving including calligraphic bands. The qubba has five receding arches forming squinches to support a true dome.

›4.4 DELHI, NIZAM-UD-DIN, JAM'AT KHANA, c. 1315: view from east.

The central pavilion was possibly conceived by the sultan as the sheikh's mausoleum: the sheikh favoured an unpretentious cenotaph which became the nucleus of one of India's most important dargahs. With semi-domes behind squinch arches, the central qubba marks an advance on the prototype but, ill-related to it in plan, structure or articulation, the wings were probably added later.

The first of the Alai Daraza's many descendants was the austere central pavilion of the Jam'at Khana in the Delhi burial ground of the *sufi* sheikh Nizam-ud-din Aulia. It was probably originally conceived by the sultan as a mausoleum for the sheikh but, whatever its original purpose, it provided the model for the sultanate tomb and it marks the advent of the domed qubba with iwan to the Indian mosque.**4·4**

THE TUGHLUQS

The last ephemeral Khalji was despatched in 1320 by Ghiyath al-Din Tughluq, Ala-ud-din's governor of the Punjab, who founded a new Turkish dynasty and a formidable Delhi seat.**4·5** Tughluq sustained his former master's imperial pretensions but had little time to do

4.5a

4.5b

›4.5 TUGHLUQABAD (SOUTH DELHI), 1320–25: (a) aerial view, (b) ramparts.

Founded on a rocky outcrop by a seasonal lake to the east of Lal Kot, the citadel containing the palace was integrated with the town defences. These are powerful fortifications of cyclopean masonry aggressively battered like the brick-built walls of the Indus valley, where Tughluq had formerly been based, but little of substance remains within them – even of the citadel.

›4.6 DAULATABAD (DEVAGIRI): general view. The fortifications built around their extraordinary conical hill fortress by the Yadavas, the Hindu rulers destroyed by Khalji forces, were restored and extended to accommodate the forced emigrées from Delhi: the Delhi sultan and his Bahamani followers were responsible at least for strengthening the double-walled, double-moated second circuit and constructing the outer ring which, well over 4 kilometres in diameter and penetrated by eight gates, is protected by moat, glacis and massive bastions. The first mosque was built for the Khalji conquerors with materials pillaged from Hindu temples, like most of the mosques built for early Muslim rulers elsewhere in India. Most of the ruined palaces are later.

much more than finish the walls of his city and his tomb before he was murdered in 1325 by his son, Muhammad.

In an exercise of extraordinary brutality, the parricide sultan moved the capital and its population to the Deccani fortress of Devagiri (renamed Daulatabad; see AIC2, pages 215–217), the better to hold a subcontinental empire.**4.6** The exercise failed as it was bound to do without a generally accepted ethos: the north revolted, the capital (and its population) moved back and, his empire disintegrating, the deranged sultan died in 1351. Bengal and the Deccan were lost.

In Delhi the *ulema* elevated Muhammad's cousin Firoz Shah (1351–88) in return for concessions which left him without adequate material or moral resources to meet any real challenge to his authority. More independent states emerged under both Muslims and Rajputs but the sultanate subsisted until Timur destroyed it – and much of Delhi – in 1398. The Tughluqs were replaced by Timur's nominee but his undistinguished Sayyid line did little more than sustain itself in Delhi for fifty years – and build tombs.

TUGHLUQ MONUMENTS

The pillaging of Hindu temples for hypostyle prayer halls was long to continue across the Indian subcontinent but the architects of the Khaljis' Tughluq successors pressed local craftsmen into translating Iranian types into Indian terms. In the medium of plastered rubble, mosque architecture ultimately went beyond the derivative form of works such as Delhi's Begampuri to explore new depths of complexity at nearby Khirki and Nizam-ud-Din. The experiments were not successful: in association with a novel form of madrasa, there was a return to the traditional courtyard mosque type in the funerary complex of Firoz Shah Tughluq at Hauz Khas. **4.7, 4.8**

›4.7 DELHI, BEGAMPURI MOSQUE, C. 1350: court and prayer hall from the north-east.

Experimental mosque planning

On a high platform, the court of the Begampuri is bordered by prayer hall and cloisters, as usual, but – no longer of pillaged materials – these are formed of arcaded bays with shallow domes carried on pendentives over simple paired piers. The qibla is marked by a great iwan. Built of coarse plastered masonry, there are traces of glazed tiling which once presumably sheathed all the exposed surfaces. The battered minarets attached to the frontispiece (as in contemporary Iran) produce an idiosyncratic pylon-like form.

The vizier of Sultan Firoz Shah (1351–85), Khan-i-Jahan Tilangani, built three mosques in Delhi varying the extension of cover at the expense of the court. The most advanced is the one at Khirki: perfectly formal in its symmetry about the cardinal axes, the three ranges of triple arcades

4.8a

4.8b

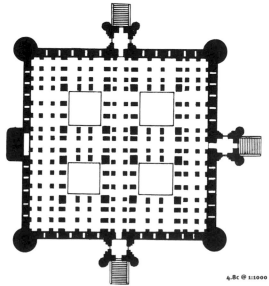

4.8c @ 1:1000

›ARCHITECTURE IN CONTEXT »BEYOND THE EASTERN PALE

›4.8 DELHI: (a–c) Khirki (c. 1375), exterior, roof detail and plan; (d) Kalan (c. 1370), arcades.

along all four sides and across the centre frame four square internal courts. With entrance pavilions on the south, north and east, a projection behind the mihrab to the west and tapering turrets at most corners, the absence of any dominant feature on the skyline reinforced the impression of homogeneity. As at Khirki, the Kalan mosque has four courts, but they are bordered by a single range of arcades to all sides except the west (before the qibla), where there are three ranges. Stout battered walls of plastered rubble pierced by relatively small screened windows give the appearance of rugged strength.[4.8d]

It was homogeneity that made the approach unworkable: it denied authority to the qibla and it is unsurprising that the experiments were not sustained. On the banks of the Hauz Khas tank, dug for Ala-ud-din, Firoz Shah built ranges of arcaded galleries and residential cells surmounted by domed chambers and pillared halls almost as austere in structure as the rock-hewn multi-storey Buddhist and Hindu masterpieces of Ellora (AIC2, pages 79–82, 115–120). The mosque, towards the north of the east range, was of the conventional court type though the east side does not seem to have been closed with colonnades. Instead of the formal four-iwan scheme favoured in post-Seljuk Iran, the court is dominated by canopied pavilions (chattris), presumably for convocation or teaching as well as cenotaphs.

4.8d

4.9

Before his translation from the Punjab to Delhi in 1320, Ghiyath al-Din Tughluq had taken the imported funerary tradition to new heights in the tomb of Sheikh Rukn-i-Alam at Multan: the sole precedent on such a scale was the tomb of Oljeitu at Sultaniya.**3.42** At his new seat in Delhi, Tughlaq renounced the octagonal form of the great Ilkhanid for the qubba developed by his Khalji predecessor. Firoz Shah retained the qubba with battered walls but not the materials; with no more enduring effect, the greatest of his ministers adopted the octagon. His Sayyid successors, on the other hand, adopted the octagon for their tombs and left the qubba to their ineffective ministers.**4.9–4.12**

Towards the great tomb

Ghiyath al-Din Tughluq was commander of the sultanate's frontier forces based at Multan in the Punjab when he commissioned one of the most magnificent tombs of the entire Muslim world. It was apparently first meant for himself, but after he seized the sultanate in 1320 he assigned it to the *sufi* Sheikh Rukn-i-Alam. Multan maintained direct ties with Iran, whose brick and tile tradition was well adapted to the conditions of the Indus plains, and the influence of the tomb of Oljeitu at Sultaniya is obvious. Further, the Samanids of Bukhara seem to be recalled by the domed turrets at the corners. There was also a Multani tradition of tomb-building which provided the steeply battered walls, octagonal clerestory and broad dome. Inlaid blue tiles are used sparingly in bands around the lower storey, more lavishly on the pilasters, frieze and clerestory window frames and to relieve the base of the great white dome. In addition, patterned brickwork and carved timber play important roles.

On its own on an island citadel connected to the palace precinct by a causeway over the seasonal lake, Tughluq's own tomb combines elements from both Multan and Delhi. The walls of both compound and qubba are battered, as at Multan. On the other hand, the qubba form recalls the central pavilion of the Juma'at Khana and beyond that, the Alai Darwaza: decorative exuberance cedes to austerity, indeed to military

4.10a

4.10b

strength in the main, but the striking contrast of red and white material is retained. The outer gate has a great arch, battered like the walls and springing from inset colonettes, enclosing a vertical screen wall with a trabeated portal below arched lancet windows. Arcades around the compound are interrupted by porticoes of a Hindu Order before towers at the corners containing subsidiary burial chambers. The white marble dome,

4.10d,e

stringcourse, prayer-mat panels, iwan voussoirs – with the spearhead valance of the Alai Darwaza – and inset screens complement the vivid red sandstone without. Inside, the plain vertical walls are relieved only by the elegant mihrab but above squinches formed of double arches, red sandstone again gives way to white marble.

4.10c

The tomb of Firuz Shah, in the extensive complex incorporating a madrasa and a palace as well as the mosque at Hauz Khas, retains the battered walls – less aggressively – but resorts to plastered and tiled rubble rather than red sandstone: the effect without the tiles is grim. Sad too are the remains of Tilangami's seminal octagonal work at Nizam ud-din: an expansion of the canopy form (the Indian chattri) on the precedent of the Dome of the Rock in Jerusalem, the dome rests on eight arcades and is surrounded by a gallery with a saucer dome over the central bay of each side. It set the precedent for the tombs of the last dynasties of Delhi sultans: their ministers made do with the square form.

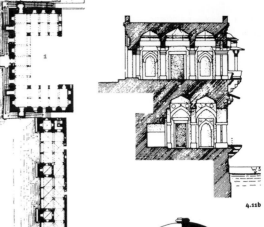

4.11b

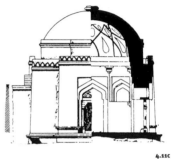

4.11c

4.11d

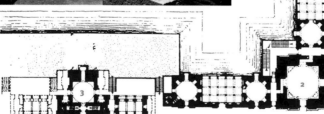

4.11a @ 1:1000

4.11e

›4.11 DELHI, HAUZ KHAS, c. 1380: (a) plan of complex with (1) mosque, (2) tomb, (3) madrasa, (b) section through gallery south of mosque, (c) half-elevation/half-section of tomb, (d, e) general views of the southern range across the tank and chattris in the southern precinct.

4.12

In Multan and in Delhi, their work at once derivative and idiosyncratic, the Tughlugs laid the foundations of the greatest funerary tradition of the Islamic world. And on the basis of several centuries of development, largely lost to us now, they set the pattern for the Indian imperial palace.

Up and down the subcontinent the ruins of citadels with traces of once-palatial apartments bear testimony to the passion of the Indian ruler for change. The most obvious examples are the sultanate seats in Delhi and Daulatabad – but we shall encounter spectacular examples in the provinces too. This passion – and war – has meant that little remains of palaces built before the Muslims achieved prominence – indeed until after the 14th century – and comprehension of secular developments is very far from complete. Yet across the gaps left by destruction and decay, one or other of the ancient native and imported types – the prasada, the apadana or talar, the iwan – appears always to dominate. And as required by the chancellor of the ancient Mauryan emperor Chandragupta, Kautilya (AIC2, page 25), there are invariably three clearly distinguished zones: the ceremonial with facilities for public audience, the king's private apartments and the zenana. Kotla Firoz Shah is the oldest substantial example.**4.13**

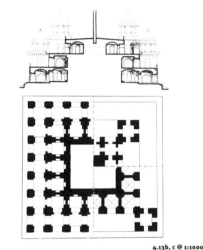

4.13b, c @ 1:1000

>**4.13 DELHI, KOTLA FIROZ SHAH:** (a) reconstruction (after Brown), (b, c) stepped pavilion, section and quartered plan (after Reuther).

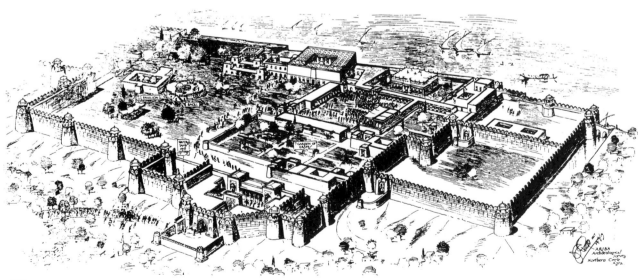

4.13a

Kotla Firoz Shah

Like most of its predecessors, Firoz Shah's new seat was protected by a citadel integrated with town defences. There are considerable denuded remains of the fort palace on an extensive terrace beside the Yamuna River. Incorporating all the constituent elements of the earliest Indian palaces, themselves derived from the Achaemenids, Kotla Firoz Shah lacks the formality and, indeed, the great vaulted structures of Abbasid or Ghaznavid complexes. Instead, trabeated pavilions of a type by no means unfamiliar in India seem to have been distributed in a way which recalls the tent palaces of central Asia, for which the Tughluqs' Turkish ancestors certainly felt as much affinity.

Within the massive battered battlements, beyond the main western gate and its stout barbican, was a vast irregular enclosure before the principal mosque. Through the enclosure, a circuitous route led to the sultan's quarters (Daulat Khana), with the court of public audience (Diwan-i-Am) dominated by a talar on its southern side, the private royal court (Diwan-i-Khas) on a riverside terrace beyond this to the east next to the conventional congregational mosque, and the harem quarters to its south.

Firoz Shah was an antiquarian and his interests extended well beyond his Muslim inheritance. Most significantly, an ancient Indian form plays a major symbolic role in the centre of his complex: a prasada, apparently once complete with chattris on its terraces, was built to support a pillar of the law credited to the Mauryan emperor Ashoka (c. 270–232 BCE), which Firoz removed to the capital from Tapra.

›4.14 CHANDERI, BADAL MAHAL: portal, 1460.

The freestanding palace portal – derived from the indigenous torana (AIC2, page 19) via the Tughluq translation of the Persian pishtaq – well represents the eclecticism of the rulers of Malwa in north-central India: the filigree screen is from neighbouring Gujarat to the west, the spearhead valance is a familiar motif of the early Delhi sultanate but the ogee profile of the arches is more pronounced than usual at Delhi, echoing practice in Jaunpur to the north and to the south in Mandu (the Malwan capital).

2 REGIONAL GRAVITY

Even the most impressive works of the late-Delhi sultanate are overawed by the riches of former provinces. The political process which conditioned the elevation of provincial patronage to sovereign significance had begun following Muhammad Tughluq's retreat from Daulatabad in 1338. Two years earlier a Hindu prince, who had been pressed into the service of the Khaljis, had himself crowned king of Hastinavati (Hampi) and founded the last great Hindu empire in the south – Vijayanagar (AIC2, pages 135–140). Within the decade, the Tughluq governor of the Deccan declared his independence as Bahaman Shah: he moved the capital from Daulatabad to Gulbarga and it was moved again in 1429 to Bidar. About the middle of the 14th century too, the governor of Bengal declared himself sultan. Kashmir followed.

After Timur's destruction of the Tughluqs in 1398, there was a further spate of secessions by provincial governors: Malik Sarwar founded the Sharqi (eastern) sultanate of Jaunpur in 1394; Dilawar Ghuri established himself in Malwa in 1401 and his successor Hoshang Shah founded a new capital at Mandu; Ahmad Shah made himself sultan of Gujarat with his capital at Ahmedabad in 1411.**4.14**

Following the usual period of pillaging Hindu temples, distinct architectural traditions developed in all these states, either in accordance with the imported proclivities of their immigrant rulers or on the basis of a rich indigenous legacy – or, indeed, from the cross-fertilization of the two. The former was the case in the Bahamani kingdom, Jaunpur and Malwa. The indigenous tradition was still virile in Kerela, Bengal, Kashmir and Gujarat and the grafting of imported forms on to it had spectacular results.

PERIPHERAL STATES

Around the periphery of the Indian subcontinent, notably in the Himalayas, Bengal and the far south-west, the need to shed prodigious quantities of rain – or snow – sponsored forms related by a common pragmatism but reflecting the local vernacular. At variance with the main streams of Hindu development, Nagara and Dravidian (AIC2, pages 135–140 and 238–239), most of these peripheral schools retained their identity until modern times: indeed, when the Muslims conquered these territories, they adopted the local vernacular.

>**4.15 CALIKUT, MISHQAL PALLI**, 16th century, restored: (a) general view, (b) detail.

4.15a

4.15b

The ports of Kerala had been entrepots of the Arabian Sea trade from time immemorial and, therefore, prime bastions of Islam in the subcontinent. However, the great Hindu empires of the south held sway there until Ala-ud-Din Khalji fatally weakened the grip of the Hoysalas (AIC2, pages 203–208) in the second decade of the 14th century. Muslim dominance was as shortlived as Muhammad bin-Tughluq's ambitions in the south and Kerala was absorbed by Vijayanagar. After the destruction of the latter by the combined forces of the Muslim Deccani sultans – heirs to the Bahamanis – it was again subject to Muslim rule for a brief period in the mid-17th century before its reabsorption into the Hindu realm of Mysore. The vernacular style was sustained throughout this chequered history, for the secular and religious purposes of Hindu or Muslim though, of course, the spatial requirements of a mosque are entirely different from those of a Hindu temple (AIC2, page 67ff.). **4.15**

4.16

At the other pole, in Kashmir way to the north, the Muslims who won the province in the fourth decade of the 14th century began with the conversion of Hindu temples and thereafter conformed to the local idiom. There were foreign imports – like the essentially Iranian brick tomb chamber of the *sufi* Pir Haji Muhammad Sahid which Sultan Zayn al-Abidin (1417-67) built in place of one designed for Hindu foundations. Far more common, however, was the form derived pragmatically from the ubiquitous timber village shrine (ziarat) – a simple square structure, usually with verandahs projecting more or less symmetrically, surmounted with a pyramidal roof and spire-like minaret. The Shah Hamdan and Jami-masjids in Srinagar may be taken as representative of the type.**4.16**

›4.16 KASHMIRI TRADITION: Srinagar, Shah Hamdan Mosque (c. 1400).

Shah Hamdan's mosque is a large but simple structure of one ziarat pavilion with a richly detailed timber interior capable of sheltering a considerable number of worshippers from the rigours of the climate. The much-restored and rebuilt Jami-masjid in the same city is a complex conforming in general to the court type with cloisters but the entrances and prayer hall are ziarat pavilions.

›4.17 BENGAL, SYNTHESIS BETWEEN THE TRADITIONAL AND THE IMPORTED: (a) Gaur, Dakhil Darwaza; (b) typical bangaldar; (c–f) Hazrat Pandua, Adina-masjid (c. 1360), prayer hall general views and interior details, plan; (g, h) Gaur, Tantipara-masjid and Ekhlakhi mausoleum (early 15th century)

In the planning of his Adina-masjid, Sultan Sikandar

4.17a

4.17b

emulated the Great Mosque of Damascus – and, implicitly, the Umayyads as instituters of legitimate rule. Three ranges of domed bays surrounded the court to the north, south and east but the five-aisled prayer hall is interrupted by an enormous iwan which clearly belongs to the tradition descended from Ctesiphon and most recently recalled in the Jami-masjid of Tabriz. Below crisply carved lotus mouldings the elaborate

In Bengal in the north-east, as in Kerala in the south-west, consistency of style prevailed across the Hindu/Muslim divide for similar reasons. When the Delhi sultan's forces conquered the province barely five years after the fall of Lal Kot, they founded their capital, Gaur, on the site of Sena Lakhnauti and maintained the splendid bulwarks of their predecessors as much to protect themselves from nature as from man but both have destroyed much where brick and bamboo are the traditional materials. Towards the middle of the 14th century the independent sultanate was ruled from Hazrat Pandua, where the first masterpiece of the regime survives in part. Gaur was revived a century later and, naturally, much more survives there to demonstrate the strength of the local tradition.

4.17c

4.17d

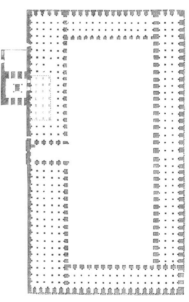

4.17e

4.17f @ 1:2000

Throughout the province the Muslims, like the Hindus before them, referred to the local vernacular for the great majority of their works: the basic form is the bamboo and mud hut with thatched roof curved to throw the water off more effectively. Despite the importation of more sophisticated types, this form (bangaldar) and its derivatives with pitched and hipped roof (do- and chou-chala), remained dominant throughout the architectural history of the province – not least because of the non-monumental nature of Bengali materials. **4.17**

4.17g

4.17h

central mihrab has a distinctly Hindu profile. Hindu artisans doubtless provided the other mihrabs, door frames, balconies and pillars – especially the squat ones with bracket capitals supporting the zenana gallery in the north wing of the prayer hall.

Below the cornice which follows the curve of the low-pitched roof in the vernacular types, elevations are consistently relieved by recessed panels in a rectilinear framework recalling the timber reinforcement of mud walls. Minarets are added at the corners. Tombs are usually square and the burial chamber rising above the curved roof may have a dome. The mosques conforming to the type are invariably rectangular, usually of two or three ranges of five arcaded and individually domed bays, but empty repetition often produced as many as ten or twelve. In later works the framework of terracotta panels is less assertive and often more monotonous, cusped arches are used for openings and a chou-chala may rise over the tomb chamber instead of a dome.

4.18a

THE BAHAMANI DECCAN

The Delhi artisans transported to Daulatabad took the sultanate style with them to the north-west Deccan but trade had long exposed the region to direct contact with western Asia. With trade came skilled immigrants and the Tughluq governor, the Shi'ite Iranian adventurer Jafar Khan, who asserted his independence at about the same time as his colleague in Hazrat Pandua, found talent from his homeland ready to hand to embellish his new seats. As Ala al-din Bahman (1347–58), he first ruled from Daulatabad, then moved the capital to Gulbarga – a Yadava fortified outpost stoutly redefended by its new masters.

The Bahamanis' Shi'ite leanings towards Iran are clearly revealed in their greatest mosques. The Jami-masjid built for Muhammad I (1358-73) by one Rafi of Qazvin at Gulbarga (c. 1360) is among the earliest in India to reflect interest in the multi-domed prayer halls of Isfahan: experiments in maximizing coverage were about to be launched by the architects of Firuzshah Delhi but none was as complete as Rafi's in Gulbarga. **4.18a–e**

The tombs of the first Bahamanis are essentially Tughluqian domed qubbas of plastered rubble with relief confined to the entrance arch. As at Delhi, the main line of development was the proliferation of bays and registers

›4.18 GULBARGA: (a–e) Jami-masjid (1368), exterior, details of entrance, inner arcades and outer arcades, plan; (f) Mujarrad Kamal's dargah-masjid, façade.

Surrounded by a moat cut from the rock, Gulbarga's doubled ramparts (16 metres thick) have stepped wallwalks and bastions with revolving platforms for cannon. The west gate, facing open country, has an extraordinary horn-shaped projection incorporating no less than four guarded courts deflecting the entrance towards maximum cover from battlements and bastions. As the site was no natural defensive eminence, the Bahamanis built the Bala Hissar, a massive block like the keeps of the Crusaders in the Holy Land and their European compatriots but outmoded in the west by the mid-14th century.

On a rectangular base, arcades two bays deep and a triple-aisled prayer hall may be distinguished in the plan of the Jami-masjid. However, the minor domed bays of the hall are extended to cover the whole court area and the cloisters are cross-spanned by great single ogee arches springing from low imposts on simple square piers between secondary domed spaces at each corner. Purely architectonic, the entire visual effect is drawn from the simple repetition of the two types of arch, which seem to float over anonymous supports. In subtle counterpoint, cusped arches make an appearance in the northern entrance, and the mihrab and squinches of the qubba have an idiosyncratic trefoil form.

4.18b

4.18c

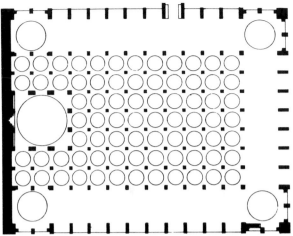

4.18e @ 1:1000

4.18d

›ARCHITECTURE IN CONTEXT »BEYOND THE EASTERN PALE

4.18f

and the stilting of domes over octagonal drums but there is a greater wealth of detail in moulded stucco or carved stone. As in the embellishment of mosques, some of the detail is distinctly Hindu in motif, particularly cornices (chadyas), the door frames, lotus-flower finials on domes and the lotus-bud caps of pinnacles. The dargah-masjid of Mujarrad Kamil goes further and incorporates flying arches below the chadya. **4.18f**

Gulbarga's formidable defences failed to reassure the Bahamanis that the site, towards the south-west frontier of their domain, was not overexposed to the threat from Vijayanagar with whose Hindu rulers they were in constant conflict. After seizing the throne, Ahmed Shah 1 (1427–35) made the strategic move to Bidar, a well-watered site with natural eminences near the centre of the kingdom. The sultanate disintegrated a century later and Bidar emerged as the capital of an independent realm under Al Barid (1543–79).

Bidar's defences, massively extended by Ahmad Shah and his successors, strengthened against artillery in the 16th century and renovated in the 17th century, are among the most impressive survivors of any medieval era anywhere in the world. The remains of the palace complexes are extensive too: there was considerable augmentation after the emergence of Bidar as a separate realm in the 16th century, but the main elements are usually dated to the second half of the 15th century. Despite the late work, it is convenient to deal with the whole complex here. **4.19a–f**

4.19a

4.19b

The Bidar fort

Bidar, formerly an outpost of the Kalyani Chalukyas (AIC2, page 190), is sited on a rising spur whose natural defences are augmented by walls 12 kilometres in extent: the town spreads over the lowest part of the site; the citadel is at the northern end where the eminence rises to 100 metres. A triple moat hewn from solid rock – probably inherited from the Chalukyas – separated the town from the citadel walls and its system of dams and sluices provided for its isolation. The walls (14 metres high) are doubled throughout their low-lying course but not above the precipitous northern slopes. The town's main southern and eastern entrances, the Fateh and Talghat Gates, are the most sophisticated of five entrances: they incorporate much of the familiar repertory of obstructive devices including octagonal towers with machicolated projections beyond a barbican and drawbridges leading to dog-leg passages closed with spiked doors. The main entrance to the citadel from the town, the Gumbad Darwaza, is a triple gate spanning the triple moat between the doubled walls.

Little survives of the palaces of Gulbarga and those of Bidar were severely damaged by imperial Mughal forces in the late-17th century but the distribution of their elements is clear and much of substance adheres to the walls. There were three main zones. The first, nearest to the Gumbad Darwaza, was probably the seat of the provincial governor before the transfer of the capital: the living quarters, in a bastion of the south-eastern range of ramparts, were transformed into the sumptuous Rangin Mahal (Coloured Palace) by Mahmud Shah c. 1490 and further embellished by the first independent ruler, Al Barid, in the mid-16th century. Second, in the centre of the complex, is the massive Solah Khumba-masjid built by Ahmad Shah's governor in 1423, before the transfer of the capital: its court was expanded to form the Lal Bagh. The watercourses of the latter linked the baths with the zenana whose main elements (developed over the century from c. 1450) are the so-called Tarkash Mahal (Turkish Palace) and Gagan Mahal (Heavenly Palace) on the southern ramparts: fountain courts are surrounded by varied chambers but in place of vaulted iwans the Gagan Mahal's dominant recession seems to have been filled with a trabeated talar. The third zone is preceded by the court of public audience and its huge apadana which are dated to the reign of Ahmad Shah I – the

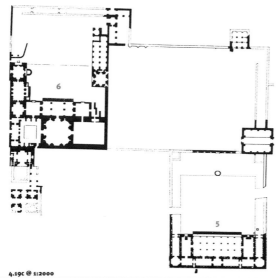

4.19C @ 1:2000

4.19e

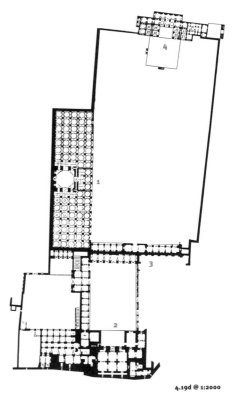

4.19d @ 1:2000

main chamber, (i, j) Solah Kumbah-masjid, exterior and interior, (k, l) Madrasa of Mahmud Gawan (1470), court and plan, (m, n) Bahamani tombs, Ahmad Shah (left) and interior, (o) tomb of Al Barid, exterior.

bases of the wooden columns remain. Beyond to the west, the contemporary court of private audience, flanked by a mosque and withdrawing rooms around fountain courts, was addressed from a recessed talar. The latter has disappeared like all the other talars in the complex except for the one attached to the Rangin Mahal and that is unrivalled as an example of the translation of a Persian form, with ancient Indian associations, into Hindu terms at the behest of a Muslim ruler. This cross-fertilization of the imported and indigenous was to prove enduringly popular with Deccani builders.

4.19f

4.19g

4.19h

4.19i

Rafi's exercise in the complete coverage of the prayer area in the Jami-masjid of Gulbarga was rarely repeated: his broad, low-slung arches rarely reappear. Bidar's main mosques, the Solah Kumbah and Jami-masjid – built just before and just after the transfer of the capital – retain the multi-domed prayer hall but combine it with the traditional open court and favour conventionally proportioned arches with minimal imposts. At Gulbarga transition from square to octagon below the springing of domes was usually effected by squinches or muqarnas but the builders of Bidar began interpolating the apex of a pointed arch in repetition of the main arcades, producing a star-shaped perimeter. Star shapes had long been popular with the Deccani Hindus but the variations favoured by the Mus-

4.19j

4.19k

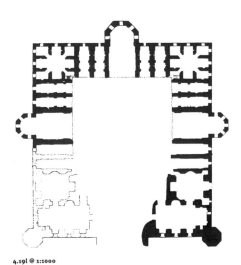

4.19l @ 1:1000

lims included lattice vaults related to those of their Timurid contemporaries.

The influence of contemporary Iran is nowhere more pervasive than in the great madrasa built by Mahmud Gawan, the Persian minister of Muhammad Shah Baaman III (1463–82) – Bidar's chief claim to architectural distinction after the fort. An elevation of three storeys of cells for students is rare, but the rigorously symmetrical four-iwan plan of Mahmud Gawan's foundation, its arcading and its revetment of brilliantly coloured tiles are related to contemporary Timurid work, the most notable intermediary between Gawan's building and the foundation of Samarkand being the lost madrasa of Gauhar Shad at Herat. As in several Timurid madrasas, the Bidar work's

4.19m

4.19n

mosque is balanced by a hall on the other side of the entrance. The monumental minarets of the eastern front are exceptional among the works of the Bahamanis. Despite the quality of the building, the type represented by this Iranian importation was not to be favoured in India.**4.19j, k**

The bulbous form of dome, as yet squatter than the Timurid norm, appears in Mahmud Gawan's work for the first important time in India. It was predominant in the Deccan in the 16th century, notably at Bidar on the canopy tomb with which Al Barid distinguished himself from his Bahamani predecessors. The latter's tombs were essentially Tughluqian domed qubbas of plastered rubble with relief confined to the entrance arch and, as at Delhi, the main line of development was the proliferation of bays and registers: the finest, especially in its interior decoration, is the tomb of Ahmad Shah I.**4.19m–o**

4.19o

4.203

JAUNPUR

The independence asserted by the governors of the Deccan and Bengal was not to be emulated in the other major provinces of the Delhi sultanate until after the destruction of the Tughluq regime by Timur. Jaunpur set the renewed

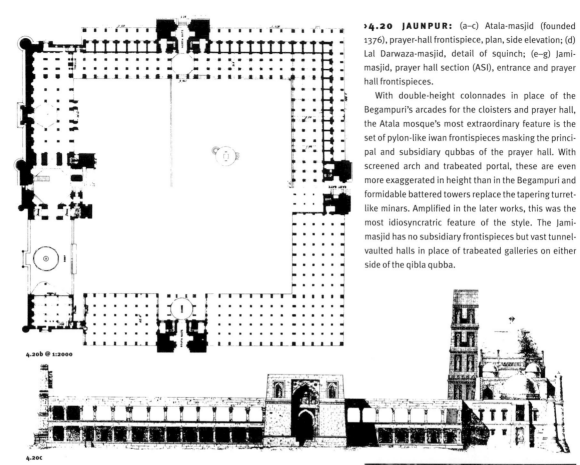

4.20b @ 1:2000

4.20c

(a–c) Atala-masjid (founded 1376), prayer-hall frontispiece, plan, side elevation; (d) Lal Darwaza-masjid, detail of squinch; (e–g) Jami-masjid, prayer hall section (ASI), entrance and prayer hall frontispieces.

With double-height colonnades in place of the Begampuri's arcades for the cloisters and prayer hall, the Atala mosque's most extraordinary feature is the set of pylon-like iwan frontispieces masking the principal and subsidiary qubbas of the prayer hall. With screened arch and trabeated portal, these are even more exaggerated in height than in the Begampuri and formidable battered towers replace the tapering turret-like minars. Amplified in the later works, this was the most idiosyncratic feature of the style. The Jami-masjid has no subsidiary frontispieces but vast tunnel-vaulted halls in place of trabeated galleries on either side of the qibla qubba.

example. The city was founded by Firoz Shah Tughluq in 1358 on an ancient Hindu site by the Gumti River. Begun soon after, the Atala-masjid initiated a series of monumental works promoted by the independent Sharqi sultans which culminated in the Jami- and Lal Darwaza masjids. Taking its departure from Delhi's Begampuri, the Jaunpur formula derives its greater monumentality not only from the adjustment of the proportions of the main elements but also from the substitution for rubble of fine grey sandstone and granite won from temples or dressed specifically for them by Hindu masons.**4.20**

4.20d

4.20e

4.20f

4.20g

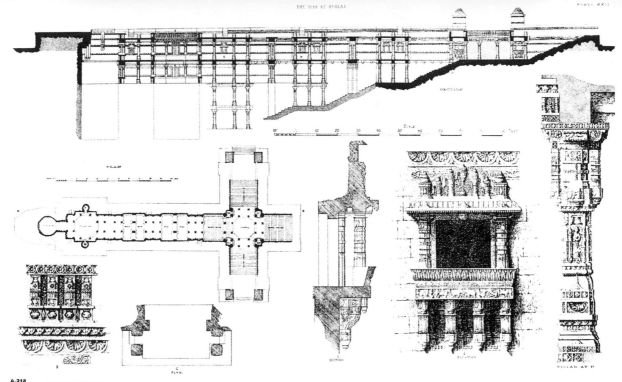

4.21a

4.21b

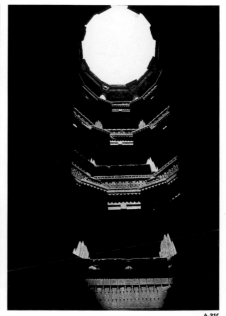

4.21c

›ARCHITECTURE IN CONTEXT »BEYOND THE EASTERN PALE

>4.21 AHMEDABAD: (a–c) plan, section, details and views of the wells of Rudabai and Dada Hari; (d–h) Jami-masjid (1423), plan with tombs of Ahmad Shah (centre) and his queens (left), exterior of the sultan's tomb, section through prayer hall, interior, exterior of queens' tomb; (i–k) mortuary complex of Rani Rupvati (1505), sections through prayer hall and tomb chamber, general view from the south-west; (l) Sidi Sayyid mosque, detail of screened arcade.

In the unsurpassed Jami-masjid, with five large chambers to its prayer hall, the arcaded façade screens only the three central zones. The slightly projecting frontispiece incorporates minarets which rise from the ground, as in contemporary Timurid Iran, but they are applied to the outer face and their bases have much of the complexity of Solanki piers. There is a clear progression in height from the trabeated outer bays to the arcaded intermediate ones and on to the central frontispiece. This responds to an increasing number of superimposed galleries within, the central chamber with its flying arches rivalling the great open halls of the Jains.

Ahmad Shah's tomb, of the canopy type but square in plan, has deep screened colonnades leading from porches at the cardinal points to the main tomb chamber, whose great corbelled vault rests somewhat haphazardly on beams extended between pilasters in the arcaded walls. The queens' tomb (Rani-ka Huira) is a raised open court surrounded by doubled colonnades with screens supported on the central range of pillars. These works inspired many others over the century and a half of the sultanate's independent existence.

GUJARAT

The earliest centres of Muslim culture in India were in Sind and the ports of Gujarat, where Arab traders had long been domesticated, but only fragments of the oldest works survive. Established in the Solanki domain when its rich cultural tradition had just reached maturity and anxious to assert their own magnificence, the Muslim rulers of Gujarat were as prolific as patrons as their Hindu predecessors and Jain contemporaries. Moreover, dependent at first on the spoils from Hindu sites and on local craftsmen always, they sustained the most prolix of Indian styles despite the change in religion.

Ahmedabad was founded as the capital of Gujarat on a Solanki site. Theory notwithstanding, in practice few Indian cities were decidedly formal in plan, but here a great axial thoroughfare, spanned by a magnificent triumphal arch, linked the citadel and its palace with the Jami-masjid, itself aligned with the tombs of the ruler and his wives. Little survives of the palace but, among utilitarian facilities, much is left of the palatial public wells (wavs) rebuilt in accordance with tradition: more than merely sources of water, they are subterranean retreats from the heat with sumptuous chambers open from superimposed galleries.**4.21a–e**

Of the capital's many mosques, some reverted to the primitive type with open prayer halls – like the original

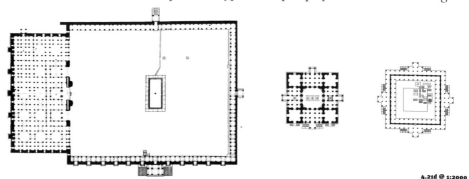

4.21d @ 1:2000

4.21e

4.21f

›ARCHITECTURE IN CONTEXT »BEYOND THE EASTERN PALE

4.21g

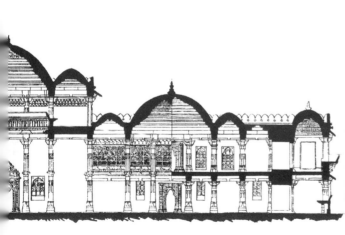

4.21h

4.21i

4.21j

4.21k

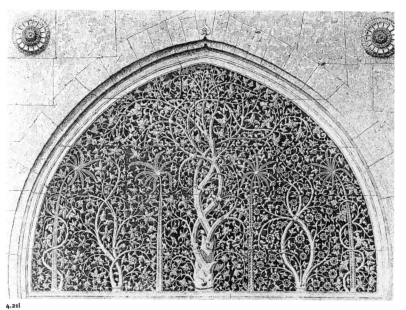

4.21l

Quwwat al-Islam – but the majority developed the arcaded screen type most popular in Delhi with Hindu pillars visible through the arcades. In the capital and elsewhere the province is exceptionally rich in survivals but the process of development culminated in Ahmad Shah's Jami-masjid.**4.21f–k**

Ahmedabad is particularly notable for its mortuary complexes (rauzas) in which tomb and mosque confront one another across an open court. Matching in exquisitely refined detail, the former usually conforms to the model provided by the tomb of Ahmad Shah, the latter, naturally, is of the old unscreened type. For want of a frontispiece to the prayer hall, minarets were applied to the front corners, but tending there to deny the composition integrity. they were progressively reduced in scale until they became mere ornamental turrets, as here. With this went the proliferation of subsidiary projections such as balconies.**4.21l**

4.22a

MALWA AND ITS HINDU NEIGHBOURS

The Tughluq governors of Malwa ruled from Dhar and the first Ghuri sultan stayed there. The second ruler, Hoshang Shah (1405–35), chose the virtually impregnable plateau of Mandu some 35 kilometres from Dhar as the site for a new capital. This had been a seat of the Hindu Paramaras and Hoshang Shah built his own royal complex on that of the Hindus around a great tank. After tortuous access to the broad plateau, a fine ceremonial route led from the Delhi Gate to the several royal enclosures past the cult centre. There the crossing of a subsidiary axis, extending the qibla of the Jami-masjid, aligned the sultan's tomb to the west

›4.22 MANDU, THE RELIGIOUS WORKS: (a–c) Jami-masjid (early 15th century), entrance pavilion and prayer hall interior, detail of mihrab and minbar; (d) tomb of Hoshang Shah (c. 1430) with the domes of the mosque in the background; (e) remains of the Ashrafi Mahal (c. 1440).

4.22b

4.22c

and, to the east, the Ashrafi Mahal – one of India's earliest formally planned madrasas.**4.22**

The axis of the Faith

The earliest Malwan mosques were largely assembled from materials pillaged from Hindu temples. However, able to attract the artisans of Delhi under-employed by the successors of Firoz Shah, Hoshang Shah was not content with mere improvisation. The prayer hall of the great mosque is of the open hypostyle type, common among the contemporary works of neighbouring Gujarat but rare in the sullanate, yet the austerity of Firuzshah forms is preferred to Gujarati floridity in a wholly arcuate context. The extended series of identical domed bays is interrupted before the qibla by three nine-bay qubbas – but no iwan or frontispiece – and by a monumental

entrance pavilion in the centre of the east range. Domed turrets mark the corners, as in the mosques of Tilangani. The piers are those of Firuzshah Delhi but the arches retain the ogee profile also favoured in the Deccan and decorative play is made with flying arches, after the non-structural principle of the native tradition but with Firuzshah restraint in practice.

Except for a modest amount of tiling, for which the Malwans had a special facility, the building relies for its effect on simple repetition and the play of light over the beautiful red sandstone , sharply delineating the elegant arches with their sturdy verticals against the depth of the void and the deep shadow line thrown by the chadya. Inside, restraint is relinquished solely in the chattri of the minbar and the several mihrabs. Etched with the spearhead valance popluar in Delhi, these are enriched with stone in contrasting colours.

The domes of the Jami-masjid's prayer hall and entrance pavilion are echoed by that of Hoshang Shah's tomb beyond the qibla to the west: among the earliest Muslim buildings in India to be sheathed entirely in white marble, the weighty qubba is relieved only by iwan arches. To the east of the mosque, little but the base remains of the Ashrafi Mahal: the open court of the original madrasa, once surrounded by cells on several levels, was filled to provide the foundation for the tomb chamber of

4.22e

Mahmud Khalji, who displaced the Ghurids in 1436. The new sultan also enlarged one of the corner pavilions to provide the base for a seven-storey tower of victory emulating the Qutb Minar in celebration of triumph over Chittor in 1443.

4.23a

Mahmud Khalji's transformation of the Ashrafi Mahal was ill-founded and menaced collapse well before the end of the next century but the insertion of a square block of large volume into a square court surrounded by living accommodation was to provide an important precedent for great works in the Mughal era. The building types involved – tomb and madrasa – were imported.

As in Firuzshah Delhi, the development of the palace at Mandu in the central decades of the 15th century was a seminal exercise in combining both the imported and indigenous traditions. The contemporary palace of the Rana Kumbha at Chittor (1433-68), Malwa's neighbour and adversary to the west, is the product of a similarly syncretic process. Knowledge of the former must inform the latter: Muslim and Hindu work is interdependent. **4.23, 4.24**

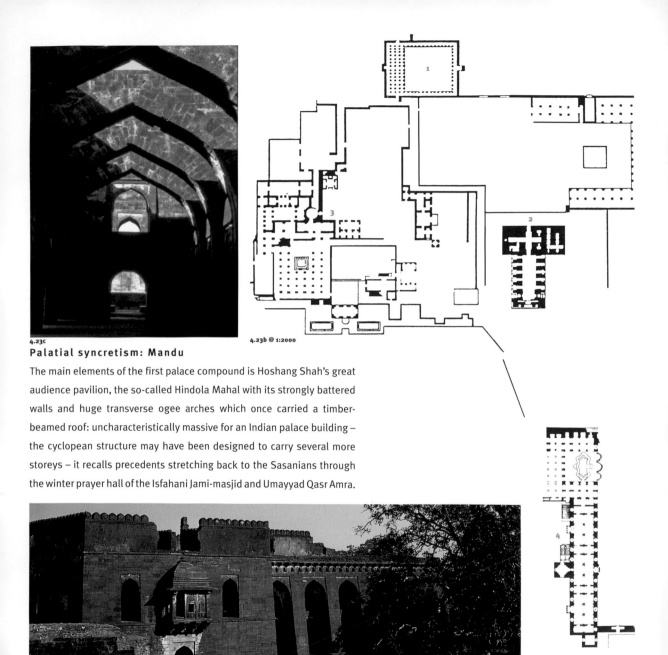

4.23c

4.23b @ 1:2000

Palatial syncretism: Mandu

The main elements of the first palace compound is Hoshang Shah's great audience pavilion, the so-called Hindola Mahal with its strongly battered walls and huge transverse ogee arches which once carried a timber-beamed roof: uncharacteristically massive for an Indian palace building – the cyclopean structure may have been designed to carry several more storeys – it recalls precedents stretching back to the Sasanians through the winter prayer hall of the Isfahani Jami-masjid and Umayyad Qasr Amra.

3d

4.23e

›4.23 MANDU, ROYAL PALACE COMPLEX, c. 1410 onwards: (a) sultan enthroned, (b) plan with (1) palatine mosque, (2) Hindola Mahal, (3) daulat khana, (4) Jahaz Mahal, (c, d) Hindola Mahal, interior and exterior, (e) daulat khana, (f) Jahaz Mahal.

More typical of India are the daulat khana, the zenana and retreats of later rulers. Generous courts surrounded by myriad small rooms, airy towers rising from screened and canopied terraces all respond to a climate in which much of life may seek open air but also wants cool, dark and varied retreat from the sun.

Sad now without the predominantly blue tiles which once masked its plastered rubble, the Daulat Khana was dominated from the uppermost level by a multi-columned hall of the indigenous mandapa type but at base the complex descends from the Parthian tradition of walled courts, iwans and irregularly disposed chambers – in contrast to Kotla Firoz Shah with its central-Asian antecedents. On the other hand, the indigenous prasada tradition is recalled in the main kiosk-crowned, balconied pavilion of the long, slender arcaded zenana of Mahmud I. When its revetment of tiles was complete, it must have been a gorgeous confection reflected in the water of the tank to either side.

.23f

Rana Kumbha's Chittor

The palace in the Chittor fort is the earliest complex built for a Hindu ruler of which much substance survives. Like the daulat khana at Mandu, walled and arcaded if embellished with trabeated elements, it seems to descend from the court and iwan tradition imported nearly 1500 years earlier by the Parthians – but the lineage has been lost. Like the zenana wing at Mandu, it acknowledges the indigenous tradition too.

Terminating the series of gates along the ascent to the acropolis, the principal entrance to Rana Kumbha's palace compound, guarded by twin octagonal towers, is embellished with serpentine brackets between post and beam in the indigenous manner and with niches in the form of the imported arch. Within is an elongated trabeated portico for the guard, the right-hand range aligned with the audience mandapa. Beyond this open public zone, in the seemingly random distribution of rooms around private courts, there is no obvious distinction between the ruler's personal quarters and the accommodation of the royal women.

Some relatively formal elements may be distinguished: on the southwestern corner of the main building, opposite the main gate, a tower rises over doubled halls which address the main inner court in the manner of iwans though they are trabeated like talars; adjacent to another tower on the north-west corner, beyond the innermost court, is a three-storey block with a rectangular hall flanked by a pair of square chambers. Hardly less than the towers themselves, this latter structure is distinct, and all three elements, with their superimposed balconies carried on elaborate brackets and piers, recall the prasada. Even more extreme superimposition produced the Tower of Victory which the Rana erected to commemorate a turn of fortune in his incessant war with his neighbour – and in answer to the victory minaret added to the Ashrafi Mahal in Mandu when Mahmud Khalji had had his turn of fortune.

4.24a

›4.24 CHITTOR: (a) Tower of Victory (1458); (b, c) Palace of Rana Kumbha (1433–68), north front and main gate (Tripolia) with the court and audience hall beyond.

The Mandu and Chittor palaces stand at the head of a series of important works for both Hindu and Muslim rulers which led to the imperial court of the Mughal emperor Akbar and beyond. The pivotal masterpieces are the late-15th century and early 16th-century Tomar palaces

4.24b

4.24c

4.25a

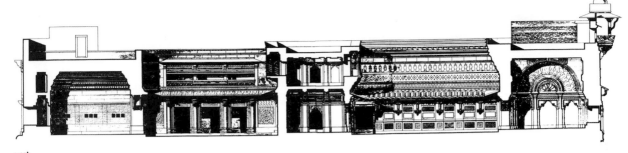

4.25b

at Gwalior. Planned around court and iwan, but recalling the prasada tradition, it represents the most fundamental synthesis of native and imported ideas.**4.25**

Man Singh's Gwalior

The palace of Man Singh in the great fort at Gwalior is the oldest Hindu secular building of any importance to come down to us virtually intact. High on the edge of the vast spur which dominates the town, access is gained by a typically tortuous route through a series of gates culminating in the precinct portal – as Kautiliya required. The splendid ramparts and Hathi Pol (Elephant Gate) are clearly in direct line of descent from those at Sanchi and the prasadas have become double-height chattris on the towers. The walls retain rich blue, white and yellow tilework in the context of a sumptuous articulation incorporating elements drawn from both the native trabeated and imported arcuated traditions, carved in relatively high relief from fine masonry.

On the principal level of the royal apartments, the halls and chambers are formally disposed about two square courts, though these are not axially aligned: the main halls are represented as mandapas though they are formally integrated with the courts in accordance with the imported tradition of the iwan. All the spaces are essentially human in scale, despite external appearances, and as richly varied in volume as in surface ornament. The zenana quarters above have communication passages to the outside and roof terraces with pavilions, and overlook the courts from screened galleries between deep eaves. Subterranean chambers recall the subterranean rooms (serdabs) long provided in Persian and Mesopotamian palaces for summer retreat.

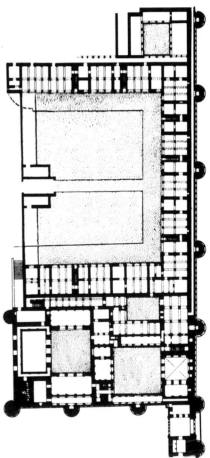

4.25c @ 1:1000

›4.25 GWALIOR: (a–g) Fort-Palace of Man Singh (1486–1516), ramparts and Hathi Pol from the south (pages 526–527), section and plan, main eastern court

4.25d

4.25e

25f

4.25g

›ARCHITECTURE IN CONTEXT »BEYOND THE EASTERN PALE

4.25h

Within the stout walls – as in their articulation – the structure is a trad-itional trabeated one, the eaves and galleries supported on particularly luxurious serpentine brackets, the piers which screen the main spaces from the courts bearing capitals descended from the forms elaborated by the Chandellas and their contemporaries. The roofing of the main western hall was achieved pragmatically by laying large slabs of stone against a raised transom, but there is a false ribbed vault over the eastern chamber.

of the private apartments, vaulted chambers; (h) Gujari Mahal (1510).

The private apartments are within the walls adjacent to the gate; the range with galleries and two-storey chattris borders the main audience (durbar) court. Beyond are four palaces of later rulers.

4.26

3 THE MUGHALS: ADVENT

After the death of Firoz Shah in 1388 more than a century is dominated by the activities of provincial rulers who took advantage of Delhi's weakness. The Tughluqs were replaced by Timur's nominee, but his undistinguished Sayyid line did little more than sustain itself in Delhi and build tombs until dispatched by the Afghan Lodis in 1451.**4.26** Sikandar Lodi (1488–1516) managed to reassemble something of an empire in north India, with its capital at Agra, and his reign has left some considerable monuments but his line was to be short-lived.**4.27, 4.28**

›4.27 TOMBS OF THE SAYYID AND LODI PERIOD IN DELHI: (a) Mubarakpur, Bare-Khan-ka Gumbad (late-15th century); (b, c) Lodi Gardens, tomb of Muhammad Sayyid (c. 1480), general view, section, half-plans at base and parapet levels; (d) Lodi Gardens, Bara Gumbad (early 16th century), general view from the north-east with its funerary mosque.

4.27a

4.27b

4.27c

The octagonal form of tomb favoured by Tilangani was adopted by the Sayyid and Lodi rulers while the qubba form was developed by countless noblemen. Muhammad Sayyid's architect reinforced the corners with battered piers, enhanced the continuous chadya, and replaced the low cupola over the central bay of each side by octagonal chattris. Qubba design involved varied stonework delineating an increasing number of bays and registers. Chattris appear on the corners. The major motif is the iwan frontispiece, with trabeated or arcaded portals.

4.27d

4.28a

›4.28 DELHI, SIRI, MOTHI-KI MOSQUE,
early 16th century: (a) exterior, (b) interior.

Rejecting the novel, satisfying but inappropriate centralized plan of the Khirki mosque, Lodi architects reverted to the arcaded prayer hall addressing an open court. Their experiments with centralization in the design of the arcade culminated here: each bay is domed and, though the arches are consistent in size and relief, the outer plane of the central one is raised with panelled piers to form an iwan frontispiece which interrupts the deep awning. The piers between the intermediate bays echo those of the frontispiece in a lower key and the whole composition is closed at the ends by broad piers pierced with elegant niches.

4.28b

THE FIRST MUGHALS

Sikandar Lodi's grandiloquent son alienated his main sup-
porters. They appealed to the Timurid prince Babur who,
dispossessed of his inheritance in central Asia by the
Shibanids but forging a kingdom in Afghanistan,
responded in the recognition of a great opportunity. He
despatched the Lodi sultan in 1526 and occupied Agra,
went on to Man Singh's Gwalior but retired from India as
soon as possible to lay out gardens in Kabul.**4.29** He died
in 1530, far from having consolidated his hold on India,

>4.29 THE FIRST MUGHALS: (a) Babur invest-
ing Gwalior; (b) Humayun in the wilderness.

>4.30 DELHI, JAMALI-MASJID, 1536: (a)
prayer hall from south-east, (b) interior detail of Jamal
Khan's tomb.

and was buried in his favourite Kabul garden. His son Humayun made a good start in campaigns against Malwa and Gujarat but lost himself to indolence and his throne to the Afghan Sher Shah in 1540. After fifteen years of exile in Iran,**4.33b** he won the throne back from Sher Shah's successor but died within the year.

WORKS OF THE INTERREGNUM

Of several mosques built during the turbulent decades in which the Mughals were establishing themselves, the Jamali-masjid at Mehrauli and the Qila-i-Kuhna in Delhi's Purana Qila are the most important followers of the Moth-ki-masjid in departing from the traditional courtyard plan. The five arches of the freestanding prayer hall are consistent in size in the earlier work but the central bay is given prominent relief with a pishtaq and there is a single dome. The centralization of the Qila-i-Kuhna's façade, through the manipulation of planes in concert with a rich palette of coloured stone inlay, is at its most subtle.**4.30, 4.31**

4.30b

4.30a

4.31a

4.31b

538   ›ARCHITECTURE IN CONTEXT »BEYOND THE EASTERN PALE

Purana Qila

The first great citadel built after the advent of the Mughals, the Purana Qila which dominated Humayun's new Delhi capital of Dinpannah, seems to have followed the precedent set ready to hand by Firoz Shah though the so-called Sher Mandal, the octagonal building used as a library in which Humayun met his death, may be seen as a miniature derivative of the hasht behist form used in Uzun Hassan's Tabriz palace. In a way typical of early Mughal works, like the Jamali-masjid at Mehrauli and the Purana's own Qala-i Kuhna, the portal set into the powerful bastions combines Persian-inspired encaustic tile work, marble mosaic possibly contributed by refugees from Mamluk Egypt and India's own finely dressed red sandstone inlaid with panels of contrasting colours or white marble.

The five arches of the Qala-i Kuhna progress in height from the sides to the centre but the elevated blind arcades are applied before each in

4.31c

counterpoint, the outer ones being taller but shallower than the intermediate ones and the central one taller still but deeper. The foremost plane of the frontispiece has a spearhead valance and this is echoed on the inner arches of the intermediate bays while the plain white marble surround of the innermost central arch echoes the blind outer arches of the side bays, both in the context of coloured inlay. Dispensing with colouristic effects and rich materials, except for the lavish mihrab, the interior relies wholly on cool lucidity in the delineation of multiple arches.

The Purana Qila and its splendid mosque were probably begun by Humayun but the achievement is generally attributed to Sher Shah and, as Babur decreed that he should be buried in his garden at Kabul, the Afghan usurper was responsible for the first great funerary work of the Mughal era: the apotheosis of the octagonal form of mausoleum inherited from the late Delhi sultanate, it is set in a lake at Sasaram in Bihar.**4.32**

›**4.31 DELHI, PURANA QILA:** (a) general view, (b, c) Qala-i Kuhna Mosque (1541), east front and interior of prayer hall.

›**4.32 SASARAM, TOMB OF SHER SHAH,** c. 1540: (a) section and half-plan, (b) entrance front with causeway (19th-century lithograph), (c) view over lake.

On a high walled platform with corner chattris and stepped terrace connected to the entrance pavilion by a causeway, the mausoleum has a chattri-crowned verandah around the high, clerestory-lit tomb chamber. The dome, on a low drum, is surrounded by eight more chattris. This superimposition of chattris in stepped tiers leading up to the great dome counter the horizontals far more effectively than formerly, producing an aspiring pyramidal composition to which the finite mass of the platform provided an admirable foil.

4.32a @ 1:1000

4.32c

4.32b

4.33a

4.33b

AKBAR

Humayun's son Akbar, born in exile and only thirteen on his accession, survived to demonstrate his worth thanks to his exceptionally able guardian, Bairam Khan. Brusquely assuming the government on attaining his majority, he spent the next forty years expanding his power with outstanding generalship and consolidating it with enlightened policies: the Rajputs were under control by 1568, Gujarat was absorbed by 1573, Bengal the following year, Kashmir in 1583, Orissa in 1592 and Sind in 1595. Though

›4.33 AKBAR: (a–f) images from the *Akbarnama* and other contemporary Mughal court sources illustrating the emperor's prowess in sport and war, his erudition and religious tolerance (specifically of the Hindu Krishna cult and Christianity).

4·33c

4·33d

he advanced against the Deccan with some success, it took
his dynasty a century to overcome Bijapur and Golconda
– the two states which had won most from Vijayanagar and
from subsequent campaigns against their neighbours. **4·33**

   Akbar constructed an exceptionally sound administrative edifice and cemented it by mollifying his Hindu subjects. Authority in provincial administration was divided
between the chief executive officer and the revenue col-
lector, and office-holders were remunerated in cash rather
than land. The Rajputs were left autonomous and invested

4.33e

4.33f

with high office, army commands and imperial honours. Akbar married a Rajput bride who bore him his heir.

Akbar's monarchy acquired an aura of sanctity derived from the ancient Vedic tradition and, indeed, his whole approach was symptomatic of his unorthodox attitude to Islam. He promulgated a new syncretic faith, the Din-i Ilahi, which acknowledged many theologies and to which the monarch was central. Apart from the imperial system itself, the most obvious expression of Akbar's syncretism was the synthesis in painting and architecture of Persian forms with which Humayun and his suite were certainly well acquainted and those traditional in India.

THE EARLY MUGHAL IMPERIAL SEAT

Babur was a man of acute aesthetic awareness, attuned to the sophisticated works of the Timurids and Safavids. In his memoirs he claims credit for several gardens and pavilions and betrays some contempt for the Indian tradition. One of the few Indian buildings he did admire was Man Singh's Gwalior palace – presumably because its architect, reducing the monumental to the exquisite, adapted the

4.35a

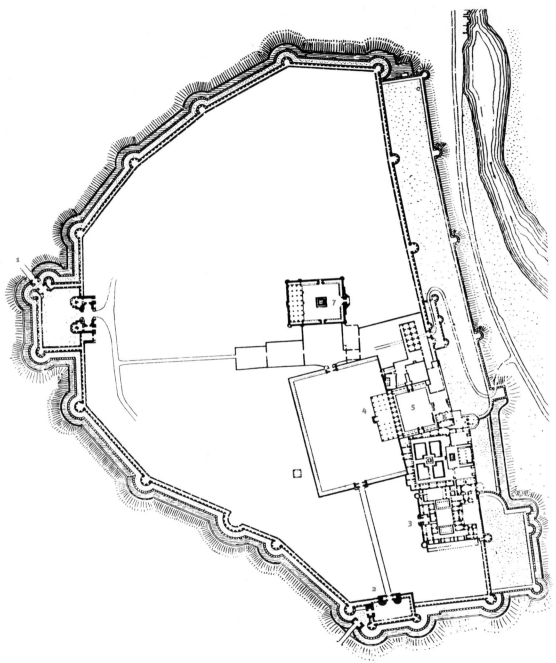

4.35b @ 1:5000

›**4.35 AGRA, RED FORT**, 1564–65: (a) entrance through the south-west barbican, (b) plan with (1) Delhi Gate, (2) Amar Singh Gate, (3) Jahangiri Mahal, (4) Diwan-i-Am, (5) Rang Mahal, (6) Diwan-i-Khas, (7) Mothi-masjid, (c) Delhi Gate, detail, (d–i) Jahangiri Mahal façade, section, river front, central court, chambers.

The Agra fort is an irregular semi-circle with its base parallel to the Yamuna River. On the river side there is a broad terrace between the two-tiered walls, breaking out into irregularly spaced bastions of which the most prominent commands a water gate. On the town side the moated, doubled walls with regularly spaced bastions are more massive and reach 30 metres in height. Between three stringcourses there are two rows of slits for marksmen, the upper ones grouped between hood machicolations. The Delhi Gate to the west is emblazoned with elephants overcome by a hybrid winged beast – a syncretic exercise of Hindu lineage symbolizing the power of the empire. Like the Amar Singh Gate to the south, it has a barbican with canted, restricted and multiple acute-angled turns.

4.35c

ubiquitous west Asian court and vaulted hall to suit a climate which Babur specifically deplored.

Like his predecessors in the unfinished Purana Qila, Akbar furthered the tradition represented by Kotla Firuz Shah in his series of metropolitan and provincial fortresses, most notably those of Agra, Lahore and Allahabad. Beyond their general distribution, the defence work is the most substantial legacy of Akbar's period in all his greatest forts. Pronounced aesthetic sensibility was brought to bear on the design of even the most utilitarian elements, achieving a compromise between oppressive power and festive display which is at its most admirable, perhaps, at Agra.

The principal royal seat was clearly designed to impress the native princes but also to win their admiration. In a way utterly typical of the Din-Illahi, moreover, much in the decorative scheme is of Islamic inspiration but much else derives from the indigenous tradition. Akbar's appreciation of the resources of indigenous artisans is explicit in the official record of the construction of 'upwards of 500 edifices of red stone in the fine styles of Bengal and Gujarat'. Of these, few survive in the major metropolitan forts: most of the main elements of these were transformed two generations later by Shah Jahan in the sumptuous style which he brought to its fruition at Delhi.

The chihil sutun of Allahabad gives some idea of Akbar's hall of public audience at Agra, lost to Shah Jahan, but by far the most important survivor is the so-called Jahangiri Mahal, the main element in the harem at Agra. Evidently sharing his grandfather's predilections, Akbar had the former modelled on the palace of Man Singh at Gwalior: representing the most fundamental synthesis of the native and the imported, as we have seen, that splendid work could hardly have failed to appeal to the emperor's syncretic sensibility.**4.34, 4.35**

4.35d

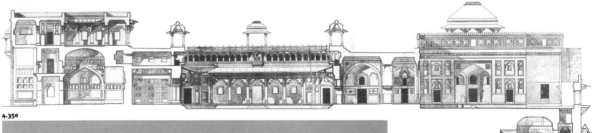

4.35e

4.35f

The Jahangiri Mahal's plan is symmetrical along the clearly defined central axis from the entrance with its striking coloured frontispiece, through the square central court to the recessed terrace overlooking the river. Something of the great caliphate tradition of palace planning survives in the way service zones isolate the central court and the main reception spaces addressing it. Inside, the rich elaboration of the indigenous trabeated system in red sandstone often varies themes stated in the palace of Man Singh at Gwalior. Outside, the effect drawn from the same material, inlaid with white marble and coloured stone, is typically early Mughal, but relief ornament is resolutely Islamic.

4.35g

4.35h

4.35i

4.36a

If continuous use meant continuous change at the principal imperial seats, the very non-viability as a permanent capital of Akbar's own foundation at Fatehpur Sikri, initiated in honour of the emperor's favoured *sufi sheikh* Selim Chishti, was the prime condition for the survival of its most important elements: the palace and the mosque beside the *sheikh*'s khanqah on a ridge above the site of the largely vanished town. Hardly had it been completed when the water supply proved inadequate: the new city was abandoned and Akbar's court thereafter moved regularly between Agra and Lahore.**4.36**

4.36b

Fatehpur Sikri

The Badshahi ('imperial') Mosque, by far the greatest of the many mosques of Akbar's reign, is traditional in its court plan: surrounded by cloisters, heightened and deepened and interrupted by a pishtaq in the same plane, it is in marked contrast to the freestanding block of the Afghan period. The qibla qubba, its dome hidden by the frontispiece, is richly decorated within with carved, painted and inlaid ornament: transition is effected by arched squinches rather than by corbelling as in the two subsidiary qubbas. The dominant element – interpolated to impress from without at some cost to the interior – is the triumphal Buland Darwaza ('lofty gate') which, bearing celebrated pantheistic inscriptions, replaced the south portal above the service quarters of the town to commemorate Akbar's conquest of Gujarat.

The incorporation of arcuate and trabeated structural elements and decorative details from both the Persian and the native repertoires is

>4.36 FATEHPUR SIKRI, 1570s: (a–c) Badshahi
Mosque, Buland Darwaza, prayer hall front and Selim
Chishti's tomb; (d) plan with (1) court of public audience, (2) emperor's quarters with private court around
the Anup Tala'o tank (Diwan-i-Khas was probably here),
(3) northern pavilion with central column (so-called
Diwan-i-Khas), (4) harem building, (5) 'House of Bir-
bal', (6) 'House of Maryam', (7) Nagina Mosque, (8)
Panch Mahal, (9) Badshahi Mosque; (e–i) emperor in
context, main palace compound looking south to
emperor's quarters with Panch Mahal right, so-called
Diwan-i-Khas pavilion exterior and interior column,
principal harem compound.

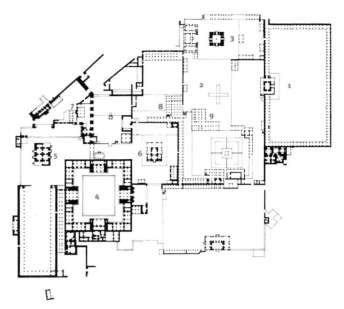

4.36d @ 1:1500

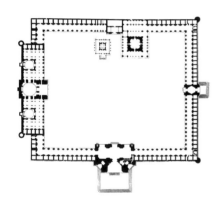

characteristic of Akbar's works. Red sandstone with coloured stone and white marble inlay are the characteristic materials. The principal exception is the marble-sheathed tomb of Selim Chishti which eclipses all else in the mosque's court: with its filigree screens and extravagant serpentine brackets springing from chevron-patterned columns below deep chadyas, it marks the triumph of the style of Ahmedabad at Akbar's eclectic court.

Walled for distinction rather than defence, the palace compound was usually entered by the emperor and his retinue through the Hathi Pol facing the lake to the north-west. The public gained entrance from the marketplace to the east through a triple gate to the outer court of the emperor's quarters, where public audience was held. The emperor entered the audience pavilion from the daulat khana garden immediately to the west.

Formerly walled, the emperor's garden shared the central zone of the tripartite daulat khana compound with a broad terrace providing the open space before the imperial apartments which was an essential feature of Timurid palaces and imperial Indian camps. Occupying the

4.36e

southern zone, once cloistered between its pavilions and cooled by the square Anup Tala'o tank, the principal court is the nucleus of the emperor's private quarters. Facilities for suspending awnings from its various pavilions make it clear that the whole covered area was often expanded into the most sumptuous of tent palaces. The main block of the apartments to the south, with an elegant baradari over walled chambers, was probably used for dining and confidential meetings: one of the chambers, distinguished by a dais, was probably the Diwan-i-Khas.

The northern zone of the emperor's quarters has a range of building to the west including a lavish Gujarati-style pavilion and the celebrated freestanding two-storey structure with balconies, deep chadyas and elegant chattris: traditionally – but almost certainly incorrectly – identified as the Diwan-i-Khas, it may have been dedicated to theological disputation. The outstanding feature of this building's interior is the central pillar

with a fantastic capital of radiating serpentine brackets which bears a circular platform, connected by narrow bridges to the corners of the surrounding gallery. The structure of the column is essentially Hindu but the introduction of Persian floral and chevron patterns was to provide the key to the evolution of the 'Order', with its fan- or bell-shaped base, most popular under Akbar's successors.

A screened viaduct once connected the emperor's private apartments with the principal building within the harem compound, a large introverted quadrangular structure where Akbar slept. Its single gate is a domestic expression of the double-bastion portal with offset entrance and exit of the type familiar in military works. The complex recalls the Gujari Mahal at Gwalior. Apartments were provided in wings separated by pavilions in the centre of each side and at the corners, the central pavilions containing a grand reception room enriched with a wide range of

4.36g

4.36h

4.36i

motifs, mainly Hindu in origin. The carving is assertively Gujarati, the tiles are Malwan and the combination of materials recalls Gwalior.

Flanking the main block to the north-east are elegant isolated pavilions which probably housed the emperor's mother and principal non-Rajput wives. The rest of the harem enclosure is occupied by a large court to the south-west, probably for attendants, by the Nagina Mosque and by gardens. Beyond the gardens to the east is the Panch Mahal: once screened to provide a secure zone of transition from the emperor's private court to the harem gardens, this structure of five diminishing tiers – yet another permutation of the prasada – dominates the entire complex.

›4.37 DELHI, NIZAM-UD-DIN AULIA, TOMB OF ADHAM KHAN, 1560s: exterior.
Persian forms were rarely so exquisitely clothed in rich Indian materials – primarily sandstone with marble mosaic inlay – as in this ministerial tomb.

4-37

THE PALACES OF THE EARLY MUGHAL DEAD

As we have noted, Babur decreed that he should be buried in one of his gardens, in a grave covered only by the earth and sky in accordance with venerable Muslim tradition. The tombs of his successors, among the greatest works of Islam, were usually modelled on palaces. Of course, palaces – whether or not destined to be tombs – are set in gardens. The Mughals were certainly not the first Indian rulers to plant gardens, but after Babur the chahar-bagh is pervasive.

The Mughals were equally obsessed with water – as were all the rulers of Islamic lands where paradise is an oasis. In the Koran, as we know, paradise is the Eden of Genesis, whose definition is related to the ancient Persian ideal order of an enclosed square divided by four rivers flowing in the cardinal directions from the source of the waters of life in the centre. As a cosmological concept – the context of blessedness emitting benign influence or grace (*baraka*) – the four-square garden is the setting for the tomb and might be enjoyed by the patron before and after he came finally to rest there.

The octagonal tomb of the Sayyid type, amplified by

Sher Shah, had once again become the preserve of the courtier: splendid examples were destined for Isa and Adham Khan in 1548 and 1562 respectively, the former at Mehrauli, the latter outside the dargarh compound of Nizam-ud-din Aulia.**4·37** Overshadowing the latter in scale and style at the same site, the first great architectural enterprise in which a chahar-bagh played a crucial role was the tomb of Humayun himself, built by his wife, the Hamida Banu Begum, well into the reign of their son Akbar. Here the mausoleum matches Babur's own description of the hasht behisht pavilion of the Tareb Khana in the palace at Herat, which the Mughals in exile would have seen, and recalls the type of the mausoleum of Mulla Hassan at Sultaniya.**4·38**

A considerable number of tombs built during Akbar's reign also retained varying degrees of Persian influence, not only in the west, around Tatta for instance, but in the heart of the empire for ministers of the Persianized court. On the other hand, the indigenous tradition – especially that of Gujarat – is also pervasive.**4·39** Most characteristically, Akbar's own tomb at Sikandra, on the outskirts of Agra, is an extraordinary synthesis of the indigenous and the imported: it was probably designed by the emperor himself.**4·40**

4.38b

›**4.38 DELHI, DINPANNAH:** (a) plan of complex, (b) tomb of Isa Khan (1547), (c) Humayun's tomb

4.38c

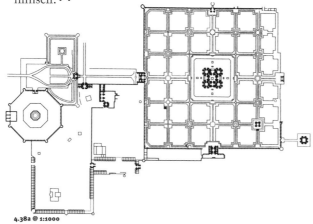

4.38a @ 1:1000

The imperial tomb: progenitors

The vast square compound of Humayun's chahar-bagh is entered from the west, but there is a monumental south gate as well: the unpretentious funerary mosque is outside beyond the main western entrance. The four quarters of the square are defined by causeways leading from these entrances – and from the pavilions which balance them at the cardinal points in the centre of the other sides – to the central square occupied by the mausoleum itself. Set into each causeway is a water channel interrupted at the junction of subsidiary axes by lily ponds except in the southeast corner, where a secondary mausoleum was constructed.

The mausoleum itself stands on a great platform like the tomb of Mahmud Khalji on the transformed Ashrafi Mahal at Mandu – a work which Akbar admired and attempted to save from dilapidation following his

complex (1560s), view of platform with domed hasht behisht superstructure.

conquest of the Khalji seat. Within, as in Humayun's tomb, arcaded and vaulted chambers surround the actual burial vault, which is entered directly along the southern axis. The crowning hasht behist is, of course, a rationalist exercise, square in plan but subdivided by vestibules beyond the great iwans on the main axes into five zones, all with their corners cut to effect contiguity – the southern iwan is blind to provide a two-storey entrance hall. The four chattri-crowned corner zones, with two storeys and superimposed arcades in the canted corners on either side of subsidiary iwans, contain the tombs of members of the imperial family.

The emperor's great arched central cenotaph chamber, recalling that of Oljeitu, rises through the full height of the building. The marble-sheathed, slightly bulbous outer profile of the splendid double dome is perhaps more Safavid than Timurid. It is suggested that the patroness imported Persian workers for the job: the beautifully dressed red sandstone and its white marble inlay lend festivity to this masterly work but never at the expense of a gravitas worthy of its distinguished lineage.

At Sikandra, Akbar adopted the chahar-bagh formula of his predecessor. The great arcaded platform in the centre – with the mortuary chamber surrounded by vaulted cells – corresponds to that of Humayun's mausoleum – equally recalling the Mandu Ashrafi Mahal – but the superstructure is resolutely indigenous: instead of a hasht behisht it is a multi-storey prasada.

With octagonal minarets crowned by chattris at each corner and an iwan frontispiece in the centre of each side, the platform is linked by causeways with water channels to pavilions with responding frontispieces in the enclosure. The one in the south, providing the only entrance, is an enormous two-storey structure with exceptional circular white marble minarets at the corners where chattris might have been expected. All the pavilions, like the platform and its frontispieces, are lavishly ornamented with painted stucco, coloured stone, marble inlay and low-relief carving, the decorative motifs include venerable Vedic symbols of regeneration (goose, lotus, the swastika of solar movement; see AIC2, page 10) and the wheel of the sacred law as well as flora, arabesques and Islamic calligraphy.

In place of the hasht behisht, the prasada has four storeys, square in

4.39a

›4.39 GWALIOR, TOMB OF MUHAMMAD GHAUS, 1564: (a) exterior, (b) central shrine.

4.40a

4.39b

plan and the lower three stepped: trabeated throughout, though with decorative arcading at regular intervals, the lower two levels break forward in the centre to support chattris. Concealed within the third level, sealed off from its terrace except for a narrow window high up in the south wall, is a grid of chambers with an enigmatic cenotaph at its centre. The top storey, of white marble in contrast with the red sandstone elsewhere, has an open court surrounded by colonnades with screens. On a central dais, the marble cenotaph is inscribed with verses in praise of Akbar or reflecting his Din-Illahi, in addition to the ninety-nine names of God. The question of whether the cenotaph was to be covered is the subject of some speculation, but given the square platform and the massive piers of the third-storey grid, a canopied pavilion would certainly have been feasible.

›4.40 SIKANDRA, TOMB OF AKBAR, 1605–13: (a) general view of mausoleum from the south-west, (b) gatehouse.

4.40b

4.41

4 THE DECCAN: THE QUTBSHAHI AND ADILSHAHI SULTANATES

4.42

By the end of the reign of Akbar in the first decade of the 17th century, the most significant independent powers in the Indian subcontinent – the only important ones, in fact – were the successors to the Bahamanis in the Deccan. After the latter had succumbed to factional rivalry in 1538, their empire was divided between their viceroys into six states – including the former palatine province of Bidar where we have already encountered the Baridids in the overwhelming context of the late-Bahamani capital works. The several sultans were constantly squabbling but united in 1565 long enough to fulfil the longstanding Bahamani ambition of destroying the Hindu empire of Vijayanagar: the effort exhausted them and left the smaller states vulnerable to the larger – and to the waxing power of the Mughals.

The new Deccani dynasties were all active patrons but the most prolific were the Adilshahis of Bijapur, closely followed by the Qutbshahis of Golconda.**4·42** They all built

4.43a

on experience of the Bahamanis and sustained their predecessors' fondness for Persian forms to varying degrees.
However, as we have seen, the Bahamani style ripened in
cross-fertilization with local Hindu tradition: the syncretic
was enjoyed by both the Qutb- and Adilshahis but, above
all others, the latter revelled in lusciousness.

GOLCONDA AND HYDERABAD

The Qutbshahis ruled from within the walls of the great
fortified palace which they built to emulate the example set
by their former masters at Bidar but the remains are less
impressive. More representative of the dynasty's early
efforts, late-Bahamani in style, are the tombs of Quli
Qutbshahi, founder of the dynasty (died 1543), and Ibrahim

4.43c

4.43b

›**4.43 GOLCONDA:** (a, b) general view of fort and overview of palace remains, (c) tomb of Muhammad Shah outside the walls (c. 1610).

The main citadel, c. 110 metres above the town, is fortified by three ranges of walls. The main gate, embellished with Hindu motifs, has a semi-circular mantlet with faceted outer walls, crenellated and box-machicolated, around a raised platform commanding the entrance. The Hindu motifs incorporated in the gates reveal the religious tolerance of the Qutbshahi. Even more tangible evidence of this is provided by the remains of both temples and mosques amid the ruins of the great palace complex begun by Sultan Quli Qutb-shahi and greatly extended by his successors.

›**4.44 HYDERABAD, CHAR MINAR,** 1592.

(died 1580). In the later works – for example, the tomb of Sultan Muhammad (died 1612) which incorporated tra-beated porticoes – the accumulation of small-scale elements such as arcaded galleries and miniature turan-topped minarets denied the monumentality of often large and simple masses.**4.43**

The tombs apart, the most important surviving works of the Qutbshahis are in Hyderabad, the new capital founded near Golconda in the late-16th century. Convolution is most apparent in the Jami-masjid there and the multiplication of forms at variance with the scale of the whole is nowhere better illustrated than in the celebrated Char Minar which marks the crossing of the two main arteries of that impressively planned city.**4.44**

monumental Jami-masjid which emulated Rafi's work at Gulbarga in commemoration of victory over Vijayanagara.

The Arh Qila, in the centre of the town, had double walls and moat, as at Bidar. The major elements of the citadel were distributed in accordance with no clear plan, also as at Bidar but, unlike the private quarters there, they are rectangular blocks each with a great hall backed and overlooked by superimposed apartments in the Safavid manner. In the Gagan and Anand Mahals – the scene of public and private audience respectively – there is a triple arched iwan, the central arch low-slung as in the Jami-masjid of Gulbarga. In the Athar Mahal, which enshrined relics of the Prophet, there is a talar. Apart from similar structures for the courts of justice and the regulatory offices, several pleasure palaces included the prasada-like Sat Manzil, once of seven storeys, and the long slender terraced Jahaz Mahal which must once have recalled the zenana of Mandu.

The dynasty maintained a secondary seat on the Arabian Sea coast at the site of modern Goa. Compensation for the latter's loss is splendidly provided by Janjira, perhaps the premier example (anywhere) of the ancient category of water fort (see AIC2, page 217). The island was first fortified in the 13th century by Abyssinian slave-traders and developed in the 16th century by their descendants who provided naval escort to the subjects of the Adilshahi sultans on pilgrimage to Mecca or trade. Still ringed by formidable ramparts, in three tiers for defence in depth, it is dominated by the shell of a multi-storey residential block: there was only one of these and as it was not a royal seat there was, of course, no imperial Safavid talar.**4.46**

Within the Bijapur Arh Qila, several small palatine mosques were built of materials from the Hindu temples of the Chalukyas and Yadavas. Apart from these, the Adil-

4.46a

4.46b

4.46c

›4.46 JANJIRA, THE MARINE FORT, 16th century: (a) view from the sea, (b) tiered ramparts, (c) detail of palace portal, (d) interior view with palace.

›4.47 THE ADILSHAHI DYNASTY (Bijapuri school, 1680): Ali I is to the progenitor's right, Ibrahim II and Muhammad are first and second left (New York, Metropolitan Museum of Art).

4.46d

4.47

4.48a @ 1:1000

4.48b

›ARCHITECTURE IN CONTEXT »BEYOND THE EASTERN PALE

4.48c

›4.48 BIJAPUR, MOSQUES: (a–d) Jami-masjid
(1565), plan and interior, section, vault plan, prayer hall
front; (e, f) Mihitari Mahal, elevations of prayer hall and
gate (ASI).

Standing on a galleried base, the Jami-masjid of Ali I
has an open arcaded prayer hall whose outer bays are
extended to define the court. The qibla is asserted by a
great hemispherical dome on a square clerestory, the
latter richly arcaded and surmounted by merlons, the
former rising like a bud from an upturned lotus. As at
Gulbarga, the cool restraint of the interior derives from
the repetition of simple recessed arcades springing low
from plain rectangular piers. The transition device of
interpenetrating arches spun from the rotated square
is at its most spectacular here.

Hindu derived embellishment is at its most lavish in
the Mihitari Mahal, though the prayer hall lacks a

4.48d

dome. The full panoply is reserved for the distinguished double-storey entrance pavilion with its extremely elegant balcony sheltered by an exceptionally elaborate chadya. The equally rich contemporary mosque at Laksmeshvar is celebrated in particular for the astonishing stone chains which swing from its chadya and minarets, rivalling the virtuoso exercises of the masons of Vijayanagara.

4.48e

4.48f

shahis built more than fifty mosques ranging in scale and embellishment from three-bay chapels to the nine-bay masterpiece of Ali I, the Jami-masjid. **4.47, 4.48a–e** As there, prayer-hall façades are usually subjected to the assertive horizontal lines of a vigorously bracketed chadya unbroken by a pishtaq of the Persian type but central arches are distinguished by spandrel medallions and increasingly assertive apex brackets. Inside, transition from square to circle or octagon is usually effected by lattice-like patterns of interpenetrating arches of the kind the Bahamanis had imported from Persia. Alternatively this is most spectacularly done by interlocking arches rising from squares rotated as in the star-shaped plans of later Hindu Deccani builders (see AIC2, page 203ff.).

The earlier works of the dynasty, up to about 1580, recall the restraint of early Gulbarga with their simple, broad, low-sprung arches. Elaboration of decorative detail – if not form – increases steadily to a crescendo about 1620. The introduction of a fringe of lotus petals to the base of domes was an early conceit and so too was the cusping of central façade arches, pre-echoing the mihrab within – after the later-Bahamani example taken up also by the Baridids.

As the style evolved, especially in more intimate contexts, cusping was augmented with rampant vine motifs and additional embellishment in finely carved stone – much of it distinctly Hindu in inspiration as in Bahamani work – includes prominent chaddyas on rich corbelled brackets, filigree balustrades, elegant chattris. Minarets became attenuated finials and domes were inflated beyond the merely bulbous till they resembled balloons rising from ever longer, more closely set, padma petals. The process is already advanced in the Jami-masjid but the scale accommodated the richness. By c. 1620 prolixity is quite overwhelming on the small scale of the Mihitari Mahal – not without fascination. **4.48f,g**

4.49a

>**4.49 BIJAPUR, RAUZAS:** (a, b) tomb complex of Ibrahim II (1580–1626), general view with mortuary chamber left, mosque right of entrance pavilion, plan;

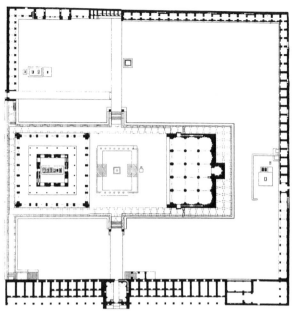

4.49b @ 1:1000

(c–e) the Gol Gumbad of Muhammad (1626–56), interior detail, exterior – and the sultan on his elephant.

The tomb complexes (rauzas) founded by the rulers and high officers of state usually consist of a three- or five-bay mosque and larger mortuary pavilion with a qubba rising high above a lofty verandah due to the extravagant disparity between the inner and outer shell of the dome. The finest surving example is that of Ibrahim II just outside the Mecca Gate: the most grandiose is that of Muhammad I – the so-called Gol Gumbad, the last statement of Adilshahi pretensions before they fell to the Mughals.**4·49**

The mosque and tomb of Ibrahim's complex, highly elaborate in decorative detail like the Mihitari Mahal, confront one another over an ornamental pool on a rectangular terrace set in a chahar-bagh with a sumptuous entrance pavilion. Seeking to surpass this but unable to conceive a richer work, Muhammad I resorted to colossal scale: the tomb was originally conceived as an amplification of Ibrahim's type but the walls of the qubba were

4.49c

moved out to the perimeter of the projected gallery and the whole vast space was covered with a dome rivalling the greatest of Europe. Between blind bays below a great chadya, the central iwan frontispieces fully accord with the scale of the powerful volume, but the seven-storey octagonal towers introduce an incongruity which is enhanced

4.49e

4.49d

in the attempt to bind them to the main mass by continuing the top storey arcades right around the building – as
in the Char Minar at Hyderabad.

In the late-19th century the Deccani Muslim style – mis-
named 'Indo-Saracenic' or even 'Moorish' – was exported
by the British to colonies with a dominant Muslim population – especially Malaya. In the process the fantasy was
certainly not diminished.**4.50**

›**4.50 KUALA KANGSAR (PERAK, MALAY-
SIA), JAMI-MASJID:** general view.

›4.51 AGRA, TOMB OF THE I'TMAD-UD-
DAULAH: detail of marble revetment with inlay of
semi-precious stones.

›4.52 THE GREAT MUGHALS, 17TH CEN-
TURY: (a) Jahangir; (b) Shah Jahan receiving
Aurangzeb at court; (c) Mughal forces investing
Daulatabad.

4.51

5 THE MUGHALS: APOGEE

4.52a

Akbar's legacy was one of Asia's greatest empires and his
heirs were impressive. Jahangir (1605–27) was perhaps the
least effective, yet expansion continued throughout his
reign and he inherited his great-grandfather's taste for laying out gardens.**4.52a** His name was given by others to two
of India's finest surviving palace buildings but he is notable
more for his interest in gardens than monuments, though
his reign contributed one of India's most exquisite tombs.

In contrast to his father, Shah Jahan (1627–59) was one
of history's greatest builders – and he produced one of the
world's most celebrated buildings. He took the empire to
its greatest height culturally and advanced his arms in
south but was less successful abroad.**4.52b** The system of
divided provincial authority began to break down, but
partnership between Persian and Hindu was largely sustained until the ailing, ageing emperor was superseded and
incarcerated by his son Aurangzeb (1659–1707). A zealous
Muslim, the latter took the empire to its widest extent by
completing the conquest of the south.**4.52c**

4.52b

4.52c

4.53a

4.53b

The frontispiece stands out from the twin arcaded bays of the prayer hall, themselves significantly higher than the blind arcades around the other sides of the court, and minarets rise from all four corners. Cells behind the north, south and east ranges of blind arcades suggest that the mosque was also a madrasa and there were shops on an internal street behind the east front. Contrary to Persian practice, variation from the base plane of the wall is provided by the blind arcades and their rectilinear framework. The dazzling effect of the exterior is derived from the brilliant Punjabi mosaic tilework in the framework of glazed red brick. Inside, the painted stucco, especially over the rich muqarnas, is equally brilliant.

4·53c

THE IMPERIAL MOSQUE AT ITS APOGEE

The example set by Akbar's Badshahi-masjid at Fatehpur Sikri was followed in several mosques built later in the reign – notably at Ajmer and Tatta. However, the influence of Persia is more pervasive in the Begum Shahi-masjid of Akbar's widow Maryam Zamani in Lahore and the Patthar Masjid of Srinagar – among the few important works of Jahangir's reign. It is pervasive too in several mosques of Shah Jahan's early years, notably those of the Nawab Gul Baqa Amir Khan's great Jami-masjid at Tatta, the Nawab Wazir Khan and Dai Anga in Lahore.**4·53**

Shah Jahan and his successor were prolific mosque builders – Aurangzeb even notorious in his iconoclastic replacement of temples. The Mothi-masjid in the Agra fort apart, the crowning masterpiece is the Jami-masjid of the new imperial seat at Delhi, Shahjahanabad: in red sandstone and white marble, it developed the iwan plan precedent of the Badshahi-masjid at Fatehpur Sikri – on an even larger scale – and set the example for India's last imperial mosques, notably Jahanara Begum's at Agra (1648) and Aurangzeb's at Lahore (1674) – and their increasingly decadent successors.**4.54-4.56**

>**4.54** DELHI, SHAHJAHANABAD, JAMI-MASJID, 1644: (a) general view from the north-east, (b) court front, (c) interior of prayer hall.

>**4.55** AGRA, MOTHI-MASJID, 1645: (a, b) prayer hall from court.

>**4.56** LAHORE, BADSHAHI-MASJID: (a) interior of prayer hall, (b) court front.

4.54b

The great Mughal mosque

Apart from the striking red and white colour scheme, the major effect of the great Delhi work is drawn from the combination of the native chattri with the imported iwan and bulbous dome – as much Deccani as Timurid in profile. Like many of its Indian predecessors, and the Agra Mothi mosque, it is raised on a platform surrounded by arcades but, with rare concern for external effect, the platform is high enough for the arcades to be left open on both sides without risk of ritual pollution.

4.54a

4.54c

Monumental flights of steps ascend to the emperor's eastern entrance, inspired by the Buland Darwaza, and to subsidiary ones for the public to the north and south. To some extent this arrangement recalls the four-iwan plan common in Iran after the Seljuks. As in the Fatehpur Sikri mosque, the cloisters return around the western side, but the more elevated prayer hall is projected into the court as a freestanding block as in the Qila-i-Kuhna and its predecessors. As in many Timurid and Safavid works, the frontispiece rises high above the five bays of each wing to mask much of the great qibla qubba's dome. There are no chadyas. Chattris are used only on the entrance pavilions, on the rear corners of the prayer hall – where they stand in for the elegant minarets of the main façade – and over slender miniature minarets applied to the sides of the frontispiece in the Safavid manner.

For the Agra Mothi-masjid, Shah Jahan's architects adopted the alternative scheme of an open arcaded prayer-hall, coterminous with the qibla

4.55b

4.55a

4.56a

wall and without frontispiece or minarets. In contrast to the cloisters in the Jami-masjid at Delhi, the arches of the prayer hall and cloisters are all cusped but the former rise to their greater height from piers, the latter from columns. Chattris are used instead of minarets on all four corners of the prayer hall, with smaller chattris between and on the axial portals. The three bulbous domes rise unobscured. As no sandstone is revealed by the white marble revetment and black marble is used only for the calligraphy, nothing disturbs the work's cool elegance.

Aurangzeb's work at Lahore is comparable to his father's Delhi Jami-masjid in importance and size but its freestanding prayer hall has a minaret at each corner and so too does the vast court. There is one portal. White marble is used only to provide relief to the red sandstone outside – perhaps too delicately for the scale of the building. The interior, too, approaches the effete with its web of gilded stucco covering virtually every surface except the mihrab.

4.56b

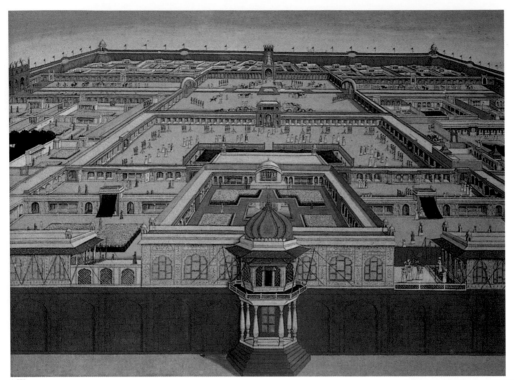

4·57a

THE IMPERIAL PALACE AT ITS APOGEE

Conceived and executed as a whole, Shah Jahan's Delhi fort is far more formal in organization than any of its predecessors in India's imperial capitals. The emperor reviewed the plans of Baghdad, and though trabeated in structure and dominated by a columned portico, his scheme recalls the great caliphate complexes in an order which extends beyond that of the individual chahar-bagh elsewhere. As usual in Shah Jahan's works, the main elements – mosques, pavilions of public and private audience or retreat aligned on riverside terraces – were executed largely in marble, with inlaid precious metal and semi-precious stones, rather than in the familiar coloured sandstone. **4·57–4·59**

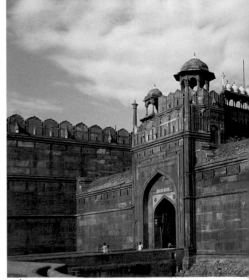

4·57b

›4.57 SHAH-JAHAN'S PALACES: (a–c) Shahja-hanabad (Delhi, begun late in the 1630s), 19th-century overview, Lahore Gate, and plan with (1) Lahore Gate, (2) naubat khana, (3) Diwan-i-Am, (4) Rang Mahal, (5) Khas Mahal, (6) Diwan-i-Khas, (7) hamam, (8) Hayat Bakhsh, (9) Shah Burj and kiosk, (10) Badoan garden pavilion, (11) haram sara, (12) Delhi Gate; (d–f) Agra, Diwan-i-Am, Nagina-Masjid exterior and interior; (g–j) Delhi, Mothi-masjid court, Diwan-i-Am throne platform and Shah-Jahan on the Peacock Throne, Nahar-i-Behist; (k) Lahore, fort, Shish Mahal; (l–r) Agra Diwan-i-Am and Diwan-i-Khas details, Shah-Jahan in the latter and on the external throne beside it, Rang Mahal and Shish Mahal, Anguri Bagh of the Rang Mahal with the Taj Mahal in the background; (s) Delhi, Shah Burj and kiosk.

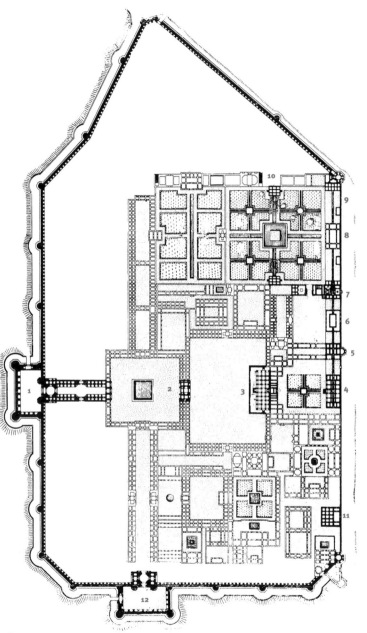

4.57c @ 1:5000

4.57d

4.57e

4.57f

4.57g

4.57h

4.57i

Pavilions of earthly paradise

Shah Jahan was to be confined to his splendid pavilions at Agra for his last melancholy years but he had intended his new fort at Delhi to be his definitive seat. A regular rectangle – except for the citadel to the north – the compound is aligned strictly north–south to avoid any discordance with the qibla of its mosques. The finely dressed red sandstone walls, 30 metres high over a splayed base on the town side, are built as much to be admired as to overawe. The Lahore Gate, with its octagonal guard chamber, opens the principal axis from the west. The Delhi Gate, west of centre in the south, opens a subsidiary axis through a bazaar. The two axes cross in a great square court before the Naubat Khana gatehouse, which leads to the court of public audience with its throne platform.

4-57j

4-57k

The great hypostyle Diwan-i-Am, its sandstone columns plastered with powdered marble, was commanded from the central bay of its eastern range by a raised platform covered by a curved canopy of white marble backed by Italian pietra-dura. Here in Shah Jahan's time stood the fabulous Peacock Throne of gem-encrusted gold. Before the throne was a dais from which the grand vizier handed petitions up to the emperor in public audience.

The emperor entered his throne platform from the garden court of his private quarters immediately to the east: still on the principal axis, the once fully screened pleasure pavilion (Rang Mahal) at the head of this garden is the first in a sequence of buildings embracing the Diwan-i-Khas and the private palace (Khas Mahal), aligned north–south on the riverside

4·57l

4·57m

4·57n

4·57o

4-57p

4-57q

terrace. It leads south to the now-destroyed harem, north to the Hayat Baksh. Running through these exquisitely chased and inlaid marble pavilions with their intricate screens is the Nahar-i-Behist ('Canal of Paradise')

4-57r

which supplied water – raised from the river in the north-east bastion – to a series of pools and fountains. The cooling effect of the water as it rippled over the white marble was crucial to this environment.

At Lahore the pavilion of private audience is positioned like the Delhi Rang Mahal on the principal axis behind the court of public audience – which was unfortunately transformed in restoration. The sequence of increasingly intimate enclosures to the west culminates in the dazzling mirror- and glass-inlaid, many-niched Shish Mahal associated with the bath house and its subsidiary bangaldar Naulakhi kiosk. At Agra the main suite of private apartments survives in better state than at either Delhi or Lahore: the court of the sumptuous Khas Mahal and its twin, gilded bangaldar kiosks is aligned with the Jahangiri Mahal to expand the facilities of the harem around the Anguri Garden – the 'Garden of Grapes'.

The pavilion of the Hayat Baksh and the white marble palatine mosque of the Delhi fort were completed under Aurangzeb. The latter, far more opulent than its predecessors at Agra and Lahore, is essentially non-architectonic in decoration: flamboyant low-relief carving, ephemeral pilasters, Bengali bowed cornice and awning, implausible miniature minarets and inflated, turban-like domes of Deccani profile all mark the turning towards the effete, anticipating decadence.

By the mid-17th century an increasingly feminine elegance tending towards over-refinement was effected with bulbous domes and semi-ogee versions of the cusped arch: these were essential ingredients in the styles of the Muslim Deccani kingdoms, with which the emperor and his forces were increasingly preoccupied, but not altogether unfamiliar in the north from the earliest phase of Indian Islamic architecture. The ribbed dome is ultimately Timurid but balloons as in Bijapur. Columns were given volutes, lotiform or muqarnas capitals, foliate or bell-shaped bases and cannelated, baluster-like shafts derived from the reed-bundle piers of Bengal, whose curved roof forms found increasing favour at court. In all the main palaces, on the other hand, the bath house shimmered with

4·57s

Persian-inspired mirror mosaics. Akbar's syncretic style was further developed in this way, though the empire was returning from tolerance to Sunni orthodoxy, and the last significant efflorescence of the Din-Illahi illuminated Shah Jahan's pavilions with a highly eclectic range of royal symbols reaching back to the ancient Vedic ideal and the quasi-divine Achaemenids.

THE GARDEN OF PARADISE AND THE APOTHEOSIS OF THE TOMB

Jahangir, who took the chahar-bagh to its apogee as the context for retreat, was not unique among the great Mughals in his obsession with flowers: his successor, in particular, managed to combine a taste for the supremely grand with a love of florid intricacy. Inlaid in semi-precious stones or painted in the borders of miniatures, flowers infiltrate his monuments in a delightfully informal way – if with increasing botanical accuracy – yet, ironically, they are pressed into the service of a rigorous formality in the chahar-bagh as inseparable from the garden image of Paradise.**4·58**

4.58a

4.58b

>4.58 GARDENS OF PARADISE: (a) Babur tending his garden; (b–d) Srinagar, Shalimar gardens (1619), site, plan and axial view.

Ascending terraces, now mostly devoid of their original pavilions, were divided into three zones: public audience, private audience (both full chahar-baghs), and the harem. The lowest terrace, immediately within the entrance, was dominated by the Diwan-i-Am through which the water flowed along the central canal, but from which access to the Diwan-i-Khas was open only to the emperor and his entourage. On the upper terrace, the inviolable harem commanded a view of the whole – and, from towers in its enclosure wall, of its unrivalled setting between lake and mountain.

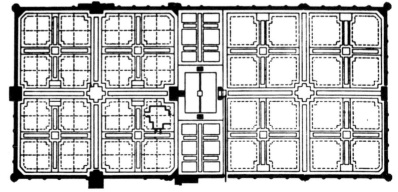

4.58c @ approximately 1:2000

4.58d

For his tomb at Shahdara, near Lahore, Jahangir dispensed with his father's overt reference to the prasada in superimposed storeys but he retained the base and the superior pavilion – and, of course, the chahar-bagh. The

formula is at its most celebrated in the exquisite miniature built for the empress's Persian father, the I'tmad-ud-Daulah Mirza Ghiyas Beg, on the left bank of the Yamuna at Agra. **4.59, 4.51**

4·59a

4·59b

›4.59 AGRA, TOMB OF THE I'TMAD-UD-
DAULAH, 1622–28: (a) view from the entrance, (b)
detail of external revetment, (c, d) details of interior
revetment, (e) detail of cenotaph chamber, (f) interior
of vestibule.

In the centre of the chahar-bagh, entered from the
west, the platform is now a low plinth and the arcaded
base of Akbar's tomb at Sikandra has become the main
element of the mausoleum itself, with chattris on circular minarets at the corners and an iwan sunk into the
mass. A screened pavilion covered by an elegant
canopy shelters the cenotaphs of the I'tmad-ud-
Daulah and his wife. In contrast with its sandstone
enclosure and the ancilliary buildings with their filigree
marble mosaics, the mortuary pavilion was the first to
be built entirely of white marble with gorgeous pietra-
dura floral ornament, Persian in inspiration.

4.59c

4.59d

4.59e

4.59f

›ARCHITECTURE IN CONTEXT »BEYOND THE EASTERN PALE

4.60

Late in Jahangir's reign, the architects of the Delhi tomb built for the vizier Abdur Rahman reverted to the Persian tradition of the hasht behisht crowned by a bulbous dome: unlike Humayun's tomb nearby, however, it is higher than it is wide and the four chattris are clustered more closely about the drum. Sorry relic though it is, its importance lies in the precedent it provided for a revision of Humayun's broad, static five-part composition to achieve the dynamic aspiring Taj Mahal which took the Muslim architectural tradition in India to its apotheosis. **4.60, 4.61**

>**4.60 DELHI, TOMB OF THE KHAN-I-KHANAN ABDUR RAHMAN,** c. 1625: view from the south.

›4.61 AGRA, TAJ MAHAL, 1631–52: (a) view from river (early 20th-century photograph), (b) entrance pavilion garden front, (c, d) resthouse, matching mosque, exterior and interior, (e, f) section through mausoleum and site plan, (g, h) detail of revetment and west face of mausoleum, (i) general view from the south.

The Taj Mahal

Founded in the fifth year of the reign of Shah Jahan to enshrine his favourite wife, Mumtaz Mahal, the main mass of the Taj Mahal is a totally integrated entity on a riverside terrace beyond its chahar-bagh. There, the culmination of a now clearly dominant axis denying the centralization of the garden, its reflected verticals are resolved in both directions. Yet, elusive in scale, it is ambiguous in form: the main arcades express the fusion of the five elements of the hasht behisht, the dome and chattris express their distinction.

Both the main causeways of the chahar-bagh have exceptionally broad, cypress-lined water channels which meet in a raised lotus pond – the cross-axis terminating in water pavilions – but only the north–south axis has fountains. The directional logic in the conception is reinforced by the triad of red sandstone buildings – the entrance pavilion, the mosque and the matching guesthouse, which flank the mausoleum on its platform with the mortuary chamber deep within – a consistent feature of the

great Mughal tombs. The superstructure emulates Humayun's hasht behisht in scale, if revising the proportions to enhance the verticals: in particular, the platform is relatively lower than in Humayun's scheme and, given the greater distance of view, the superstructure stands out unmasked on first appearance from the entrance gate.

As in the prototype, vestibules behind the great iwans are linked by corridors to the great central chamber and to subsidiary chattri-crowned chambers superimposed on the diagonals. As in the shrine of Khwaja Abu Nasr at Balkh, the compression of the hasht behisht denies autonomy to these corner elements: here they have both orthogonal and diagonal arcades but no centralizing iwans or re-entrant inner bays. The arcading of sides and centre is defined by slender shafts enhancing the verticals without vigorous changes in plane – apart from the canted corners opposite which the minarets stand detached. The dome, more elevated, more bulbous and with a steeper profile more clearly reminiscent of the mature Timurids, rises high over the closely associated chattris and frontispieces

4.61c

4.61d

because of the enormous disparity between its inner and outer shells – as in the Gir-i Amir.

A dado of unsurpassed richness incorporating a flowering-plant motif – as of the living paradise – runs around and through the mausoleum, ringing the sumptuous screened cenotaphs of the empress and emperor below the dome. The exquisite floral and geometric ornament in low-relief carving and semi-precious stone inlay, which textures vaults and spandrels, like the black marble calligraphic bands of the frontispieces, hardly becomes legible before the relationship between solid and void is no longer appreciable in its totality. And it is the materials – the water of canal and river as much as the substance on the terrace – which take this incomparable work beyond the realm of rational analysis. In sharp contrast with the red sandstone mosque and guesthouse flanking it, the mausoleum is built entirely of marble of legendary beauty, passing through a range of colours from peach to pearl according to the light of sun, moon or stars.

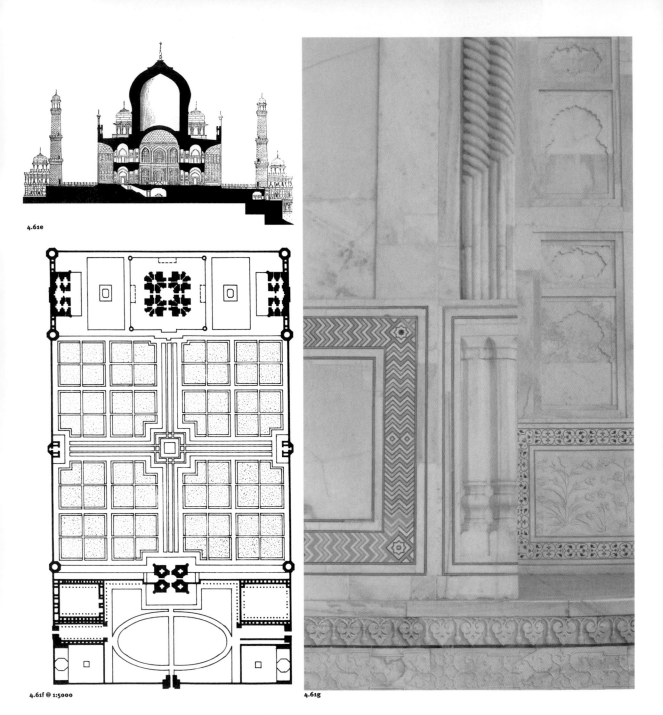

4.61e

4.61f @ 1:5000

4.61g

4.61h

4.61i

That the composition of the Taj Mahal admitted of no improvement is demonstrated by the only two significant attempts at its emulation: the tomb of Rabi Daurani, wife of Aurangzeb, built at Aurangabad less than thirty years later, and the tomb of Safdar Jang, Nawab of Oudh, built in Delhi in the mid-18th century. Still aiming at aspiration, but confusing architecture and ornament, Aurangzeb's architect miscalculated by stressing the corners with

›4.62 AURANGABAD, TOMB OF RABI DAU-RANI, 1680: view from the south.

additional minarets. Safdar Jang's architect realized this but the logic of his static conception is elementary and the whole is unfortunately reduced to the effete by the fussy detail which provides mere relief instead of virile differentiation – as in the neighbouring masterpiece of Humayun which set the standard so astonishingly emulated by his great-grandson.**4.62, 4.63**

4.64a

EPILOGUE: HINDUSTANI SYNCRETISM

At the height of Mughal power, the imperial synthesis had naturally appealed to those indigenous rulers who sought advantage from Akbar's tolerance and the cross-fertilization of indigenous and imported traditions was certainly no less important in developments under Shah Jahan. Rajput rulers, long familiar with the imperial court, vied with one another in the embellishment of their own courts. The prime example was set by the Rajas of Budelkhand. Thereafter, none surpassed Jai Singh I of Amber (1623–68).

ORCHHA, DATIA AND AMBER

At Orchha the century from c. 1520 saw the construction of three great palaces: the Ramji Mandir, the Raj Mahal and the Jahangiri Mahal. The series was completed at nearby Datia. In all these works arch and dome join post and beam. All four have square courts surrounded by apartments, like the most formal four-iwan type of madrasa – specifically the Mandu Ashrafi Mahal – and the Gwalior Gujari Mahal which inspired the principal building in the harem sera of Fatehpur Sikri. All have balconied towers and tiered terraces in the manner of the prasada. At Datia, however, a freestanding prasada rises from the centre of the court – just as a tomb had been interpolated

4.64b

4.64c

›4.64 ORCHHA: (a) Raj Mahal (c. 1520) with Jahangiri Mahal (c. 1610) background; (b, c) Jahangiri Mahal, exterior and north-east corner of court; (d, e) Chaturbhuja (c. 1560), exterior from south-east and interior.

The Raj Mandir of the town's founder, Raja Rudra Pratap (1501–31) was unfinished and converted into a temple. The Raj Mahal of Raja Madhukar (1554–91) is damaged but its adjunct, the enormous palace which Raja Bir Singh Deo (1607–27) named after Akbar's heir Jahangir, still gives some impression of its former opulence. Of its five storeys, the main ones are the third and fourth, with the court raised over superimposed arcades and overlooked by a broad gallery from which the eight prasada-like pavilions stand out. At the third-floor level the main rooms of these pavilions are linked with antechambers and served by screened corridors hung on the outer walls. On the fourth level the apartments are separated by courts. Above that are the domed and balconied kiosks of the roof terraces reached by the narrow screened galleries crowning the perimeter walls.

Until the advent of the Muslims, orthodox Hinduism had not required large covered congregational space: the mystic cults with which the indigenous religion

in the centre of the Ashrafi Mahal at Mandu by Mahmud Khalji. And at Orchha the synthesis was redeployed – extraordinarily – to accommodate a congregation in a novel form of Hindu worship.**4.64, 4.65**

challenged sufism were radically different and predominant among the initiates were the hymn-singing devotees of Krisha's *bakhti* who congregated en masse. Devised by the architects of Raja Madhukar to accommodate such a congregation with an abundance of light and space, uncharacteristic of the Hindu temple, the Orchha Chaturbhuja is audacious in concept and colossal in scale: the side arms are elongated and crowned with sikharas but the bays are domical and the crossing is covered by a huge dome. The cruciform example was followed without elongation or corner chambers at Brindaban, the centre of the Krishna cult where the Bundela rajas, like other Rajput magnates, were active as patrons.

4.64d

4.64e

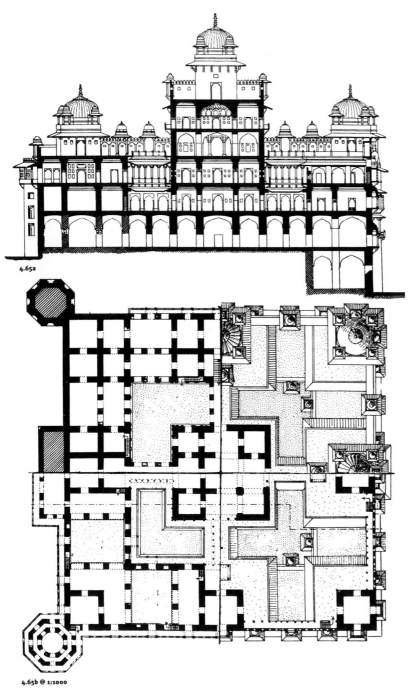

4.65a

4.65b @ 1:1000

c. 1620: (a, b) section and quartered plan, (c) bridge to central pavilion, (d) general view from south-west.

The outer walls of the Govind Mahal at Datia are more massive than those of its Orchha precedent – or, rather, the lower storeys are devoid of relief except on the entrance front – but the galleries and balconies are retained in similar positions on the upper levels and the ribbed domes, which distinguish the corners at Orchha, crown all the axial towers as well as the extra-ordinary central pavilion. There, however, the Hindu architect dispenses with severe walls and monumental arches in favour of the indigenous post, beam and bracket, balcony, chadya and chattri – more graphically even than in the corner pavilions of Orchha: indeed, linked to the axial pavilions by elegant bridges, the four-storey tower containing the royal apartments and durbar hall transforms the four-square solidity of Orchha into one of majestic aspiration.

4.65c

4.65d

4.66a

Jai Singh lived long enough to take works of both Akbar and Shah Jahan as precise models for the major elements he inserted into the courts inherited from his predecessors. The Diwan-i-Am is comparable with the grandest halls produced for Akbar by his indigenous artisans. The Diwan-i-Khas, the bangaldar Jass Mandir above it, and the Shish Mahal, covered by canopies of flowers or dazzling mirror mosaic and addressing a chahar-bagh, are modelled on the most intimate works of Shah Jahan: mirror mosaic, Persian floral ornament, garden murals and the chahar-bagh itself are the richest of Mughal contributions to the court style which owed so much else to native India.**4.66, 4.67**

›**4.66 AMBER, FORT:** (a) general view from the south-west, (b) Diwan-i-Am, (c) plan with (1) Singh Pol, (2) Diwan-i-Am, (3) Ganesha Pol, (4) Sukh Niwas and chahar-bagh, (5) Jai Mandir, (6) Shish Mahal with Jass Mandir above, (d) Ganesha Pol, (e) Shish Mahal, (f, g) Jai Mandir and Sukh Niwas.

Beyond the entrance court and its temples, the court of public audience is overawed by the great apadana with its vaulted canopy carried on doubled rows of vigorously carved columns and elephant capitals. To the south the Ganesh Pol – crowned by the exquisite Sohag Mandir – leads to the garden court of private audience: to the left, beyond the chahar-bagh, are the private apartments; to the right is the Jai Mandir with the Diwan-i-Khas and Shish Mahal.

4.66b

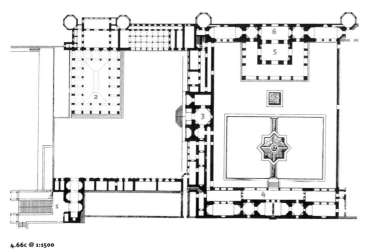

4.66c @ 1:1500

4.66d

4.66e

4.66f

4.66g

4.67

MUGHAL DECADENCE AND POLITICAL FRAGMENTATION

The measure of unity achieved in the subcontinent under the great Mughals gave way before the sectarian division promoted by orthodox Muslim opposition to Akbarian 'heresy'. Matters came to a head under the ageing Aurangzeb. On the one hand, hard-pressed on campaign in the Deccan for the last decades of his reign, the emperor pursued an uncompromising Sunni revival. On the other hand, Hindu *bhakti* enthusiasm had elevated the Krishna cult to pre-eminence centred on Brindaban by the Yamuna River. Moreover, opposition from the Mughals forged several new faiths into militant religious sects, in particular

›4.67 MAHARAJA RAO JAGAT SINGH OF KOTAH IN HIS CHAHAR-BAGH (Kotah school, c. 1670).

4.68a

›4.68 SHIVAJI'S FORTS: (a) Sinhagarh (Simha-
gad), Kalyani Gate; (b) Sindhurdurga, outer ramparts.

Sinhagarh, an ancient fortified site captured by
Muhammad Tughluq in 1328, strengthened by the Adil
Shahis of Bijapur, guards the route through the pass in
the Western Ghats from the coast to Pune – the seat of
Shivaji's father as a vassal of Bijapur from 1604. Taken
by the Mughal forces of Aurangzeb in his conflict with
Bijapur, it was recaptured with legendary daring by
Shivaji's forces in 1670 and thereafter achieved its
definitive form. Sindhurdurga was built about the same
time to guard the naval base at Malvan: Janjira is the
obvious model but the walls follow the entire perimeter
of a larger island and the accommodation towards the
centre was utilitarian.

the Sikhs of the Punjab and the Maharashta of the Western Ghats.

Aurangzeb's short-lived heir, Bahadur Shah (1707–12)
was the last impressive Mughal emperor. The regime was
undermined by succession stuggles after 1712 and was
impotent in the face of repeated disaster. A former main-
stay, the Nizam-ul-mulk Asaf Jah, carved out a virtually
indpendent kingdom in the eastern Deccan based on the
Qutb Shahis' old capital, Hyderabad. The charismatic
Maratha leader, Shivaji, asserted his control over what is
now Maharashtra from his formidable chain of fortresses
in the Western Ghats and the Arabian Sea coast.**4.68**
The Marathas ultimately overran much of central India,

4.68b

plundered the outskirts of Delhi in 1738 and forced the cession of Malwa. In 1739 the Persian Nadir Shah humiliated the emperor, occupied Delhi and stole the Peacock Throne.

Under pressure from the Persians the Mughals lost their grip on Gujarat in 1750, Oudh and Punjab in 1754 and Delhi was invaded again in 1756. Distinct Maratha factions emerged in Maharashtra, Baroda, Nagpur, Indore and Gwalior. The Rajputs had lost what faith they had in the Mughal imperial ideal – indeed for most Hindus it had turned sour under Aurangzeb – and reasserted their independence. The Muslim magnates resorted either to refuge in fatalism or to carving out kingdoms for themselves.

During the period of Mughal ascendency Jai Singh of Amber was not alone among client princes in enlarging

›4.69 AMRITSAR, THE GOLDEN TEMPLE: general view.

The typical gurdwara, set in a sacred tank, is a two- or three-storey cubicle building enshrining a holy text or the remains of a teacher (*guru*). Over the central reliquary chamber a dome usually emerges from a fringe of pinnacles and chattris. The principal Sikh shrine is the Golden Temple at Amritsar which enshrines the holy book bequeathed by the last of the *gurus*, Govind Singh: it was built towards the end of the 16th century and rebuilt in 1764 after it had been sacked by the invading Persians.

his seat in a manner befitting the new dignity bestowed by the emperor. During the period of Mughal decline, especially after Hindu and Muslim magnates reasserted or established their independence, there was a plethora of new palace building. There was also a revival of temple building which reiterated the traditional types – except at centres of the Krishna *bakhti* cult and in the sanctuaries of the Sikhs.**4.69** And the Hindu princes, who had learned from the Muslims to erect monuments to the dead, built canopied cenotaphs at their cremation sites.**4.70** Naturally, too, the major Muslim magnates eclipsed the flagging efforts of the debilitated imperial court in endowing their capitals with mosques and mausoleums – though none surpassed Safdar Jang and his heirs at Lucknow.**4.71**

>**4.70 MANDOR:** cenotaphs of the Maharajas of Jodhpur and associated temples.

4.71a

4.71b

›4.71 LUCKNOW: (a, b) Great Imambara of Nawab Asaf-ud-daulah (1775–97), main compound and entrance; (c) Jami-masjid of Muhammad Ali Shah (1837–42), court front.

Dedicated to the first three *imams*, Ali and his sons Hasan and Husayn, the Great Imambara was built in 1784 to accommodate the Muharram festival of Ashura which marks the anniversary of Husayn's martyrdom: the main element is one of the largest vaulted halls in the world.

4.71C

PRINCELY PROLIXITY

Into the service of this wide range of building types was pressed the inflated, convoluted, hybrid style of the late religious and secular essays of the Mughals, which was drawn from the cross-fertilization of the indigenous and imported traditions in form and structure. The indigenous multi-storey residential prasada with attached audience mandapa is combined with the imported court and iwan – as in 15th-century Mandu and Chittor but in a far more fantastic context. Cusped arches, bangaldar roofs and ribbed domes with lotus-flower finials were predominant but the post, bracket and beam, chadya, chattri, balcony and screen all played their parts – and all were assembled with increasingly flagrant opulence as the 18th century progressed.**4·77**

Muslim and native builders alike, working primarily in plaster and wood, shared the imperial court's general inclination towards Gujarati floridity and specific appreciation of the decorative value of Bengali and Deccani forms. Persian motifs were given a conspicuous role in delicate inlay work of ivory and mirror or elegantly moulded stucco – not to mention the chahar-bagh. And at the turn of the century, repetition and inversion of forms, syncopated rhythms and exaggerated floridity mark the triumph of the vegetal over the architectonic when columns became baluster-like bundles of reeds and arches were overcome by creeper-like cusps.

Muslim princes were certainly not immune to the virus,**4.71b** but most prolific were the Rajputs. Usually constrained by existing fortifications from reproducing the formal qualities of Orchha or Datia, their palaces delight instead in a picturesque contrast between the exigencies of defence and the excesses of retreat. Apart from the fortifications incorporating all the sophistications produced by the stormy past, most of the early work was obliterated in 17th- or 18th-century rebuilding. By then, as much due to prodigal rivalry with one another as to familiarity with the grand scale of the imperial court, most Rajput rulers had extended their seats to incorporate at least three zones, varied in their differentiation but invariably knit together by a defensible network of corridors and galleries: an outer service court, flanked by armoury and temple as at Amber, led to the court of public audience addressed by the durbar hall; beyond that, as usual, the ruler's private apartments; and beyond those, sealed to a greater extent than seems previously to have been the Hindu norm, was the women's rawala of myriad small chambers, screened courts and roof terraces.

The combination of stout traditional defences and palace building – royal, noble and merchant – at its most

convoluted is nowhere better represented than in the walled desert city of Jaisalmer. **4.72** Of the many ancient hill forts embellished with prasadas, none exceeds the spectacle of Jodhpur. Of the even greater number of sites where

4.73a

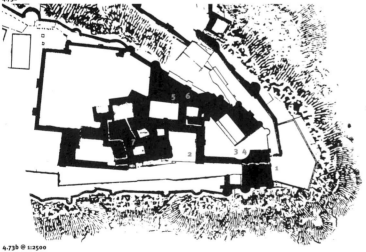

4.73b @ 1:2500

>4.73 JODHPUR FORT PALACE: (a) general view, (b) plan of palace complex with (1) Loha Pol (at the head of tortuous path), (2) Singar Choki Chowk (durbar court), (3, 4) Jhanki Chowk (ruler's private reception court) and Phul Mahal (with private audience hall), (5, 6) Khabka and Mothi Mahal Chowks (courts of ruler's private apartments), (7) rawala, (c, d) Singar Choki Chowk and durbar hall, (e) Mothi Mahal Chowk, (f, page 615) Shish Mahal decoration.

4.73c

4.73d

4.73e

4.74a

4.74b

4.74c

›4.74 BIKANER, DURBAR COURT, DIWAN-
I-KHAS: (a) general view from the south-west showing external galleries, (b) durbar hall, (c) gallery
interior.

the device of man was needed to supplement nature for defence, Bikaner may be called on for extreme opulence of marbled court and gilded hall. Udaipur, protected by lake and surrounding hills with narrow passes rather than by desert or elevation, must also be included as archetypical: the palace there, moreover, demonstrates that imperial pretension was not the preserve of the emperor's allies but also of the most resolutely independent of magnates.**4.73–4.76**

The archetypical Rajput palace

Jodhpur's eminence, like isolated Jaiselmer, provides a commanding view of the surrounding desert, and the walls rising from the rocky face were unassailable. Multi-storey prasada-like blocks and mandapa-like iwans are wholly integrated into a complex of courts, again as at Jaiselmer and many other Rajput seats.

Jodhpur's tortuous access route, guarded by seven gates, leads to the durbar court. Centred, as at Bikaner and elsewhere, on the ruler's marble throne, this is enclosed on three sides by 17th-century buildings (restored after asssault by Aurangzeb) but the nucleus of the complex is 15th century. Beyond, to the south-west is a wholly enclosed court addressed by a magnificent hall which was probably originally built in the mid-17th century: the size suggests a Diwan-i-Am but the position at the heart of the ruler's apartments and its mirror-mosaic ceiling suggests a Diwan-i-Khas – as we have noted, the lack of clear distinction between public and private zones is not untypical of the early Rajput palace. A Diwan-i-Khas was incorporated in the mid-18th-century Phul Mahal to the north-west of the durbar court.

Over the cusped arcading on all sides of the 17th-century ranges – and the 18th-century additions to their north – are multi-storey prasadas hung with galleries and balconies carried on extremely rich corbels. They are screened with a profusion of jalis, dazzling in their intricacy, which provide an outer skin to protect the living spaces from the rigours of the desert climate. Few of the smaller rooms preserve their original decoration intact but the Shish Mahal retains an early scheme of Krishna Lilas in

4.75a

4.75b

>4.75 UDAIPUR, CITY PALACE: (a) processional entry of the Maharana into his palace, (b) main entrance to the royal apartment block, (c) Mor Chowk (mid-17th century with 19th-century embellishment), (d) general view from the north with Trapolia Gate foreground, (e, f) roof terrace garden with Rana Ari Singh and his entourage (Mewari school, 18th century).

coloured glass and mirror mosaic: other rulers, like Bikaner, preferred the Safavid-inspired Mughal style in this and other secluded contexts.

The Udaipur palace was begun on the lines laid down by Rana Khumba at Chittor when Udai Singh retreated to its remote valley to escape Akbar in 1567. A second building campaign, begun after the Rana had made peace with the Mughals and continuing into the 17th century, developed the ruler's apartments by adding rooms and courts for the rawala over the original work. That first formed the towers – prasada-like, as at Chittor – of the Dilkush and Chandra Mahals. New work on a hillock to the north achieved similar elevation as the Badi Mahal. Succeeding generations of builders integrated the blocks and extended the rawala with further superstructures – trabeated, arcaded, corbelled, canopy-vaulted or domed – on and between them. As in most other Rajput palaces, many of the rooms and courts were reworked and redecorated in the debased styles of the 19th century. However, the Chandra Mahal preserves the earliest manifestations in the complex of the court style of Shah Jahan. And in the roof garden added to the Badi Mahal nearly a century later, courtiers real and painted might still enjoy the shade of real and painted trees under arcades in the exquisitely refined style of the late-Mughal court.

4.75c

4.75d

4.75e

4.75f

second half of the 18th century: hall and gallery.

›4.77 DUNGARPUR, UDAI VILLAS, late-18th
century and later: central prasada.

The elaborate confection on which the design pivots
– in the centre of the central court – is the ultimate variation on the theme developed at Datia and first stated
in the entirely different context of Mahmud Khalji's
transformation of the Ashrafi Mahal at Mandu.

4.76

4.77

4.78a

4.78b

›4.78 JAIPUR, CITY PALACE: (a) mural decoration with miniature image of the complex, (b) Chandra Mahal from the court of the Diwan-i-Am, (c) plan, (d) Jantar Mantar astrological park, (e) Hawa Mahal (1799).

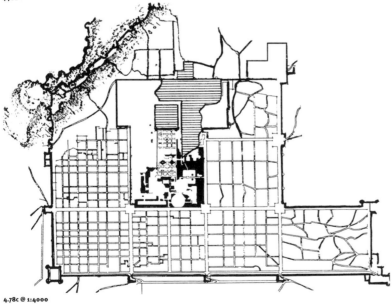

4.78c @ 1:4000

A considerable power by the early 18th century, Maharaja Jai Singh II of Amber (1699–1744) descended from his fort to lay out a modern capital in the plain: abstruse astrological calculation played its age-old part and left its bizarre but tangible mark. Like Kautilya's ideal town, Jaipur was regularly planned – though the contours of the site inhibited the complete realization of the ideal square. Within the walls the garden palace was also conceived in strict accordance with Kautilya, with outer court preceding the great raja-bhavana for public audience and, beyond, the

4.78d

inner raja-nivesana with the ruler's private apartments in a multi-storey prasada. The rawala is located on the upper floors of the seven-storey structure but the ladies of the court were given their own prasada, the Hawa Mahal, whose veil of infinitely repeated bangaldars assimilates it to the age-old prototype.**4.78**

The Jaipur Hawa Mahal was built in 1799. By then Europeans were contributing to the rich mix of imported and indigenous ingredients in India's late architectural style. The fantasy which was the charm of that style gave way to delirium as the 19th century progressed under the *Pax Britannica*: peace meant plenty and princes had fabulous resources to refashion their courts on Western lines at least in part to astonish the potentates of the Raj – but that belongs to another book.

4.78e

GLOSSARY

ABLAQ masonry wall in coloured stripes.

AEDICULE ornamental niche housing a sacred image, for example.

AISLE side passage of a church or temple, running parallel to the nave and separated from it by columns or piers.

AJIMEZ paired windows with a shared central column, characteristic of Muslim Spain.

ALCAZAR castle or palace built by the Moors in southern Spain (from the Arabic *al-qasr*).

AMBULATORY semi-circular or polygonal arcade or walkway surrounding, for example, a sanctuary.

APADANA columned hypostyle hall, usually square in plan, with a portico to one or more sides.

APSE semi-circular domed or vaulted space, especially at one end of a basilica, hence **APSIDAL**, in the shape of an apse.

ARABESQUE decorative element consisting of leaves and tendrils interlaced to form a geometric system.

ARCADE a series of arches supported by columns, sometimes paired and covered so as to form a walkway.

ARCHITRAVE one of the three principal elements of an entablature, positioned immediately above the capital of a column, and supporting the frieze and cornice.

ARCUATE shaped like an arch. Hence (of a building) **ARCUATED**, deploying arch structures (as opposed to trabeated).

ARTESONADO type of wooden ceiling in Spanish Islamic building, with intricate patterns of carved beams and panels.

ATRIUM entrance hall or courtyard, usually open to the sky.

AZULEJO small Spanish glazed tiles.

BAB gate (or door).

BADGIR wind tower, a structure projecting above a building to evacuate warm air during the day and introduce cool air at night.

BAGH (Arabic/Persian) garden or garden pavilion.

BALUSTER short column or pillar, usually bulbous towards the base, supporting a rail.

BALUSTRADE a row of balusters supporting a rail.

BANGALDAR Bengali form of roof with a central curved ridge, highest in the centre. Derivatives are **DO-CHALA**, a roof curving down from the centre in two segments, and **CHOU-CHALA**, curving down in four segments (hipped).

BARADARI 'twelve-doored' pavilion, a summer house with triple arcades on all four sides.

BARBICAN fortified structure at the entry to a town or city, often straddling a gateway.

BASILICA temple or other public building, consisting principally of a colonnaded rectangular space with an apse at one end, generally enclosed by an ambulatory, or having a central nave and side aisles, and lit by a clerestory.

BASTION structure projecting from the angle of a defensive wall enabling enhanced vision and mobility for a garrison.

BATTERING reinforcement of walls and column bases by building sloping supporting structure.

BAY one of a series of compartments of the interior of a building, the divisions being created by piers or columns, for example.

BAYT apartment, or paired apartments characteristic of Umayyad domestic building.

BAYT AL-MAL 'house of money', a mosque treasury, usually a small structure on columns sited in the mosque courtyard.

BAZAAR market.

BEAM horizontal element in, for instance, a trabeated structure.

BEDESTAN enclosed form of market intended to protect commerce in valuable goods. Usually a long two-storey structure with shops facing on to the street.

BELVEDERE open-sided roofed structure, freestanding or sited on the roof of a building so as to command a view.

BEMA sanctuary of a church, especially Byzantine.

BEYLIK small Anatolian principalities, an area governed by a 'bey'.

BIMARISTAN hospital.

BIT HILANI columned portico, originating in the 1st millennium BCE in Syria.

BURJ fortified tower.

BUTTRESS support, usually stone, built against a wall to reinforce or take load.

CAMI in Turkish, congregational mosque.

CAPITAL top part of a column, supporting the entablature.

CARAVANSERAI arcaded enclosure providing overnight accommodation for travellers and their goods.

CENOTAPH funerary monument remote from the location of the remains of those commemorated.

CESME fountain or other source of drinking water often associated in a charitable way with Ottoman monuments.

CHADYA awning, eave.

CHAHAR-BAGH formal garden, ideally square and divided into four smaller squares by axial paths or canals.

CHAHAR-SUQ market sited around a square.

CHAHAR-TAQ square domed structure characteristic of Zoroastrian fire temples and adapted for use in other circumstances.

CHASED ornamented with embossing or engraving.

CHATTRI umbrella-shaped dome or pavilion, sometimes acting as a turret on the roof of a stupa.

CHIHIL SUTUN many-columned (literally forty columns) pavilion or hall.

CHOU-CHALA hipped variant of bangaldar roof.

CIBORIUM canopy raised on columns to cover a tomb or altar.

CITADEL fortress, usually at the highest part of a town.

CLERESTORY windowed upper level providing light for a double-storey interior.

CLOISTER covered arcade, often running around the perimeter of an open courtyard.

COLONNADE line of regularly spaced columns.

COLONNETTE small column, decorative and/or functional.

COLUMN vertical member, usually circular in cross-section, functionally structural or ornamental or both, usually comprising a base, shaft and capital.

CORBEL course of masonry or support bracket, usually made of stone, for a beam or other horizontal member. Hence **CORBELLED**: forming a stepped roof by deploying a series of progressively overlapping corbels.

CORNICE projecting moulding forming the top part of an entablature. More generally, a horizontal ornamental moulding projecting at the top of a wall or other structure.

CRYPT underground chamber, often beneath the chancel of a church.

CUSP projection formed between two arcs, especially in stone tracery, hence cusped.

CYMA REVERSA wave-shaped moulding, the upper part concave and the lower convex.

DADO the middle part, between base and cornice, of a pedestal, or the lower part of a wall when treated as a continuous pedestal.

DAR AL-IMARA regional governor's palace or administrative centre.

DARGHA Muslim saint's tomb complex.

DARWAZA door, gate or portal, especially of monumental proportions.

DAULAT KHANA 'abode of majesty', a securely walled residence, but particularly a sultan's palace enclosure.

DERSHANE room in a madrasa in which study or lectures take place.

DIAPERWORK repeated pattern in brick or tile, for instance, often involving diamond shapes.

DIWAN royal court or audience place, hence **DIWAN-I-AM**, court of public audience in an Islamic palace or **DIWAN-I-KHAS**, court of private audience in an Islamic palace.

DO-CHALA pitched variant of bangaldar roof.

DURBAR royal assembly, a court or audience hall.

ENTABLATURE part of the façade immediately above the columns, usually composed of a supportive architrave, decorative frieze and projecting cornice.

FASTIGIUM pediment or other structure in the shape more or less of the gable end of a house, especially when dignifying the entrance to a temple precinct or palace, hence a place of epiphany.

FILIGREE decorative work formed from a mesh or by piercing material to give the impression of a mesh.

FINIAL ornament at the top of a gable or roof, for example.

FRESCO painting done on plaster which is not yet dry.

FRIEZE middle part of an entablature, above the architrave and below the cornice; more generally any horizontal strip decorated in relief.

FRONTISPIECE principal entrance and its surround, usually distinguished by decoration and often standing proud of the façade in which it sits.

GLACIS slope or ramp in front of, typically, a defensive wall.

GUNBAD domed tomb.

GURDWARA Sikh temple (literally 'guru's door or house'), typically a simple domed building which, for theological reasons, can be entered from all sides.

HAMAM a bath house or public bathing complex.

HAN relatively small, usually urban, inn or caravanserai.

HAREM private family or women's quarters; **HAREM SERA**, palace compound exclusively for the royal women.

HASHT BEHISHT 'eight paradises', an octagonal palace pavilion, usually with axial iwans alternating with chambers at the corners.

HAUZ pool, usually in the courtyard of a mosque.

HAVELI mansion or merchant's house.

HAZARBAF type of ornate brickwork.

HAZAR SUTUN 'thousand-pillared hall'.

HAZIRA tomb within an enclosure, often with a mosque.

HEMICYCLE semi-circular recessed structure on a grand scale.

HYPOSTYLE HALL hall with a roof supported by numerous columns, more or less evenly spaced across its area.

IMAMZADA tomb of an *imam*, hence shrine.

IMARET Ottoman kitchen, part of a religious complex, supplying food to various deserving groups.

IMPOST structural member – usually in the form of a moulding or block – at the top of a pillar, for instance, on which an arch rests.

INTRADOS curve defined by the lower surface of an arch.

IWAN large vaulted hall or recess opening off a court.

JALA net, hence **JALAKA**, grilled or screened window; and **JALI**, lattice or filigree-patterned screen.

JAMB the inner side of a door frame.

JAMI-MASJID mosque in which the Friday prayers can be held, as well as the five daily congregational prayers.

KHAN building providing facilities for trade and accommodation.

KHANQAH hermitage or retreat.

KHAS MAHAL private palace.

KIOSK small open pavilion, often pillared.

KUFIC SCRIPT originating in Kufa in Iraq, a stylized form often featured in Islamic painting and carving.

KULIYE large complex centred on a mosque and which might include libraries, madrasas, khanqas and a kitchen providing meals to the needy.

LINTEL horizontal member over, for example, a window or doorway or bridging the gap between two columns or piers.

LOBE projection formed between two arcs, especially in stone tracery; larger form of cusp.

MADRASA Islamic school or college generally associated with a mosque.

MAHAL summer house or pavilion.

MAIDAN open field before a fort or palace, hence civic park or polo ground.

MAMLUK a slave brought from central Asia, then trained and freed before entering military service.

MAQAD a loggia overlooking the courtyard of a house.

MAQSURA the area in a mosque within which the caliph worshipped: also, the protective screen enclosing that area.

MASHHAD memorial, in the form of a shrine or mosque, commemorating a martyr or marking the site of a holy vision.

MASHRABIYA in Islamic domestic architecture, windows or grills with latticework screens of turned or carved wood. They combine a measure of privacy with ventilation.

MASJID small mosque used for the five daily congregational prayers.

MAUSOLEUM tomb, usually of a dignitary, built on a grand scale.

MECIT small domed Ottoman prayer hall.

MEDINA settlement, city, often used to indicate the old part of a city.

MERLONS raised elements of a battlement, alternating with embrasures.

MIHRAB niche or marker in a mosque indicating the direction of Mecca.

MINAR freestanding monumental tower, mainly used to call Muslims to the mosque to prayer.

MINARET tower attached to a mosque, from which Muslims are called to prayer.

MINBAR type of pulpit, usually consisting of a small dais with a throne reached by steps.

MIRADOR a belvedere.

MOSAIC decoration formed by embedding small coloured tiles or pieces of glass in cement.

MOSQUE Muslim temple/complex used for public worship.

MUQARNAS miniature squinch forms used in combination functionally in effecting transition from, for instance, polygonal chamber to domed roof; and/or used decoratively to produce a honeycomb effect.

NAGINA-MASJID 'jewel mosque', palatine chapel of the harem sera in a Mughal palace.

NARTHEX chamber adjunct to the nave of a building, usually a Christian church.

NASHKI a cursive style of script.

NAUBAT KHANA place for beating drums to mark the hours and important events at court.

NECROPOLIS cemetery, literally a community of the dead.

NICHE recess in a wall, often containing a statue.

OCULUS circular window.

OGEE arch composed of two cyma reversa mouldings meeting head to head at the apex.

PADMA lotus, hence also moulding with a lotus-shaped profile.

PASTOPHERIA in the Byzantine church, areas to the sides of the rear of the sanctuary, used by priests for preparations for ritual.

PAVILION lightly constructed building, often tent-like and set in a garden.

PENDENTIVE curved concave triangular member used at the corners of a square or polygonal structure so as to enable reconciliation with a domed roof.

PIER supporting pillar for wall or roof, often of rectangular cross-section.

PILASTER a pier of rectangular cross-section, more or less integral with and only slightly projecting from the wall which it supports.

PISHTAQ a frontispiece or monumental portal standing proud of the façade.

PLINTH rectangular base or base support of a column or wall.

POL gateway.

PORTAL doorway, usually on a grand scale.

PORTICO entrance to a building, featuring a colonnade.

POST vertical element in, for instance, a trabeated structure.

PRASADA multi-storey structure: mansion, palace or temple.

PYLON monumental tower, often associated with a temple gateway.

QASR palace or fortress.

QIBLA orientation of a mosque such that prayer is directed towards Mecca: also, of a mosque, the wall that faces towards Mecca.

QUBBA domed cubical chamber with open sides, often a mausoleum or shrine.

RAMPART defensive earthwork, usually surrounding a fortress or citadel, often with a stone parapet.

RANG MAHAL pleasure palace (literally 'painted palace').

RAUZA mortuary complex comprising a courtyard with a tomb and mosque.

RAWALA women's quarters in a palace.

REGISTAN parade ground.

RELIEF carving, typically of figures, raised from a flat background by cutting away more (high relief) or less (low relief) of the material from which they are carved.

REVETMENT decorative reinforced facing for a wall.

RIB raised band on a vault or ceiling.

RIBAT fortified enclosure, usually square, associated with Muslim holy warriors.

RIWAQ arcade along one or more sides of a courtyard.

SABIL public fountain, either attached to a mosque or freestanding.

SABIL-KUTTAB a building with a public fountain at ground level and a Koranic school above.

SAHN a courtyard in a mosque or domestic building, surrounded by rooms and/or an arcade.

SARCOPHAGUS type of outer coffin, usually of highly decorated stone.

SARDIVAN fountain in the middle of the courtyard of a mosque.

SCENAE FRONS flat wall forming the back of the stage in a semi-circular Roman theatre.

SEBIL drinking fountain.

SEMEHANE room, often octagonal and roofed with a dome, attached to an Ottoman mosque in which dervishes danced.

SERAI palace.

SERDAB underground room in a Mesopotamian or Persian palace providing respite from summer heat.

SHISH MAHAL room usually decorated with mirror mosaics, especially a bath house in a palace compound.

SOUK market, often within a covered arcade.

SPANDREL triangular space formed by the outer curve of an arch and the horizontal and vertical elements of the rectangle within which the arch sits.

SQUINCH arch placed across the corner of a square structure so as to form a polygon capable of being roofed by a dome.

STALACTITE form of ornament consisting of multi-tiered niches used, for instance, in domes and portals.

STRINGCOURSE projecting horizontal course of structural elements or moulding.

STUCCO type of plaster, especially used where decoration is to be applied.

STUPA Buddhist monument, tumulus, burial or reliquary mound.

SUFI Muslim ascetic holy man.

TABHANE hostel attached to a mosque to accommodate travelling religious types.

TALAR multi-columned portico or open hypostyle hall backed by a wall.

TEKKE building providing accommodation for dervishes, usually attached to a mosque complex.

TETRACONCH quatrefoil structure with four apses open to the centre.

TIM warehouse.

TRABEATED structurally dependent on rectilinear post and beam supports.

TURBE tomb in the form of a tower.

TURKISH TRIANGLE pendentive transformed into long, narrow triangles.

TURRET small tower, often at the angle of a building.

TYMPANUM triangular area of a pediment, enclosed by raking cornices above and entablature below; more generally, the area, usually recessed, formed by a window- or door-lintel below and an arch above.

ULEMA Muslim legal scholar, more generally the body of Muslim clerical scholars.

ULU CAMI Turkish Friday mosque.

VAULT structure forming an arched roof over a space.

VERANDAH roofed colonnade attached to one or more sides of a building.

VESTIBULE courtyard in front of the entrance to a house; hallway to a building; space adjunct to a larger room.

VIADUCT walkway or road elevated on arches.

VOLUTE scroll or spiral ornamental and/or support member.

VOUSSOIR wedge-shaped stone deployed in building an arch. Hence **VOUSSOIR ARCH**, where such stones are used.

WALI in North Africa, the tomb of a Muslim saint or holy man.

WAV Gujarati public step-well, palatial and often with heavily ornamented walls.

ZAWIYA (Turkish **ZAVIYE**) a building in which a *sufi* scholar disseminates theology to followers.

ZENANA enclosed accommodation for women.

ZIARAT small timber shrine of Kashmir, square in plan with projecting verandahs, a pyramidal roof and a spire-like minaret.

ZONE OF TRANSITION area in which the change from the vertical walls of a square or polygonal space to a dome is effected.

FURTHER READING

This set of volumes, *Architecture in Context*, is based on a survey series of lectures covering the whole spectrum of architectural history developed over a quarter of a century at the Canterbury School of Architecture. It is therefore impossible, even if it were desirable, to enumerate all the books that I have consulted and, in one way or another, depended on, over that period. Beyond students of architecture, for whom this whole process was initiated, I hope that the present work will provide the general reader with a broad but also reasonably deep introduction to the way our environment has been moulded over the past five thousand years. With this in mind, rather than a bibliography, I hope it will be useful if I provide a rough guide to how I would go about developing a course in further reading, were I starting now.

First, I would consult the *Grove Dictionary of Art*, as much for the bibliographies attached to each section of each subject as for the individual articles – inevitably some are better than others as different authors naturally bring different standards of scholarship to bear on their products. Second, for greater depth and breadth, I would consult *The Pelican History of Art*, now published by Yale University Press. Notable for the scope of this book are Richard Ettinghauser, Oleg Grabar and Marilyn Jenkins-Madina, *Islamic Art and Architecture 650–1250* (New Haven and London 2001) (and the original text of Ettinghauser and Grabar published as *The Art and Architecture of Islam* by Pelican in 1987), and Sheila S. Blair and Jonathan M. Bloom, *The Art and Architecture of Islam 1250–1800* (New Haven and London 1994). Again, the bibliographies appended to each volume will be an invaluable guide to even broader and deeper reading.

Taschen (under the indefatigable editorship of Henri Stierlin) and Könemann have both published lavishly illustrated multi-volume series that have perhaps been over-ambitious and therefore incomplete: the Könemann volume on Islam, edited by Markus Hattstein and Peter Delius (Cologne 2000) offers a particularly sumptuous, comprehensively illustrated coverage of both art and architecture.

Third: specific histories of architecture. As any student of the subject knows, the inescapable primer is the work first published in 1896 by Sir Banister Fletcher as *A History of Architecture on the Comparative Method*: that was essentially a catalogue arranged roughly chronologically by area but as the method was gradually superseded more room was found in the later-20th-century editions for essential analysis of the architecture of Islam and other non-European traditions. Beyond that, from my view in the 1970s the most useful general survey of architectural history was the multi-volume series initiated by Electa in Milan, edited by Pier Luigi Nervi and published in English by Abrams (and later by others): it had its flaws, not least in the relationship of text to illustrations, and much was lost in translation from the authors' native languages into English. However, the range of scholars involved was impressive and, despite their age, some of the material not otherwise easily available is still essential reading: John D. Hoag's volume on *Islamic Architecture* (New York 1977) is one of the best.

In particular, I would recommend the following monographs and their bibliographies: K.A.C. Creswell, *A Short Account of Early Muslim Architecture* (Harmondsworth 1958); Robert Hillenbrand, *Islamic Architecture* (Edinburgh 1994); G.S.P. Freeman-Grenville and Stuart C. Munro-Hay, *Historical Atlas of Islam* (New York 2002); Andrew Petersen, *Dictionary of Islamic Architecture* (London 1996); K.A.C. Creswell, *The Muslim Architecture of Egypt* (Oxord 1952, reissue New York 1978); Marianne Barrucand and Achim Bednorz, *Moorish Architecture in Andalusia* (Cologne 2002); Godfrey Goodwin, *A History of Ottoman Architecture* (London 1971 and reprints); Edgar Knobloch, *Monuments of Central Asia* (London 2001); Edgar Knobloch, *The Archaeology and Architecture of Afghanistan* (Stroud 2002); Thomas W. Lentz and Glenn D. Lowry, *Timur and the Princely Vision* (Los Angeles and Washington, DC 1989); Sheila R. Canby (ed.), *Safavid Art and Architecture* (London 2002); Philip Davies, *The Penguin Guide to the Monuments of India*, volume II, *Islamic, Rajput, European* (London 1989); and the Islamic section of my *The History of Architecture in India* (London 1990, 1994).

My own dependence on the contributors to the series cited in the second and third paragraphs above – and relevant works inadvertently omitted from the list in the fourth paragraph – will be apparent to many readers – especially the authors themselves to whom I apologize for any unwitting offence.

THE SPREAD OF ISLAM

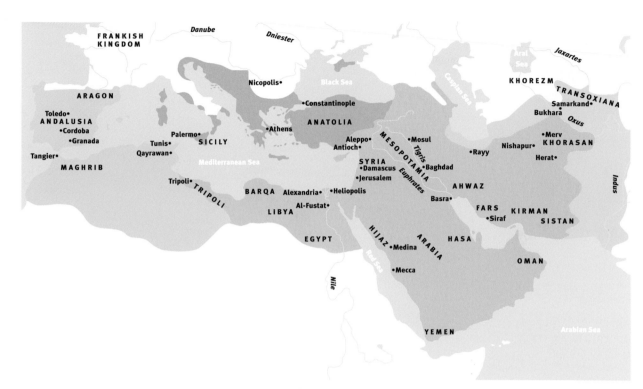

FRANKISH KINGDOM

Danube

Dniester

Nicopolis•

Black Sea

•Constantinople

Jaxartes

Aral Sea

KHOREZM

TRANSOXIANA

ARAGON

ANATOLIA

Samarkand•

Bukhara•

Oxus

Toledo•
ANDALUSIA

•Cordoba

•Granada

Palermo•

Tunis•

Qayrawan•

SICILY

•Athens

Aleppo•

Antioch•

MESOPOTAMIA

•Mosul

Tigris

•Merv

KHORASAN

Nishapur•

•Rayy

Herat•

Tangier•

MAGHRIB

Mediterranean Sea

SYRIA

•Damascus

•Jerusalem

Euphrates

Baghdad•

AHWAZ

Indus

Tripoli•

TRIPOLI

BARQA

Alexandria•

•Heliopolis

Basra•

FARS

KIRMAN

•Siraf

SISTAN

LIBYA

Al-Fustat•

HIJAZ

ARABIA

HASA

EGYPT

Red Sea

•Medina

OMAN

Nile

•Mecca

YEMEN

Arabian Sea

AREA CONQUERED BY THE DEATH OF MUHAMMAD, 632

AREA CONQUERED UNDER THE FIRST FOUR CALIPHS BETWEEN 632 AND 661

AREA CONQUERED UNDER THE UMAYYADS BETWEEN 661 AND 750

BYZANTINE EMPIRE IN THE EARLY 11TH CENTURY

THE MUSLIM WORLD C. 1020

SUNNI STATES

SHI'ITE STATES

BYZANTINE EMPIRE

THE MUSLIM WORLD C. 1200

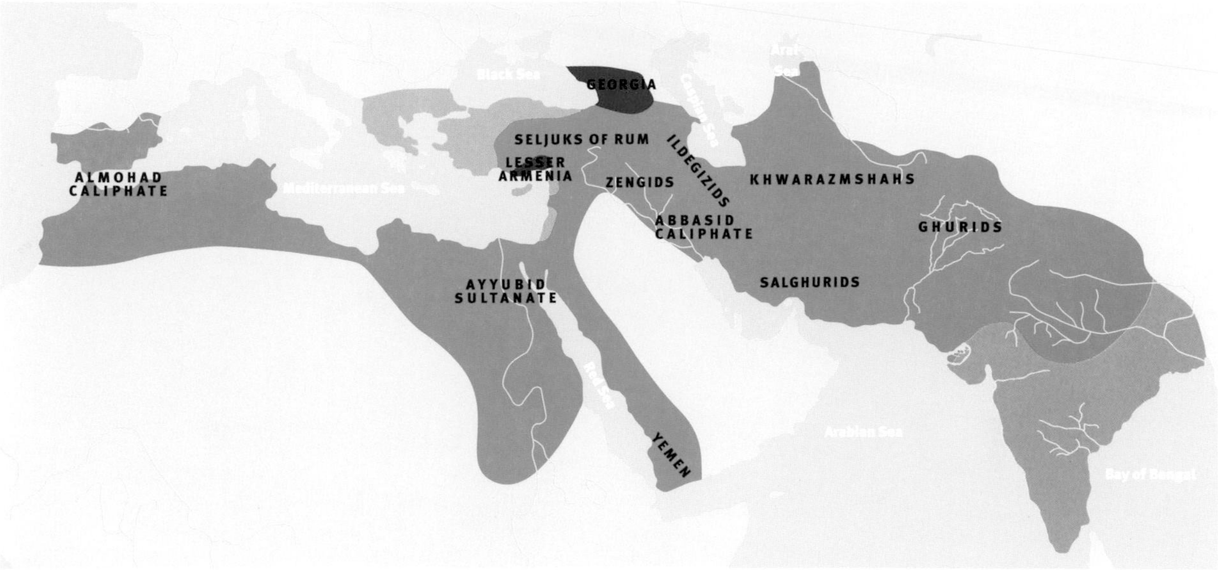

GEORGIA
SELJUKS OF RUM
LESSER ARMENIA
ILDEGIZIDS
ZENGIDS
KHWARAZMSHAHS
ALMOHAD CALIPHATE
ABBASID CALIPHATE
GHURIDS
SALGHURIDS
AYYUBID SULTANATE
YEMEN
Black Sea
Caspian Sea
Aral Sea
Mediterranean Sea
Red Sea
Arabian Sea
Bay of Bengal

MUSLIM STATES

HINDU STATES

CHRISTIAN STATES

CRUSADER STATES

BYZANTINE EMPIRE

THE TIMURID EMPIRE C. 1405

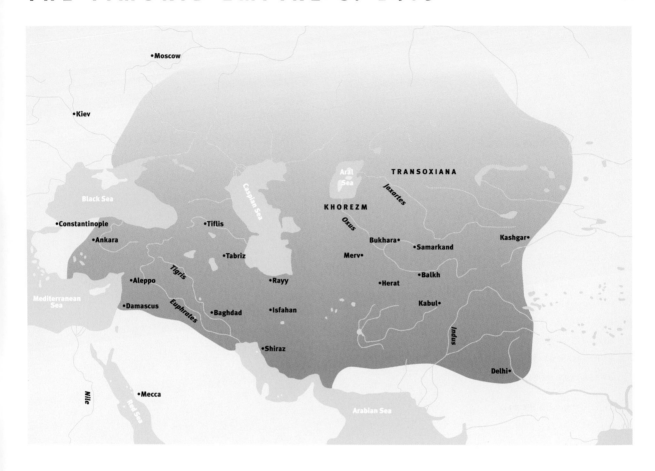

Moscow

Kiev

Black Sea

Constantinople

Ankara

Mediterranean
Sea

Aleppo

Damascus

Nile

Red Sea

Mecca

Tigris

Euphrates

Baghdad

Tiflis

Tabriz

Rayy

Isfahan

Shiraz

Caspian Sea

Aral
Sea

KHOREZM

Oxus

Merv

Herat

TRANSOXIANA

Jaxartes

Bukhara

Samarkand

Balkh

Kabul

Indus

Kashgar

Delhi

Arabian Sea

GROWTH OF THE OTTOMAN EMPIRE

TRANSYLVANIA
MOLDAVIA
BESSARABIA
Dniester
CRIMEAN KHANATE (TRIBUTARY STATE)
Don

WALLACHIA (TRIBUTARY STATE)
Belgrade•
•Bucharest
Danube
DOBRUJA
Black Sea
GEORGIA

BOSNIA
SERBIA
•Nicopolis
Sofia•
BULGARIA
•Amasra
•Samsun
Trebizond•
TREBIZOND

Edirne•
ERTENA
Constantinople•
ALBANIA
•Thessaloniki
Gallipoli•
•Nicaea
KURDISTAN
•Canakkale
Bursa•
A N A T O L I A
KERMIAN
Lepanto•
SARUKHAN
Smyrna•
KARAMAN
•Athens
AIDIN
•Konya
CILICIAN ARMENIA
MESOPOTAMIA
MOREA
HAMID
MENTESHE
TEKKE
Euphrates

Mediterranean Sea

Adriatic Sea

- ■ **INCORPORATED BY 1307**
- ■ **INCORPORATED BETWEEN 1307 AND 1359**
- ■ **INCORPORATED BETWEEN 1359 AND 1451**
- □ **INCORPORATED BETWEEN 1451 AND 1481**

THE DELHI SULTANATE

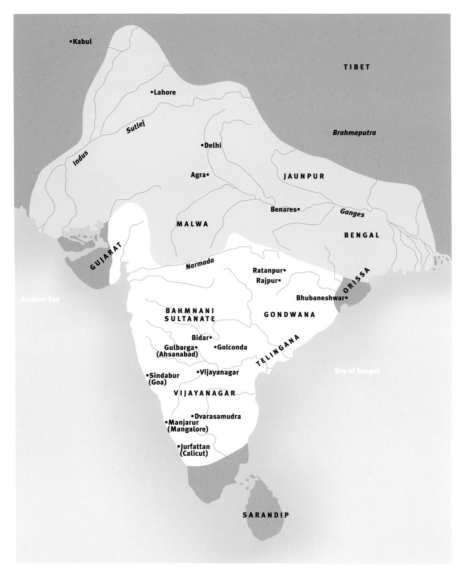

•Kabul

TIBET

•Lahore

Sutlej

Brahmaputra

Indus

•Delhi

Agra•

JAUNPUR

MALWA

Benares•

Ganges

BENGAL

GUJARAT

Narmada

Ratanpur•
Rajpur•

ORISSA

Arabian Sea

Bhubaneshwar•

BAHMNANI
SULTANATE

GONDWANA

Bidar•

Gulbarga•   •Golconda
(Ahsanabad)

TELINGANA

•Sindabur
(Goa)

•Vijayanagar

Bay of Bengal

VIJAYANAGAR

•Dvarasamudra

•Manjarur
(Mangalore)

•Jurfattan
(Calicut)

SARANDIP

SULTANATE IN 1236

AREA ADDED BY 1335

HINDU AREAS

INDEX

Ferdinand of Aragon 248
Ferdinand I of Castile 220
Ferghana 138
Fertile Crescent 30, 45, 49, 75
Fez 120, 199, 220, 220–1, 221, 223, 226, 241; capture of by Berbers (1248) 230; Marinid madrasas 234, 235–7; Qarawiyin 220, 221
fire temple 35–6, 109, 145
Firoz Shah, Sultan 475, 476, 477, 479, 481, 487, 508, 517, 533, 539, 547
Firozabad 30–1, 65, 74–5
First World War 331
Firuzkuh 159
flowers: and Mughals 598
forts: Adilshahi 567; Bahamani 498, 498–9, 500–1, 501–2, 503; Berber 230, 230–1; Marinid (Berber) 230, 230–1; Mughal 545, 546, 547, 547, 622–5; Ottoman 324, 324–5; Rajput 633, 634–5; Seljuk 141–2; Shivaji 626–7; Syrian desert 60, 61; Zengi 164, 164; see also water forts
fountains 360, 435
four-iwan plan 288, 405, 479, 505, 586; and court 30, 65, 134, 142, 287, 377, 384, 391, 401, 416, 443; and madrasa 154–7, 155, 157, 234, 292, 401, 405; and mosque 144–53, 292, 401, 445–6; and mosque-madrasa 292, 293, 297
four-square fort 41
four-square garden 216, 557
funerary complex: Bahri Mamluk 282–91, 284–91; Burji Mamluk 292–3, 293–7; Ottoman 332–3; Timurid 392–400; see also mashhad; mausoleums; tombs
Fustat 16, 53, 120, 122; Mosque of Amr 88, 89, 89; Mosque of Ibn Tulun 89, 90–1, 92–3

Gabriel, Archangel 5, 6
garden palace 392, 462–3, 645–6
gardens 45, 82, 134, 216, 250–1, 262–5; four-square 216, 557; Mughal 557, 579
Gardens of Paradise 598–613
Garjistan: Shah-i Mashhad 155, 156
gatehouses 44
Gaur 493, 495; Dakhil Darwaza 493, 493; Tantipara-masjid and Ekhlakhi mausoleum 495
Gawharshad 389
Genghis Khan see Ghingiz Khan

Gerasa 37
Ghana 230
Ghassanids 67
Ghazan Khan 373, 374
ghazis 103, 178
Ghazna: minaret of Mas'ud III 158
Ghaznavids 133–4, 159
Ghazni 133, 134, 467
Ghengis Khan 139, 270–1, 373, 387, 407
Ghurids 159, 465, 467, 519
Gira 34
Goa 568
Golconda 542, 563; fort and palace remains 564–5; tomb of Muhammad Shah 564
Golden Horde 271, 387
Granada 230, 248, 252; Alhambra 252–61, 252–60, 262–5, 266, 267
Great Khan see Ghengis Khan
Greeks: conception of order 36
Guinea 223, 230
Gujarat 466, 489, 511–14, 517, 537, 542, 558, 628
Gulbarga 489, 496, 496–7, 498, 567, 568; Jami-masjid 496, 496–7, 504; Mujarrad Kamal's dargah masjid 498, 498
Gunbad-i Qabus 114–15, 114
gurdwara 628
Gwalior 536, 536; Gujari Mahal 555, 615; palace of Man Singh 526–7, 528, 528, 529, 530–1, 532, 532, 545, 547; tomb of Muhammad Ghaus 560–1

hadith 9, 12, 27
Hafsids 233
al-Hakam I 199
al-Hakam II 208
Hamadan (city) 136
Hamadan, Shah: mosque of (Srinagar) 492
hans 323, 324, 384
harem 329, 330, 363, 364, 368, 369–70, 383, 547, 555, 556, 557, 597, 598
Harun al-Rashid 72, 105
Hasan (Ali's son) 10–11
Hasan, sultan 278, 288, 292
hasht behisht 392, 406, 431, 435, 440–1, 444, 539, 560, 604, 606
Hatra 34, 121
Hazara: Masjid-i-Diggarun 109, 109, 374, 377

Hazrat Pandua 493; Adina Masjid 493, 494–5
Hellenistic 30, 34, 165
Heraclius, Emperor 7
Herat 137, 159, 389, 407, 409; Gauhar Shad madrasa 401, 405, 505; palace at 392, 558; Tareb Khana 406, 558
hermits 102
Hindu temples 476, 489, 491, 492, 517
Hinduism 616
Hisham I 49
Hisham II 199, 201
Holy Land 120–1, 139, 275
Hoshang Shah 489, 516, 517, 520
hostels see caravanserai
houses 413, 413, 432; Ayyubid 173; courtyard 13, 13, 143, 432; Seljuk 143; Shibanid 413
Hoysalas 491
Hulagu 271, 373
Humayun 536, 537, 539, 540, 544; tomb complex (Delhi) 558, 558–9, 559
Huns 72
Husayn I, Shah 458
Husayn (Ali's son) 10–11, 27, 117, 130; shrine of (Kerbala or Karbala) 27, 429
Husayn Baykara 407, 427
Hyderabad 563, 565, 627; Char Minar 565, 566, 578
hypostyle hall 36, 40, 53, 67, 75, 94, 125, 144, 147, 149, 185, 185, 201, 306–7, 476, 517

Iberia 216, 248
Ibn Sina of Bukhara 105
Ibn Tulun: mosque of 124
Ibrahim II: tomb complex of (Bijapur) 564–5, 567, 574–5, 575
Idris bin Abdullah 198–9
Ifriqiya (modern Tunisia) 88, 94, 96, 101, 105, 198, 230
Ikhshidid dynasty 101
Ilkhanids 309, 373–85, 418
Iltutmish 466, 468
Imam Dur 159, 166; tomb of Muslim bin Quraish 116, 116
imams 9, 10, 18, 104–5, 445
imperial mosque: India's first 467–72; Mughal 583–7; Ottoman 332–61; Safavid 447–56

madrasas 166, 171–2, 233, 305–6; Ayyubid 172, *172–3*, 173–4; Bahamani 505–6, *505*; Burji Mamluk 300–1; and four-iwan plan 154–7, *155, 157,* 234, 292, 401, 405; Ilkhanid 377; Malwan 517, 518–19, *519*; Marinid 234–6, *235, 236–7*; Ottoman 311–12, *333*; Sa'di 241, *242–3*; Safavid 445–6, 458–61, *458, 459, 460*; Seljuk 154–7, 182–3, 184, 188, *188,* 190–1, 193, 377; Shibanid 409, 414–15, 416–18, *416–17*; Timurid 401–6, *404, 405*; Tughluq 476; Tuqay-Timurid *422,* 423

Maharashtra 627

mahdi 71

Mahdia *118,* 119

Mahmud Gawan 505, 506, *506*; madrasa of (Bidar) 505–6, *505*

Mahmud of Ghazni 133–4

Mahmud Shah 501

maidan scheme *433*

Malacca: Kampung Keling Mosque *23*

Malaya 578

Mali 230, 232–3; Djenne *23, 24–5*

al-Malik al-Kamal, sultan 174

Malik Sarwar 489

Malik-shah, sultan 149, 179

Malikshah 137–8, 163

Malulah (Syria): courtyard house *13*

Malwa 489, 516, 517–19, 537, 628

Mamluks 133, 135, 170, 271–8, 312, 327, 389; defeat of by Timurids 389; extension of rule 278; funerary complex 282–9, *284–91*; palaces 298, 300, *300*; tombs *275,* 287–8; *see also* Bahri Mamluks; Burji Mamluks

al-Ma'mun, caliph 72, 73, 89

Man Singh: palace of (Gwalior) 526–7, 528, *528, 529, 530–1,* 532, *532,* 545, 547

Manarat Mujda 112

mandapa type 521

Mandor *629*

Mandu 489, 516–17, 559, 631; Ashrafi Mahal *521,* 615; palace complex 519–21, *520, 521, 522–3*; religious works 516–17, *516–17,* 518, *519*; tomb of Mahmud Khalji 559

Mangu 271

Manisa *321,* 322; great mosque and zaviye *308, 309*

al-Mansur, Ahmad 244

al-Mansur, Yacoub 223, 233

al-Mansur, caliph 71–2, 74, 75

Manzikert 137, 162

maqsara 16, 55, 202, 204, *204–6*

Maragha: Gunbad-i Qabud 159, *160*; Gunbad-i Surkh 159

Marathas 627–8

marble 129, 215, 333, *340,* 553, 560, 587, *602,* 607

al-Maridani, Amir Altinburgha 279

Marinids 229–30, 233–9, 241

Marrakesh 219, 223, 230, 241; Bab Agnaou *226,* 229; Kutubiya mosque and minaret 226, *226, 227,* 229; madrasas 241, *242–3*; Qubbat al-Barudiyin 221, *222,* 223; Sa'di necropolis 241, *244*

martyria 36, 49–50, 111

al-Marwan II, Caliph 71

mashhad 27, 102–3, 129, 130–1, *131,* 405, 429, 445

Mas'ud I 179

mausoleums 27, 36; Ayyubid 171–2; development of 110–16; Fatimid 130–1, *130*; Ilkhanid 374, *374, 375*; Mamluk *275*; Mughal *540–1*; Seljuk 158–61; *see also* tombs

Mecca 5, 7, 219, 327; Ka'ba 4, 5, 7, *15,* 16, *18*; pilgrimage to (*hadj*) 12

mecit form 319

Medina 14, 53, 327; Prophet's Mosque 14–16, *15,* 18, 26, 53, *53,* 59

Medina al-Zahra 209–16, *209–15,* 261

Mehmet Aga 357

Mehmet I 311, 317; Yesil Cami of (Bursa) 317, *318, 319, 319*

Mehmet II, the Conqueror 326–7, *326, 327,* 332, 363, 364

Mehmet III 331

Mehrauli: Jamali-masjid 537

Meknes 241; Bab al-Mansur *246, 247*; granaries *246*; great mosque *218–19,* 220; tomb of Moulay Ismail *245*

Merv 8, 75, 137, 142, 271; Seljuk palace *142*; tomb of Sultan Sanjar 159–60, *160–1*

Mesopotamia 133, 428

mihrab 16, 18, 40, *40,* 53, 59, *147, 173, 186,* 206, *224–5,* 283, 285, *376,* 495

minarets 40, *40,* 114, 127, 134, 145, 511; Adilshahi 573, *573*; Almohad 226, *226, 228,* 229; Bahamani 506; cylindrical *106*; Ghurid 467, 469, *470*; Gujarat 515; Mamluk 279, 289; Mughal 560, *583,* 586; Ottoman 322, 323, 353, 357; Seljuk 137, 158–61, *158–9, 186,* 193, *195*; spiral 87, *87,* 89, 92; stepped 95, *95*; Timurid 393, 401, *404,* 405; Tughluq 477; Umayyad 59

minbar 16, 40, *40*

Miranshah 389

mirror: Anatolian bronze *178*

Mongolia 271

Mongols 167, 170, *268–9,* 270, *270,* 466; building 372–85; conquest of 136, 139, 179, 270–1; *see also* Ilkhanids

Moorish style 248–9

Moriah, Mount 27, 49

Moroccan sultanates 219–67

Morocco 120, 198, 240

mortuary complexes: Gujarat 515; *see also* funerary complexes

mosaics 43, 45, *46–7,* 51, *51,* 56, 68, 208, 435, 598

Moscow 387

mosque-madrasa 292; four-iwan 292, *293,* 297

mosques 40; Abbasid 84–7, 89–99; Adilshahi 567–8, *568, 570–1, 572, 573*; Almohad 224–9, *224–8*; Almoravid 220; Ayyubid 171; Bahamani 496, *496–7,* 504; Bahri Mamluk 278–9, *279, 280–1*; Bengali 493, *493, 494–5, 495*; Burji Mamluk 300; development of 14–25; early Iranian 106–10; Empyrean *335*; Fatimid 119, 122–9, *124–8*; Gujarat 511, 515; Ilkhanid (Mongol) 374, *376–81,* 377–82; Indian 473; Kashmiri *492*; Lodi *535*; Malwan *516,* 517–18; Marinid 233–4; Mughal 537, *537,* 539, *540,* 550–1, 552–3; Mughal imperial *583–7*; Ottoman 306, *306–7, 307,* 311, 312, 313–23, *313–21*; Ottoman imperial 332–61; Sa'dis 241; Safavid 445–7, *446, 447, 448–51,* 452–3, *452, 453, 454–7,* 456; Seljuk 137, 144–53, 182–3, 184–6, *185, 186–7,* 193; Shibanid 414, *414–15*; Timurid 401–6, *401, 402–3, 407*; Tughluq 476–9, *476–7, 478, 479*; Umayyad 52–9, 199–207, 220, 221–2; Zengi 163–4, 165–6, *165*

Mosul 162; mashhad of Awn al-Din 167; minaret *163,* 164; traditional house *143* mother of pearl 285

motifs 34, 261; Adilshahi 573; animal 194–5; 'arabesque' 42; Bahamani 498; Buyid 109; Fatimid 129; floral 43, 59, 229; 'grotesque' 117; Ilkhanid 374; Mughal 560; Persian 632; Sa'di 241; Seljuk 144, 160, 186, 194; Umayyad 59, 65

Moulay Abdallah 247

Moulay Idris 240–1, 241

Moulay Ismail 241; tomb of (Meknes) 245

Moulay Rashid 241

mourning cults 105

Mshatta 62, 65, 66, 67

Mu'awiya, caliph 8–10, 49, 89

Mu'ayyad Sheikh, sultan 293

mud-brick 45, 81, 84, 134, 141

Mudejar 249

Mughals 524, 533–59, 563, 579–613, 579, 580–1; and see Akbar, emperor; decadence and political fragmentation 626–9; early imperial seat 545–57; fall of Adilshahis to 575; first 536–7, 536; forts 545, 546, 547, 547, 622–5; Gardens of Paradise 598–613; imperial mosque 583–7; imperial palace 588–98; mosques 537, 537, 539, 540–1, 550–1, 552–3; obsession with water 557; palaces 548–9, 553–5, 554–5, 556, 557, 615–16, 616–17, 618–21; tombs 540–1, 553, 557–61, 557, 558–62, 598–601, 602–4

Muhamad Karim Khan Zand 461

Muhammad Ali Shah: Jami-masjid of (Lucknow) 631

Muhammad Ghaus: tomb of (Gwalior) 560–1

Muhammad Ghuri 465

Muhammad I (1232–72) 253

Muhammad I (1626–56): Gol Gumbad of 575–6, 576

Muhammad ibn Tumart 223, 224

Muhammad II 253

Muhammad, Prophet 4–7, 5, 7, 8, 11, 14–16, 102; Mosque (Medina) 14–16, 15, 18, 26, 53, 53, 59

Muhammad Shah Bahaman III 505

Muhammad Shah, sultan: tomb of (Golconda) 564, 564

Muhammad Sultan 393

Muhammad V 254, 255, 257, 261

Mullah Hasan: tomb of (Sultania) 444, 444, 558

Multan: tomb of Sheikh Rukn-i-Alam 480, 481

al-Muntasir, caliph 111

muqarnas 114, 130, 152, 174, 224, 283, 406, 441, 453

Murad I, sultan 310, 311, 313, 319; mosque of (Bursa) 360

Murad II, sultan 319, 322

Murad II, sultan 331

Murad VI, sultan 429

Murad V, sultan 331

Muslim bin Quraish: tomb of (Imam Dur) 116

al-Mustansir, caliph 157

al-Musta'sim, caliph 271

al-Mu'tasim 73, 75

al-Mutawakkil, caliph 84, 101, 104, 110; mosque of (Samarra) 84, 84–5, 86

Mu'tazilitism 104

Muzaffarids 373

Mysore 491

mysticism 102, 103

Nadir Shah 430, 628

Nagara 489

Najaf 429; shrine of Imam Ali 429

Najm al-Din Ayyub, Salih 176–7, 274, 275; tomb of (Cairo) 176–7

Naqqash Ali 319

Naqsh-i Rustam 34, 114

al-Nasir Muhammad, sultan 277–8, 279, 286

Nasr bin Ali 161

Natanz: khanqah of Sheikh Abd al-Samad 382, 382–3

nave 59, 86–7, 95, 107

Nayin: Jami-masjid 106, 107–8, 107, 108, 145

Nebuchadnezzar 4

Nicopolis 316

Nigde: Ala ad-Din mosque 186, 186

Night of Destiny 5

Night Journey to Heaven 6, 6

Nile, floods 121

nine-square scheme 67, 208, 321

Nineveh 44

Niriz 145

Nishapur 106, 155, 271

Nizam al-Mulk 137, 149, 155, 156

Nizamiyas 155

Nur al-Din Zengi 163, 166, 167; complexes of (Damascus) 166, 166

observatories 383, 388

octagonal minaret 20

octagonal tombs 374, 444, 444, 469, 471, 471, 481, 534, 540, 557–8

octagonal towers 576, 577, 578

Oghuz 73, 309

Ogoday 271

Oljeitu 373, 374, 374; tomb of (Sultaniya) 374, 374, 375, 481

Omar, caliph 8, 10, 65, 67

opus mixtum 313

Orchha 615, 616, 616–17; Chaturbuja 617; Jahangiri Mahal 615, 616; Raj Mahal 614–15, 615

Orhan Ghazi, sultan 310, 312, 313, 317; mosque of (Bursa) 311, 311, 313, 313, 316

Orissa 542

orthodoxy, assertion of 48–99

Osman 309, 317

Othman 8

Ottomans 296, 326–71, 389, 428; advent of 304–25; bathing complexes 322, 323–4, 336; bridges 323, 324; civil works 332–3, 333–4; dealing with revolts 326; decline 331; defeat of by Timur 389; early building 311–24; early foundation plans 311; expansion of and conquests 309–11, 326–7, 329–30; forts 324, 324–5; imperial mosque 332–61; imperial palace 363–70; madrasas 311–12; mosques 306–7, 307, 311, 313–23, 313–21; roads 324; and Safavids 428, 429, 430; tombs 312, 316–17, 319

Oudh 628

Ozbeks 429

padma 467

paganism 4

Pakubuono III, sultan 22

palaces 30, 42, 43, 43; Abbasid 74, 75, 76–7, 78–9, 79–82, 80–3; Almohad 249; Ayyubid 170, 170, 171, 173, 174; Bahamani 501, 502, 503; Burji Mamluk 302–3, 303; Chittor 519, 524, 525; Fatimid 119, 122; Ghaznavid 134, 134; Gwalior 526–7, 528, 528, 529, 530–1, 532, 532, 545, 547; Ilkhanid 383–4, 384; Malwan 519–21; Mamluk 298, 300, 300; Mughal 548–9, 553–5, 554–5, 556, 557, 615–16, 616–17,